THE MAKING OF THEATRE

From Drama to Performance

Theater is the only form of art that deals in life as it happens or may not happen. . . . The theater evolves in front of the person who is receiving it and who will accept it or not.
— From "For Barrault, Wonder and Astonishment"
by Sylvie Drake, *Los Angeles Times,* June 8, 1980.

THE MAKING OF THEATRE

From Drama to Performance

Robert W. Corrigan
The University of Wisconsin–Milwaukee

Scott, Foresman and Company   Glenview, Illinois

Dallas, Tex.   Oakland, N. J.   Palo Alto, Cal.
Tucker, Ga.   London, England

Library of Congress Cataloging in Publication Data

The Making of Theatre.

   Includes bibliographical references.
   1. Drama—Collected works. 2. Theater—Collected
works. I. Corrigan, Robert Willoughby, 1927–
PN1655.M15   809.2   80–19046
ISBN 0–673–15403–3

1 2 3 4 5 6-RRC-86 85 84 83 82 81 80

Cover: Mila (Gorlanoff Studio), The American Shakespeare Festival Theatre.

Acknowledgments

Part 1 "How Drama Is Born Within Us" from *The Theatre of Jean-Louis Barrault.*
Translated by Joseph Chiari. First published in 1959 by Flammarion, Paris under the title
Nouvelles Reflexions sur Le Theatre. English translation first published and © 1961 by
Barrie and Rockliff (Barrie Books Ltd.) 2 Clement's Inn, London WC2. Reprinted with the
permission of Joseph Chiari and Hill and Wang (now a division of Farrar, Straus and
Giroux, Inc.).   Claude Lévi-Strauss: "The Many Faces of Man." As published in *World
Theatre,* Spring, 1963. Vol. X, No. 1. Date of original publication, December 10, 1959.
Reprinted by permission of the author.   Robert E. Sherwood: "The Dwelling Place of
Wonder." *Theatre Arts Anthology: A Record and a Prophecy.* Copyright, 1941, by Theatre
Arts, Inc. Reprinted by permission of Theatre Arts Books.   Used by permission of
Atheneum Publishers and Granada Publishing Ltd. from *The Empty Space* by Peter Brook.
Copyright © 1968 Peter Brook.   Eugène Ionesco: "Experience of the Theatre." *Notes
and Counter Notes.* Translated from the French by Donald Watson. Reprinted by
permission of Grove Press, Inc. and Calder and Boyars Ltd.
Part 2   Tennessee Williams: *The Rose Tattoo.* Copyright 1950, 1951 by Tennessee
Williams. Reprinted by permission of New Directions.   Jean Vilar: "Secrets." *The
Tradition of the Theatre,* Paris, 1955. Tr. by Christopher Kotschnig. First published in *The
Drama Review,* Vol. 3, No. 3, 1959, pp. 24–30. © 1959 by *The Drama Review.* Reprinted
by permission. All Rights Reserved.   "The Dramatic Illusion." Used by permission of
Charles Scribner's Sons from *Feeling and Form* by Susanne K. Langer. Copyright 1953
Charles Scribner's Sons.   From *The Actor's Freedom* by Michael Goldman. Copyright ©
1975 Michael Goldman. Reprinted by permission of Viking Penguin Inc.   Copyright ©
1975 by David Cole. Reprinted from *The Theatrical Event* by permission of Wesleyan
University Press.

Preface

The purpose of this collection of writings is to illumine the complex process of "making theatre." What is the nature of a dramatic script, and how is that script transformed by a group of artists into a theatrical event that provides enjoyment for an audience while at the same time fulfilling some of the audience's deepest inner needs? It is my hope that these writings by some of the theatre's most distinguished theorists and practitioners will enable students to appreciate more fully the dynamic interaction that always exists between performers and audiences. Furthermore, they will be introduced to the ideas, attitudes, and the wisdom and experience—in all their rich variety —of the makers and shapers of our contemporary theatre, for the essays in this book reflect the important changes in how we have come to think about theatre in recent years. It is significant, I think, that nearly half the essays included here were written since 1970. This is not prompted by a desire to be up-to-date. The fact is, during the past ten years or so, the theatre—like most institutions in our society—has been undergoing a penetrating self-scrutiny.

The theatre of the 1970s can best be characterized perhaps as being wildly eclectic in its search for new forms and rigorously committed to a reexamination of its own nature. The theatre of that period literally opened up. There were experiments in mixed media, improvisation, and new kinds of texts. The action moved out of the traditional proscenium stage (or the, by then, nearly as conventional thrust stage) into garages, gymnasiums, and churches. Before long, theatre was taking place everywhere and anywhere in environments as diverse as New York City's Times Square and the grape vineyards of California. Training of the actor became the central concern for some of the theatre's most powerful and imaginative practitioners. Yet there was something nervous and self-conscious about all of this activity. As all of the established boundaries and conventions came crashing down, it became increasingly apparent that much of what was going on were the flailings of artists who had lost their bearings; one sensed that in all of this experimentation there was as much hokum as there was genuine creative achievement. As a result, by the middle of the decade more and more people in theatre began to ask themselves, as if for the first time, some basic questions about the nature of the theatrical event. Interestingly enough, this kind of critical questioning proved to be the most significant accomplishment of the decade. It was truly radical in that it brought the theatre into touch once again with its old and long-established roots, and in so doing it not only enlarged our understanding of what theatre is but also created a new sense of purpose and direction. As we enter the 1980s, I perceive the theatre as having both great energy and its usual diversity, but I don't sense any of that splintered destructiveness which dominated so much of the last twenty years. This condition of wholeness is the most important fruit of theatre's self-examination of its nature and purpose.

The aim of this collection of essays and excerpts from longer works is to reflect the broad dimensions of this self-examination. Many points of view are represented, but each piece has been chosen because some aspect of the transformational nature of the theatrical event is its central concern and because it speaks directly and clearly to what is involved in the "making of theatre." Some of the "classic" documents of twentieth-century theatre history are here as are several pieces from the frontiers of contemporary theatrical theory. All of them, however, underscore the central fact of theatre: whenever drama is transformed into living theatre, it engenders an amazing vitality which has the power to awaken and enlarge the mind, spirit, and imagination of audiences and performers.

This book can be used in several ways in courses in theatre and dramatic literature. For those teachers of an Introduction to Theatre course who want to teach the course "their way" without working within the constraints of someone else's text, this volume will provide a large resource for assigned readings. For teachers of dramatic literature or play analysis, the essays will serve as a valuable adjunct to the reading of plays—particularly for those who are concerned with how drama on the page is transformed into a play on the stage. Certainly, it will be an ideal text for courses in theatre theory and criticism. Finally, I believe various sections of the book can be combined in any number of ways to serve as additional readings for most advanced theatre courses, from modern trends in theatre to such practice-oriented courses as directing or playwriting.

I must thank several people who have helped me in the shaping of this book. Robert Bechtold Heilman, J. L. Styan, and Julian Olf were advisors to the project and their suggestions were most helpful. My secretary, Margaret Rotter, was her usual indispensable self. She helped prepare the manuscript and handled the arduous task of obtaining the permissions. Finally, thank you to the staff of Scott, Foresman and especially Tana Vega-Romero and JoAnn Johnson.

Robert W. Corrigan

Contents

9 Audiences and Critics

10 The Theatre and Society

1

THE THEATRICAL IMPULSE

◆ . . . a dream dreamt . . .   . . . a world
of magic . . .   . . . evoked by myths . . .
. . . beyond the humdrum . . .   . . . the mask brings
the god on earth . . .   . . . the Invisible-Made-Visible . . .
. . . invoke the supernatural . . .   . . . takes place
in the present . . .   . . . masks are living things . . .
. . . climax of celebration . . .   . . . lived and relived
with each performance . . .   . . . a certain silence . . .

Jean-Louis Barrault
How Drama Is Born Within Us

JEAN-LOUIS BARRAULT (1910–   ) is the legendary actor-director of the twentieth-century French theatre. Always interested in the nature of the theatrical impulse,
in this essay he examines those qualities of human nature that enable the mysterious
communication between performers and audience to take place.

◆   Drama is as old as man; it is as closely linked to him as his double for
the theatrical game is inherent in the existence of any living being. Man has
invented fire, together with Dionysian and Apollonian arts, and that is what
makes him different from the animal, but man and animals have one thing
in common, they both love playing. Animals, like men, know how to play, and
as soon as they begin to do so they display a kind of imagination which one
would not credit them with. A dog does not know how to draw, a horse cannot
sculpt, a cat does not show any sign of deep delight when the radio plays Bach,
and a beaver will not think of adding decorations to the house which it builds,
but when it comes to dancing, singing, or to mimicking a fright or enjoyment,
all the animals can do that.

Observe a dog playing with a ball or a cat playing with a piece of paper
held by a thread, and see how it enjoys the merry-go-round of faked fears,
feints, pseudo panics and wild excitements. Suddenly in the middle of all that,
an abrupt stop! An imaginary enemy has been seen, and one has to crawl, hold
one's breath, and approach it with precaution. This is a tense moment! The
climax is near, the price of it may be life itself! Ready: the enemy is now within
reach! One, two, three, and the dog makes a sudden pounce on the deadly
enemy represented by the ball with which he was playing. He catches it, holds
it prisoner, he bites but without killing it, he throws it in the air, barks with
joy and performs a swift victory dance around it. Five minutes later, this very
same dog will come to you pretending to be in agony because of an imaginary
thorn in his paw, or adopt an attitude of perfect indifference if he sees you
with a suitcase in your hand. To superimpose an imaginary reality upon actual
reality is a tendency shared by all living beings—whether men or animals.
What's the cause of it? Does the reason for it lie in the desire to live imaginatively a story which could not be lived if this story were true? One has all kinds
of courage in imaginary situations. It is pleasant to play with the notion of fear
when there is no real cause for fear. This desire for 'acting' comes perhaps from
the urge to get a full grasp of real life and its problems through an artificial
re-creation of life, something which is really 'filtered' life, or life at one remove.
This is something in which attitudes and behaviour are more clearly outlined

and lucidity is not blinded by the urgency of decision. It is therefore a training ground for virtual actions which can be beneficial in cases of incapacity to act; it is a school of energy, a place where one recharges one's batteries.

All men are double, that is a well-known fact, and one would not be surprised to hear that men are multiple: 'there are many men in one man.' Yet if each of us is a compound of many personalities, the fact that another self seems to be always present in us, makes us say that we are double. Our double has its own individual life; it is he who at night lives our dreams. Life on the stage is a dream dreamt when one is awake. There has been in recent years a good deal of talk about the lie of the theatre. It is frequently said that the actor when acting deludes himself and lies, and the spectator does the same and lies when he believes what he sees. Diderot's famous paradox of the comedian or of the spectator is supposed to be the result of a connivance between two liars. That is very possible; but what of it? Dreams also are supposed to be lies but in fact nobody knows anything about it. Let us content ourselves with saying that the theatre, like life, is a dream, without caring too much about the question of lie.

The whole history of the theatre shows us that it has its source in imitation, which of course is not the lifeless copying of nature, but the re-creating of life through artificial means. The artist gives life to a kind of magic object which has more life than any ordinary object. A picture, a bust, a symphony, ought in fact to belong to the living world. 'Creation' is for the artist a kind of sexual action at the end of which he gives life to something. If life is a symphony of colours it is normal to invent the painter; if it is a dance of forms then a sculptor must be born; and if it is a pattern of sounds then it is clear that music exists as well as man. What appearances will life take in order to justify the invention of an 'imitator'? Painting, sculpture, architecture, music, poetry, are historically valid; can we also say that the art of the 'imitator' deserves a history? Our friend Fluchère in a fascinating study of Shakespeare and the Elizabethan theatre said two things which deeply impressed me: 'The theatre which interests us,' he said, 'is the spoken theatre, the theatre which belongs to literature,' and he added: 'the theatre is above all an experimental art of language whose primary mission of entertaining and instructing rests on the success of the ceaseless verbal experiments and on the actor who endeavours to convey these experiments to the public.' From these two sentences, I retain two points:

1. The 'spoken' theatre, considered as 'an experimental art of language,' deserves its history which will be a branch of the history of literature.
2. The author, bent upon his primary task of entertaining and instructing, will adopt as a means of expression, that is to say of creation or procreation— speech, that is to say language with which he will experiment ceaselessly.

These two points imply that the history of the theatre does not date from the origins of man. Man in his struggle for life began with dances, shouts, songs, incantations and warlike mimes meant to bring to him the strength of his ancestors and power over his enemies. These manifestations do not belong to art, which implies gratuitousness, but to the world of magic; they were part of a profound, mysterious and metaphysical reality which was at one with life. When men began to trace graffiti of animals on walls, it was in order to protect themselves from animals, to master them in order to eat them or to make use of them. It was therefore a form of magic. When men sculpted their first masks, they aimed at giving form to their inner face or to the traits of their assumed role; they were trying to bring to light the appearances of their most mysterious instincts. The primary aim of these attempts was not art but efficacy. Whatever art there was lay in the technical perfection of these magic acts (the drawings made with powders, upon the earth, during voodoo ceremonies in Haiti have a kind of perfection which is due not to their beauty, but to their efficacy; yet it just happens that one serves the other).

Human behaviour is made of gestures, songs, dances, drawings, masks, sculptures, choices of perfumes, incantations accompanied with drum and bells, or simply of human bodies clashing one against the other in frenzies, of trances or possessions, which have nothing to do with literature but have everything to do with man. The origin of the theatre lies in the attempt to imitate and to re-create these forms of human behaviour. If we ask ourselves how the theatre is born in us and what it endeavours to re-create, I should be inclined to answer instinctively—a certain silence. Let us see what this means. When the arts reach our senses, they satisfy them one by one. For instance, we might be deaf and appreciate painting, we might be blind and appreciate music, and sometimes we even shut our eyes in order to hear better. Life, when re-created by the artist, reaches us in a kind of 'specialized' form, and only through one sense at a time. In normal life, on the contrary, we absorb the outside world simultaneously through all the senses and pores of our body; there is not a single nerve in us which does not record some kind of contact. While the outside world is thus impinging on us, we perceive at the same time all the various aspects of an internal life—memories from our past, the industrious agitation of our blood, the noise of saliva in our mouths, the crackings of our joints, the bellows of our breathing, etc. etc. . . . If we concentrate our attention on any one of these moments in the present when the outside world continuously impinges on our internal world, we soon perceive beyond that medley of noises and distant sights and sounds a kind of faint murmur which is caused by the slight and surreptitious breeze of the present-on-the-move upon silence. Claudel used to say that the stars make a noise, and he used to call the sky the celestial kettle. The present causes silence to vibrate. Time flows, the present moves on, life passes, silence trembles, and we do the same, we tremble with anguish at the continuous movement, flow and vibration, which is irrevocable and which terminates in death. Consciousness of the tragic rolling carpet condemned to end in the dark abyss, tightens up the throat, and sends the blood buzzing to our head; one has at once a feeling of claustrophobia and of being stifled under blankets, yet the machine has been set in motion and cannot be stopped. Silence, the present, and all the perceptions which reach us, plunge us into a panic; anxiety nearly chokes us, and there is only one way of getting out of this terrifying state, it is by breaking this silence and making the present inaudible, so we plunge into talk, noise, whirls of ideas and discussions of all kinds. We try to become conscious of life in order to do away with the consciousness of death. Action is not enough, we plunge into agitation, we think of the future, and of the past, but we no more mention the word present than we would mention the word rope in the house of a man who has been hanged. We prefer to live in a world drowned in noise than in the real world where a kind of silence unavoidably leads to Nothingness . . . or to God . . . two notions equally terrifying. To become conscious of the present is to become conscious of death, for the present is continuous death. The only real and concrete thing in life is the present, yet as if to torment us, the present is impossible to grasp and to hold. The present ever lies between something which is not yet, and something which has already been, and it changes ceaselessly. Nothing can hold this march towards death, and what is more, everything truly real in life takes place at that very moment which, so to speak, is nothing, and outside such a moment nothing is real. This is a terrifying enough statement and it is not surprising that we whistle with bravado in order to hide our fear. To re-create life, seen from this angle, is to go back to the source of the theatre.

Theatre is basically the art which takes place in the present and appeals simultaneously to all the senses, all the nerves, all the instincts, all at the same time. It is essentially the art of sensation, the art of the present, therefore of reality in all its aspects, from hell to heaven, as they would have said in the Middle Ages. It is also the art of putting to death, that is why there is a bull's head on our emblem. Recently Montherlant told me, 'I have understood at last the deep meaning of bull fights! They represent the history of man, the bull plays the part of man, and it is the very art of Life.' The actor receives life through the present, which is simultaneity and a 'kind of silence,' from that he decomposes life and re-creates it. How does he decompose it? The present is the ephemeral spark of which we are the image; through its continuous births and deaths it is ceaseless movement of exchanges, rejections and absorptions according to an implacable pattern which cannot alter its rhythm. The actor who observes life is struck by whatever is movement and exchanges and by whatever transports itself into a rhythm. He is so close to real and complete life and to the life of sensations that he cannot use for his creations media so remote as abstract writing, two-dimensional painting or the massiveness of stone. Music is what is closest to him, but even music cannot convey the impression of physical reality which he obtains from the contact of the present.

If man could truly become an instrument worthy of art, he would be the ideal artificial means of recreating the life of the present. That should be possible, for man has in his body the seat of movement (which is his spine, pliable as a whip), the centre of exchange (which is his respiratory apparatus and the continuous comings and goings of appetites and refusals) and the seat of rhythm (his heart which is also his magician). In order to translate the intoxicating sensation of man caught in the life of the universe, one has only to plunge man into space, the individual into the world, the one into the infinite and the being into the whole. That is why drama is essentially the conflict between the individual and the collective, between inner and external forces. Whenever the 'chosen' man or the ideal actor becomes conscious of the silent murmurs of his space-present, he will, as we suggested, first feel anguish, then, according to his temperament or his humour, he will either turn his anguish into metaphysical or divine drama attuned to esoteric liturgy, or in order to reassure himself he will take to whistling, telling stories or dancing 'in order to forget his fright.' Then his theatre adopts the free forms which one finds in farce, satyric drama and Bacchic ceremonies. Confronted with the type of life which strikes us as if it were an apparition, we adopt two lines of behaviour, both dictated by our emotions. We either transform it into something divine which we can face and which is tragedy, or we pretend to ignore it, and we can then indulge in all types of merriment, and that is comedy. In the first case we trust life, and in the second case we rather fly away from it. That is why tragedy is exalting while comedy is not so gay after all.

Honorius said: 'The priest is a tragic actor who re-enacts in front of his Christian audience in the theatre of the church, the struggles of Christ and the victory of Redemption.' This is all the more striking in that it was said in the twelfth century. Mass can be divided into three acts which are:

1. The proclamation of the Faith;
2. The tragedy of the order of the Mass;
3. Communion and joy.

The order of the Mass follows the pattern of a symphony: there is the first movement which is rapid, there is the anguish-laden and opaque andante and there is the joy of the third movement. Bearing in mind Menander's sayings in one of his comedies: 'Joy prevents me from knowing where I am,' one could conclude that tragedy and comedy are the two faces of this very same thing which is precisely the 'kind of silence' which only appears in the present. Tragedy and comedy are the two opposite faces of terror or sterile anguish: 'Gods, free me from my sterile anguish,' says Aeschylus in the *Oresteia.* In fact, until Aeschylus, every poet ended his tragic trilogies with a satyric drama which dealt with the same subject. We therefore had the face and the obverse of the same medal. *Proteus* was a kind of farce which went with the *Oresteia,* and it described Menelaus's return with Helen, it was a burlesque song accompanying the funeral of a whole race. When, after Sophocles, poets began writing satyrical dramas which were unrelated to the tragic themes of their trilogies, comedy and tragedy ceased to be connected one with the other, and they were uprooted. The single cell which they formed originally was divided into two which assumed independent lives from then on. When they were one, they were connected by a religious attitude. If art blossoms as soon as the profane is separated from the sacred, its decadence is not very far. This is true of all ages and of all countries. When the religious spirit disintegrates, art for art's sake appears and flourishes. A whole heritage, a golden age, is squandered and replaced by a slow period of decadence. 'We have kissed away kingdoms and provinces,' says Shakespeare in *Antony and Cleopatra.* Like life the theatre evolves in cycles. A new religion born from a period of dark depression revives existence and gives rise to a new civilization. For a while, the theatre which had decayed during the period of decadence, is rejected and condemned to go through its 'purgatory.'

But the theatre does not die easily, and it leaves its prison for a clandestine existence: peripatetic comedians, minstrels and tumblers keep the flame alive in inns and pub courtyards. Once the new religion is well established it feels the need to recreate the theatre which finds its place again in liturgical ceremonies. It begins with a voice and a chorus, then 'imitation' progresses, the acting is perfected, and one day dialogue is invented. The theatrical ceremony moves away from the altar, passes into the nave, comes out in front of the church, and in no time it is again in the public square. The theatre becomes a social art; it is the acme of collective art; all the various corporations take part in it. The gods and the city enter the dance, and politics bring a new life to it. The priests are overtaken by events and satyrical farce and carnivals are an excellent means of letting out human exuberance. Tragedy becomes more and more refined and comedy more and more teeming with life. Meanwhile religion keeps growing and getting old, and people become more educated and tend towards emancipation. One day, comedy goes off to live its own life, leaving tragedy on its own. Civilization becomes more refined, and people tire of holy wars. Politics corrupt everything and sow confusion everywhere. The more taste develops, the more the revolt towards the collective and the social element increases. Then the theatre concentrates on domestic dramas. Psychology makes its appearance, drama loses its violence and becomes 'bourgeois.' The people try to react but unfortunately they, too, have lost their religious feelings, so drama decays. In the early religious phase, while drama was still connected with magic, the Dionysian element was called eroticism, and phallic art was part of religious life; they were in fact two aspects of the same physical rite.

Now that religion is no longer part of life, and the profane is independent of the sacred which has become an abstraction, eroticism becomes obscurity and corruption spreads like a disease. The day is not far off when a new religion will appear and the theatre will be again banned, excommunicated and condemned to take to clandestine living. Whether religion is called Christianity, Buddhism, or otherwise, the cycles and the fate of the theatre are the same and they belong to the phases of life. One might sum up by saying that the theatre is the first serum that man invented in order to protect himself against anxiety. In order to combat solitude, men come together and sometimes form the magnetic gathering called the public; they gather in order to live together dramas of life which have been rendered 'harmless' through imagination. In the course of the performance everyone is injected with the serum of the disease which is anguish. Art consists in transforming the disease into a serum, otherwise the injection communicates the disease. Naturalism is the disease which propagates itself by contagion. The poetic theatre is on the contrary the beneficent serum which brings health to man. The art of the theatre has therefore since the beginning been a means of defence and not a gratuitous or debased form of entertainment. Since man has existed the theatre has always been something of public utility. In order to preserve life, man sleeps, eats, procreates (so as to maintain the race alive) and plays. To play is to struggle against anguish and to invent happiness which suppresses it. In order to play, man has since the beginning, relied upon himself.

[Translated by Joseph Chiari]

Claude Lévi-Strauss
The Many Faces of Man

CLAUDE LÉVI-STRAUSS (1908–   ), the social anthropologist, is best known for his studies on the structures of primitive societies. In this little-known review of an exhibition of primitive masks, he reveals why the mask has always been the primary symbol of the theatre.

◆   In the word "cosmetic", there is "cosmos"; and it is not by chance that the word "mask" has been included in the vocabulary of the beauty specialist. A head of hair which we call bushy has always presented the picture of wild and savage Nature as evoked by myths of the time before the creation of man and the dawn of society. By dressing her hair, "masking" her face with cream, powder and various colours, by correcting with the aid of tweezers and pencil irregular features to give them "chic", the woman of fashion is executing, without knowing it, on her face—the universe in miniature—the gestures of the Demiurge, organiser of the cosmos, destroyer of monsters, herald of the arts of civilization.

Man believes that he is at variance with the rest of creation: he has, in any case, done enough damage for thousands of years to justify this conviction. But, in the same way, man's face is at variance with man's body; in the same way that the state of society is at variance with the state of Nature. The natural functions belong to the body: breathing, circulation, assimilation, generation and over these we have little control. The face, on the other hand, is the seat of the "socialised" functions, or should I put it, "socialising": first language, articulated by the mouth; then that other system of signs which constitutes the expression of feelings, of natural origin, no doubt, but which each culture has remodelled in a special range and style. It is by reason of the face and by the face that man communicates with man. It is by disguising or transforming his face that he interrupts that communication, or diverts it to other ends.

Hair brushed forward and covering the face, here we undoubtedly have the prototype of the mask, as found in certain rites. Such a simple gesture and yet so full of meaning. The well-organized microcosm symbolised by the eyes, nose and mouth and their established order, gives way to a disordered universe; the social instruments of expression and communication give way to triumphing Nature; the individual identifiable as a person becomes an anonymous being; he escapes from classification in the group, he is no longer a parent or a relative, a fellow-citizen or a foreigner, a master or a servant; he is set free to make contact with other powers, other worlds, those of love and death. The distance is not so very great between this rudimentary mask and the black velvet one of our masked balls, which for its wearer and for those who make its brief acquaintance, symbolises adventure and the chance to overthrow the daily order of things.

A Fabulous Variety

The exhibition, "The Mask", which was held at the Musée Guimet in Paris, the guidebook to which, drawn up by a dozen authorities, is a veritable treatise on the mask, hitherto lacking—broached, through the medium of objects, a problem which covers the whole field of ethnology. If makeup and tattooings are included under the definition of the mask, then it is found among all societies. And rare are they which, as in the case, it seems, of Australia and Polynesia, have not known the mask which is applied to the face.

In the entrance hall several showcases introduced the visitor to the different varieties of mask. Here and there, masks displayed in pairs emphasise contrasts and help one to realise the variety—which may be legitimately described as fabulous—which exists supremely in the world of masks. Some are enormous, the two biggest on show at the exhibition are more than fifteen and eighteen feet high respectively. They are Dogon masks from the Sudan; alongside one of them can be seen the smallest, an Eskimo mask about five inches long made to be worn on the finger like a ring. An extremely complicated Yoruba mask representing two faces surmounted by an armed man on horseback and his retinue, is seen beside a Brazilian mask, roughly executed with half of a calabash. A precious mask in tortoiseshell from Torres Strait is contrasted with an Iroquois mask in humble, plaited straw.

A Mediator

Some masks have a utilitarian purpose: a hunting disguise, a war helmet to protect its wearer; others, a magic one, like the Chinese masks which are put on children to ward away diseases, or the masks worn by Siberian hunters to try and escape the vengeance of the game; some are realistic, others fantastic. Masks may be attractive or fearful, human or animal, sacred or secular, solemn or comic. Some masks only disguise the features like the simple vizier of black feathers of the Borero Indians of Central Brazil, worn over the face. Its principle is the opposite of that which inspires the fine, polychrome, wooden mask of the Kwakiutl Indians of British Columbia, with movable parts which swing open at a certain moment to reveal the almost human face of the cannibal god concealed behind his outward guise of a raven.

All these different types constitute so many intermediate forms between extremes which not a single society has not known; but which not all can boast with equal success. On the one hand, the mask is a god, on the other, the man is not a man since he is able to wear a mask—notwithstanding the amazing discoveries of Pasyryk: horses wearing the masks of reindeer. For social man is in essence masked: he bears a name, inherits a status, holds a position. One can therefore understand the place and importance of the mask in human societies.

Imbued with life by its wearer, the mask brings the god on earth, it establishes his reality, mingles him with the society of men; inversely, by masking himself, man testifies to his own social existence, manifests it, classifies it with the aid of symbols. The mask is both the man and something other than the man: it is the mediator par excellence between society, on the one hand, and Nature, usually merged with the Supernatural, on the other.

It was the mask which deified the Egyptian gods and also certain pre-Colombian Mexican gods. The masks of the Duk-Duk, a large Melanesian initiation society, are supposed to procreate the initiates. Moreover, the masks "beget" each other. Thus, each year, two masks called *tubuan* beget two Duk-Duk masks, thus ensuring the perpetuity of the mask species. The masks are living things: it is impossible to enumerate, so many are they, the societies in which the masks, entrusted to the care of priests or other qualified persons, are daily prayed to, cared for and given food. As I have said above, the mask diverts communication from its human, social and secular function in order to establish contact with a sacred world. In consequence, the mask does not speak, or if it does it uses its own special language which is opposed phonetically and semantically to that which enables men to communicate with each other. An ill-treated mask or one desecrated by the impiety of its wearer, will wreak vengeance upon him and kill him, for instance, by contracting until the culprit is strangled or suffocated.

These beliefs are so strong that they sometimes account for the reason why certain types of mask are unrepresented in the museums. The natives refuse to give them up for fear that the mask will regard being displayed in a showcase as neglect. The exhibition in the Guimet Museum included a very fine collection of Pueblo Indian masks from the south-west of the United States. It would have been even richer if the museums of the region, when solicited by the organisers, had not replied that the Indians continued to watch jealously over the masks which these museums had been able to procure and that the people would be indignant if the masks left what was formerly the tribe's sacred territory.

Even where the divine character of the masks is not clearly attested, they remain the medium for man to enter into relation with the supernatural world. The Eskimo masks of Alaska dazzle with their lightness and grace combined with the most prodigious freedom of invention that any art form has undoubtedly ever known. However, these beings of arbitrary appearance, creations it seems of an unbridled imagination, these double faces, human on one side, animal on the other, these dangling attachments twirling round with the dancer, only go to illustrate and even methodically apply, a metaphysical doctrine: that of the *inua*, human double of the animal, whose joint presence recalls the time when separation was not yet irrevocable, when the two natures mingled. Whether the mask thus seeks to invoke the supernatural or to capture it in order to possess it or, on the contrary, to deceive it by representing a false appearance, the supernatural is always there.

"Somebody"

Here from the supernatural we pass by a barely perceptible transition to the social. In modelling the clay on the head of the dead person to make a faithful portrait of him, the natives of the New Hebrides are not executing the mask of an already present god; but through the medium of the mask, they deify by immortalising him an important member of the group, whose ghost they hope, having been paid a last tribute, will refrain from returning to torment the living. Thus begins a series which, through the intermediary of funeral masks, already materially distinct from the corpse, then Greek and Roman or Mediaeval tomb figures, still faithful to the last appearance, finally ends in the statues which we erect to the memory of great men. In all these cases, the mask is never nor ever principally, a mere physical resemblance. It includes emblems, insignia and symbols representing social rank, position and honours. Furthermore, in many societies these could not be assumed or affirmed without wearing the corresponding mask; in America, Africa and Melanesia masks exist of herald, policeman, tax collector, spy and beggar. Do not the role and prestige constitute that "face" which man risks to lose when the support of society is withdrawn?

For the Iroquois medicine-man, protected and justified by a "false face" of wood with convulsed features which represents the immoderate rival of the Creator, as for the eighteenth-century beauty, more coated with white and red than a geisha, the face strangely marked with black velvet patches and blue pencil marks simulating the network of veins beneath the skin, as, finally, for the famous man, continually heedful of his person, to be oneself is to be "somebody". Somebody, therefore a mask: a being, not merely existing but significant.

The history of the true mask ends in the sorry confections of a Mardi gras which no longer arouses any enthusiasm even in the children. However, and even though their functions are almost the opposite, masks are no less indispensable to the group than words. A society which believes it has dispensed with masks can only be a society in which masks, more powerful than ever before, the better to deceive men, will themselves be masked.

Robert E. Sherwood
The Dwelling Place of Wonder

ROBERT E. SHERWOOD (1896–1955), a three-time Pulitzer prize-winning playwright, presidential speech writer, and government official, was always deeply concerned about the role the theatre plays in its society. This brief statement affirming this relationship first appeared in *Theatre Arts*, the country's most influential theatre magazine during the first half of this century.

◆ . . . The theatre is the spiritual home of one who is barred from the church by distaste for dogma but who still requires and demands expression of great faith.

Does that sound a bit pretentious?

All right.

But I persist in thinking of the theatre as the workshop of Sophocles and Shakespeare rather than a mere testing ground for the movies. I still persist in believing that although the fate of any play that I may write will be decided by the verdict of the most frivolous and inattentive of juries, the New York first-night audience, I must go on trying to say what I want to say in the one way that is best for me to speak.

Sophocles wrote:

Never to have been born is much the best;
And the next best, by far,
To return thence, by the way speediest,
Where our beginnings are.

Which is certainly a confession of abysmal despair. But Sophocles also wrote:

Wonders are many and none is more wonderful than man.

The theatre is the dwelling place of wonder.

The essence of Shakespeare's philosophy is in Hamlet and the essence of Hamlet is in the speech:

What a piece of work is man! How noble in reason! how infinite in faculty! in form and moving how express and admirable! in action how like an angel! in apprehension how like a god! the beauty of the world! the paragon of animals! And yet, to me, what is this quintessence of dust? man delights not me; no, nor woman neither.

Was there ever a more magnificent summing up of all human hopes and misgivings? "How like an angel"—and—"this quintessence of dust." And when you read those lines you know that they were written to be spoken from a stage by an actor—preferably an actor not averse to hamming it up a bit.

That is writing for the theatre—bitterness and confidence—exaggerating both, but not illegitimately. Actors and actresses are in themselves fabulous beings and therefore qualified to express that which print can never adequately convey.

What Shakespeare said—what all the great dramatists have said—is that man is frail, man is vain, man is mortal but that he is still capable of reaching, as did Prometheus, into the highest heaven and snatching the very fire from the hand of God.

That is what the theatre has been for, from its very beginning—to make credible the incredible, to awaken the king that dwells in every humble man, the hero in every coward. The Athenian dramatists first attempted and achieved this at a time when men trod warily in a tiny world which was completely surrounded and beset by the supernatural, the divine, the inexplicable. The sun had not then been measured and analyzed chemically. It was a god in a chariot. The wind that blew over Hymettus and the sea that beat against Sunium were dread beings. And yet, in the midst of this fearful bewilderment, in the face of a generally hostile and entirely incalculable Nature, the Athenian dramatists managed to assert for the first time on earth the dignity of man.

"We easily believe that which we wish," said Corneille.

The dramatist cannot be dismissed as merely a successful merchant of wish fulfillment. For there is historical proof that every age which has produced great dramatists—in Greece, in England and Germany and France—has presaged an age of renewed, vigorous assertion of human rights.

For it is in his wishes that man becomes like an angel, like a god. And the assurance that his wishes can and will be fulfilled is the supreme source of inspiration to man.

A great play, then, is a great inspiration, and its performance is a kind of revivalist meeting. The great dramatist is one who knows that in the tragedy of blindness Oedipus discovered the inward power to see the ultimate truth. . . .

Peter Brook
The Holy Theatre

PETER BROOK (1925–　), the English director and former director of the Royal Shakespeare Company, has been one of the most influential innovators in the contemporary theatre. His experiments include developing a style for the "Theatre of Cruelty," creating performances in nontheatrical spaces, and working with nonverbal modes of expression.

◆ I am calling it the Holy Theatre for short, but it could be called The Theatre of the Invisible-Made-Visible: the notion that the stage is a place where the invisible can appear has a deep hold on our thoughts. We are all aware that most of life escapes our senses: a most powerful explanation of the various arts is that they talk of patterns which we can only begin to recognize when they manifest themselves as rhythms or shapes. We observe that the behaviour of people, of crowds, of history, obeys such recurrent patterns. We hear that trumpets destroyed the walls of Jericho, we recognize that a magical thing called music can come from men in white ties and tails, blowing, waving, thumping and scraping away. Despite the absurd means that produce it, through the concrete in music we recognize the abstract, we understand that ordinary men and their clumsy instruments are transformed by an art of possession. We may make a personality cult of the conductor, but we are aware that he is not really making the music, it is making him—if he is relaxed, open and attuned, then the invisible will take possession of him; through him, it will reach us.

This is the notion, the true dream behind the debased ideals of the Deadly Theatre. This is what is meant and remembered by those who with feeling and seriousness use big hazy words like nobility, beauty, poetry, which I would like to re-examine for the particular quality they suggest. The theatre is the last forum where idealism is still an open question: many audiences all over the world will answer positively from their own experience that they have seen the face of the invisible through an experience on the stage that transcended their experience in life. They will maintain that *Oedipus* or *Berenice* or *Hamlet* or *The Three Sisters* performed with beauty and with love fires the spirit and gives them a reminder that daily drabness is not necessarily all. When they reproach the contemporary theatre for its kitchen sinks and cruelties, this, honourably, is what they are trying to say. They remember how during the war the romantic theatre, the theatre of colours and sounds, of music and movement, came like water to the thirst of dry lives. At that time, it was called escape and yet the word was only partially accurate. It was an escape, but also a reminder: a sparrow in a prison cell. When the war was over, the theatre again strove even more vigorously to find the same values.

The theatre of the late '40s had many glories: it was the theatre of Jouvet and Bérard, and of Jean-Louis Barrault, of Clavé at the ballet, *Don Juan, Amphitryon, La Folle de Chaillot, Carmen,* John Gielgud's revival of *The Importance of Being Earnest, Peer Gynt* at the Old Vic, Olivier's *Oedipus*, Olivier's *Richard III, The Lady's not for Burning, Venus Observed;* of Massine at Covent Garden under the birdcage in the *The Three-Cornered Hat* just as he had been fifteen years before—this was a theatre of colour and movement, of fine fabrics, of shadows, of eccentric, cascading words, of leaps of thought and of cunning machines, of lightness and of all forms of mystery and surprise —it was the theatre of a battered Europe that seemed to share one aim—a reaching back towards a memory of lost grace. . . .

Certainly, we still wish to capture in our arts the invisible currents that rule our lives, but our vision is now locked to the dark end of the spectrum. Today the theatre of doubting, of unease, of trouble, of alarm, seems truer than the theatre with a noble aim. Even if the theatre had in its origins rituals that made the invisible incarnate, we must not forget that apart from certain Oriental theatres these rituals have been either lost or remain in seedy decay. Bach's vision has been scrupulously preserved by the accuracy of his notations: in Fra Angelico we witness true incarnation: but for us to attempt such processes today, where do we find the source? In Coventry, for instance, a new cathedral has been built, according to the best recipe for achieving a noble result. Honest, sincere artists, the 'best', have been grouped together to make a civilized stab at celebrating God and Man and Culture and Life through a collective act. So there is a new building, fine ideas, beautiful glass-work—only the ritual is threadbare. Those Ancient and Modern hymns, charming perhaps in a little country church, those numbers on the wall, those dog-collars and the lessons—they are sadly inadequate here. The new place cries out for a new ceremony, but of course it is the new ceremony that should have come first —it is the ceremony in all its meanings that should have dictated the shape of the place, as it did when all the great mosques and cathedrals and temples were built. Goodwill, sincerity, reverence, belief in culture are not quite enough: the outer form can only take on real authority if the ceremony has equal authority—and who today can possibly call the tune? Of course, today as at all times, we need to stage true rituals, but for rituals that could make theatre-going an experience that feeds our lives, true forms are needed. These are not at our disposal, and conferences and resolutions will not bring them our way.

The actor searches vainly for the sound of a vanished tradition, and critic and audience follow suit. We have lost all sense of ritual and ceremony—whether it be connected with Christmas, birthdays or funerals—but the words remain with us and old impulses stir in the marrow. We feel we should have rituals, we should do 'something' about getting them and we blame the artists for not 'finding' them for us. So the artist sometimes attempts to find new rituals with only his imagination as his source: he imitates the outer form of ceremonies, pagan or baroque, unfortunately adding his own trappings— the result is rarely convincing. And after the years and years of weaker and waterier imitations we now find ourselves rejecting the very notion of a holy stage. It is not the fault of the holy that it has become a middle-class weapon to keep children good. . . .

. . . If we understood more about rituals, the ritual celebration of an individual to whom we owe so much might have been intentional, not accidental. It might have been as powerful as all his plays, and as unforgettable. However, we do not know how to celebrate, because we do not know what to celebrate. All we know is the end result: we know and we like the feel and sound of celebrating through applause, and this is where we get stuck. We forget that there are two possible climaxes to a theatre experience. There is the climax of celebration in which our participation explodes in stamping and cheering, shouts of hurrah and the roar of hands, or else, at the other end of the stick, the climax of silence—another form of recognition and appreciation for an experience shared. We have largely forgotten silence. It even embarrasses us; we clap our hands mechanically because we do not know what else to do, and we are unaware that silence is also permitted, that silence also is good.

It is only when a ritual comes to our own level that we become qualified to deal in it: the whole of pop music is a series of rituals on a level to which we have access. Peter Hall's vast and rich achievement in his cycle of Shakespeare's 'Wars of the Roses' drew on assassination, politics, intrigue, war: David Rudkin's disturbing play *Afore Night Come* was a ritual of death: *West Side Story* a ritual of urban violence, Genet creates rituals of sterility and degradation. When I took a tour of *Titus Andronicus* through Europe this obscure work of Shakespeare touched audiences directly because we had tapped in it a ritual of bloodshed which was recognized as true. And this leads to the heart of the controversy that exploded in London about what were labelled 'dirty plays': the complaint was that the theatre today is wallowing in misery; that in Shakespeare, in great classical art, one eye is always on the stars, that the rite of winter includes a sense of the rite of spring. I think this is true. In a sense I agree wholeheartedly with our opponents—but not when I see what they propose. They are not searching for a holy theatre, they are not talking about a theatre of miracles: they are talking of the tame play where 'higher' only means 'nicer'—being noble only means being decent—alas, happy endings and optimism can't be ordered like wine from cellars. They spring whether we wish it or not from a source and if we pretend there is such a source readily at hand we will go on cheating ourselves with rotten imitations. If we recognize how desperately far we have drifted from any-thing to do with a holy theatre we can begin to discard once and for all the dream that a fine theatre could return in a trice if only a few nice people tried harder.

More than ever, we crave for an experience that is beyond the hum-drum. Some look for it in jazz, classical music, in marijuana and in LSD. In the theatre we shy away from the holy because we don't know what this could be—we only know that what is called the holy has let us down, we shrink from what is called poetic because the poetic has let us down. Attempts to revive poetic drama too often have led to something wishy-washy or obscure. Poetry has become a meaningless term, and its association with word-music, with sweet sounds, is a hangover of a Tennysonian tradition that has somehow wrapped itself round Shakespeare, so that we are conditioned by the idea that a verse play is half-way between prose and the opera, neither spoken nor sung, yet with a higher charge than prose—higher in content, higher somehow in moral value.

All the forms of sacred art have certainly been destroyed by bour-geois values but this sort of observation does not help our problem. It is foolish to allow a revulsion from bourgeois forms to turn into a revulsion from needs that are common to all men: if the need for a true contact with a sacred invisibility through the theatre still exists, then all possible vehicles must be re-examined. . . .

In Haitian voodoo, all you need to begin a ceremony is a pole and people. You begin to beat the drums and far away in Africa the gods hear your call. They decide to come to you, and as voodoo is a very practical religion, it takes into account the time that a god needs to cross the Atlantic. So you go on beating your drum, chanting and drinking rum. In this way, you prepare yourself. Then five or six hours pass and the gods fly in—they circle above your heads, but it is not worth looking up as naturally they are invisible. This is where the pole becomes so vital. Without the pole nothing can link the visible and the invisible worlds. The pole, like the cross, is the junction. Through the wood, earthed, the spirits slide, and now they are ready for the second step in their metamorphosis. Now they need a human vehicle, and they choose one of the participants. A kick, a moan or two, a short paroxysm on the ground and a man is possessed. He gets to his feet, no longer himself, but filled with the god. The god now has form. He is someone who can joke, get drunk and listen to everyone's complaints. The first thing that the priest, the Houngan, does when the god arrives is to shake him by the hand and ask him about his trip. He's a god all right, but he is no longer unreal: he is there, on our level, attainable. The ordinary man or woman now can talk to him, pump his hand, argue, curse him, go to bed with him—and so, nightly, the Haitian is in contact with the great powers and mysteries that rule his day.

In the theatre, the tendency for centuries has been to put the actor at a remote distance, on a platform, framed, decorated, lit, painted, in high shoes—so as to help to persuade the ignorant that he is holy, that his art is sacred. Did this express reverence? Or was there behind it a fear that something would be exposed if the light were too bright, the meeting too near? Today, we have exposed the sham. But we are rediscovering that a holy theatre is still what we need. So where should we look for it? In the clouds or on the ground?

Eugène Ionesco
Experience of the Theatre

EUGÈNE IONESCO (1912–   ), the French playwright of Rumanian origin, has been a major force in the theatre since the early 1950s. In addition to his many plays, he has also written brilliantly on the nature, meaning, and methods of the contemporary theatre. He is often credited as being one of the founding fathers of the Theatre of the Absurd.

◆   Drama is one of the oldest of the arts. And I can't help thinking we cannot do without it. We cannot resist the desire to people a stage with live characters that are at the same time real and invented. We cannot deny our need to make them speak and live before our eyes. To bring phantoms to life and give them flesh and blood is a prodigious adventure, so unique that I myself was absolutely amazed, during the rehearsals of my first play, when I suddenly saw, moving on the stage of the *Noctambules,* characters who owed their life to me. It was a terrifying experience. What right had I to do a thing like that? Was it allowed? And how could Nicolas Bataille, one of my actors, turn into Mr. Martin? . . . It was almost diabolical. And so it was only when I had written something for the theatre, quite by chance and with the intention of holding it up to ridicule, that I began to love it, to rediscover it in myself, to understand it, to be fascinated by it: and then I knew what I had to do.

I told myself that the too intelligent playwrights were not intelligent enough that it was no use for thinkers to look to the theatre for the idiom of a philosophical treatise; that when they tried to bring too much subtlety and refinement into the theatre it was not only too much but not enough; that if the theatre was merely a deplorable enlargement of refined subtleties, which I found so embarrassing, it merely meant that the enlargement was not sufficient. The overlarge was not large enough, the unsubtle was too subtle.

So if the essence of the theatre lay in magnifying its effects, they had to be magnified still further, underlined and stressed to the maximum. To push drama out of that intermediate zone where it is neither theatre nor literature is to restore it to its own domain, to its natural frontiers. It was not for me to conceal the devices of the theatre, but rather make them still more evident, deliberately obvious, go all-out for caricature and the grotesque, way beyond the pale irony of witty drawing-room comedies. No drawing-room comedies, but farce, the extreme exaggeration of parody. Humor, yes, but using the methods of burlesque. Comic effects that are firm, broad and outrageous. No dramatic comedies either. But back to the unendurable. Everything raised to paroxysm, where the source of tragedy lies. A theatre of violence: violently comic, violently dramatic.

Avoid psychology or rather give it a metaphysical dimension. Drama lies in extreme exaggeration of the feelings, an exaggeration that dislocates flat everyday reality. Dislocation, disarticulation of language too.

Moreover, if the actors embarrassed me by not seeming natural enough, perhaps it was because they also were, or tried to be, *too* natural: by trying not to be, perhaps they will still appear natural, but in a different way. They must not be afraid of not being natural.

We need to be virtually bludgeoned into detachment from our daily lives, our habits and mental laziness, which conceal from us the strangeness of the world. Without a fresh virginity of mind, without a new and healthy awareness of existential reality, there can be no theatre and no art either; the real must be in a way dislocated, before it can be reintegrated.

To achieve this effect, a trick can sometimes be used: playing against the text. A serious, solemn, formal production or interpretation can be grafted onto a text that is absurd, wild and comic. On the other hand, to avoid the ridiculous sentimentality of the tear jerker, a dramatic text can be treated as buffoonery and the tragic feeling of a play can be underlined by farce. Light makes shadows darker, shadows intensify light. For my part, I have never understood the difference people make between the comic and the tragic. As the "comic" is an intuitive perception of the absurd, it seems to me more hopeless than the "tragic." The "comic" offers no escape. I say "hopeless," but in reality it lies outside the boundaries of hope or despair.

Tragedy may appear to some in one sense comforting, for in trying to express the helplessness of a beaten man, one broken by fate for example, tragedy thus admits the reality of fate and destiny, of sometimes incomprehensible but objective laws that govern the universe. And man's helplessness, the futility of our efforts, can also, in a sense, appear comic.

I have called my comedies "anti-plays" or "comic dramas," and my dramas "pseudo-dramas" or "tragic farces": for it seems to me that the comic is tragic, and that the tragedy of man is pure derision. The contemporary critical mind takes nothing too seriously or too lightly. In *Victims of Duty* I tried to sink comedy in tragedy: in *The Chains,* tragedy in comedy or, if you like, to confront comedy and tragedy in order to link them in a new dramatic synthesis. But it is not a true synthesis, for these two elements do not coalesce, they coexist: one constantly repels the other, they show each other up, criticize and deny one another and, thanks to their opposition, thus succeed dynamically in maintaining a balance and creating tension. The two plays that best satisfy this condition are, I believe: *Victims of Duty* and *The New Tenant.*

Similarly, one can confront the prosaic and the poetic, the strange and the ordinary. That is what I wanted to do in *Jack, or the Submission,* which I called "a *naturalistic* comedy" too, because after starting off in a naturalistic tone I tried to go beyond naturalism.

In the same way *Amédée, or How to Get Rid of It,* where the scene is laid in the flat of a *petit bourgeois* couple, is a realistic play into which fantastic elements have been introduced, a contrast intended at one and the same time to banish and recall the "realism."

In my first play, *The Bald Soprano,* which started off as an attempt to parody the theatre, and hence a certain kind of human behavior, it was by plunging into banality, by draining the sense from the hollowest clichés of everyday language that I tried to render the strangeness that seems to pervade our whole existence. The tragic and the farcical, the prosaic and the poetic, the realistic and the fantastic, the strange and the ordinary, perhaps these are the contradictory principles (there is no theatre without conflict) that may serve as a basis for a new dramatic structure. In this way perhaps the unnatural can by its very violence appear natural, and the too natural will avoid the naturalistic.

May I add that "primitive" drama is not elementary drama; to refuse to "round off the corners" is a way of providing a clear outline, a more powerful shape; drama that relies on simple effects is not necessarily drama simplified.

If one believes that "theatre" merely means the drama of the word, it is difficult to grant it can have an autonomous language of its own: it can then only be the servant of other forms of thought expressed in words, of philosophy and morals. Whereas, if one looks on the word as only *one* member of the shock troops the theatre can marshal, everything is changed. First of all, there is a proper way for the theatre to use words, which is as dialogue, words in action, words in conflict. If they are used by some authors merely for discussion, this is a major error. There are other means of making words more theatrical: by working them up to such a pitch that they reveal the true temper of drama, which lies in frenzy; the whole tone should be as strained as possible, the language should almost break up or explode in its fruitless effort to contain so many meanings.

But the theatre is more than words: drama is a story that is lived and relived with each performance, and we can watch it live. The theatre appeals as much to the eye as to the ear. It is not a series of pictures, like the cinema, but architecture, a moving structure of scenic images.

Nothing is barred in the theatre: characters may be brought to life, but the unseen presence of our inner fears can also be materialized. So the author is not only allowed, but recommended to make actors of his props, to bring objects to life, to animate the scenery and give symbols concrete form.

2

THE OTHER WORLD
OF THE PLAY

◆   . . . a world without time . . .   . . . surrender
ourselves . . .   . . . passion for knowing . . .
. . . distorting mirror . . .   . . . that boundless realm . . .
    . . . transfigured image . . .. . . the reality of
their dreams . . .   . . . great with things to come . . .
. . . perpetual present moment . . .   . . . mode of
Destiny . . .   . . . passions issue in words and deeds . . .
. . . illusion of Destiny . . .   . . . histrionic imagination . . .
. . . poetry in the mode of action . . .   . . . a complete
unfolding . . .   . . . exits and entrances . . .

Tennessee Williams
The Timeless World of a Play

TENNESSEE WILLIAMS (1911–   ) has been America's most prolific, and perhaps most honored, playwright for the past forty years. Although he has given countless
interviews and written a great deal about the theatre, this essay (his preface to *The Rose
Tattoo*) is still his fullest statement concerning the nature of the theatrical event.

◆   Carson McCullers concludes one of her lyric poems with the line:
"Time, the endless idiot, runs screaming 'round the world." It is this continual
rush of time, so violent that it appears to be screaming, that deprives our actual
lives of so much dignity and meaning, and it is, perhaps more than anything
else, the *arrest of time* which has taken place in a completed work of art that
gives to certain plays their feeling of depth and significance. In London notices
of *Death of a Salesman* a certain notoriously skeptical critic made the remark
that Willy Loman was the sort of man that almost any member of the
audience would have kicked out of an office had he applied for a job or
detained one for conversation about his troubles. The remark itself possibly
holds some truth. But the implication, that Willy Loman is consequently a
character with whom we have no reason to concern ourselves in drama, reveals
a strikingly false conception of what plays are. Contemplation is something
that exists outside of time, and so is the tragic sense. Even in the actual world
of commerce, there exists in some persons a sensibility to the unfortunate
situations of others, a capacity for concern and compassion, surviving from a
more tender period of life outside the present whirling wire-cage of business
activity. Facing Willy Loman across an office desk, meeting his nervous glance
and hearing his querulous voice, we would be very likely to glance at our wrist
watch and our schedule of other appointments. We would certainly *ease* him
out with more expedition than Willy had feebly hoped for. But suppose there
had been no wrist watch or office clock and suppose there had *not* been the
schedule of pressing appointments, and suppose that we were not actually
facing Willy across a desk—and facing a person is *not* the best way to *see* him!
—suppose, in other words that the meeting with Willy Loman had somehow
occurred in a world *outside* of time. Then I think we would receive him with
concern and kindness, even with respect. If the world of a play did not offer
us this occasion to view its characters under the special condition of a *world
without time*, then, indeed, the characters and occurrences of drama would
become equally pointless, equally trivial, as corresponding meetings and happenings in life.

     The classic tragedies of Greece had tremendous nobility. The actors
wore great masks, movements were formal, dance-like, and the speeches had

an epic quality which doubtless were as removed from the normal conversation of their contemporary society as they seem today. Yet they did not seem false to the Greek audiences: the magnitude of the events and the passions aroused by them did not seem ridiculously out of proportion to common experience. And I wonder if this was not because the Greek audiences knew, instinctively or by training, that the created world of a play is removed from the element which makes people little and their emotions fairly inconsequential.

Great sculpture often follows the lines of the human body: yet the repose of great sculpture suddenly transmutes those human lines to something that has an absoluteness, a purity, a beauty, which would not be possible in a living mobile form.

A play may be violent, full of motion: yet it has that special kind of repose which allows contemplation and produces the climate in which tragic importance is a possible thing, provided that certain modern conditions are met.

In actual existence the moments of love are succeeded by the moments of satiety and sleep. The sincere remark is followed by a cynical distrust. Truth is fragmentary, at best: we love and betray each other not in quite the same breath but in two breaths that occur in fairly close sequence. But the fact that passion occurred in *passing*, that it then declined into a more familiar sense of indifference, should not be regarded as proof of its inconsequence. And this is the very truth that drama wishes to bring us . . .[1]

Whether or not we admit to ourselves, we are all haunted by a truly awful sense of impermanence. I have always had a particularly keen sense of this at New York cocktail parties, and perhaps that is why I drink martinis almost as fast as I can snatch them from the tray. This sense is the febrile thing that hangs in the air. Horror of insincerity, of *not meaning*, overhangs these affairs like the cloud of cigarette smoke and hectic chatter. This horror is the only thing, almost, that is left unsaid at such functions. All social functions involving a group of people not intimately known to each other are always under this shadow. They are almost always (in an unconscious way) like that last dinner of the condemned: where steak or turkey, whatever the doomed man wants, is served in his cell as a mockingly cruel reminder of what the great-big-little-transitory world has to offer.

In a play, time is arrested in the sense of being confined. By a sort of legerdemain, events are made to remain *events*, rather than being reduced so quickly to mere *occurrences*. The audience can sit back in a comforting dusk to watch a world which is flooded with light and in which emotion and action have a dimension and dignity that they would likewise have in real existence, if only the shattering intrusion of time could be locked out.

About their lives people ought to remember that when they are finished, everything in them will be contained in a marvellous state of repose which is the same as that which they unconsciously admired in drama. The

---

[1]This punctuation is in the original, as are similar punctuations elsewhere in this essay as printed here. The essay is complete; the punctuation does not indicate omissions.

rush is temporary. The great and only possible dignity of man lies in his power deliberately to choose certain moral values by which to live as steadfastly as if he, too, like a character in a play, were immured against the corrupting rush of time. Snatching the eternal out of the desperately fleeing is the great magic trick of human existence. As far as we know, as far as there exists any kind of empiric evidence, there is no way to beat the game of *being* against *non-being,* in which non-being is the predestined victor on realistic levels.

Yet plays in the tragic tradition offer us a view of certain moral values in violent juxtaposition. Because we do not participate, except as spectators, we can view them clearly, within the limits of our emotional equipment. These people on the stage do not return our looks. We do not have to answer their questions nor make any sign of being in company with them, nor do we have to compete with their virtues, nor resist their offenses. All at once, for this reason, we are able to *see* them! Our hearts are wrung by recognition and pity, so that the dusky shell of the auditorium where we are gathered anonymously together is flooded with an almost liquid warmth of unchecked human sympathies, relieved of self-consciousness, allowed to function . . .

Men pity and love each other more deeply than they permit themselves to know. The moment after the phone has been hung up, the hand reaches for a scratch pad and scrawls a notation: "Funeral Tuesday at five, Church of the Holy Redeemer, don't forget flowers." And the same hand is only a little shakier than usual as it reaches, some minutes later, for a highball glass that will pour a stupefaction over the kindled nerves. Fear and evasion are the two little beasts that chase each other's tails in the revolving wire-cage of our nervous world. They distract us from feeling too much about things. Time rushes toward us with its hospital tray of infinitely varied narcotics, even while it is preparing us for its inevitably fatal operation. . . .

So successfully have we disguised from ourselves the intensity of our own feelings, the sensibility of our own hearts, that plays in the tragic tradition have begun to seem untrue. For a couple of hours we may surrender ourselves to a world of fiercely illuminated values in conflict, but when the stage is covered and the auditorium lighted, almost immediately there is a recoil of disbelief. "Well, well!" we say as we shuffle back up the aisle, while the play dwindles behind us with the sudden perspective of an early Chirico painting. By the time we have arrived at Sardi's, if not as soon as we pass beneath the marquee, we have convinced ourselves once more that life has as little resemblance to the curiously stirring and meaningful occurrences on the stage as a jingle has to an elegy of Rilke.

This modern condition of his theater audience is something that an author must know in advance. The diminishing influence of life's destroyer, time, must be somehow worked into the context of his play. Perhaps it is a certain foolery, a certain distortion toward the grotesque, which will solve the problem for him. Perhaps it is only restraint, putting a mute on the strings that would like to break all bounds. But almost surely, unless he contrives in some way to relate the dimensions of his tragedy to the dimensions of a world in which time is *included*—he will be left among his magnificent debris on a dark stage, muttering to himself: "Those fools . . ."

And if they could hear him above the clatter of tongues, glasses, chinaware and silver, they would give him this answer: "But you have shown us a world not ravaged by time. We admire your innocence. But we have seen our photographs, past and present. Yesterday evening we passed our first wife on the street. We smiled as we spoke but we didn't really see her! It's too bad, but we know what is true and not true, and at 3 A.M. your disgrace will be in print!"

Jean Vilar
Secrets

JEAN VILAR (1912–1970), French director, actor, and producer became the head of the Théâtre National Populaire in Paris in 1951. As director of TNP he presented the great masterpieces of the classic repertoire to large, and often uneducated, audiences. His productions of both ancient and modern plays were simple and pared down, yet stunningly beautiful. He recorded his quest for a popular theatre in his influential book *The Tradition of the Theatre.*

◆ The art of theatre was not born one day in the heart of that drunken fellow who, at a Greek crossroads, sang his joys and sufferings. The art of theatre is also the product of the passion (serene or driven, depending on the individual) for knowledge.

Bacchus, I know, is often the boon companion of actors and playwrights. Dramatic creation remains, nonetheless, a matter of control, for actor as well as playwright. Wilde's stricture is law in this craft: "Only the critical spirit is creative." No work of art (and no acting or direction) can depend on inspiration alone without damage to itself. Inspiration, a necessary evil, provides, in theatre as in architecture, only a rough sketch for a masterpiece which must be *built.*

Playwright! You cannot employ the novelist's resource of description and explanation; and what real good would his palette of true details from life be to you? Your characters must talk, whether in prose or verse, and you know that you have only one effective weapon: the spoken word.

The dialogue of Dostoyevsky's characters has but one accent, a common identity. Balzac sought to differentiate the speaking styles of his characters—was it necessary? Stendhal cared not a fig for such idle foolery.

The speaking style of Alceste, however, is not like that of Dandin; Hamlet's cadences are not those of Macbeth. And the basic reproach that may be levelled against Racine is that the language of his heroes and heroines is too absolutely controlled by the master prosodist: Hermione's cry is that of Phaedra; Antiochus' lament is echoed in Titus'. Prosody, prosody above all, alas! We admire and are astonished by the spareness of this perfect Hellenist's vocabulary: let us not praise him for having so little variety in the range of his cadences, for having compelled all his powdered monsters to employ an identical syntax. A dramatist is not only a poet.

The stage accommodates itself with difficulty to the overstrict rules of the perfect stylist. Character must always remain free with respect to the dramatist's prosody.

Back to our subject.

The art of theatre, then, is ruled by the passion for knowing. Granted, playwright and actor are not Cuvier and Socrates. Neither ever frees himself from the demands of his imagination or from the mythomaniac demons who possess him. Which is to say that the speculative bent of the philosopher or the laboratory researcher are never to be found in him. Illusion, if not lies, rules his professional life.

Actors spend their time in pursuits filled with obsessions and hallucinations regulated by an often less than blithe mythomania. Malraux spoke truly when he said: "Theatre is not serious; mythomania is." And Talma, following his son's corpse to the cemetery, realized at the graveside that he had been *observing* the behavior of a bereaved father all the way.

I know that this is not exactly mythomania. It is more, really: the professional imaginer at his exercises. The pathological liar is the actor's innocent brother; true mythomania is only a risky game compared with the psychic life of the actor. There are many actors—more than one would think —who in the course of time lose their grasp on reality. Some end their days in asylums, victims of their own fantasies.

The spectator, too, is a mythomaniac. The movies have made clear the nature of his myth. The little hunchback, coming out of his neighborhood theatre, feels in his body the easy grace of Gary Cooper. And his wife, when he becomes enterprising in the night, first refuses him, then sighs, when he insists: "Put out the light, then." A story by Carette.

Smile, if you will. But don't forget that the art of theatre attracts and seduces to the extent that it pictures to man and woman a momentary vitality from which the imagination derives a pleasure often more durable than that of sex.

Vitality and pleasure; and, just as for the mythomaniac, an all-embracing, constant, daily need for untruth. The spectator who fails to yield to these understandable follies is rare: Let's face it, he's a theatre professional.

Yes, the deception of ourselves by others and of others by ourselves is that natural demon in us which leads to theatre, calm or hectic, no matter.

For creatures and things deceive us constantly, even the most faithful and sure. Few, if any, of our admirations and loves are free of illusion; that is, of errors of judgment, if not of outright lies. Everything in the realm of the senses and imagination (hence, of artistic creation) is subject to vagaries, hesitations, instability. There is no human work or creature which, in the light of some revealing happening, is not finally seen in its true contradictions. And there is no art which more necessarily unites illusions and reality than theatre; a fact unknown to the public though plain to see. Accomplices?

Truth and lies. Secrets and exposure. Theatre, in its essence, is made of our essence. It will never die.

As often as we disguise our thoughts and actions, so often are we caught by the obsession to know and to see the truth. This is the cruel, incisive weapon of genius. Truth is often inhuman for those who lack the courage or passion to confront it. All of us flee it, often.

The search for truth, however, this insatiable need to penetrate to the very depths of the hidden existence of all beings, is at once poison and antidote to us. Oh, you can be a good actor without these preoccupations; but I don't believe there are any great actors who are not forced by the demands of their art to pursue this quest, this frequently painful interrogation of oneself in relation to others, of the masks of others in relation to oneself.

Are the distorting mirror and the mask the only human states reflected in the theatre's inner secrets? No, another mode of theatre exists in us all: the desire to reveal. Who has not thrilled to the strong, pure emotion of confession, the more so when confession must bring catastrophe. "The players tell all," Hamlet assures us. Drama above all, when it is conceived by Shakespeare.

Let's talk about the spectator.

It is by searching for truth and, along the way, learning the realities of others, their motives and individual passions, that we create ourselves. To know the truth at last strengthens our confidence in ourselves, in the validity of our experience, in the soundness of our judgment; in a word, in our understanding of creatures and things. It seems to me, too—fortunately for the continuance of our art—that this knowledge is the most common there is, acquired by everyone who has passed beyond adolescence. It is our common property, not the special gift of the exceptionally intelligent.

Which is why we must never despair of the natural genius of the audience. Why, also, we need not despair of the quality of their judgment, since we may be sure of the existence of private, often remarkable dramas in the life of every man and woman.

And understanding. Yes, understanding, too. For the theatre, in its masterpieces, is not only the enchanted circle of poetry, cruelty and beauty of gesture. Intellectual understanding; for a genius always distills a meaning comprehensible to all from the stories—exceptional as they are in themselves—of his heroes. If this meaning is not clear, don't try to tell me, "But he has genius." All men and women understand the universal joys and sufferings. Everything else is argumentation, academic fustian, manifestoes, quibbles, dust in the eyes. For men and women come to the theatre prepared, whoever they are, and their private world is a richer soil than even Aeschylus' and Shakespeare's naked monsters. Life, their life, has forced them to understand; not just to hate remorselessly or forgive at once, but to understand. It has bound them to suffering, to chastisement, to cowardice, to what you will, and we have in us a memory that retains it all. We are the sum of those memories, and our memory prepares us and compels us to accept the masterpiece.

The theatre, like our passions, is illusion. It is also action.

If there are no pathetic plays that are not first plays of action, there are equally no verisimilar plays which are not in fact illusory, dead with the last word set down by the poet. A play must be neither all action, nor all imagination. A masterpiece must have reality.

> Let [me] command a mirror hither straight,
> That it may show me what a face I have. . .
> —(Shakespeare, *Richard II,* IV, i.)

The theatre is that mirror. It reflects, in its masterpieces as well as in its plays of a day, our innermost life. A woman, however calm in appearance, in whom are passions of the heart and senses, discovers in the theatre a part of what she knows herself to be and cannot suppress, and feels the weight of another. Such honorable adultery is committed by our most faithful companions: They love, enduringly, a Romeo or a Chimène; not necessarily the actual person of the actor or actress who plays Romeo or Chimène.

Truth and phantom—a mirror, that is theatre.

Projects, yet realization; reflection, yet action; dreaming in the chimney-corner, yet struggle for life—that is our lot in the theatre. By unremitting effort, we have to resist the charms of illusion, which draws us like a vacuum; we have to wed it to the sun of everyday.

Oh, I know! illusion is not dreaming, for the level head. Napoleon reminds us that, where the destiny is great, calculation enters the world of imagination and is not far from dreams. Imagination is not only the artist's tool. At night, at least, the realistic mind drowses in its meditation.

> At home, I repair more often to my library. . . . It is on the third floor
> of a tower. . . . That is my castle. I try to keep it for my sole empery
> and to remove this only corner from the conjugal, filial and civil

community. Unhappy he! to my view, who has not in his home a private home, where he may woo his solitary self, and hide.

—*(Montaigne)*

If imagination is "mistress of error," it is nonetheless necessary before, after, and during action. As de Retz said, it is incumbent on us then to distinguish between the "unusual and the impossible"; a dilemma more refined than Hamlet's "To be or not to be."

Imagination, tool of man and artist's world, is that boundless realm which the stage, and only the stage, can represent. And that is why (this is my conclusion from the preceding lines), just as imagination is abstract and unlimited, even so the stage must be unlimited, unconfined and, if possible, bare. Then the imagination delights and rejoices: the playwright's, the spectator's, the actor's.

That is, is it not, the lesson taught by those masterpieces which are not purely literary? It is the lesson taught by the Greek amphitheatre, the trestle-boards of Spain, the Elizabethan platform and the French tennis court. It is also the example given, in its own way, by that new art of our times, the delight of our fellow-creatures of today—the cinema, with its boundless freedom of montage and fields of vision.

Give me the glass, and therein will I read.
No deeper wrinkles yet? hath sorrow struck
So many blows upon this face of mine,
And made no deeper wounds? O flattering glass,
Thou dost beguile me!
—(Shakespeare, *Richard II*, IV, i.)

And how marvelously skillfully this mirror of man, the theatre, beguiles us! It must beguile us, and it must *flatter* us. It is not for nothing that the great poetic works of the stage end with a transfigured image of the hero, be he a devil.

The hero is, in truth, always a monster. The laws of the stage require it which, among others, require unity of thought in function of the unity of character: that is, the unity of *obsession*. Chimène is as monstrous as Shylock.

Let's get back to our beguilements.

Is there any more perfect example of our imaginative self-deception than Richard II's coffin brought onto the stage and opened? Then the spectator indeed fools himself. Illusion calls the tune; *imaginatio generat casum*. No need for the actor. And let the corpse not show his face! After three hours of the play, the hero is so completely become myth that there is, God knows!

no need for his physical presence. Basta! The actor who played Richard can go smoke his first cigarette of the evening in his dressing room and return to his private life. And yet, out on the stage, the hero continues. No need, at the final and culminating point of this masterpiece, for the actor's voice, or mask, or presence. The symbol alone suffices. The coffin alone is enough—the empty coffin.

I was working on this essay when I had occasion to view an actor's face in the final petrifaction of its mask.

A hospital room. The bare walls whitewashed. Naked. Real. Aggressive. Flowers around the well-loved dead preserved something of our tenderness, something of the life of our sorrowing hearts. He lay with his upper body raised up, chin lifted, the hair still black and plentiful, the lips thinner than ever, dressed in an ordinary suit, without collar, tie or shirt, the undershirt high at the neck. His hands were folded on his stomach, holding a bunch of violets.

He was unrecognizable.

Yet those were his body and hands and face; his nose, his mouth, his angular bones. The lids were lowered over the eyes which had reflected his heart. No smile animated his face. We were looking at a mannequin.

Death does not magnify actors.

Our art is movement; death freezes us. We are incarnation; it destroys our flesh. We attempt to grasp the soul of a character; it takes our own. More eloquently, often, than words, our eyes express suffering and joy; the lids close. Moving and at rest, our hands on stage live with the life of the character; they are forever immobile. We are supple, expansive, sensitive; we become stiff and aloof.

If death claps on the actor's face the mask of a reality without illusion, without flattery; if this cruel, truthful visage belies our dreams; just so does crude reality in theatre plant a desert in our hearts. It affronts our need for flattering illusion, our lighthearted desire to see ourselves other than we are. For theatre, I believe, is unreality, dreams, psychic magic, mythomania. And if it is also reality, at least it must drug and intoxicate us, speed us from the theatre with a heart quickened, the mind full of wonders, and life strong within us.

Cover the dead actor's face.

Hamlet deceives himself. He is a big boy ashamed of his solitude. Hamlet has difficulty convincing us of the tragedy of his situation; of the tragic-ness of his tragedies. His personal drama is too vast—or too simple. Fresnay has said: "I don't know why he comes on the stage, nor why he leaves it." It is the most obscure of all the great roles.

So Hamlet deceives us.

The play's the thing to confound the guilty? To make him confess? No, Your Highness; the culprit is too much a realist and too familiar with the very particular circumstances of his crime to betray himself at its parody. No, my Prince, it is the honest man—if such there be—who trembles before the parable of a fault or a criminal life. Neither perfectly good, nor wholly evil, the honest man alone is capable of betraying himself. As for the remorse aroused in the criminal's bosom by the spectacle of his crime, let's have no illusions. Don't flatter the actor, please! We aren't all conceited fools. Macbeth would have bored Weidmann or Landru, you may be sure. Nor do they put on plays in the *rue des Saussaies.* And don't try to tell me that the re-enactment of the crime is theatre; the murderer may be upset by it, but he doesn't confess.

Let me assure you, my Prince, Himmler cared little enough for our gestures and paint, for our eyes dilated by passion or lining color. He wasn't fond of Shakespeare: found him too gory, or too wordy. He wept tenderly over the death of a canary. These are not like Macbeth-like niceties of feeling.

It is the honest men and women, those in whom the sense of guilt is not worn out, who follow with feverish attention the destinies of our bloody heroes. We know they always have some faults to expiate, and they hear in the masterpieces the faint echo of their vices, their faults, their secret lives.

Stage illusion is the reality of their dreams.

[*Translated by Christopher Kotschnig*]

Susanne Langer
The Dramatic Illusion

SUSANNE LANGER (1895–1978) was one of the great American philosophers of the twentieth century. The comprehensive approach to art which she developed in *Feeling and Form*—first published in 1953—still stands as one of the landmarks of modern aesthetic theory.

◆ Most theoretical treatments of literature draw their material and evidence as much from drama as from lyric and narrative works. A serious analysis of literary art with only an occasional, passing mention of Shakespeare may have seemed to many readers a curious innovation. The reason for it, however, is simple enough, . . . Shakespeare is essentially a dramatist, and drama is not, in the strict sense, "literature."

Yet it is a poetic art, because it creates the primary illusion of all poetry —virtual history. Its substance is an image of human life—ends, means, gains and losses, fulfillment and decline and death. It is a fabric of illusory experience, and it is the essential product of poesis. But drama is not merely a distinct literary form; it is a special poetic mode, as different from genuine literature as sculpture from pictorial art, or either of these from architecture. That is to say, it makes its own basic abstraction, which gives it a way of its own in making the semblance of history.

Literature projects the image of life in the mode of virtual memory; language is its essential material; the sound and meaning of words, their familiar or unusual use and order, even their presentation on the printed page, create the illusion of life as a realm of events—completed, lived, as words formulate them—events that compose a Past. But drama presents the poetic illusion in a different light: not finished realities, or "events," but immediate, visible responses of human beings, make its semblance of life. Its basic abstraction is the act, which springs from the past, but is directed toward the future, and is always great with things to come.

In using common words, such as "event" or "act," as analytic terms, one runs the danger of suggesting far less general concepts, and indeed a variety of them, all equally inadequate to the purpose in hand. "Event," . . . is used in the sense given it by Whitehead, to cover all space-time occurrence, even the persistence of objects, the repetitious rhythms of life, the occasion of a thought as well as of an earthquake. Similarly, by "act" I mean any sort of human response, physical or mental. The word is commonly used, of course, in more specialized senses. It may mean one of the major divisions of a play—Act I, Act II, etc.; or it may refer to overt behavior, rushing about, laying hands on someone, taking or surrendering an object, and so forth; or it may mean a piece of dissembling, as when one says of a person that he feels one way and acts another. In the general sense here employed however, all *reactions* are acts, visible or invisible; so in drama, any illusion of physical or mental activity is here called an "act," and the total structure of acts is *a virtual history in the mode of dramatic action.*

An act, whether instinctive or deliberate, is normally oriented toward the future. Drama, though it implies past actions (the "situation"), moves not toward the present, as narrative does, but toward something beyond; it deals essentially with commitments and consequences. Persons, too, in drama are purely agents—whether consciously or blindly, makers of the future. This future, which is made before our eyes, gives importance to the very beginnings of dramatic acts, i.e. to the motives from which the acts arise, and the situations in which they develop; the making of it is the principle that unifies and organizes the continuum of stage action. It has been said repeatedly that the theater creates a perpetual present moment[1]; but it is only a present filled with its own future that is really dramatic. A sheer immediacy, an imperishable direct experience without the ominous forward movement of consequential

---

[1]For example, R. E. Jones in *The Dramatic Imagination,* p. 40, says: "This is drama; this is theatre—*to be aware of the Now.*" And Thornton Wilder, in "Some Thoughts on Playwriting," lists as one of the "four fundamental conditions of the drama" that "its action takes place in a perpetual present time."—"On the stage it is always now." (*The Intent of the Artist,* p. 83.)

action, would not be so. As literature creates a virtual past, drama creates a virtual future. The literary mode is the mode of Memory; the dramatic is the mode of Destiny.

The future, like the past, is a conceptual structure, and expectation, even more obviously than memory, is a product of imagination.[2] The "now" created by poetic composition is always under the aegis of some historical vision which transcends it; and its poignancy derives not from any comparison with actuality, but from the fact that the two great realms of envisagement —past and future—intersect in the present, which consequently has not the pure imaginative form of either memory or prophecy, but a peculiar appearance of its own which we designate as "immediacy" or "now."

In actual life the impending future is very vaguely felt. Each separate act is forward-looking—we put on a kettle expecting it to boil, hand someone a bill and expect to be given change, board a bus with casual confidence that we shall leave it again at an intended point, or board an airplane with somewhat more conscious interest in our prospective exit from its inside. But we do not usually have any idea of the future as a total experience which is coming because of our past and present acts; such a sense of destiny arises only in unusual moments under peculiar emotional stress.

In drama, however, this sense of destiny is paramount. It is what makes the present action seem like an integral part of the future, howbeit that future has not unfolded yet. The reason is that on the stage, every thought expressed in conversation, every feeling betrayed by voice or look, is determined by the total action of which it is a part—perhaps an embryonic part, the first hint of the motive that will soon gather force. Even before one has any idea of what the conflict is to be (i.e. before the "exposition" has been given), one feels the tension developing. This tension between past and future, the theatrical "present moment," is what gives to acts, situations, and even such constituent elements as gestures and attitudes and tones, the peculiar intensity known as "dramatic quality."

In a little-known volume, bearing the modest, impersonal title: *Essays by Divers Hands* (a volume of "Transactions" of the Royal Society of Literature in England),[3] there is a very thoughtful philosophical essay by Charles Morgan, called "The Nature of Dramatic Illusion," in which he seems to me to have both stated and answered the question of what is created in the full-fledged work of dramatic art—the enacted play.

"With every development of dramatic technique," he wrote there, "and every departure from classical structure, the need increases for a new discussion which . . . shall establish for the stage not indeed a formal rule but

---

[2]Compare the observations of George Mehlis, . . . Mehlis mistook the nature of the "distancing" effect of memory and expectation, which he thought rested on people's tendency to leave out the unpleasant, and a consequent "aesthetic improvement" of the facts; but despite this error he noted truly the transformational power of both projections.

[3]From "The Nature of Dramatic Illusion" by Charles Morgan, Essays by Divers Hands. Royal Society of Literature in England, N. S. Vol. 12, ed. by R. W. Macan, 1933. Reprinted by permission of Roger Morgan.

an aesthetic discipline, elastic, reasoned, and acceptable to it in modern circumstances.

"It is my purpose, then, to discover the principle from which such a discipline might arise. This principle I call the principle of illusion."[4]

"Illusion, as I conceive it, is form in suspense. . . . In a play form is not valuable *in itself,* only the suspense of form has value. In a play, form is not and cannot be valuable in itself, because until the play is over form does not exist. . . .

"A play's performance occupies two or three hours. Until the end its form is latent in it. . . .

"This suspense of form, by which is meant the incompleteness of a known completion, is to be clearly distinguished from common suspense—suspense of plot—the ignorance of what will happen, . . . for suspense of plot is a structural accident, and suspense of form is, as I understand it, essential to the dramatic form itself. . . .

"What form is chosen . . . matters less than that while the drama moves *a* form is being fulfilled."[5]

"Fulfilled" is here the key word to the idea of dramatic form. Everything, of course, has a form of some sort: the famous million monkeys playing a million typewriters for a million years, turning out chance combinations of letters, would be rendering countless phonetic forms (though some of these might not encourage pronunciation); similarly, the most aimless conglomerate of events, acts, utterances, or what not, would *produce* a form when taken together; but before such collections were complete (which would be simply when, for any reason, one stopped collecting), no one could imagine their form. There has to be a sense of the whole, some anticipation of what may or even must come, if the production of new elements is to give the impression that "a form is being fulfilled."

Dramatic action is a semblance of action so constructed that a whole indivisible piece of virtual history is implicit in it, as a yet unrealized form, long before the presentation is completed. This constant illusion of an imminent future, this vivid appearance of a growing situation before anything startling has occurred, is "form in suspense." It is a human destiny that unfolds before us, its unity is apparent from the opening words, or even silent action, because on the stage we see acts in their entirety, as we do not see them in the real world except in retrospect, that is, by constructive reflection. In the theatre, they occur in simplified and completed form, with visible motives, directions, and ends. Since stage action is not, like genuine action, embedded in a welter of irrelevant doings and divided interests, and characters on the stage have no unknown complexities (however complex they may be), it is possible there to see a person's feelings grow into passions, and those passions issue in words and deeds.

---

[4]Ibid., p. 61.
[5]Ibid., pp. 70–72.

We know, in fact, so little about the personalities before us at the opening of a play that their every move and word, even their dress and walk, are distinct items for our perception. Because we are not involved with them as with real people, we can view each smallest act in its context, as a symptom of character and condition. We do not have to find what is significant; the selection has been made—whatever is there is significant, and it is not too much to be surveyed *in toto*. A character stands before us as a coherent whole. It is with characters as with their situations: both become visible on the stage, transparent and complete as their analogues in the world are not.[6]

But what really assures the artistic unity Morgan called "form in suspense," is the illusion of Destiny itself that is given in drama, and that arises chiefly from the way the dramatist handles circumstance. Before a play has progressed by many lines, one is aware not only of vague conditions of life in general, but of a special situation. Like the distribution of figures on a chessboard, the combination of characters makes a strategic pattern. In actual life we usually recognize a distinct situation only when it is reached, or nearly reached, a crisis; but in the theater we see the whole setup of human relationships and conflicting interests long before any abnormal event has occurred that would, in actual life, have brought it into focus. Where in the real world we would witness some extraordinary act and gradually understand the circumstances that lie behind it, in the theater we perceive an ominous situation and see that some far-reaching action must grow out of it. This creates the peculiar tension between the given present and its yet unrealized consequent, "form in suspense," the essential dramatic illusion. This illusion of a visible future is created in every play—not only in very good plays, but in everything we recognize as a play, and not as dance, pageantry, or other non-dramatic "theater act."[7] It is the primary illusion of poetry, or virtual history, in the mode peculiar to drama. The future appears as already an entity, embryonic in the present. That is Destiny.

Destiny is, of course, always a virtual phenomenon—there is no such thing in cold fact. It is a pure semblance. But what it "resembles" (or, in the Aristotelian language which has been lately revived, what it "imitates") is nonetheless an aspect of real experience, and, indeed, a fundamental one,

---

[6]A German critic, Peter Richard Rohden, saw this difference in our understanding of illusory and actual persons, respectively, as something of a paradox. "What," he wrote, "distinguishes a character on stage from a 'real' person? Obviously the fact that the former stands before us as a fully articulated whole. Our fellowmen we always perceive only in fragmentary fashion, and our power of self-observation is usually reduced, by vanity and cupidity, to zero. What we call 'dramatic illusion' is, therefore, the paradoxical phenomenon that we know more about the mental processes of a Hamlet than about our own inner life. For the poet-actor Shakespeare shows not only the deed, but also its motives, and indeed more perfectly than we ever see them together in actual life." (See "Das Schauspielerische Erlebnis," in Ewald Geissler's collection of essays, *Der Schauspieler,* p. 36.)

[7]On this point Mr. Morgan might not agree with me. Having stated that "form in suspense" is the dramatic illusion itself, and the suspense of form something "without which drama is not," he speaks elsewhere of the dramatic illusion as a rare experience, "the highest reward of playgoing." I do not know whether he uses two concepts or only one, somewhat different from mine.

which distinguishes human life from animal existence: the sense of past and future as parts of one continuum, and therefore of life as a single reality.

This wide awareness, which we owe to our peculiarly human talent of symbolic expression, is rooted, however, in the elementary rhythms which we share with all other organisms, and the Destiny which dramatic art creates bears the stamp of organic process—of predeterminate function, tendency, growth, and completion. . . . In every art [the abstraction of those vital forms] is differently achieved; but in each one, I think, it is equally subtle—not a simple reference to natural instances of that form, but a genuinely abstractive handling of its reflection in non-living or even non-physical structures. Literally "organic process" is a biological concept; "life," "growth," "development," "decline," "death"—all these are strictly biological terms. They are applicable only to organisms. In art they are lifted out of their literal context, and forthwith, in place of organic processes, we have dynamic forms: instead of metabolism, rhythmic progression, instead of stimulus and response, completeness, instead of maturation, fulfillment, instead of procreation, the repetition of the whole in the parts—what Henry James calls "reflection" in the parts,[8] and Heinrich Schenker "diminution,"[9] and Francis Fergusson "analogy."[10] And in lieu of a law of development, such as biology sets up, in art we have destiny, the implicit future.

The purpose of abstracting vital forms from their natural exemplifications is, of course, to make them available for unhampered artistic use. The illusion of growth, for instance, may be made in any medium, and in numberless ways: lengthening or flowing lines, that represent no live creatures at all; rhythmically rising steps even though they divide or diminish; increasing complexity of musical chords, or insistent repetitions; a centrifugal dance; poetic lines of gradually deepening seriousness; there is no need of "imitating" anything literally alive in order to convey the appearance of life. Vital forms may be reflected in any elements of a work, with or without representation of living things.

In drama the *situation* has its own "organic" character, that is to say, it develops, or grows, as the play proceeds. That is because all happenings, to be dramatic, must be conceived in terms of acts, and acts belong only to life; they have motives rather than causes, and in turn motivate further and further acts, which compose integrated *actions.* A situation is a complex of impending acts. It changes from moment to moment, or rather, from move to move, as the directly imminent acts are realized and the future beyond them becomes distinct and fraught with excitement. In this way, the *situation* in which characters act differs from their "environment"—a term with which it is sometimes confused, through the influence of the social sciences that invaded the theater a generation ago and bred a teeming, if shortlived progeny of

---

[8] *The Art of Fiction,* p. 170.
[9] Cf. Chap. 8, p. 129.
[10] *The Idea of a Theater,* p. 104.

sociological plays, with a few real dramas among them. The environment wherein characters have developed, and whereby they are stunted or hardened, refined or falsely veneered, is almost always implicit (*almost* always, i.e. except where it becomes a conscious factor of interest to someone in the play). The situation, on the other hand, is always explicit. Even in a vague romantic world like that of Pelléas and Mélisande, removed from all actual history, and so ungeographical that the environment is really just castle walls and a forest, without population (the chorus of women in the death-scene simply springs up *ex nihilo*—there were no inhabitants in the background before, as there are in Shakespeare's castles), the situation that elicits the action is clear.

The situation is, indeed, part of the action; it is conceived entirely by the dramatist, and is given by him to the actors to understand and enact, just as he gives them the words to be spoken. The situation is a created element in the play; it grows to its climax, often branching out into elaborate detail in the course of its development, and in the end it is resolved by the closing of the action.

Where "environment" enters into drama at all, it enters as an idea entertained by persons in the play, such as the slum visitors and reformers of the "radical" problem play. They themselves, however, do not appear in an environment, because that sociological abstraction has no meaning for the theater. They appear in a setting. "Environment" is an invisible constant, but "setting" is something immediate, something sensuously or poetically present. The playwright may utilize a setting as Strindberg did in his earlier plays, to establish the feeling of everyday life, or he may put it to the opposite purpose of removing the scene from all familiar associations, as Wagner sought to do by his extravagant stage demands. The setting is a highly variable factor, which the poets of former ages used to entrust to those who put their plays on the boards; a practice which harbors dangers, but also speaks of a healthy faith in the power of the script to guide the theatrical imagination that is to project it. There is a grand freedom given with the simple indication: "Thebes."

Drama is more variable, more tolerant of choices made by performing artists, than any other art and mode. For this reason, the "commanding form," which is established by the playwright, must be clear and powerful. It has to govern the crisscross of many imaginative minds, and hold them all—the director, the actors, the designers of sets and lights and costumes—to one essential conception, an unmistakable "poetic core." But the poet must give his interpreters scope, too; for drama is essentially an enacted poem, and if the acting can only duplicate what the lines already effect, there will be unintended redundancy, and an apparent clutter of superfluous elements that makes the total form impure and opaque (such failures of clear conception, not the use of materials "belonging" to other arts, not bold secondary illusions, are the source of impurity in a work; if the commanding form is organic and its realization economical, the most abnormal materials will be assimilated, the most intense effects of abstracted space, time, or power will become part of the pure dramatic work).

If drama is not made of words as a piece of literature is, how can the poet, who composes only the "lines," be said to create the commanding form? "Lines" in a play are only the stuff of speeches; and speeches are only some of the acts that make drama.

They are, however, acts of a special sort. Speech is a highly specialized activity in human life, and its image in all modes of poetry, therefore, has peculiar and powerful uses. Verbal utterance is the overt issue of a greater emotional, mental, and bodily response, and its preparation in feeling and awareness or in the mounting intensity of thought is implicit in the words spoken. Speech is like a quintessence of action. Edith Wharton described its relation to the rest of our activities very aptly, when she indicated its use in her own poetic medium, prose fiction: "The use of dialogue in fiction . . . should be reserved for the culminating moments, and regarded as the spray into which the great wave of narrative breaks in curving toward the watcher on the shore."[11]

Mrs. Wharton's metaphor of the wave is more apt than her literal statement, because one naturally thinks of "culminating moments" as rare moments, high points of the story, whereas the culmination of thought and feeling in speech is a frequent occurrence, like the culmination and breaking of each wave in a constant surf.

If, moreover, one contemplates the metaphor a little more deeply, it conveys a further relation of speech to the poetic elements that surround it, namely: that it is always of the same nature as they, subject to the basic abstraction of the mode in which it is used. In narrative it is an event, like all the events that compose the virtual Past—the private events that culminate in "direct discourse," the public events that intersect in the speaker's experience, and those which the speech, as a new event, engenders. In drama speech is an act, an utterance, motivated by visible and invisible other acts, and like them shaping the oncoming Future.

A playwright who writes only the lines uttered in a play marks a long series of culminating moments in the flow of the action. Of course he indicates the major non-verbal acts, but that may be done with the fewest possible words: *enter So-and-so, exit So-and-so,* or such laconic directions as: *dies, they fight, excursions and alarums.* Modern playwrights sometimes write pages of instructions to the actors, even describing the heroine's figure and face, or the style of some character's motions and postures (Strindberg tells the leading actor in *Miss Julia* to look like a half-educated man!). Such "stage directions" are really literary treatments of the story—what Clayton Hamilton called, "the sort of stage directions which, though interesting to the reader, are of no avail whatever to the actor,"[12] because they do not partake of the dramatic form. Ibsen prefaced his opening scenes with minute descriptions of persons and set;

---

[11] *The Writing of Fiction,* p. 73.
[12] *The Theory of the Theatre,* p. 307. A few paragraphs later he remarked on Granville-Barker's plays: "Barker's printed stage directions are little novels in themselves."

but his greatest interpreters have always made free with them. The lines of the play are the only guide a good director or actor needs. What makes the play the author's work is that the lines are really the highlights of a perpetual, progressive action, and determine what can be done with the piece on stage.

Since every utterance is the end of a process which began inside the speaker's body, an enacted utterance is part of a virtual act, apparently springing at the moment from thought and feeling; so the actor has to create the illusion of an inward activity issuing in spontaneous speech, if his words are to make a dramatic and not a rhetorical effect. As a very interesting German writer, Ferdinand Gregori, expressed it, "Gesture is older than words, and in the actor's dramatic creation, too, it must be their herald. Whether it is visible to the audience or not, it must always be the pacemaker. Anyone who starts with the words and then hunts for the appropriate gesture to accompany them, lies to the face of art and nature both."[13]

The need of preparing every utterance by some elements of expression and bearing that foreshadow it, has led many theorists and almost all naive spectators to the belief that an actor must actually undergo the emotive experiences he renders—that he must "live" his part, and produce speech and gesture from a genuine passion. Of course the stage-occurrence is not his own life, but (according to this view) he must pretend to be the individual he represents, until he actually feels the emotions he is to register. Oddly enough, people who hold this belief do not ask whether the actor must also actually have the motives and desires of his alter ego—that is, whether he must really intend or at least wish to kill his antagonist, or to divulge a secret.

The imputation of bona fide feelings and emotions to the actor on stage would be only a negligible popular error, were it not part and parcel of a broader fallacy—the confusion of theatrical representation with "make-believe," or pretense, which has always led both playwrights and directors to misconceive the relation of the audience to the play, and saddled them with the gratuitous and silly problem of the spectator's credulity. The classic expression of concern is, of course, Castelvetro's warning in his *Poetics,* published in 1570: "The time of the representation and that of the action presented must be exactly coincident. There is no possibility of making the spectators believe that many days and nights have passed, when they themselves obviously know that only a few hours have actually elapsed; they refuse to be so deceived."[14] Corneille, a generation later, still accepted the principle, though he complained that to limit a dramatic action quite strictly to one room and the time span of a theater visit "is so awkward, not to say impossible, that some enlargement of place must of necessity be found, as also of time."[15]

---

[13]"Die Vorbildung des Schauspielers," in Ewald Geissler's collection *Der Schauspieler.* See p. 46.

[14]Reprinted in *The Great Critics, An Anthology of Literary Criticism,* edited by J. H. Smith and E. W. Parks. See p. 523.

[15]Ibid., p. 531. From *A Discourse on the Three Unities.*

An art principle that cannot be fully and wholeheartedly applied, but requires compromises and evasions, should be immediately suspect; yet the principle of making the spectators believe that they are witnessing actual happenings has been accepted down to our own day,[16] and though most theorists have seen its error, it still crops up in contemporary criticism, and —worse yet—in theater practice. We have fairly well recovered from the epidemic of naturalism, the stagecraft that sought to dispense with all artifice, and consequently borrowed living material from the actual world—"drugstore clerks drafted to impersonate themselves in real drugstores transferred bodily to the stage," as Robert Edmond Jones described this sort of dramaturgy. Now it is true that real art *can* be made with such devices; no device in itself is taboo, not even putting stagebeggars in clothes begged from real beggars (Edward Wothern, in his autobiography, recalls his acquisition of one such alluring treasure). But the theory that a play is a game of "make-believe" designed by the poet, carried on by actors, and supported by an audience willing to pretend that the stage history is actual, which still persists, and with it its practical counterpart—the principle of deluding the audience, aiding the public "make-believe" by making the play seem as real as possible—is another story.

The whole conception of theater as delusion is closely linked with the belief that the audience should be made to share the emotions of the protagonists. The readiest way to effect this is to extend the stage action beyond the stage in the tensest moments, to make the spectators feel themselves actually present as witnesses of the scene. But the result is artistically disastrous, since each person becomes aware not only of his own presence, but of other people's too, and of the house, the stage, the entertainment in progress. Rosamond Gilder reported such an experience in her comment on Orson Welles' staging of *Native Son;* describing the scene wherein Bigger Thomas is cornered by his pursuers, she said: "Here flashing lights, gun-play, shouting and shooting converge on the stage from balcony and boxes. The theatrical illusion, far from being increased, is shattered, and the scene becomes nothing more than a nineteen-forty-one version of Eliza crossing the ice."[17]

I, too, remember vividly to this day the terrible shock of such a recall to actuality: as a young child I saw Maude Adams in *Peter Pan.* It was my first visit to the theater, and the illusion was absolute and overwhelming, like

---

[16]Strindberg, for instance, was convinced that the spectators in the theater let themselves be deluded, tricked into believing or making-believe that what they saw was actual life going on in their presence, and he was seriously afraid of what popular education, and the general enlightenment it was expected to bring, would do to people's credulity. In the famous preface to *Miss Julia* he observes that "the theater has always served as a grammar school to young people, women, and those who have acquired a little knowledge, all of whom retain the capacity for deceiving themselves and being deceived," but that "in our time, when the rudimentary, incomplete thought-processes operating through our fancy seem to be developing into reflection, research, and analysis, the theater might stand on the verge of being abandoned as a decaying form, for the enjoyment of which we lack the requisite conditions."

[17]"Glamor and Purpose," in *Theatre Arts*, May 1941, pp. 327–335.

something supernatural. At the highest point of the action (Tinkerbell had drunk Peter's poisoned medicine to save him from doing so, and was dying) Peter turned to the spectators and asked them to attest their belief in fairies. Instantly the illusion was gone; there were hundreds of children, sitting in rows, clapping and even calling, while Miss Adams, dressed up as Peter Pan, spoke to us like a teacher coaching us in a play in which she herself was taking the title role. I did not understand, of course, what had happened; but an acute misery obliterated the rest of the scene, and was not entirely dispelled until the curtain rose on a new set.

The central fallacy in such play production, and in the concept of drama that it assumes, is the total disregard of what Edward Bullough, in an essay that has become deservedly famous,[18] called "psychical Distance." All appreciation of art—painting, architecture, music, dance, whatever the piece may be—requires a certain detachment, which has been variously called the "attitude of contemplation," the "aesthetic attitude," or the "objectivity" of the beholder. As I pointed out in an early chapter of this book,[19] it is part of the artist's business to make his work elicit this attitude instead of requiring the percipient to bring an ideal frame of mind with him. What the artist establishes by deliberate stylistic devices is not really the beholder's attitude —that is a by-product—but a relation between the work and its public (including himself). Bullough terms this relationship "Distance," and points out quite rightly that "objectivity," "detachment," and "attitudes" are complete or incomplete, i.e. perfect or imperfect, but do not admit of degrees. "Distance, on the contrary, admits naturally of degrees, and differs not only according to the nature of the *object,* which may impose a greater or smaller degree of Distance, but varies also according to the *individual's capacity* for maintaining a greater or lesser degree."[20]

He describes (rather than defines) his concept, not without resort to metaphor, yet clearly enough to make it a philosophical asset:

"Distance . . . is obtained by separating the object and its appeal from one's own self, by putting it out of gear with practical needs and ends. . . . But it does not mean that the relation between the self and the object is broken to the extent of becoming 'impersonal'. . . . On the contrary, it describes a *personal* relation, often highly emotionally colored, but *of a peculiar character.* Its peculiarity lies in that the personal character of the relation has been, so to speak, filtered. It has been cleared of the practical, concrete nature of its appeal. . . . One of the best-known examples is to be found in our attitude towards the events and characters of the drama. . . ."[21]

---

[18] "'Psychical Distance' as a Factor in Art and an Aesthetic Principle," *British Journal of Psychology,* June, 1912.

[19] See Chap. 4.

[20] *Op. cit.,* p. 94.

[21] *Op. cit.,* p. 91. The attitude referred to is, of course, the famous "aesthetic attitude," here treated as an index to the proper degree of distance.

This relation "of a peculiar character" is, I believe, our natural relation to a symbol that embodies an idea and presents it for our contemplation, not for practical action, but "cleared of the practical, concrete nature of its appeal." It is for the sake of this remove that art deals entirely in illusions, which, because of their lack of "practical, concrete, nature," are readily distanced as symbolic forms. But delusion—even the quasidelusion of "make-believe"—aims at the opposite effect, the greatest possible nearness. To seek delusion, belief, and "audience participation" in the theater is to deny that drama is art.

There are those who do deny it. There are very serious critics who see its essential value to society not in the sort of revelation that is proper to art, but in its function as a form of ritual. Francis Fergusson and T. S. Eliot have treated drama in this vein,[22] and several German critics have found in the custom of hand clapping a last vestige of the audience participation that is really the public's lost birthright.[23] There are others who regard the theater not as a temple, but primarily as an amusement hall, and demand of drama that it shall please, delude us for a while, and incidentally teach morals and "knowledge of man." Brander Matthews extended the demand for amusement—any or every sort of amusement—to all the arts; but as his renown rests entirely on his dramatic criticism and teaching, his view of "art" is really a view of the theater casually extended to all other realms. "The primary purpose of all the arts is to entertain," said Matthews, "even if every art has also to achieve its own secondary aim. Some of these entertainments make their appeal to the intellect, some to the emotions, and some only to the nerves, to our relish for sheer excitement and for brute sensation; but each of them in its own way seeks, first of all, to entertain. They are, every one of them, to be included in the show business."[24]

Here we have certainly two extremes of dramatic theory; and the theory I hold—that drama is art, a poetic art in a special mode, with its own version of the poetic illusion to govern every detail of the performed piece—this theory does not lie anywhere between these extremes. Drama is neither ritual nor show business, though it may occur in the frame of either one; it is poetry, which is neither a kind of circus nor a kind of church.

Perhaps the greatest snare in the course of our thinking about theater is its free trafficking with the standard materials of all the other arts. People are so used to defining each art by its characteristic medium that when paint is used in the theater they class the result as "the painter's art," and because the set requires building, they regard the designer of it as an architect. Drama,

---

[22]Cf. Francis Fergusson, *The Idea of a Theater.* A book so full of ideas, scholarship and discernment that even in taking issue with it I would recommend it to every reader.

T. S. Eliot, in "A Dialogue on Dramatic Poetry" (in *Selected Essays, 1917–1932*), p. 35, lets "E" say, "The only dramatic satisfaction that I find now is in a High Mass well performed."

[23]E.g., Theodor Wiesengrund-Adorno, "Applaus," *Die Musik,* 23 (1930–31), p. 476; also A. E. Gunther, "Der Schauspieler und wir," in Geissler's *Der Schauspieler,* p. 144.

[24]*A Book About the Theater,* p. 6.

consequently, has so often been described as a synthesis of several or even all arts that its autonomy, its status as a special mode of a great single art, is always in jeopardy. It has been treated as essentially dance, by confusion with pantomimic dances that have a dramatic plot; it has been conceived as tableau and pageantry heightened by speech and action (Gordon Craig held that the designer of its visual aspects was its real creator), and as poetic recitation accompanied by gestures, sometimes by dance-gestures. This last view is traditional in India, where it is supported by the obvious epic sources of Hindu plays (as usual, finding the source of a phenomenon is supposed to reveal its "real" nature). Hindu aestheticians, therefore, regard drama as literature, and judge it by literary standards.[25] Nietzsche found its origin in "the spirit of music" and consequently regarded its true nature as musical. Thornton Wilder describes it as an exalted form of narrative: "The theater," he writes, "carries the art of narration to a higher power than the novel or the epic poem. . . . The dramatist must be by instinct a story-teller."[26]

But story-telling, narration, is something quite different from story-enactment in a theater. Many first-rate story-tellers cannot make a play, and the highest developments of narration, such as the modern novel and short story, show devices of their own that have no meaning for the stage. They project a history in retrospect, whereas drama is history coming. Even as performed arts, narration and dramatization are distinct. The ancient rhapsodist, for all his gesticulations and inflections, was not an actor, and today, too, people who are known as good readers of poetry or prose need not therefore have any aptitude for the theater.

The concept of drama as literature embellished with concurrent appeals to the sense of sight is belied most convincingly in the very society where it enjoys its traditional vogue; the fact that in India the classic drama survived as a popular art for centuries after both the Sanskrit and the various Prakrits in which it was composed had become dead languages, understood only by scholars, proves that the stage action was no mere accompaniment, but was instinctively developed by the actors to the point of self-sufficiency, making the precise word meanings of the speeches dispensable; that this drama is, in fact, what Cocteau called "a poetry of the theater," as well as "poetry in the theater."

As for dance, though it probably preceded drama on the boards, and though it uses dramatic plots after its own fashion, it does not give rise to drama, not even to true pantomime. Any direct dramatic action tends to suspend the balletic illusion. The fact that Greek drama arose amidst ritual

---

[25]Cf. Sylvain Levi, *Le théâtre indien*, p. 257: 'They [Indian theorists] are wont to consider drama as the juxtaposition of two arts, which simultaneously pursue their respective ends, namely poetry and mimetic dance. . . . Dance and mummery, stagecraft and scenery combine to heighten the illusion and pleasure by appealing to several senses. Representation, therefore, surpasses reading by a quantitative difference of emotion; there is no qualitative difference between them." See also A. B. Smith, *The Sanskrit Drama*, pp. 294–295.

[26]"Some Thoughts on Playwriting," p. 86.

dancing has led several art historians to consider it as a dance episode; but the dance was, in fact, only a perfect framework for the development of an entirely new art; the minute the two antagonists stepped out of the choric ensemble and addressed not the deity, nor the congregation, but each other, they created a poetic illusion, and drama was born in midst of the religious rite. The choric dance itself was assimilated to the world of the virtual history they presented.

Once we recognize that drama is neither dance nor literature, nor a democracy of various arts functioning together, but is poetry in the mode of action, the relations of all its elements to each other and to the whole work become clear: the primacy of the script, which furnishes the commanding form; the use of the stage, with or without representational scenery, to delimit the "world" in which the virtual action exists; the need of making the scene a "place," so that often the designer produces a plastic illusion that is secondary here, but primary in the art of architecture;[27] the use of music and sometimes of dance to keep the fictitious history apart from actuality and insure its artistic abstraction;[28] the nature of dramatic time, which is "musical" instead of practical time, and sometimes becomes strikingly evident—another secondary illusion in poetry, but the primary one of music. The guiding principle in the use of so many transient borrowed illusions is the making of an *appearance,* not under normal circumstances, like a pretense or social convention, but under the circumstances of the play. Its total emotional tone is like the "palette" of a picture, and controls the intensity of color and light, the sober or fantastic character of the sets, the requirements such as overture, interludes, and what not.

Above all, that emotional tone guides the style of the actors. The actors are the chief interpreters—normally, the only indispensable ones—of the poet's incomplete but commanding creations. An actor does not undergo and vent emotions; he conceives them, to the smallest detail, and enacts them.

Some of the Hindu critics, although they subordinate and even deprecate dramatic art in favor of the literary elements it involves, understand much better than their Western colleagues the various aspects of emotion in the theater, which our writers so freely and banefully confuse: the feelings experienced by the actor, those experienced by the spectators, those presented as undergone by characters in the play, and finally the feeling that shines through the play itself—the vital feeling of the piece. This last they call *rasa;* it is a state of emotional knowledge, which comes only to those who have long studied and contemplated poetry. It is supposed to be of supernatural origin,

---

[27]Cf. Jones, *op. cit.,* p. 75: "The energy of a particular play, its emotional content, its aura, so to speak, has its own definite physical dimensions. It extends just so far in space and no farther. The walls of the setting must be placed at precisely this point."

George Beiswanger, in a little article entitled "Opera for the Eye" (*Theatre Arts,* January, 1943, p. 59), makes a similar remark: "Each opera has its own ideal dimensions, and their illusion must be created whether the actual stage be large or small."

[28]Schiller, in his famous preface to *Die Braut von Messina,* called the Greek Chorus, which he revived in this play, "a living wall" to preserve the Distance of the work.

because it is not like mundane feeling and emotion, but is detached, more of the spirit than of the viscera, pure and uplifting.[29]

Rasa is, indeed, that comprehension of the directly experienced or "inward" life that all art conveys. The supernatural status attributed to its perception shows the mystification that beset the ancient theorists when they were confronted with the power of a symbol which they did not recognize as such. Audiences who can dispense with the helps that the box stage, representational setting and costumes, and sundry stage properties lend to our poetic imagination have probably a better understanding of drama as art than we who require a potpourri of means. In Indian, Chinese, and Japanese drama—but most consistently in the Far Eastern—not only events and emotions, but even *things are* enacted. Stage properties exist, but their use is symbolic rather than naturalistic. Even the simulation of feeling may be sacrificed to enhance the formal value, the emotional effect of the play as a whole. Objects involved in the action are simply implied by gesture.[30] In India, some stage properties do occur—carts, dragons, even elephants—and are elaborately made of paper, bamboo, lacquer, etc.; others are left to the imagination. The deciding factor seems to be whether the action turns on the non-human element, or not. A king who quite incidentally mounts a chariot merely indicates its existence by an act, but in *The Little Clay Cart* the cart is really put upon the stage. European spectators at Chinese plays always find it surprising and offensive that attendants in ordinary dress come and go on the stage; but to the initiated audience the stagehand's untheatrical dress seems to be enough to make his presence as irrelevant as to us the intrusion of an usher who leads people to a seat in our line of vision.

On the Japanese stage, an actor may step out of his part by giving a signal and address the audience, then by another formal sign resume his role.

A public that enjoys such pure acting gives itself up to the dramatic illusion without any need for sensuous delusion. But sensuous satisfaction it does want: gorgeous robes and curtains, a rich display of colors, and always music (of a sort that Westerners often find no asset). These elements make the play dramatically convincing precisely by holding it aloof from actuality; they assure the spectator's "psychical Distance" instead of inviting him to consider the action as a piece of natural behavior. For in the theater, where a virtual future unfolds before us, the import of every little act is heightened, because even the smallest act is oriented toward the future. What we see, therefore, is not behavior, but the self-realization of people in action and passion; and as every act has exaggerated importance, so the emotional responses of persons in a play are intensified. Even indifference is a concentrated and significant attitude.

---

[29]Sylvain Levi, *op. cit.,* p. 295.

[30]See Jack Chen, *The Chinese Theater;* A. E. Zucker, *The Chinese Theater;* Noel Peri, *Cinq no: Drames lyriques japonais.* The last-named gives the most detailed account of this technique.

As every act and utterance set down in the poet's script serves to create a perceptible destiny, so all plastic, choreographic, or musical elements that are added to his play in the theater must support and enhance that creation. The dramatic illusion is poetic, and where it is primary—that is to say, where the work is a drama—it transmutes all borrowings from other art into poetic elements. As Mr. Jones says in *The Dramatic Imagination,* "In the last analysis the designing of stage scenery is not the problem of an architect or a painter or a sculptor or even a musician, but of a poet."[31] It is the painter (or architect, or sculptor) turned poet who understands the commanding form which the author has composed by writing the lines of the play, and who carries this form to the further state of visibility, and it is the actor-poet who takes the whole work—words, setting, happenings, all—through the final phase of its creation, where words become utterances and the visible scene is fused into the occurrence of the virtual life.

Histrionic imagination is the same fundamental talent in the playwright, the leading actors, the performers of even the smallest parts in so far as they are genuine actors, the scene and light designer, the costumer, the light controller, the composer or selector of incidental music, the ballet master, and the director who surveys the whole to his satisfaction or despair. The work on which they are engaged is one thing—an apparition of Destiny.

"From the Greeks to Ibsen the actor has represented, by elocution as well as by movement, human character and human destiny. . . . When drama takes on the abstract character of music or pure dance it ceases to be drama. . . .

"The dramatist . . . is a writer, a poet, before he is a musician or a choreographer. Wagner of course showed that many dramatic elements can be embodied in orchestral music; silent movies showed how much can be done with the visual element alone; but if you add Wagner to Eisenstein and multiply by ten you still do not have a Shakespeare or an Ibsen. This does not say that drama is better than music, dancing, or the visual arts. It is different.

"The defenders of the arts of the theater must be infected by the commodities of the theater if they can forget that all 'theater arts' are means to one end: the correct presentation of a poem."[32]

---

[31]P. 77.
[32]From E. R. Bentley, "The Drama at Ebb," *Kenyon Review,* VII, 2 (Spring, 1945), 169–184.

Michael Goldman
The Actor's Freedom

MICHAEL GOLDMAN (1936–   ), actor, director, and scholar, is a professor at Princeton. His book, *The Actor's Freedom,* has proven to be one of the most significant theories of drama published in the past decade. Drawing on many diverse sources—primitive shamanism, contemporary psychiatric theory, and a wide range of plays—he has boldly reexamined the ways we experience drama in performance.

◆ . . . The art of the theater—and the nature of its appeal—cannot be separated from the mechanism of appearance and disappearance. Theater is exits and entrances. Resurrections and rehearsals, the dimming of lights, curtain calls, the curtain itself, the structure of the scene, wings, traps, the clown's head around the cardboard tree, the deus ex machina, prologues and epilogues—are all refinements and recurrences of the one pervasive motif. Wherever we have theater, we have hiding and surprise, appearance and disappearance. Among many primitive tribes, the sudden rush of the performers into the playing area and the concealment of important props and costumes are essential elements in presentation, in which the audience often actively participates:

> This stage moving is done with rather remarkable expedition and the dancers contrive to keep the stage furniture from the spectators' view. This attempt at secrecy is rather noteworthy. Women spectators, for instance, may seize their mats and rush forward to help in concealing the stage properties as they are brought on, already well enough concealed as they are by the throng of stage-movers.

Among children, games of appearance and disappearance, hiding and finding, now-you-see-it-now-you-don't are ubiquitous and powerful. And like the child's games of imitation, they spring from the experience of fear. For their purpose is twofold: to make what is lost return and to master the experience of being lost. When we are left behind—as our mothers and fathers constantly leave us—we experience not losing-someone, but being-lost. The little boy in *Beyond the Pleasure Principle* who reacts to his mother's frequent absence by developing a game in which he throws his toys under the bed is enacting losing-of-the-baby; he is mastering it, as Erik Erikson suggests. The same little boy, we recall, also played a game with his mirror, making himself appear and disappear. R. D. Laing's young daughter would make him put his hands over his eyes, then remove them and crow with delight over what she had accomplished: nothing less than her own obliteration and renewal.

Of course all works of art that unfold in time involve appearances and disappearances. Characters in a novel have their exits and entrances too. But only in the theater do actual people and objects appear, disappear, and reappear. The show goes *on*, it is repeated and rehearsed, what is lost can be brought back. Drama is full of recognitions and reconciliations, reunions and dispersals, deaths and entrances. It is not like a movie, where the product's permanence gives it an obsessive quality, as in dreams. The star dies but we can screen him indefinitely. If we need theater it's because, as we often casually say, we need "live" entertainment, and specifically because of the promise in the word "live"—it can't be dead. The immortality of the stage actor is different from that of the screen actor, who is simply preserved by a mechanical process, an indestructible illusion summoned from the past. The stage actor, while he is acting, cannot die—he must be alive. On stage, all losses can be restored.

Thus theater springs from the games we play with fear and loss. All art does this, but theater is closest to the root: to the shaman, the maenad, the obsessive child; to the first loomings of our parents; to ghosts and spirits; to the full physicality of the game and the apprehensions the game springs from; to the actual matter and mastery of our fears. Not that the subjects of drama are inevitably unpleasant, or that the greatest plays contain the greatest horrors. But the source of theatrical excitement lies close to our most primitive awareness of threat; the vitality of the dramatic artist springs from the inherent threatening nature of the materials he handles. Both in the process of impersonation and his relation to the audience, the actor's art never ceases to handle—with an unparalleled immediacy—the haunting volatility of a menacing world.

There is good reason why imitation, of the dead, with the aim of propitiating and expelling them, is a fundamental element in so much primitive drama. Such ceremonies bring together many of drama's essentials—the impulse to act and behold acting, the mystery and appeal of exits and entrances, the dramatic excitement of ghosts, the general thrust to handle terror. And impersonating the dead has an interesting relation to aggression—a relation, we may speculate, with a significant bearing on drama. When we act out the hostile aggression of our dead toward us, we draw of course on our aggression toward them. Like the little boy in *Beyond the Pleasure Principle*, we make them go away because they have lost *us*. But by making them go away, by transforming them from malign to benevolent spirits, we also transform or banish our aggression toward them, which would otherwise remain with us undischarged. It, too, ceases to haunt us. Each year among the Tangkul of northern Burma, actors who for days have impersonated the dead, having been repeatedly feasted and heaped with gifts, are led in rich costumes and with the greatest show of respect out of their little village to a tree on the outskirts of the community—thence, it is understood, to disappear beyond the river and toward the hills, happily and forever. We may think of the *Oresteia*, which ends with a similar procession—for the Furies, before they are propitiated, feted, and renamed as the benevolent Eumenides, are themselves the threatening representatives of dead men scorned.

The transformation of ghosts, the transformation of our aggressions: In primitive mourning ritual (as in psychiatric theory) it seems impossible to separate them. Perhaps, in some useful sense, this will apply to sophisticated drama too. In the connected movements and transformations of haunting and aggression, it may be possible to discover many of the patterns and pleasures of the stage. . . .

"Theory" and "theater" derive from the same source. The theater is a *theatron*, a seeing place, but the kind of seeing involved is legitimately *theorein* as opposed to other seeing—an inspection, a looking at with a distinctive intensity, as a traveler or ambassador looks at things. Not a coming into the range of vision, nor a staring, but a process by which the mind inspects and possesses in inspection, as it possesses its own thoughts. The theater is thus, though not a place for contemplation, nevertheless a mind-place. For Plato and Aristotle, *theorein* was the mode for self-discovery or radical change.

What the mind inspects and possesses in the theater is action in performance in a scene, actors doing things in a special world which yet bears upon our own. The acting area is both a sacred field and a condensation of the known world, a place where the actor cannot die, the space where his gestures exhibit their eloquence because of the special charging of the place, because of its investment with significance. The place exhibits the actors and holds the audience. It is always in some form a great reflector, helping to receive and throw back—as the performers receive and throw back—the aggressions of the audience.

Quasimodo has defined eloquence in poetry as "discourse with a world gathered up into a narrow landscape." Some intense condensation of the world is a feature of all literature. It is what William Empson has called "the pastoral," a landscape apparently small enough to be familiar and yet somehow containing the world. The actions of the Elizabethan hero gained resonance from being performed on a stage that had the recognizably condensed presence of the world. The same is true of the sacred bull's-eye of Greek drama and the balanced aquarium of fourth-wall realism. In this sense the physical setting of the theater—the theater building, stage, scenery—is a kind of eloquence itself, an eloquence at least *in posse* which the proper discourse can realize. It is a place for the mind, for "learning to think" in the sense that the symbolic play of a very young child is a way of learning to think—a place, that is, where we can assimilate freely so much that reminds us of the most traumatic adaptations. . . .

Hamlet is the most interesting play ever written—and one reason for this is that it is immediately concerned with the nature of theatrical interest itself, with the relation of the actor's art to life. So it is no surprise that it pays special attention to the process of identification on-stage and off, and that it is alert to the connections between the two, to the ways in which the problems of establishing an effective self in dramatic performance illuminate the more general problem of establishing identity in a mortal world. I want to take advantage of this now, and treat the play as a commentary on our appetite for drama, particularly on the meaning and nature of acting as a mode of experience.

To say, as Hamlet does when we first see him, "I have that within which passeth show," is to challenge provocatively the value of drama; it is to say that no performance can adequately express the self. Hamlet suggests that anything that can be performed may be, indeed is likely to be, a mere pretense ("They are actions that a man might play"). The defiance in Hamlet's assertion exposes a doubt as to identity, for to claim that what is within cannot be shown is to doubt that the self can ever be whole in action or utterance. It is to confess to a weight on the self that the self cannot master; Hamlet's belief in the unactability of what is within him is at one with the overwhelming depression he confesses to in his first soliloquy:

> How weary, stale, flat, and unprofitable
> Seem to me all the uses of this world.

The world disgusts him, and all actions in it are meaningless. His position is similar to Cordelia's initial refusal of all show at the beginning of *Lear*. In both plays, these anti-theatrical refusals are preludes to an upheaval and chaos in the visible world we feel reflects an inner upheaval of the self.

In Hamlet's case the upheaval—which causes him to question the very foundations of being and to wish he had never been born—comes about because he is enjoined to *act*. Just as his profound attachment to his father has driven him to find all actions meaningless, it now leads him to devote himself to pursuing his father's instructions to act—and to act as a revenger, which means constructing an action of a peculiarly elaborate, meaningful, and self-consciously theatrical kind. It is theatrical in many senses, but perhaps most of all in that, against the background of a world in which all actions are ambiguous, in which a gesture of love may be a springe to catch a woodcock, in which it is hard to tell the difference between a spirit of health and a goblin damned, in which even to be and not to be are ambiguously intertwined— against this background, Hamlet as a revenger is called upon to construct an action whose climax must be an emblematic punishment, as clear as it is satisfying. It must not only achieve its immediate end—the death of Claudius —and do so through disguise and plotting, but it must be, as the revenge genre requires, a properly significant killing, vengeance for a foul and unnatural murder. Its meanings must be made unambiguously visible to an on-stage audience, in this case the Danish court.

Hamlet's efforts to accomplish his task lead him, of course, into the most elaborate disguises and scenarios. Starting as a man who rejects all activity as play-acting, he becomes not only an actor—assuming the antic disposition, speaking daggers but using none—but a playwright, and even an instructor of actors. Significantly, the kind of growth required of him strikingly resembles a process that may be observed both in the psychic development of children and the training of professional actors. Psychologists describe this process as the movement from "play-action" to "play-acting," from the immediate expression of emotion in action, to the transformation of emotions into impersonations, "scripted" and controlled:

> Play *action* is characterized by the unmodified expression of the instincts of love and hate in the form of play. Play *acting* utilizes a more mature . . . process of mental functioning in which the instinctual expression is subservient to the specific play. . . . Normally, as the child grows, play action gives way to play acting. Stage acting encompasses both activities. However, the actor who is limited to the play-action level of his art is usually an inferior, exhibitionistic artist and may be emotionally disturbed. The play-acting actor controls and regulates his acting technique and therefore is likely to be a competent professional.

Hamlet makes a similar distinction to the actors:

> Nor do not saw the air too much with your hand, thus, but use all gently, for in the very torrent, tempest, and (as I may say) whirlwind of your passion, you must acquire and beget a temperance that may give it smoothness.

Otherwise, as he points out, some necessary question of the play may be neglected. The smoothness and temperance Hamlet requires here are the professional regulation of emotion the play-acting actor has mastered. It is the technique Hamlet himself must master in order to respond successfully to his own cue for action. The play-action of the earlier scenes, the sulky silences and wild outbursts, are gradually left behind when, in response to the Ghost's injunction, he learns he must behave like a trained actor and even a writer of plays.

The unregulated outbursts do not vanish entirely. Hamlet's rage and anguish are always close to the surface and he finds it difficult to control them, but we soon see him struggling to accommodate his painful emotions to play-acting. At the end of the second act, when Hamlet contrasts the Player's feigned passion over Hecuba with his own real emotion, he flies into a fury in which he rants like a conventional stage revenger, but then he suddenly stops and sees his outburst as a kind of performance:

> Bloody, bawdy villain!
> Remorseless, treacherous, lecherous, kindless villain!
> O, vengeance!
> Why, what an ass am I! This is most brave,
> That I, the son of a dear father murdered,
> Prompted to my revenge by heaven and hell,
> Must, like a whore, unpack my heart with words
> And fall a-cursing like a very drab,
> A scullion! Fie upon't, foh!

This shift of focus, which enables him to see his play-action as play-acting, apparently allows him to go a step further, for, now, he realizes that he can use drama itself as part of his plot for revenge:

> . . . Fie upon't, foh! About, my brains.
> Hum—
> I have heard that guilty creatures sitting at a play . . .
> . . . The play's the thing
> Wherein I'll catch the conscience of the King.

In our own lives, too, the transition from play-action to play-acting is never complete, and as with Hamlet or the perpetually struggling actor, it is repeated constantly in the effort to build a coherent and effective self.

The child develops "character" (control over his emotions, power over other people's) as the actor develops the power to play characters. Like the child's, the actor's play-acting grows out of play-action. The leap by which he takes on another identity depends, to begin with, on his capacity for emotional expressiveness, his ability to act out the aggression inside him ("unmodified expression . . . of love and hate"), the play of intense reactions to the external world. But the leap is complete only when he applies some regulation—some governing aggression, we might say—to this instinctive play. Once more we come upon the paradox of acting, and here we may see that it involves a peculiarly ambiguous relation to sincerity. Only when you "modify" your emotions, that is, alter them, can you "play" them successfully. Not surprisingly, sincerity presents a problem Hamlet must struggle with too. When we first see him he is positively tongue-tied with sincerity, oppressed by a sense that all action must falsify what he feels. Polonius puts the problem glibly— the important thing, he says, is to be true to one's self. But for Hamlet sincerity in action is no simple matter. As the play progresses, we encounter a number of characters who are obviously true to themselves, who enjoy a simple relation of inner feeling to outward act. They make the conventional gestures with no sense of ambiguity. But the obvious "sincerity" of Laertes, Fortinbras, and the First Player leaves Hamlet either irritated or envious. Their simple directness or simple artifice—attractive as it may at moments seem—is not adequate to his difficulty, any more than it would be to an actor who wanted to play Hamlet's part.

Hamlet's development is a paradigm of the problem of sincerity in its radical form, the form which connects the problem of sincerity with our appetite for drama. What Hamlet, children, and actors have in common is that they are haunted—and compelled by what haunts them to "act." Feeling incomplete, robbed, or betrayed, they are driven by some ghostly, elusive force —almost against their will—from play-action to play-acting; they must make up for the grief that passes show with a series of passionately maintained disguises. Surely they experience, in aggravated form, a struggle within the self that goes on ceaselessly in each of us, that drives us all to some kind of concocted selfhood, thrown together to meet the slings and arrows of daily life, and leaves always some residue of longing for a clearer self, for fuller freedom, for sharply defined and true identity. I said earlier that the self discovers its identity in fear and deprivation. It is through our relationship with the ghosts who arise at that discovery—with unstable, inexorable, haunting presences disturbingly like our parents, as disturbing in their sorrow as in their anger, arousing fear and urgency and guilt—that we begin to learn, like Hamlet, about the dangerous forces lying within us and around us. What these ghosts are, psychology still struggles to learn. They are, perhaps, instinctive or ac- quired fears, innate aggressions, scars left by various traumas—the shocks that flesh is heir to—suppressed desires, memories of our parents, patterns and relations we are doomed to repeat (or, as we say, to "re-enact"). They may be some or all of these, or perhaps something entirely different. For our purposes, it is only necessary to acknowledge that, whatever they are, they haunt us, and begin to haunt us as we begin to discover that we are separate, beleaguered selves. It is our ghosts who force us to take action and to make the pretenses, true or false, that taking action requires. It is our ghosts—all the hauntedness we carry around inside us—who make it hard for us, impossible really, to be true to ourselves, to that within which passes show. For no matter what it does, the self cannot achieve the identification it desires in real life, it can only approximate it, and usually at the kind of cost that tragedy suggests. The theatricality of daily life, however necessary, is always at least partially a withdrawal, a compromise, a falsification, a way of covering up. In the theater, however, it can become a way of opening out, without that sense of compro- mise. This is not to deprecate real life in order to make a case for theater, nor to deny that it is through the great leaps of role playing and play-acting, through imperfect masks and partial truths, that we must blossom into action in our lives, if blossom we can. It is merely to note that the special awareness of a complete identification in the present, which our daily play-acting both points toward and recognizes as impossible, does become available to us in the theater when we respond to and participate in the actor's art. Our ghosts make play-actors of us all, but they also attract us to actors and the theater. We turn to drama as the Tangkul and Orokolo did, to drive our ghosts away. Even the blandest commercial play does this, though in the most obvious, least satisfying fashion—for example, an old baddy is defeated, and his money and his daughter are given to some nicely cosmeticized version of ourselves. What more could we want? Only when we get more do we know. In better hands, we find that ghosts can be expelled from regions much closer to our hearts— closer to the wounds where our identities began. What all drama, of whatever quality, works to drive away are the ghosts that keep us blurred and incomplete, longing for and frightened by completion.

But this is only half the story. For the aim of drama, as we have seen, is not simply to expel ghosts but to win their power for the living, to invest the self with the power of what frightens it, keeps it incomplete, hunts it down. One could say that, in the theater, we join the actors in repeating that step into selfhood-through-play-acting which we first made as children. Only now we can step, as we could not then and cannot elsewhere, into a free and full identity. The tragic process makes it possible for Hamlet, in the teeth of everything, to be true to himself in the audience's mind, to have an actor-like definiteness that seems nevertheless to be in contact with the most painful confusions and uncertainties of our existence. He achieves a complete unfolding—as drama generally makes it possible for actors-as-characters to achieve some kind of unique truth-to-self in which the audience participates. Truth-to-self, hauntingness, identification, freedom—I have used all these terms, at different times, to suggest the kind of strangeness-in-action that affects us in the theater, and I have also suggested that they may be used as touchstones in the analysis of individual plays or the drama of particular eras. The words are so interrelated as at times to be nearly interchangeable, for they all serve to express the powerful yet elusive claim which the processes of acting exercise upon us. I have said that Hamlet haunts Elsinore as the Ghost has haunted him; it is the power of ghosts to act and be free that actors take on in performance, and that we ourselves take on, watching them perform.

It seems a given quality of human consciousness to imagine a clarity of self of which the self is incapable, and to judge, guide, criticize the self, indeed to lead one's life, in terms of achieving this ideal clarity. In *Hamlet* all the fundamental conditions of pain, loss, and failure that define the self against its will and make impossible the triumphant self-definition for which the self is destined to long—all these conditions are heightened and pressed forward on the audience's consciousness. They are familiar to the psyche from infancy: the labyrinth of our attachment to parents; the horror of death; our fear of darkness, poison, cold, and the unknown; the sense of indefinable corruption at work in everything; the sinister ambiguity of all gestures. Against this we watch the career of Prince Hamlet, learning the need for theater in his life—playing role upon role, adopting disguise within disguise—in order to be true to himself. These are all "actions that a man might play," but they are the only actions available, and life needs this giving and hazarding, this thrust toward self-definition in action.

To possess genuine identity, to achieve a free and unbewildered clarity of being, to define oneself through action in the world though every action threatens to compromise the self because it exposes the self as fundamentally unclear and incomplete—this is the continuing project of the self, in one sense necessary, in another impossible. It is also the project, as Hamlet discovers, that only theater accomplishes, and for this reason, identification, as I have been calling it, stands at the center of the uniqueness of dramatic art, and bears decisively upon the human needs drama satisfies, the kind of meaning it makes, the special relation it establishes between ourselves and the world. . . .

David Cole
The Theatrical Event

DAVID COLE (1941–   ) is a playwright, theorist, and sometime teacher of drama. Drawing on the wide range of new scholarship in shamanism, he has sought to redefine the theatrical event in terms of myth and ritual as it is manifest in shamanist performance.

◆ . . . The suggestion that the actor is a kind of shaman gains in plausibility from the fact that, in most cultures, the shaman is a kind of actor.

Many witnesses have been struck by the theatrical nature of the séances in which a shaman sends his spirit forth to the *illud tempus*. The mere fact that these séances are usually performed in public, for onlookers—an unusual setting for ecstatic experience—gives them the aura of a performance situation. But the resemblances go far beyond that. In fact, it is difficult to think of a single aspect of theatre that cannot also be an aspect of shamanic "performance."

The most basic respect in which these events resemble theatre is the considerable amount of mimed action and spoken dialogue they contain. The shaman laboriously mimes the ascent or descent to the other world which his soul is at that moment making. This may involve, if it is an ascent, his climbing a mountain or flying like a bird; or, if it is a descent, his opening the earth and passing through it, crossing a narrow bridge, or swimming to the bottom of the sea. Once arrived in the other world, he uses mime to transmit back to his onlookers the adventures he is, psychically, having there: battles against divine animals or demons, social contact with gods. The latter often gives rise to dialogues, in which the shaman speaks for both himself and the deity. The shaman must be something of an expert in vocal characterization, for in the course of one of these dialogues he may be called upon to produce everything from the sound of a horse drinking to the hiccups of a god. In addition to mime and dialogue, the shaman may draw on such incidental performance skills as ventriloquism and puppetry to help render his adventures in the other world.

Shamanic performance also has a scenic dimension that allies it with theatre. The shaman employs costumes, properties, music, even primitive lighting effects and scene-changes. Shamans' costumes range from animal suits to stylized representations of the human skeleton, and often display elaborate color symbolism. A shaman's properties can include such diverse items as baskets of paper flowers, brooms, and flags. Music is provided both by accompanying drummers and by the shaman himself, who may play upon a trumpet-like or violinlike instrument, or simply shake rattles and bells. (Seed pods and bells are sometimes sewn right into his costume, making him a virtual one-man band.) Brilliant lamps, sinking hearth-fires, lighted candles, gun flashes, and sparking brands tossed aloft into the air are among the lighting effects employed in shamanic performance. Set-changes are accomplished by the rearrangement of objects in the room to correspond to each new site the shaman visits in his "wanderings."

Two sure signs of dramatic impulse in any ritual are the interpolation of comic episodes and the appearance of additional actors. Both these tendencies are in evidence in shamanic séances. For example, Siberian shamans mime such comic scenes as the offering of tobacco to a bird. And in Koniag and Toba séances, large segments of the audience join in the song and dance, sometimes taking the performance out of the shaman's hands.

Finally in this connection, it is interesting to note what personality traits are thought, in many cultures, to mark one as a potential shaman: "Frequent fainting-fits, excitable and sensitive disposition, taciturnity, moroseness, love of solitude and other symptoms of a susceptible nervous system." This profile closely corresponds to our own notion of the "star" temperament as sensitive, volatile, and moody.

But it is not enough to show that shamanism is, in some peripheral respects, theatrical. We want to know whether acting is, in any essential respect, shamanic. We have already seen that in his public role, as a community's envoy to an *illud tempus,* the actor performs a function distinctly parallel to that of the shaman. We must now go on to enquire whether the parallel extends to the inner experience of each as he goes about fulfilling this public role.

Primitive peoples believe the *illud tempus* to be an actual historical period and not merely, as in our view, a constellation of mental archetypes. Nonetheless, for them, too, the *illud tempus* is within—not, as for us, *only* within, but *also* within. Consequently, any voyage there is going to have to be pursued through outer and inner space simultaneously, through the cosmos and through the mind.

From the point of view of the community that sends him, the space through which the shaman journeys is cosmological. Shamans are thought of as "going up to the sky" via a "central opening," which they penetrate by means of a ladder, rope, bridge, or mountain—all objects which figure prominently in shamanic rite and imagery.

But for the shaman himself, whose means of "ascent" is ecstasy, not rockets, the space traversed is interior: "What for the rest of the community remains a cosmological ideogram, for the shamans . . . becomes a mystical itinerary." And the means of traversing it (shamanism and modern psychology are at one on this point) is the dream:

> It is in dreams that the pure sacred life is entered and direct relations with the gods, spirits and ancestral souls are reestablished. It is always in dreams that historical time is abolished and the mythical time regained.

> The pattern of shamanism is primarily the dream journey to the house of the supernatural being.

The *illud tempus* which the actor seeks is likewise at once without and within; and for him, too, the "space" through which he must travel to get there is both external and inner. Considered in his public role—as a community's envoy to a script—the actor makes a journey between two points external to himself: from his audience's mental life to the script *illud tempus.* But the actor himself experiences this journey as inward, as what Grotowski calls a "self-penetration." For the actor as for the shaman, an inward journey is the sole means by which a journey can be performed on behalf of others. The shaman can explore the archetypal world of the *illud tempus* only by seeking those archetypes in his own fantasies, memories, and dreams. The actor can explore an *illud tempus* which is the work of another man's imagination only by exploring his own psyche for answering impulses, shared fantasies, common symbolisms: "In the beginning his understanding of the inner significance of a play is necessarily too general. Usually he will not get to the bottom of it until he has thoroughly studied it by following the steps the author took when he first wrote it." The way to the Image lies through the self. In searching for the life of a role, it is one's own life one searches. . . .

3

THE MAKING OF DRAMA

◆　　. . . imitation of an action . . .　　. . . dramatic
shorthand . . .　. . . from ignorance to knowledge . . .
. . . language is the wine . . .　　. . . characters are
identities with roles . . .　　. . . excitement of discovery . . .
. . . purgation of the passions of fear and pity . . .
. . . conventions are essential . . .　　. . . to hear
expressed what they cannot express themselves . . .
. . . working out of a motive . . .　　. . . act of
judging . . .　　. . . particular words and phrases . . .
. . . composed of events . . .　　. . . conjure up
a fictitious world . . .

Francis Fergusson
Aristotle's *Poetics* and the Modern Reader

FRANCIS FERGUSSON (1904–   ) has probably done more than anyone to illuminate Aristotle's *Poetics* in terms of modern theatre theory and practice. In his very important book, *The Idea of a Theater,* he examines such key Aristotelian ideas as "imitation," "reversal," "discovery," and "catharsis," as they relate to ten major plays. His Introduction to *The Poetics,* included here, is a comprehensive analysis of Aristotle's theories.

I. The *Poetics* and the Modern Reader

◆   The *Poetics,* short as it is, is the most fundamental study we have of the art of drama. It has been used again and again, since the text was recovered in the early Renaissance, as a guide to the techniques of play-making, and as the basis of various theories of drama. In our own time the great Marxist playwright, Bertolt Brecht, started with it in working out his own methods. He thought that all drama before him was constructed on Aristotle's principles, and that his own "epic drama" was the first strictly non-Aristotelian form.

When Aristotle wrote the *Poetics,* in the fourth century B.C., he had the Greek theater before his eyes, the first theater in our tradition. Perhaps that is why he could go straight to the basis of the dramatic art: he "got in on the ground floor." There is a majestic simplicity about the opening sentence, which we (in our more complex world) can only envy: "I propose to treat of Poetry in itself and of its various kinds, noting the essential quality of each. . . ." It still appears that, for tragedy at least, his favorite form, he did just that.

But the *Poetics* is not so simple for us as that sentence suggests. In the two thousand years of its life it has been lost, found again, and fought over by learned interpreters in every period. The modern reader, approaching it for the first time, may benefit from a little assistance.

The text itself is incomplete, repetitious in spots, and badly organized. It probably represents part of a set of lecture notes, with later interpolations. Our text is the translation of the late S. H. Butcher, who also edited the Greek from the sources. It is one of the standard texts, probably the best now available in English. The reader will find Butcher's "Analytical Table of Contents" on pages 45–48 a useful guide on a first reading. Each chapter is summarized, and the main interpolations and omissions are indicated.

In writing the *Poetics* Aristotle apparently assumed that his readers would know his own philosophy, and also the plays and poems he discusses. Certain key terms, like "action," "pathos," "form," can only be fully understood in the light of Aristotle's other writings. Moreover, his whole method is empirical: he starts with works of art that he knew well, and tries to see in them what the poet was aiming at, and how he put his play or poem together. He does not intend the *Poetics* to be an exact science, or even a textbook with strict laws, as the Renaissance humanists tried to make out with their famous "rules" of the unities of time, place, and action. He knew that every poet has his unique vision, and must therefore use the principles of his art in his own way. The *Poetics* is much more like a cookbook than it is like a textbook in elementary engineering.

The *Poetics* should therefore be read slowly, as an "aid to reflection"; only then does Aristotle's coherent conception of the art of drama emerge. In what follows I shall offer a short reading of this kind: bringing out the main course of his thought; pausing to see what he means by his notions of human psychology and conduct; and illustrating his artistic principles by actual plays. For the sake of convenience I shall use Sophocles' *Oedipus Rex*, Aristotle's own favorite tragedy, as my main illustration. But of course the art of drama is the matter in hand, and the more plays one analyzes in the light of Aristotle's principles, the better one understands the scope and value of the *Poetics*.

II. Preliminary Observations on Poetry and Other Arts (Chapters I–V)

The opening chapters of the *Poetics* appear to be an introduction to a longer work (which has not survived) on the major forms of Poetry known to Aristotle, including comedy, epic, and dithyrambic poetry, as well as tragedy. The *Poetics* as it has come down to us, however, is devoted mainly to tragedy, and it is in Aristotle's analysis of that form that his general theory of art is most clearly illustrated. The first five chapters should be read, therefore, as a preliminary sketch which Aristotle will fill in when he gets down to business in Chapter VI.

Poets, like painters, musicians, and dancers, Aristotle says, all "imitate action" in their various ways. By "action" he means, not physical activity, but a movement-of-spirit, and by "imitation" he means, not superficial copying, but the representation of the countless forms which the life of the human spirit may take, in the media of the arts: musical sound, paint, word, or gesture. Aristotle does not discuss this idea here, for it was a commonplace, in his time, that the arts all (in some sense) imitate action.

The arts may be distinguished in three ways: according to the *object* imitated, the *medium* employed, and the *manner*. The object is always a particular action. The writer of tragedy (as we shall see) imitates a "serious and complete action"; the writer of comedy, one performed by characters who are "worse"—by which Aristotle may mean "sillier"—than the people we know in real life. By "medium" he simply means the poet's words, or the painter's colors, or the musician's sound. By "manner" he means something like "convention." Thus the manner of the writer of epics (or novels) is to represent the action in his own words; that of the playwright to represent it by what characters, acted on a stage, do and say. One may use the notions of object, medium, and manner still, to give a rough classification of the varied forms of poetry we know in our day.

In Chapter IV Aristotle briefly raises the question of the origin and development of poetry, which includes all the forms of literature and drama. He thinks it comes from two instincts in human nature itself, that of *imitation* and that of *harmony and rhythm*. The pleasure we get from the imitations of art is quite different from direct experience: it seems to come from *recognizing* what the artist is representing; some experience or vague intuition which suddenly seems familiar. It satisfies our need to know and understand; imitation has to do with the intellectual and moral content of art, and is therefore related to philosophy. Harmony and rhythm, on the other hand, refers to the pleasures of form which we usually consider "purely esthetic." It is characteristic of Aristotle to recognize both the content and the form of art.

After this short but suggestive passage, Aristotle sketches the historic development of the dithyramb, comedy, epic, and tragedy, in Greece. The passage is important, for it is the starting point of modern investigations of the sources of literature and the theater in our tradition, but Aristotle has, at this point, very little to say. It has been left to modern anthropologists and historians to fill in the details as well as they could . . . .

Aristotle did not have our interest in history, nor did he believe, as we often do, that the most primitive forms of human culture were the most significant. He thought that the only way to understand man, or his institutions, or his arts, was in their most fully developed, or "perfected" state. In the *Poetics* he seeks the highest forms of the art, and the masterpieces within each form, in order to see, in them, what poetry may be; and so he is led to tragedy. "Whether Tragedy has as yet perfected its proper types or not . . . raises another question," he writes (IV.11); but tragedy was the form known to him which best fulfilled the aims of poetry, and most fully employed the resources of that art. He leaves room (in his usual cautious way) for the possible appearance of other forms; meanwhile he takes Greek tragedy, and especially Sophocles' masterpiece, *Oedipus Rex,* as his main instance of what poetry can be.

In Chapter V Aristotle begins a discussion of comedy, but this part is fragmentary, and not enough survives to tell us what he thought of that art. In Chapters XXIII and XXVI he discusses epic, but he thinks the principles of epic are only corollaries of those of tragedy, the more complete form. It is his analysis of tragedy, which begins in Chapter VI, that constitutes the main argument in the *Poetics.*

III. Tragedy: An Imitation of an Action

In Chapter VI.2, Aristotle starts his analysis of the art of tragedy with his famous definition:

> Tragedy, then, is an imitation of an action that is serious, complete, and of a certain magnitude; in language embellished with each kind of artistic ornament, the several kinds being found in separate parts of the play; in the form of action, not of narrative; through pity and fear of effecting the proper purgation of these emotions.

This definition is intended to describe tragedy, and also to distinguish it from other forms of poetry. Greek tragedy employed a verse form near to prose, like our English blank verse, for the dialogue, and elaborate lyric forms with musical accompaniment for the choruses; that is what Aristotle means by the different kinds of language. It is "in the form of action"—that is, it is acted on a stage—unlike epic, which is merely told by one voice. The "purgation of pity and fear" is Aristotle's description of the special *kind* of pleasure we get from tragedy.

The play itself, as we read it or see it performed, is the "imitation" of an action, and in what follows Aristotle devotes his attention, not to the action, but to the making of the play which represents an action. He is concerned with the *art* of tragedy; the phases of the poet's work of play-making. The six "parts of Tragedy" which he discusses are, in fact, part of the poet's creative labor, and should be translated, "plot-*making*," "character *delineation*," and so forth. But before one can understand Aristotle's account of the poet's *art*, one must know what the art is trying to represent: the vision, or inspiration, which moves the poet to write or sing, i.e., the "action."

The concept of "action"; action and passion

Just after the definition of tragedy (VI.5) Aristotle tells us that action springs from two "natural causes," character and thought. A man's character disposes him to act in certain ways, but he *actually* acts only in response to the changing circumstances of his life, and it is his thought (or perception) that shows him what to seek and what to avoid in each situation. Thought and character together *make* his actions. This may serve to indicate the basic meaning of "action," but if one is to understand how the arts imitate action, one must explore the notion a little further.

One must be clear, first of all, that *action (praxis)* does not mean deeds, events, or physical activity: it means, rather, the motivation from which deeds spring. Butcher[1] puts it this way: "The *praxis* that art seeks to reproduce is mainly a psychic energy working outwards." It may be described metaphori-

---

[1]*Aristotle's Theory of Poetry and Fine Art*, by S. H. Butcher. 4th ed., London: Dover, 1932.

cally as the focus or movement of the psyche toward what seems good to it at the moment—a "movement-of-spirit," Dante calls it. When we try to define the actions of people we know, or of characters in plays, we usually do so in terms of motive. In the beginning of *Oedipus Rex,* for instance, Oedipus learns that the plague in Thebes is due to the anger of the gods, who are offended because the murderer of old King Laius was never found and punished. At that point Oedipus's action arises, i.e., his motive is formed: "to find the slayer." His action so defined continues, with many variations in response to changing situations, until he finds the slayer, who of course turns out to be himself. When Aristotle says "action" *(praxis)* in the *Poetics,* he usually means the whole working out of a motive to its end in success or failure.

Oedipus's action in most of the play is easy to define; his motive is a clear and rational purpose. That is the kind of action which Aristotle usually has in mind in discussing tragedy, and his word *praxis* connotes rational purpose. The common motive "to find the slayer" accounts for the main movement of *Oedipus Rex;* and most drama, which must be instantly intelligible to an audience, depends on such clearly defined motivation. But we know that human motivation is of many kinds, and in *Oedipus Rex,* or any great play, we can see that the characters are also moved by feelings they hardly understand, or respond to ideas or visions which are illusory. When one thinks of the other arts that imitate action, it is even more obvious that "rational purpose" will not cover all action: what kind of "movement-of-spirit" is represented in music, or painting, or lyric verse? "The unity of action," Coleridge wrote,[2] "is not properly a rule, but in itself the great end, not only of drama, but of the lyric, epic, even to the candle-flame of the epigram—not only of poetry, but of poesy in general, as the proper generic term inclusive of all the fine arts as its species." That is exactly Aristotle's view. He sees an action represented in every work of art, and the arts reflect not only rational purpose but movements-of-spirit of every kind.

In the *Poetics* Aristotle assumes, but does not explain, his more general concept of action. Thus when he writes (VI.9), "life consists in action, and its end is a mode of action," he is referring to the concept as explained in his writings on ethics. The word he uses there to cover any movement-of-spirit is *energeia.* In his studies of human conduct he speaks of three different forms of *energeia,* which he calls *praxis, poiesis,* and *theoria.* In *praxis* the motive is "to do" something; we have seen that Oedipus's action, as soon as he sees that he must find the slayer, is a *praxis.* In *poiesis* the motive is "to make" something; it is the action of artists when they are focused upon the play, or the song, or the poem, which they are trying to *make.* Our word "poetry" comes from this Greek word, and the *Poetics* itself is an analysis of the poet's action in making a tragedy. In *theoria* the motive is "to grasp and understand" some truth. It may be translated as "contemplation," if one remembers that, for Aristotle, contemplation is intensely active. When he says (VI.9) that the

---

[2]In his essay on *Othello.*

end of life is a mode of action, he means *theoria*. He thought that "all men wish to know," and that the human spirit lives most fully and intensely in the perception of truth.

These three modes of action—doing, making, and contemplation— provide only a very rough classification of human actions, and Aristotle is well aware of that. For every action arises in a particular character, in response to the particular situation he perceives at that moment: every action has its own form or mode of being. Moreover, in Aristotle's psychology, both action and character (which he defines as *habitual action*) are formed out of ill-defined feelings and emotions, which he calls *pathos*. In any tragedy, which must represent a "complete action," the element of pathos is essential. If we are to understand the action in our example, *Oedipus Rex*, we must reflect upon the relationship between the pathos with which the play begins and ends, and the common purpose, to find the slayer, that produces the events of the story.

In Aristotle's philosophy, and in many subsequent theories of human conduct, the concepts "action" and "passion" (or *praxis* and *pathos*), are sharply contrasted. Action is active: the psyche perceives something it wants, and "moves" toward it. Passion is passive: the psyche suffers something it cannot control or understand, and "is moved" thereby. The two concepts, abstractly considered, are opposites; but in our human experience action and passion are always combined, and that fact is recognized in Aristotle's psychology. There is no movement of the psyche which is pure passion—totally devoid of purpose and understanding—except perhaps in some pathological states where the human quality is lost. And there is no human action without its component of ill-defined feeling or emotion; only God (in some Aristotelian philosophies) may be defined as Pure Act. When Aristotle says "life consists in action," he is thinking of action, in its countless forms, continually arising out of the more formless pathos (or "affectivity," as we call it) of the human psyche. Even in pain, lust, terror, or grief, the passion, as we know it, acquires some more or less conscious motive, some recognizably human form. That is why Aristotle can speak (XVIII.2) both of "pathetic" motivation, which is closer to the passionate pole of experience, and "ethical" motivation, which is closer to reason and the consciously controlled will.

With these considerations in mind, one can see more clearly what Aristotle means by the "complete action" which a tragedy represents. In the Prologue of *Oedipus Rex*, Thebes is suffering under the plague, and the Citizens beseech King Oedipus for help: the common purpose, "to cure Thebes," arises out of the passion of fear. When Creon brings the Oracle's word, the action is more sharply defined as "to find the slayer." Each Episode is a dispute between Oedipus and one of his antagonists about the quest for the slayer, and each one ends as the disputants fail to agree, and new facts are brought to light. The Chorus is left a prey to its fear again. The Choral Odes are "pathetic" in motivation, but their pathos, or passion, is given form through the continued effort *to see* how the common purpose might still be achieved. When Oedipus at last finds himself to be the culprit, his action is shattered, and even his character as an ethically responsible man along with it. The Chorus suffers with him; but through the laments and terrible visions of the end of the play, their action moves to *its* end: they see the culprit, and thereby the salvation of the city. Moreover, they see in self-blinded Oedipus a general truth of the human condition:

> Men of Thebes: look upon Oedipus.
>
> This is the king who solved the famous riddle
> And towered up, most powerful of men.
> No mortal eyes but looked on him with envy.
> Yet in the end ruin swept over him.
>
> Let every man in mankind's frailty
> Consider his last day; and let none
> Presume on his good fortune until he find
> Life, at his death, a memory without pain.[3]

This marks the end of the action in more ways than one. The common purpose has reached its paradoxical success, and the Chorus (and through it, the audience) has attained that mode of action, *theoria,* contemplation of the truth, which Aristotle regarded as the ultimate goal of a truly human life.

The complete action represented in *Oedipus Rex* is (fortunately for our purposes) easy to see. But all human actions which are worked out to the end, passing through the unforeseeable contingencies of a "world we never made," follow a similar course: the conscious purpose with which they start is redefined after each unforeseen contingency is suffered; and at the end, in the light of hindsight, we see the truth of what we have been doing. Mr. Kenneth Burke has used this "tragic rhythm of action," as he calls it, Purpose, to Passion, to Perception, in his illuminating analyses of various kinds of literature. All serious works of fiction or drama represent some complete action, even so complex a form as Shakespearean tragedy. In short, Aristotle's notion is useful still; for his lore of "action" is a kind of natural history of the psyche's life.

How plot-making imitates the action

Plot-making is in bad odor with contemporary critics of poetry, because they think of it as the mechanical ingenuity of whodunits and other "plotty" entertainments. Aristotle saw the usefulness of that kind of plot-making, and offers suggestions about how to do it; but his own primary conception of plot is "organic." He sees the plot as the basic *form* of the play, and in that sense one might speak of the "plot" of a short lyric.

---

[3] *The Oedipus Rex of Sophocles.* An English Version by Dudley Fitts and Robert Fitzgerald. (New York: Harcourt Brace Jovanovich, Inc., 1949.)

But he is discussing the making of the plot of tragedy, and his first definition of it (VI.6) applies only to drama: "the arrangement of the incidents." This definition is very useful, as a beginning, because it enables one to distinguish the plot both from the story the poet wishes to dramatize, and from the action he wishes to represent.

The *story* of Oedipus was known to Sophocles as a mass of legendary material covering several generations. In making his *plot,* he selected only a few incidents to present onstage, and represented the rest through the testimony of Tiresias, Jocasta, the Messenger from Corinth, and the old Shepherd. The distinction between plot and story applies to all plays, including those whose story is invented by the poet. The story of an Ibsen play, for instance, might be told as a three-decker novel, but Ibsen always "arranges the incidents" in such a way as to show only a few crucial moments directly.

The purpose of plot-making is to represent one "complete action," in the case of *Oedipus Rex* the quest for the slayer which I have described. We must suppose that Sophocles saw a quest, a seeking motive, in the sprawling incidents of the Oedipus legend. That would be his poetic vision or "inspiration," the first clue to the play-to-be. He saw this action as tragic: as eventuating in destruction, suffering, and the appearance of a new insight. At that moment plot-making begins; the incidents of the story begin to fall into a significant arrangement.

"Plot, then," says Aristotle (VI.15), "is the first principle, and, as it were, the soul of a tragedy." This is the organic metaphor which is so useful in the analysis of a work of art. By "soul" Aristotle (who was a biologist) means the formative principle in any live thing whether man, animal, or plant. Consider an egg, for instance: it is only potentially a chicken until the "soul" within it, through the successive phases of embryonic development, makes it *actually* a chicken. Similarly, the action which the poet first glimpses is only potentially a tragedy, until his plot-making forms it into an *actual* tragedy. Aristotle thought that when the incidents of the story are arranged in their tragic sequence, they already produce some of the tragic effect, even though the characters are hardly more than names. That stage would correspond to the embryo when it is first recognizable as a chicken. But the chicken is not fully actual until it has plumage and a squawk, and the tragedy is not fully actual until all the dramatis personae are characterized, and all the language is formed to express their changing actions, moment by moment. The plot, in other words, is the "first" or basic form of the play, but it is by character delineation and the arts of language that the poet gives it the final form which we read, or see and hear.

The Parts of the Plot

A complete action (as we have seen) passes through the modes of purpose and pathos to the final perception, and the plot therefore has "parts" —types of incidents in the beginning, middle, and end of the play—resulting from the various modes of action. Aristotle discusses the parts of the plot in several ways, in connection with various playwriting problems.

In Chapter XII he lists and defines the "quantitative parts" of a tragedy, by which he means the sections (rather like the movements of a symphony) in which Greek tragedies were traditionally written: Prologue, Episode, Exode, and Choric song. This chapter is probably a late interpolation, and defective; but in the light of modern studies of the relation between tragedy and the ritual forms from which it was derived, it is important. The table on page 41 shows the "quantitative parts" of *Oedipus Rex* in relation to the action, and to the supposed form of the Dionysian ritual.

Aristotle devotes most of his attention to the "organic parts" of the plot, by which he apparently means those which represent a tragic action, and best serve to produce the specifically tragic effect. They all represent the action at the moment when it is reaching its catastrophic end: Reversal of the Situation, Recognition, and Pathos, which Butcher translates "Scene of Suffering." In the best tragedies, reversal, recognition, and pathos are inherent in the basic conception of the plot, and depend upon one another, as in *Oedipus Rex*.

"Reversal of the Situation," Aristotle says (XI.1), "is a change by which the action veers round to its opposite. . . . Thus in the *Oedipus*, the Messenger comes to cheer Oedipus and free him from his alarms about his mother, but by revealing who he is, he produces the opposite effect." Notice that the objective situation does not change, for Oedipus was, in fact, Jocasta's son all along. What changes is the situation as the thought of the characters makes it out at that moment; that is why Oedipus's action changes before our eyes. The action which seemed to be about to reach a happy end is seen to be headed for catastrophe, and Oedipus's final pathos follows.

"Recognition," Aristotle writes (XI.2), ". . . is a change from ignorance to knowledge." Oedipus's change from ignorance to knowledge occurs as he cross-questions the Messenger, and then the old Shepherd. By plotting this crucial moment in this way, Sophocles has, as it were, spread out before our eyes the whole turn of Oedipus's inner being, from the triumph which seems just ahead to utter despair. The tremendous excitement of this passage is partly due to the fact that what Oedipus "recognizes" is the reversal: "The best form of recognition is coincident with a Reversal of the Situation, as in the *Oedipus*," says Aristotle (XI.2). And it is due also to the fact that this moment of enlightenment was inherent in the whole conception of the Tragic Plot: ". . . of all recognitions," says Aristotle (XVI.8), "the best is that which arises from the incidents themselves, where the startling discovery is made by natural means. Such is that in the *Oedipus* of Sophocles."

Aristotle offers the recognition scenes in *Oedipus* and in Sophocles' *Electra* (where the situation onstage turns from despair to triumph) as models of their kind. He also briefly analyzes other more mechanical and superficial ways of plotting the passage from ignorance to knowledge. He is certainly right in calling the recognition scene an "organic part" of the tragic plot, for in good drama down to our own day such scenes are essential to the tragic effect. Consider old Lear's gradual recognition of Cordelia, as he wakes in Act V; or Mrs. Alving's recognition of her son's mortal illness at the end of *Ghosts.* The action of perceiving, passing from ignorance to knowledge, is near the heart of tragedy, and the masters of that art all know how to "arrange the incidents" in such a way as to represent it on the stage.

Pathos also is an essential element in tragedy. We have seen that the whole action of *Oedipus Rex* arises out of the passion of fear; sinks back into pathos in each of the Choral Odes, and ends in the long sequence when the Chorus finally sees the meaning of Oedipus's suffering. Aristotle has little to say about plotting the "scene of suffering," perhaps because in Greek tragedy the element of pathos is usually represented in the musically accompanied verse of the Choral Odes. His most important point is in Chapter XIV.1: "Fear and Pity may be aroused by spectacular means; but they may also result from the inner structure of the piece. . . . He who hears the tale told will thrill with horror and melt to pity at what takes place. This is the impression we should receive from hearing the story of the *Oedipus.*" When Oedipus yells in agony, when he appears with bleeding sockets for eyes, pathos is certainly represented by "spectacular means"; but by that moment in the play we understand Oedipus's plight so deeply that the sights and sounds are only symbols of the destruction of his inner being.

In discussing the "organic parts of the Plot" Aristotle has nothing to say about the Episodes. In *Oedipus Rex* the Episodes are the fierce disputes between Oedipus and his antagonists, whereby the quest for the slayer moves to its unforeseen end; they are essential in the unfolding of the story. Perhaps the text is again defective here, or it may be that Aristotle thought the Episodes less essential to the tragic effect than reversal, recognition, and pathos. However that may be, the inner structure of the Episodes, which are public debates, struggles of mind against mind, may best be considered under the heading of Thought and Diction, and I shall have something to say of them on page 75.

Kinds of Plots

Since the vision which the poet is trying to represent in his play is a certain action, there are various kinds of plot-making appropriate to the various kinds of action. The *Oedipus* is (in Aristotle's view) the best model: the action is "complete" and the plot represents it almost perfectly. The plot is "Complex," by which Aristotle means that it includes reversal and recognition, but there are "Simple Plots" which do not include these elements. The plot of *The Death of a Salesman,* for example, is simple, for poor Willy Loman proceeds straight down to his sordid end without ever passing from ignorance to knowledge. The action of *Oedipus Rex* takes the form of "ethical" motivation as Oedipus pursues his rational and morally responsible purpose of finding the slayer, as well as "pathetic" motivation at the beginning and end of the play. But Aristotle also recognizes plays of essentially pathetic motivation, and plays of essentially ethical motivation. In our time, Chekhov's plays are pathetic in motivation, and the plot, or basic form, is more like that of a lyric than that of traditional "drama." Ibsen's plays are mainly ethical in motivation, and consist chiefly of disputes like the Episodes in *Oedipus*.

Aristotle never forgets that a play must, by definition, hold and please an audience in the theater, and his whole discussion of plot-making is interspersed with practical suggestions for the playwright. The story must seem "probable," and Aristotle has canny recipes for making it seem so. The supernatural is hard to put over, and it is wiser to keep the gods off the stage. In Chapter XVIII.1, Aristotle points out that any plot may be divided into two main parts, the Complication, which extends from the prologue to the turning point, and the Unraveling or denouement, from the turning point to the end. This way of describing the structure of a plot will sound familiar to anyone who has learned the mechanics of the "well-made play." It is a useful formula for the practical playwright, because it has to do, not with the dramatist's vision, but with the *means* of making any action clear and effective in the theater.

Aristotle's practical suggestions are still valuable, but they require no explanation, and I return to his main theory.

The Unity of the Play; Double Plots

The most fundamental question one can ask about any work of art is that of its unity: how do its parts cohere in order to make *one* beautiful object? Aristotle's answer, which he emphasizes again and again, is that a play or poem can be unified only if it represents *one action.* The poet, in building his form, conceiving his characters, writing his words, must make sure that everything embodies the one movement-of-spirit. That, as Coleridge says, is a counsel of perfection, "not properly a rule," but rather what all the arts aim at.

The plot of a play is the first form of the one action; what then are we to say of plays, like many of Shakespeare's, in which several plots, often taken from different stories, are combined?

Aristotle of course did not have Shakespeare's plays, but he did have Homer, who also combined many stories, many plot sequences, both in the *Iliad* and the *Odyssey.* And he recognized that Homer unified that more complex scheme by obeying the fundamental requirement of unity of action: (VIII.3): ". . . he made the *Odyssey,* and likewise the *Iliad,* to center round an action that in our sense of the word is one." Aristotle returns to this point in Chapter XXIII, where he takes up the epic. Lesser poets, he says, have tried to unify an epic by basing it upon one character, or one great historic event, like the Trojan War. Only Homer had the vision to discover one action in the wide and diversified material of his epics. The action of the *Iliad* (as the first lines suggest) is "to deal with the anger of Achilles." The action of the *Odyssey* is "to get home again," a nostalgic motive which we feel in Odysseus's wanderings, in Telemachus's wanderings, and in Penelope's patient struggle to save her home from the suitors. The interwoven stories, each with its plot, are analogous; and in the same way the stories which Shakespeare wove together to make a *Lear* or a *Hamlet* are analogous: varied embodiments of one action.

Aristotle did not think that tragedies plotted like the *Odyssey* with "a double thread of plot" (XIII.7) were the best tragedies. He preferred the stricter unity of the single plot and the single catastrophe. Perhaps if he had read *Lear* or *Hamlet* he would have modified this view. Even so, his principle of the unity of action is still the best way we have to describe the unity of a work of art, including the vast and complex ones with two or more plots.

How character delineation imitates the action

In Aristotle's diagrammatic account of play-making, the poet works on characterization after the action has been plotted as a tragic sequence of incidents. Characters are of course implicit from the first, since all actions are actions of individuals. But, as Aristotle reminds us again and again, ". . . tragedy is an imitation, not of men, but of an action and of life" (VI.9), and therefore "character comes in as subsidiary to the actions." The poet sees the action of the play-to-be first; then its tragic form (or plot), and then the characters best fitted to carry it out with variety and depth.

One must remember that in Aristotle's psychology, character is less fundamental than action. *Character* is defined as "habitual action," and it is formed by parents and other environmental influences out of the comparatively formless pathos (appetites, fears, and the like) which move the very young. As the growing person acquires habitual motives, he begins to understand them rationally, and so becomes ethically responsible: we say that he is a good or bad *character*. When we first meet Oedipus, he is a fully-formed character: a responsible ruler who (apparently in full awareness of what he is doing) adopts the rational motive of finding the slayer of Laius. But his discovery that he is himself the culprit destroys, not only his motive, but the "character" of knowing and responsible ruler; and passion, or pathos, takes over. Old Lear, at a similar point in his story, describes the experience accurately:

> O, how this mother swells up toward my heart!
> Hysterica passio! Down, thou climbing sorrow,
> Thy element's below.

After the catastrophes both Lear and Oedipus are "pathetically" motivated, like children, and like children ask for help and guidance. In tragedy, character is often destroyed; and at that moment we can glimpse "life and action" at a deeper level.

It is easy to see how the character of Oedipus, as imagined by Sophocles, is admirably fitted to represent the main action of the play, and carry it all the way to the end. With his intelligence, his arrogant self-confidence, and his moral courage, he is the perfect protagonist. But the other characters are almost equally effective for this purpose: Tiresias, who knows the will of the gods all along, but cannot himself take the lead in cleansing the city; or Jocasta, who obscurely fears the truth, and so feels that Thebes would be better off in ignorance. The contrasting characters reveal the main action in different ways, and their disagreements make the tense disputes of all the Episodes. But all this diversity of characterization, all this conflict of thought, is "with a view" to the action of the play as a whole: that common motive which I have said is "to save Thebes from its plague, by finding the unknown culprit."

It is, of course, by the plot that this main action, or common motive, is established. It is very clear in the Prologue, when everyone wants only to save Thebes. We forget it in the excitement of the disputes, and in the fascination of the contrasted characters; but we are reminded of it again in each Choral Ode. It is the Chorus which most directly represents the action of the *play;* and the Chorus can do that just because it has less "character" than Oedipus or his antagonists. In the Chorus we can sense the action at a deeper-than-individual level, and its successive Odes, with music and dance, mark the life and movement of the *play.*

We must suppose that the actions of Tiresias, Jocasta, even Oedipus, would be quite different if we saw them apart from the basic situation of the play—the plague in Thebes. We see them only in relation to that crisis, and that is why their actions, different though their characters are, are analogous. Aristotle has a good deal to say (VI.11 and 12) about less successful kinds of character delineation. Some of our "modern poets," he says, do not make effective characters, and so their works are devoid of ethical quality. Others develop character for its own sake—for local color, perhaps, or glamour, or amusement—thereby weakening the unity of the play, which can only be achieved when the action is one. In *Oedipus Rex* this problem is beautifully solved: the characters, sharply contrasted, are full of individual life and varied "ethical quality," yet the action of the *play* underlies them all.

Aristotle offers many other ideas about character delineation, based on his observation of the theater he knew, notably in Chapters XIII and XV. They are essentially practical rules of thumb, intended to assist the playwright to succeed with his audience, like his insistence on "probability" and consistency in characterization, or his notion that the tragic protagonist should usually be a ruler or leader. His observations are shrewd; but to be of assistance now they must be translated into terms of the modern theater.

How "thought and diction" imitate the action

In Chapter XIX Aristotle takes up "Thought" and "Diction" together, for they are both aspects of the language of the play. By *Diction,* he tells us, he means "the art of delivery": diction or speech as it is taught in modern schools of acting. Diction is one of the six parts of tragedy, for tragedy is by definition acted on a stage, and the actors must know how to handle its language. But Aristotle has little to say about it, because he is studying the art of the poet, who does not have to know how to speak as actors do.

Thought, however, concerns the poet directly, for thought is one of the "causes" of action. The poet works it out after the situations of the plot, and the characters, are clearly conceived. The word "thought" *(dianoia)* refers to a very wide range of the mind's activities, from abstract reasoning to the perception and formulation of emotion; for it is thought that defines all the objects of human motivation, whether they are dimly seen or clear and definite, illusory as dream, or objectively real. In the play, thought is represented by what the characters *say* about the course to be pursued, in each situation. That is why Aristotle identifies thought with the arts of language. "Under Thought," he says (XIX.2) "is included every effect which has to be produced by speech, the subdivisions being—proof and refutation; the excitation of the feelings, such as pity, fear, anger, and the like; the suggestion of importance or its opposite." At this point Aristotle refers us to his *Rhetoric,* where these modes of discourse are analyzed in detail.

In that work he writes (I.2), "Rhetoric may be defined as the faculty of observing in any given case the available means of persuasion. . . ." (Jowett's translation.) He is thinking primarily of a public speaker, a lawyer or statesman, whose action is "to persuade" his audience to adopt his opinion. He considers the various means the speaker may use to persuade his audience: his attitudes, his use of voice and gesture, his pauses—in short, such means as actors use. But his main attention is devoted to arts of language, from the most logical (proof and refutation) where the appeal is to reason, to more highly colored language intended to move the feelings. The *Rhetoric* is an analysis of the forms of "Thought and Diction" which the action of persuading may take.

This analysis may be applied directly to the Episodes in *Oedipus,* i.e., to the thought-and-language of Oedipus and his antagonists, in the successive situations of the plot. They meet to debate a great public question, that of the welfare of Thebes; and they try to persuade not only one another, but the listening Chorus, and beyond that the frightened city. They are thus situated as Aristotle's user of rhetoric is, and they resort to the same arts of language. They begin with a show of reason ("proof and refutation"); but as this fails to persuade, they resort to more emotional language, and when that too fails the dispute is broken off in dismay.

Sophocles' Athenian audience, which was accustomed to the arts of public speaking, would presumably have enjoyed the skill of Oedipus and his antagonists. In modern drama we find neither the sophisticated formality of Greek tragedy, nor the rhetorical virtuosity which Aristotle analyzes. But the principles, both of tragedy and of classical rhetoric, are natural, and disputants in our day—politicians or mere amateur arguers—resort to rhetorical forms, whether they have ever heard of them or not. Disputing characters in all drama—especially drama of "ethical" motivation like Ibsen's—instinctively use the stratagems of rhetoric, as they try to overcome each other with thought-and-language. The structure of great scenes of conflict, in Neoclassic French drama, in Shakespeare, in Ibsen, is in this respect similar to that of the Episodes in *Oedipus*.

At this point the logic of Aristotle's scheme seems to require an analysis of the language of the Choral Odes which follow each Episode. In glossing his definition of tragedy he explains (VI.3), "By 'language embellished' I mean language into which rhythm, 'harmony,' and song enter"— which must refer to the Odes with their musical accompaniment. And he emphasizes the importance of the Chorus in the structure of the play (XVIII.7): "The Chorus too should be regarded as one of the actors; it should be an integral part of the whole, and share in the action, in the manner not of Euripides but of Sophocles." We know from his remark on *Mousiké*, which includes both music and lyric verse (in his *Politics*, VIII) that he thought the modes of *Mousiké* imitated the modes of action with singular directness and intimacy. But he does not analyze either music or the language of lyric poetry in any of his extant writings. Perhaps the relevant passages are lost, for the texts of both the *Politics* and the *Poetics* are incomplete.

One may, however, find the basis for an Aristotelian analysis of lyric language in some parts of the *Rhetoric,* and in Chapters XXI and XXII of the *Poetics.* I am thinking especially of his brief remarks on analogy and metaphor, which he regards as the basis of poetic language (XXII.9): "But the greatest thing by far is to have a command of metaphor. This alone cannot be imparted by another; it is the mark of genius, for to make good metaphors implies an eye for resemblances." His analysis of kinds of metaphors is dull, and he never demonstrates the coherent metaphors in a whole poem, as modern critics of lyric verse do; yet the basic conception is there. His definition of analogy is austere (XXI.6): "Analogy or proportion is when the second term is to the first as the fourth to the third. We may then use the fourth for the second, or the second for the fourth." But this conception of analogy has also proved fertile, far beyond what Aristotle could have foreseen. It is the basis of the subtle medieval lore of analogy, which underlies the poetry of Dante's *Divine Comedy*.

The Choral Odes in *Oedipus* may, like all lyrics, be analyzed in terms of metaphor and analogy. Take for example the first Strophe of the Parode, as translated by Fitts and Fitzgerald:

> What is the god singing in his profound
> Delphi of gold and shadow?
> What oracle for Thebes, the sunwhipped city?
>
> Fear unjoints me, the roots of my heart tremble.

Now I remember, O Healer, your power and wonder:
Will you send doom like a sudden cloud, or weave it
Like nightfall of the past?

Ah no: be merciful, issue of holy sound:
Dearest to our expectancy: be tender!

The main metaphors here are of light and darkness: "gold and shadow," "sunwhipped city," "sudden cloud," "nightfall of the past." In the rest of the Ode light and darkness appear in many other metaphors, and are associated with Apollo, the god of light, of healing, and also of disease; it was he who spoke through the Oracle of Delphi. The imagery of light and darkness runs through the whole play, stemming from Tiresias's blindness, and Oedipus's blindness at the end. It is based on the *analogy* between the eye of the body and the eye of the mind—sight:blindness::insight:ignorance. We may then, as Aristotle points out, use the fourth term (ignorance) for the second (blindness), and vice versa. Physical blindness and the darkness of nightfall express the seeking-action of the play, the movement-of-spirit from ignorance to insight. The Chorus "shares in the action," as Aristotle puts it. The Chorus cannot *do* anything to advance the quest, but as it suffers its passions of fear and pity it can grope through associated images of light and darkness, healing and disease, life and death, toward the perception of the truth.

It is not my intention, however, to attempt a full analysis of the poetic language of *Oedipus Rex*. I merely wish to suggest that, with the aid of the Aristotelian notions of metaphor and analogy, one can see how the Odes also imitate the action. The same principles apply to the poetic language of any good play, and the best modern critics (experts in the lyric) have made such analyses of the language of poetic drama, from Shakespeare to Yeats and Eliot.

Song and spectacle; action and acting

The three basic parts of the art of tragedy are, as we have seen, plot-making, character delineation, and thought-and-language, for by these means the poet gives the action its tragic form, and its concrete actuality. The other three parts, *speech*, in the sense of the art of delivery, *song*, and *spectacle*, all have to do with the production of the play. They are thus essential to the art of tragedy, but concern the poet less directly than the other three, and Aristotle has little to say about them. He apparently did not feel qualified to discuss music and its performance (as one gathers from his remarks on *Mousiké* in *Politics*, VIII), and he seems to have had a low opinion of theatrical production in his time. When he wrote, the great dramatists were gone; and he seems to have known a number of egoistic actors, like some of our modern stars, who made the plays into vehicles for their own personalities.

But Aristotle knew that the poet, in the very act of making his tragedy, had to be an actor. The poet does not need the techniques of voice, diction, and bodily movement, but he must, as he writes, imitate each character in his own inner being and "believe" the situations, just as a good actor does. For tragedy, as he says in his basic definition, is "in the form of actions," i.e., acted by characters. In Chapter XVII.1 and 2, he gives the poet some practical suggestions about achieving this essential quality:

> In constructing the plot and working it out with the proper diction, the poet should place the scene, as far as possible, before his eyes. . . . Again, the poet should work out his play, to the best of his power, with appropriate gestures; for those who feel emotion are most convincing through natural sympathy with the characters they represent; and one who is agitated storms, one who is angry rages, with the most lifelike reality. Hence poetry implies either a happy gift of nature, or a strain of madness. In the one case a man can take the mold of any character; in the other, he is lifted out of his proper self.

The purpose of any good technique of acting is to help the actor to perceive the action of the character he is portraying, and then re-create it in his own thought and feeling, as Aristotle says the playwright must do. The best-known acting technique of this kind is that of the Moscow Art Theater, which is widely cultivated (in several versions) in this country. The late Jacques Copeau taught such a technique, and so did the best theater schools in Germany, before Hitler. Each school tends, unfortunately, to develop its own technical vocabulary, but I think their basic assumptions may all be expressed in Aristotelian terms. They all assume that the actor's art consists in "taking the mold" of the character to be portrayed, and then responding to the situations of the play as they appear to that character. Only in that way can the actor achieve "lifelike reality." Superficial mimicry cannot produce psychological truth, fidelity to the playwright's imagined people and situations, or emotional effect on the audience. The masters of acting technique have a subtle and practical lore of action. There is no better way to understand "action," as that concept is used in Aristotle's *Poetics,* than by studying its practical utility in the art of acting.

IV. The End of Tragedy: Pleasure, the Universal, and the Purgation of the Passions of Fear and Pity

The question why tragedy, with its images of conflict, terror and suffering, should give us pleasure and satisfaction, has been answered in many ways. Aristotle's answers, cautious and descriptive as they are, have interested his readers more than anything else in the *Poetics,* and produced more heated controversies among his interpreters. The appeal of tragedy is in the last analysis inexplicable, rooted as it is in our mysterious human nature, but Aristotle's observations of the effect which tragedy has upon us are as illuminating as anything we have on the subject.

He accepted, to begin with, the Greek notion that the fine arts have no end beyond themselves. The useful arts, shipbuilding, carpentry, and the like, provide transportation or shelter, but a play or a symphony cannot be used for anything but "pleasure." And we have seen that in his introductory remarks Aristotle suggests that the arts give pleasure because they satisfy the instincts, or needs, of "imitation" and of "harmony" and "rhythm."

When we recognize the movement-of-spirit "imitated" in a play or poem, we get the satisfaction of knowledge and understanding. The joy of Romeo when he hears Juliet's voice saying his name, the despair of Macbeth when he sees that his mad race is lost, seem to confirm something we half-knew already. The creatures of the poet's imagination do not literally represent anything in our own experience; it must be that *through* word, character, and situation we glimpse something common to men in all times and places. That is why Aristotle writes, (IX.3): "Poetry . . . is a more philosophical and a higher thing than history: for poetry tends to express the universal, history the particular."

"Harmony and rhythm" must refer, not only to music, but to the accords and correspondences that we enjoy in any beautifully formed work of art. Stephen Daedalus, in Joyce's *Portrait of the Artist as a Young Man,* explaining his own Aristotelian conception of art, offers a general definition of rhythm: "Rhythm is the first formal esthetic relation of part to part in any esthetic whole or of an esthetic whole to its part or parts or of any part to the esthetic whole of which it is a part." Young Stephen's formula is laughably pedantic, but (if one thinks it out) extremely accurate. Stephen's whole discussion shows the right way to use Aristotle's ideas: as guides in one's own thinking about art.

Why do harmony and rhythm please us? We do not know; we can only note that they do. "There seems to be in us a sort of affinity to musical modes and rhythms," says Aristotle (*Politics,* VIII), "which makes some philosophers say that the soul is a tuning, others that it possesses tuning." The notion of the human psyche as itself a harmony and rhythm reappears again and again in our tradition, notably in Shakespeare, who often uses music to suggest the health of the inner being.

Such are the pleasures we find in all the fine arts; but the special quality of our pleasure in tragedy may be more closely defined. It comes, says Aristotle, from the purgation of the passions of fear and pity. At this point Stephen's meditations may help us again: "Aristotle has not defined pity and terror. I have. . . . Pity is the feeling which arrests the mind in the presence of whatsoever is grave and constant in human sufferings and unites it with the human sufferer. Terror is the feeling which arrests the mind in the presence of whatsoever is grave and constant in human sufferings and unites it with the secret cause." Notice that these passions must be stirred by the grave and *constant.* A particular calamity with no general meaning—a street accident for example—does not produce the tragic emotion, but only meaningless pain. Here we meet once more the universality of art: the passions of tragedy must spring from something of more than individual, more than momentary, significance. Moreover, the cause of our terror must be "secret." Tragedy, like the Dionysian ceremonies from which it was derived, touches the dark edge of human experience, celebrates a mystery of our nature and destiny.

It would seem (on thinking over the effects of a few tragedies) that pity and fear *together* are required. Pity alone is merely sentimental, like the shameless tears of soap opera. Fear alone, such as we get from a good thriller, merely makes us shift tensely to the edge of the seat and brace ourselves for the pistol shot. But the masters of tragedy, like good cooks, mingle pity and fear in the right proportions. Having given us fear enough, they melt us with pity, purging us of our emotions, and reconciling us to our fate, because we understand it as the universal human lot.

Aristotle's word for this effect is "purgation" or "catharsis." The Greek word can mean either the cleansing of the body (a medical term) or the cleansing of the spirit (a religious term). Some interpreters are shocked by it, because they do not wish to associate poetry with laxatives and enemas; others insist that Aristotle had the religious meaning in mind. I think it is more sensible to assume that Aristotle did not mean either one *literally:* he was talking about tragedy, not medicine or religion, and his use of the term "purgation" is analogical. There are certainly bodily changes (in our chemistry, breathing, muscular tensions, and the like) as we undergo the emotions of tragedy, and they may well constitute a release *like* that of literal purgation. But tragedy speaks essentially to the mind and the spirit, and its effect is *like* that which believers get from religious ceremonies intended to cleanse the spirit. Aristotle noticed (Politics, VIII) that, in religious rituals that he knew, the passions were stirred, released, and at last appeased; and he must have been thinking partly of that when he used the term "purgation" to describe the effect of tragedy.

In the *Poetics* Aristotle does not try to show how the various effects which the art of tragedy aims at, as its "end," are united in an actual play. The pleasures of imitation, harmony, and rhythm; the universal quality of art, and the release and cleansing of the passions, are things he observed, and mentioned in different contexts. But we may, if we like, confirm them in any good tragedy. The effect of *Oedipus Rex,* for example, depends upon its subtle and manifold "rhythm" as Joyce defines the word; upon the pity and fear which are stirred in us, and upon our recognition, at the end, of something both mysterious and universal in Oedipus's fate. Aristotle had a consistent and far-reaching conception of the art of tragedy, and of its end; but his conception only emerges gradually as one thinks over his observations in the light of one's own experience of drama. . . .

Bertolt Brecht
The Street Scene

BERTOLT BRECHT (1898–1956), German poet, playwright, director, theoretician of the theatre, was one of the most influential people in twentieth-century theatre. "The Street Scene" was chosen from the great mass of his theoretical writings because in it he so succinctly formulates his ideas about the nature of the Epic Theatre.

◆ In the decade and a half that followed the World War a comparatively new way of acting was tried out in a number of German theatres. Its qualities of clear description and reporting and its use of choruses and projections as a means of commentary earned it the name of 'epic'. The actor used a somewhat complex technique to detach himself from the character portrayed; he forced the spectator to look at the play's situations from such an angle that they necessarily became subject to his criticism. Supporters of this epic theatre argued that the new subject-matter, the highly involved incidents of the class war in its acutest and most terrible stage, would be mastered more easily by such a method, since it would thereby become possible to portray social processes as seen in their causal relationships. But the result of these experiments was that aesthetics found itself up against a whole series of substantial difficulties.

It is comparatively easy to set up a basic model for epic theatre. For practical experiments I usually picked as my example of completely simple, 'natural' epic theatre an incident such as can be seen at any street corner: an eyewitness demonstrating to a collection of people how a traffic accident took place. The bystanders may not have observed what happened, or they may simply not agree with him, may 'see things a different way'; the point is that the demonstrator acts the behaviour of driver or victim or both in such a way that the bystanders are able to form an opinion about the accident.

Such an example of the most primitive type of epic theatre seems easy to understand. Yet experience has shown that it presents astounding difficulties to the reader or listener as soon as he is asked to see the implications of treating this kind of street corner demonstration as a basic form of major theatre, theatre for a scientific age. What this means of course is that the epic theatre may appear richer, more intricate and complex in every particular, yet to be major theatre it need at bottom only contain the same elements as a street-corner demonstration of this sort; nor could it any longer be termed epic theatre if any of the main elements of the street-corner demonstration were lacking. Until this is understood it is impossible really to understand what follows. Until one understands the novelty, unfamiliarity and direct challenge to the critical faculties of the suggestion that street-corner demonstration of this sort can serve as a satisfactory basic model of major theatre one cannot really understand what follows.

Consider: the incident is clearly very far from what we mean by an artistic one. The demonstrator need not be an artist. The capacities he needs to achieve his aim are in effect universal. Suppose he cannot carry out some particular movement as quickly as the victim he is imitating; all he need do is to explain that *he* moves three times as fast, and the demonstration neither suffers in essentials nor loses its point. On the contrary it is important that he should not be too perfect. His demonstration would be spoilt if the bystanders' attention were drawn to his powers of transformation. He has to avoid presenting himself in such a way that someone calls out 'What a lifelike portrayal of a chauffeur!' He must not 'cast a spell' over anyone. He should not transport people from normality to 'higher realms'. He need not dispose of any special powers of suggestion.

It is most important that one of the main features of the ordinary theatre should be excluded from our street scene: the engendering of illusion. The street demonstrator's performance is essentially repetitive. The event has taken place; what you are seeing now is a repeat. If the scene in the theatre follows the street scene in this respect then the theatre will stop pretending not to be theatre, just as the street-corner demonstration admits it is a demonstration (and does not pretend to be the actual event). The element of rehearsal in the acting and of learning by heart in the text, the whole machinery and the whole process of preparation: it all becomes plainly apparent. What room is left for experience? Is the reality portrayed still experienced in any sense?

The street scene determines what kind of experience is to be prepared for the spectator. There is no question but that the street-corner demonstrator has been through an 'experience', but he is not out to make his demonstration serve as an 'experience' for the audience. Even the experience of the driver and the victim is only partially communicated by him, and he by no means tries to turn it into an enjoyable experience for the spectator, however lifelike he may make his demonstration. The demonstration would become no less valid if he did not reproduce the fear caused by the accident; on the contrary it would lose validity if he did. He is not interested in creating pure emotions. It is important to understand that a theatre which follows his lead in this respect undergoes a positive change of function.

One essential element of the street scene must also be present in the theatrical scene if this is to qualify as epic, namely that the demonstration should have a socially practical significance. Whether our street demonstrator is out to show that one attitude on the part of driver or pedestrian makes an accident inevitable where another would not, or whether he is demonstrating with a view to fixing the responsibility, his demonstration has a practical purpose, intervenes socially.

The demonstrator's purpose determines how thoroughly he has to imitate. Our demonstrator need not imitate every aspect of his characters' behaviour, but only so much as gives a picture. Generally the theatre scene will give much fuller pictures, corresponding to its more extensive range of interest. How do street scene and theatre scene link up here? To take a point of detail, the victim's voice may have played no immediate part in the accident. Eye-witnesses may disagree as to whether a cry they heard ('Look out!') came from the victim or from someone else, and this may give our demonstrator a motive for imitating the voice. The question can be settled by demonstrating whether the voice was an old man's or a woman's, or merely whether it was high or low. Again, the answer may depend on whether it was that of an educated person or not. Loud or soft may play a great part, as the driver could be correspondingly more or less guilty. A whole series of characteristics of the victim ask to be portrayed. Was he absent-minded? Was his attention distracted? If so, by what? What, on the evidence of his behaviour, could have made him liable to be distracted by just that circumstance and no other? Etc., etc. It can be seen that our streetcorner demonstration provides opportunities for a pretty rich and varied portrayal of human types. Yet a theatre which tries to restrict its essential elements to those provided by our street scene will have to acknowledge certain limits to imitation. It must be able to justify any outlay in terms of its purpose.[1]

The demonstration may for instance be dominated by the question of compensation for the victim, etc. The driver risks being sacked from his job, losing his license, going to prison; the victim risks a heavy hospital bill, loss of job, permanent disfigurement, possibly unfitness for work. This is the area within which the demonstrator builds up his characters. The victim may have had a companion; the driver may have had his girl sitting alongside him. That would bring out the social element better and allow the characters to be more fully drawn.

---

[1]We often come across demonstrations of an everyday sort which are more thorough imitations than our street-corner accident demands. Generally they are comic ones. Our next-door neighbour may decide to 'take off' the rapacious behaviour of our common landlord. Such an imitation is often rich and full of variety. Closer examination will show however that even so apparently complex an imitation concentrates on one specific side of the landlord's behaviour. The imitation is summary or selective, deliberately leaving out those occasions where the landlord strikes our neighbour as 'perfectly sensible', though such occasions of course occur. He is far from giving a rounded picture; for that would have no comic impact at all. The street scene, perforce adopting a wider angle of vision, at this point lands in difficulties which must not be underestimated. It has to be just as successful in promoting criticism, but the incidents in question are far more complex. It must promote positive as well as negative criticism, and as part of a single process. You have to understand what is involved in winning the audience's approval by means of a critical approach. Here again we have a precedent in our street scene, i.e. in any demonstration of an everyday sort. Next-door neighbour and street demonstrator can reproduce their subject's 'sensible' or his 'senseless' behaviour alike, by submitting it for an opinion. When it crops up in the course of events, however (when a man switches from being sensible to being senseless, or the other way round), then they usually need some form of commentary in order to change the angle of their portrayal. Hence, as already mentioned, certain difficulties for the theatre scene. These cannot be dealt with here.

Another essential element in the street scene is that the demonstrator should derive his characters entirely from their actions. He imitates their actions and so allows conclusions to be drawn about them. A theatre that follows him in this will be largely breaking with the orthodox theatre's habit of basing the actions on the characters and having the former exempted from criticism by presenting them as an unavoidable consequence deriving by natural law from the characters who perform them. To the street demonstrator the character of the man being demonstrated remains a quantity that need not be completely defined. Within certain limits he may be like this or like that; it doesn't matter. What the demonstrator is concerned with are his accident-prone and accident-proof qualities.[2] The theatrical scene may show more fully-defined individuals. But it must then be in a position to treat their individuality as a special case and outline the field within which, once more, its most socially relevant effects are produced. Our street demonstrator's possibilities of demonstration are narrowly restricted (indeed, we chose this model so that the limits should be as narrow as possible). If the essential elements of the theatrical scene are limited to those of the street scene then its greater richness must be an enrichment only. The question of border-line cases becomes acute.

Let us take a specific detail. Can our street demonstrator, say, ever become entitled to use an excited tone of voice in repeating the driver's statement that he has been exhausted by too long a spell of work? (In theory this is no more possible than for a returning messenger to start telling his fellowcountrymen of his talk with the king with the words 'I saw the bearded king'.) It can only be possible, let alone unavoidable, if one imagines a street-corner situation where such excitement, specifically about this aspect of the affair, plays a particular part. (In the instance above this would be so if the king had sworn never to cut his beard off until . . . etc.) We have to find a point of view for our demonstrator that allows him to submit this excitement to criticism. Only if he adopts a quite definite point of view can he be entitled to imitate the driver's excited voice; e.g. if he blames drivers as such for doing too little to reduce their hours of work. ('Look at him. Doesn't even belong to a union, but gets worked up soon enough when an accident happens. "Ten hours I've been at the wheel." ')

Before it can get as far as this, i.e. be able to suggest a point of view to the actor, the theatre needs to take a number of steps. By widening its field of vision and showing the driver in other situations besides that of the accident the theatre in no way exceeds its model; it merely creates a further situation on the same pattern. One can imagine a scene of the same kind as the street scene which provides a well-argued demonstration showing how such emotions as the driver's develop, or another which involves making comparisons between tones of voice. In order not to exceed the model scene the theatre only

---

[2]The same situation will be produced by all those people whose characters fulfil the conditions laid down by him and show the features that he imitates.

has to develop a technique for submitting emotions to the spectator's criticism. Of course this does not mean that the spectator must be barred on principle from sharing certain emotions that are put before him; none the less to communicate emotions is only one particular form (phase, consequence) of criticism. The theatre's demonstrator, the actor, must apply a technique which will let him reproduce the tone of the subject demonstrated with a certain reserve, with detachment (so that the spectator can say: 'He's getting excited —in vain, too late, at last. . . .' etc.). In short, the actor must remain a demonstrator; he must present the person demonstrated as a stranger, he must not suppress the *'he* did that, *he* said that' element in his performance. He must not go so far as to be wholly transformed into the person demonstrated.

One essential element of the street scene lies in the natural attitude adopted by the demonstrator, which is two-fold; he is always taking two situations into account. He behaves naturally as a demonstrator, and he lets the subject of the demonstration behave naturally too. He never forgets, nor does he allow it to be forgotten, that he is not the subject but the demonstrator. That is to say, what the audience sees is not a fusion between demonstrator and subject, not some third, independent, uncontradictory entity with isolated features of (a) demonstrator and (b) subject, such as the orthodox theatre puts before us in its productions.[3] The feelings and opinions of demonstrator and demonstrated are not merged into one.

We now come to one of those elements that are peculiar to the epic theatre, the so-called A-effect (alienation effect). What is involved here is, briefly, a technique of taking the human social incidents to be portrayed and labelling them as something striking, something that calls for explanation, is not to be taken for granted, not just natural. The object of this 'effect' is to allow the spectator to criticize constructively from a social point of view. Can we show that this A-effect is significant for our street demonstrator?

We can picture what happens if he fails to make use of it. The following situation could occur. One of the spectators might say: 'But if the victim stepped off the kerb with his right foot, as you showed him doing. . . .' The demonstrator might interrupt saying: 'I showed him stepping off with his left foot.' By arguing which foot he really stepped off with in his demonstration, and, even more, how the victim himself acted, the demonstration can be so transformed that the A-effect occurs. The demonstrator achieves it by paying exact attention this time to his movements, executing them carefully, probably in slow motion; in this way he alienates the little subincident, emphasizes its importance, makes it worthy of notice. And so the epic theatre's alienation effect proves to have its uses for our street demonstrator too; in other words it is also to be found in this small everyday scene of natural street-corner theatre, which has little to do with art. The direct changeover from representation to commentary that is so characteristic of the epic theatre

---

[3]Most clearly worked out by Stanislavsky.

is still more easily recognized as one element of any street demonstration. Wherever he feels he can the demonstrator breaks off his imitation in order to give explanations. The epic theatre's choruses and documentary projections, the direct addressing of the audience by its actors, are at bottom just this.

It will have been observed, not without astonishment I hope, that I have not named any strictly artistic elements as characterizing our street scene and, with it, that of the epic theatre. The street demonstrator can carry out a successful demonstration with no greater abilities than, in effect, anybody has. What about the epic theatre's value as art?

The epic theatre wants to establish its basic model at the street corner, i.e. to return to the very simplest 'natural' theatre, a social enterprise whose origins, means and ends are practical and earthly. The model works without any need of programmatic theatrical phrases like 'the urge to self-expression', 'making a part one's own', 'spiritual experience', 'the play instinct', 'the story-teller's art', etc. Does that mean that the epic theatre isn't concerned with art?

It might be as well to begin by putting the question differently, thus: can we make use of artistic abilities for the purposes of our street scene? Obviously yes. Even the street-corner demonstration includes artistic elements. Artistic abilities in some small degree are to be found in any man. It does no harm to remember this when one is confronted with great art. Undoubtedly what we call artistic abilities can be exercised at any time within the limits imposed by our street scene model. They will function as artistic abilities even though they do not exceed these limits (for instance, when there is meant to be no complete transformation of demonstrator into subject). And true enough, the epic theatre is an extremely artistic affair, hardly thinkable without artists and virtuosity, imagination, humour and fellow-feeling; it cannot be practised without all these and much else too. It has got to be entertaining, it has got to be instructive. How then can art be developed out of the elements of the street scene, without adding any or leaving any out? How does it evolve into the theatrical scene with its fabricated story, its trained actors, its lofty style of speaking, its make-up, its team performance by a number of players? Do we need to add to our elements in order to move on from the 'natural' demonstration to the 'artificial'?

Is it not true that the additions which we must make to our model in order to arrive at epic theatre are of a fundamental kind? A brief examination will show that they are not. Take the *story*. There was nothing fabricated about our street accident. Nor does the orthodox theatre deal only in fabrications; think for instance of the historical play. None the less a story can be performed at the street corner too. Our demonstrator may at any time be in a position to say: 'The driver was guilty, because it all happened the way I showed you. He wouldn't be guilty if it had happened the way I'm going to show you now.' And he can fabricate an incident and demonstrate it. Or take the fact that the text is learnt by heart. As a witness in a court case the demonstrator may have written down the subject's exact words, learnt them by heart and rehearsed them; in that case he too is performing a text he has learned. Or take a rehearsed programme by several players: it doesn't always have to be artistic purposes that bring about a demonstration of this sort; one need only think of the French police technique of making the chief figures in any criminal case re-enact certain crucial situations before a police audience. Or take making-up. Minor changes in appearance—ruffling one's hair, for instance—can occur at any time within the framework of the non-artistic type of demonstration. Nor is make-up itself used solely for theatrical purposes. In the street scene the driver's moustache may be particularly significant. It may have influenced the testimony of the possible girl companion suggested earlier. This can be represented by our demonstrator making the driver stroke an imaginary moustache when prompting his companion's evidence. In this way the demonstrator can do a good deal to discredit her as a witness. Moving on to the use of a real moustache in the theatre, however, is not an entirely easy transition, and the same difficulty occurs with respect to *costume.* Our demonstrator may under given circumstances put on the driver's cap—for instance if he wants to show that he was drunk: (he had it on crooked)—but he can only do so conditionally, under these circumstances; (see what was said about borderline cases earlier). However, where there is a demonstration by several demonstrators of the kind referred to above we can have costume so that the various characters can be distinguished. This again is only a limited use of costume. There must be no question of creating an illusion that the demonstrators really are these characters. (The epic theatre can counteract this illusion by especially exaggerated costume or by garments that are somehow marked out as objects for display.) Moreover we can suggest another model as a substitute for ours on this point: the kind of street demonstration given by hawkers. To sell their neckties these people will portray a badly-dressed and a well-dressed man; with a few props and technical tricks they can perform significant little scenes where they submit essentially to the same restrictions as apply to the demonstrator in our street scene: (they will pick up tie, hat, stick, gloves and give certain significant imitations of a man of the world, and the whole time they will refer to him as *'he'!*) With hawkers we also find *verse* being used within the same framework as that of our basic model. They use firm irregular rhythms to sell braces and newspapers alike.

Reflecting along these lines we see that our basic model will work. The elements of natural and of artificial epic theatre are the same. Our streetcorner theatre is primitive; origins, aims and methods of its performance are close to home. But there is no doubt that it is a meaningful phenomenon with a clear social function that dominates all its elements. The performance's origins lie in an incident that can be judged one way or another, that may repeat itself in different forms and is not finished but is bound to have consequences, so that this judgment has some significance. The object of the performance is to make it easier to give an opinion on the incident. Its means correspond to that. The epic theatre is a highly skilled theatre with complex contents and far-reaching social objectives. In setting up the street scene as a basic model for it we pass on the clear social function and give the epic theatre criteria by which to decide whether an incident is meaningful or not. The basic model has a practical significance. As producer and actors work to build up a performance involving many difficult questions—technical problems, social ones—it allows them to check whether the social function of the whole apparatus is still clearly intact.

Harold Rosenberg
Character Change and the Drama

HAROLD ROSENBERG (1906–1978) was best known as a critic of the visual arts. For many years he was art critic for *The New Yorker* magazine. However, he was always interested in the drama and played an important role in bringing painters and poets together to form The Artists Theatre, which flourished in New York in the 1950s. His book, *Act and the Actor,* is a fascinating study of the nature of identity both in and outside of the theatre.

> *"We have already seen Bernard change; passions may come that will modify him still more."*—André Gide, *The Counterfeiters*

◆   An egg with an ancestry, developing, changing its form, maturing; later, degenerating, dying, decaying, again changing its form; always in a slow gradual way except for the shocks of birth and death—such is the broadest metaphor of the human personality developed by the organic point of view and expressed in such studies of mutation as biology, biography, history, psychology. Whatever unity an organism maintains at the base of its transformations is something mysterious: the single being may be compared with other organisms which it resembles, it may be classified, accounted for statistically, subsumed under a type; but its individuality can only be "felt." To the human person himself his own coherence is, as Herbert Read once put it, "an organic coherence intuitively based on the real world of sensation."

On the other hand, the concepts of morality or social law, applying exclusively to human beings and ignoring possible analogies with other living creatures, tend to define the individual not as an entity enduring in time but by what he has done in particular instances. A given sequence of acts provokes a judgment, and this judgment is an inseparable part of the recognition of the individual. Here too there is no final comprehension of the single person; but whereas the organic approach points towards the existence of individuals, each of whom can be grasped only by a nonrational operation, social legality operates as if it were unaware of them altogether, except as they are totally defined by their "overt acts." If the law is not always satisfied with itself, it is not because it feels the need at any time to discover more about the nature of individuals, but for the reason that it realizes all at once that acts are being performed for which it has no means of holding them responsible.

The law is not a recognizer of persons; its judgments are applied at the end of a series of acts. With regard to individuals the law thus creates a fiction, that of a person who is identified by the coherence of his acts with a fact in which they have terminated (the crime or the contract) and by nothing else. The judgment is the resolution of these acts.[1] The law visualizes the individual as a kind of actor with a role whom the court has located in the situational system of the legal code.

In contrast with the person recognized by the continuity of his being, we may designate the character defined by the coherence of his acts as an "identity." Representing the human individual as an actor, the term stands against the biological or historical organism-concept, which visualizes action as a mere attribute of, and clue to, a being who can be known only through an intuition.

The modern novel has more in common with the biological or historical view of character than with the legal. *Remembrance of Things Past* and *The Magic Mountain* are models of a literature of character metamorphosis, *Finnegans Wake* a high point in the rendering of organic texture.

As for the legal definition, its way of shaping personae with a hatchet causes it to seem at first glance far removed from the needs of imaginative writing. Without considering the symbolic, collective or residual ingredients of feeling or motive, the law comprehends its "characters" in terms of the most commonly ascertainable elements of their acts. Only information relevant and material to the legal "cause of action" may be introduced as bearing on the parties and their transactions. The law is forever fixed to that edge of individuality where particulars are caught in the machinery of the abstract and pulled into an alien orbit. Yet in the old tragedy, the individual was similarly torn away from himself by the force of an impersonal system.

There too, however, distinctions must be made: social law is not dramatic law. That the persons who stand before the bar of justice are identities, that they appear to be personifications of, and completely explainable by, the logic of their crimes, is the effect of a visible artifice of judicial thinking. In fact, of course, a man who has committed a murder may not have acted in a manner recognizable as murderous until that last instant when he pulled the trigger. That he meant to kill at that moment satisfies the law's demand for premeditation and homicidal malice; but since all the acts of the criminal were not of a criminal quality, there is forced upon our consciousness a lifetime of extenuating circumstances. All those common details of existence, gestures in every way resembling our own, even including those preceding the murder—

---

[1]Raskolnikov, for example, in *Crime and Punishment* sought judgment so that his act would be completed and he could take on a new existence.

entering an automobile, stepping on the gas, obeying the traffic lights—to say nothing of receiving certain influences, being molded by certain values, which go more to form part of the criminal in the innocence or "alegality" of his animal duration than of the relevant *res gestae* of his crime, the law takes into account only to fill in the scenic accompaniments of the last act and the rationale of its intent. So that dealing with identities rather than with personalities, the law is enabled to do so only by willfully converting persons with histories into emblems of unified actions of a given order. In other words, the law, like its victims, suffers from the discrepancy between being and action, the failure of the individual to conform in every respect to his role. Were this not so, law and justice could be synonymous.

If, however, the old drama, as contrasted with biographies of actual or of fictitious persons, succeeded, as has been asserted by ethical critics, in supplying a picture of action in which a kind of justice and a kind of law conform to each other, it must be because the dramatist started with identities. Like the judge he left aside personalities, their growth, their structural peculiarities; like the judge he established the particularity of a character only on the basis of the coherence of his acts with a chosen fact; like the judge he was interested in psychological phenomena not for themselves but only as bearing on the plausibility of the judgment with which he terminated the action. But unlike that of the judge, the dramatist's definition of the character was not an arbitrary superimposition that exchanged the emotional, intellectual and mechanical characteristics of a biological and social organism for some one deed that concerned the court; it constituted instead the entire reality of the character, avoiding the ruinous abstractness of the law by determining in advance that his emotions, his thoughts and his gestures should correspond with and earn in every respect the fate prepared for him . . . In short, because the dramatist had created his characters he could maintain the relation between their emotions, their thoughts and their destinies; while those who confront the judge on his dais were, unfortunately, born.

Its distinction between personality and identity, quietly implied by its mode of defining the individual as an identity, is what dramatic thought has in common with the legal. The characters of biography and the novel are persons with histories, but in the drama the characters are identities with roles. The distinction relates to a difference in purpose of biography and tragedy. Biography aims to picture a life as fully and precisely as possible with the type of exactness which is proper to history, that is to events visualized as successive in time. But drama, as a "poetical picture of life," is composed of events which, though seemingly related sequentially and causally, are chosen with reference to the application of specific laws leading to a judgment: the conventional coherence of these events, the suggestion to the spectator that they have actually happened or are at least within the range of probability, is superficial, and far from determining the outcome of the action serves only to connect in the mind of the audience the natural world of causal determination with the dramatic world of judgment. Those psychological explanations of the motivations of dramatic figures which form so large a part of criticism apply to this layer of causality which is the outer form of dramatic movement; they do not touch on the dramatist's act of judging,[2] derived from his conception of how the world is ordered, by which his characters are moved. Psychology can establish the plausibility of Macbeth's or Lear's behavior, but for the sufficiency of his motivation we must refer not to a possible Macbeth or Lear in "real life" but to the laws of the Shakespearean universe.

It is with respect to these laws that drama reaches objectivity, that the dramatist's image mirrors the lives of actual people. In "nature" individuals may evade any system of ends; but a dramatic identity is a creature in whom a judgment is involved at birth, a judgment which delivers him to pathos and gives meaning to it. In thus substituting identities, whose motor organs are judgments,[3] for personalities who live erratically within the freedom and hazard of moral laws not yet discovered, drama brings into being figures who are at once particular and general and its account of events appears as "more philosophical than history."

Conor A. Farrington
The Language of Drama

CONOR A. FARRINGTON (1928–   ) is an Irish playwright living in Dublin. This essay, originally published in the *Tulane Drama Review*, discusses the verbal processes involved in dramatic writing.

◆ When one rides out to do battle with the ogre of Realism it is at first dismaying to see how many noble shields and lances already litter the field. Rostand, Maeterlinck, Hofmannsthal, Yeats, Lorca, Claudel, Auden, Eliot, Fry . . . one had not thought there were so many. Not that they were all

---

[2]Instead of the "dramatist's act of judging" we might refer to the "dramatist's act of seeing judgment as involved in and carried out by action." From the naturalistic point of view, there is no judgment impressed upon action, and the presence of judgment in the drama must therefore be attributed to an act of the dramatist; but from the "dramatic viewpoint" there is no action that is not an effect of judgment, whether of the gods, the fates or history, and the judgment is therefore seen as present in the real formula of the action, is said to be discovered by the dramatist, and not to be the result of his act.

[3]The moral judgments of drama may, of course, not seem moral at all in the conventional sense; the dramatist may choose to execute a character because he is powerful rather than because he is wicked.

dishonorably unhorsed, but—the ogre still rules. And there are the critics too, like captured squircs, bending to serve the one in power, always wistful and alert for liberation, it is true, but not actively encouraging to further challengers. And they have good reason for their hesitation since some who came to set them free are now among their persecutors.

A recent challenger, T. S. Eliot, has summed up his aims with regard to the drama, in several critical essays, notably one entitled "Poetry and Drama" and his statements can be taken as fairly representative and indeed more clearly, though modestly, expressed than most. "What we have to do," he says, "is to bring poetry into the world in which the audience lives and to which it returns when it leaves the theatre." "Audiences should be made to hear verse from people dressed like ourselves, living in houses and apartments like ours and using telephones and motor cars and radio sets."

One is conscious of two things on reading these sentences; firstly that the author has a somewhat chemical attitude to the problem. Audiences should be "made to hear verse," poetry is to be "brought into the world in which the audience lives." The essay indeed might be subtitled "How to Introduce Poetry into the Drama without Coloring the Liquid or Producing a Taste." Even the title as it stands, "Poetry and Drama" hints at the way the author's mind works; there they are, detached as if they could be considered wholly separately and also could be, with great tact and ingenuity, rewed. It is doubtful, however, if the robust drama of the past will be reborn from such an artificial union.

The second thing one notices is how close the poetic dramatist has come to the Ibsenite commandment to use "the genuine language spoken in real life." Eliot, however, is not the only poetic playwright to have been hypnotized, as it were, by this commandment; others, too, have tended to tone down their poetry progressively, to beat their lances into teaspoons; it is true of Lorca, Fry, even of Yeats to some degree. We are faced with the paradox that Eliot is less poetic in *The Confidential Clerk* than Ibsen in *The Wild Duck*, Lorca less poetic in *The House of Bernarda Alba* than Chekhov in *The Three Sisters*.

When we look back at Ibsen and Chekhov, who were themselves the spearheads of the last successful revolution in dramatic language, we find they wrote as they did not because they had aesthetic theories about the language most suitable for their art; they wrote realistic dialogue simply because they had certain characters in mind who could not express themselves in the idiom audiences currently accepted in the theatre. Eliot recommended that drama should be written in the idiom of the audience: Ibsen and Chekhov, like all true dramatists, wrote in the idiom of their characters. The distinction is crucial.

It was an instinctive striving towards a fitter means of expression that brought realistic dialogue into the theatre and it will be a similar striving that will bring in its overdue successor, not willed attempts to create a poetic theatre by administering verse like vitamins, specially made up in a palatable form. This last is what Eliot recommends, he proposes to lower his language to the audience's idiom rather than draw up the audience to his own. It may be pointed out that he lowers his language in order later to draw up his audience with it. I can only say this reminds me of those clergymen who spend a great part of their time ingratiating themselves by playing football with the boys, golf with the men, having cocktails with the women, exhibiting to all their manly laugh and occasional studied swearword, to gain indulgence for the inevitable talk of Higher Things. The procedure is somehow faithless and undignified in man of God or dramatist and audiences will not be moved by it, nor souls be won.

The truth is that if any of the modern literary dramatists had one half of the broad human concern and the urgency to express it that Ibsen or even Zola had, realism would have been driven out long ago, and driven out with the same words that Zola used proclaiming of the drama of his day, "It is dying of extravagances, lies and platitudes."

Before we leave the realists it is worth noting that the poignancy of effect they undoubtedly achieved quite often was achieved by a process of reaction and contrast. They had said to poetry "Get thee behind me," and poetry did just that. It follows all their characters about like shadows and speaks in overtones through every shrug and sigh. Firs' weary speech at the end of *The Cherry Orchard* derives its poignancy from the contrast between its subject, the apparent inconsequence of living, and its manner, a semi-incoherent murmur. The contrast between what the realists wrote and what their more explicit, not to say verbose, predecessors might have written, also lends freshness to their dialogue. This was a time when reticence itself was a convention, when implicitness and inarticulacy were dramatically significant. Shakespeare of course knew all about the value of homely idiom, of contrast between mood and utterance; Lear's "Pray you, undo this button" in his dying speech is perhaps the most poignant line in the play, but Shakespeare also knew better than to write the whole play in that tone and idiom.

Unfortunately, however, recent realists have not been so sensible. Reticence, inarticulacy, homely idiom and, so to speak, the undoing of buttons have been elevated into articles of the current dramatic creed—a reticence which is no longer a healthy reaction but a lazy abdication, an inarticulacy which is not dramatically significant but is the inarticulacy of characters who have nothing to say. In so far as it can be held responsible for the one-dimensional banality that now passes for dramatic language Ibsen's demand for "the genuine language spoken in real life" is the most stultifying injunction ever to rule in the theatre.

There is one dramatist, Synge, whom Eliot discusses briefly in his essay and dismisses as a special case since Synge's plays are "based upon the idiom of a rural people whose speech is naturally poetic." This will not quite do; it might have been a valid dismissal if Synge had been writing for a closed society, if his audience had also been that rural people. But the people of Galway, Mayo, and the Western Islands are not and were not his audience.

His audience was first the Dublin public—complete with houses, motor cars, and telephones, to whom the idiom was comparatively strange—and later the public of most civilized cities of the world. Synge succeeded not because he wrote in a style attuned to the ear of his audience, but because the rural idiom provided a convention within which they could accept language more expressive than their own.

It is worth noting too that Synge is the only modern poetic dramatist whose style grows richer and more highly wrought from play to play. Unfortunately this rural idiom, together with Synge's own defensive modesty, has obscured the significance of his development to the extent that critics can say, like Ronald Peacock, that he is an isolated figure of no universal significance. At the risk of seeming chauvinist, I suggest his example is of great significance indeed. True, in his first play *The Shadow of the Glen* he could write sentences like: "It's proud and happy you'd be if I was getting my death the day I was shut of yourself." Now this is almost a word for word transliteration from Gaelic; in writing thus he was awkwardly following rural idiom, the slave of dialect. But soon, in *The Playboy of the Western World* his speech has developed the carriage of a thoroughbred wherever we sample it; for instance, "He'd beat Dan Davies' circus, or the holy missioners making sermons on the villainy of man!" Already the specifically native idiom is fading, and in the tragic peak of his last play *Deirdre of the Sorrows* it is barely perceptible:

> I see the flames of Emain starting upward in the dark night and because of me there will be weasels and wild cats crying on a lonely wall where there were queens and armies and red gold, the way there will be a story told of a ruined city and a raving king and a woman will be young for ever.

This is not local speech at all but universal. This "idiom of a rural people" was nothing more than a liberating convention. It is interesting to observe, too, that in this last play Synge combined it with another time-honored convention, that of the historical or legendary play, a mode Eliot employed in what many, including myself, consider his most successful venture into the theatre, *Murder in the Cathedral.*

There is one place, even today, where that poised unification of an audience, which is what all drama is bent upon achieving, still regularly occurs and that is the opera house. It is no coincidence either that the opera house is the place where dramatic convention most robustly survives. Opera, fortunately, cannot exist without it; whatever new developments in *sprechgesang* are introduced singing will never sound plausibly like the chatter we have just heard in the foyer. As it is, Wolfram, Fiordiligi, or Radames finish a passage and stand transmogrified against a gale of cheers, or perhaps they even take a bow; but when the conductor raises his baton they step back into the world of illusion and the audience, without the slightest difficulty, follows them. Perhaps we smile a little scornfully at this procedure, but it is a tribute to the robustness of an embracing convention and we should rather be full of envy.

For dramatic conventions are not a limiting but a liberating factor in the drama. They liberate because they permit selection of manner and matter to suit the characters and issues of the play. The conventions of the Elizabethan theatre in particular permitted the use of all kinds of dramatic shorthand which enable playwrights to encompass vast areas of action and depths of expression not only by obvious means like soliloquies and asides, but also by scenes like that between Beatrice and Alsemero in Middleton's *Changeling* or that between Gloucester and Lady Anne in *Richard III,* each of which is more a concentrated résumé of a process of wooing than a single occasion.

The dramatist attempting a representation of contemporary life and language is, on the other hand, rigidly limited. Eliot himself confesses that in writing *The Family Reunion,* he spent far too much time establishing a situation. This is a typical drawback in the representational play. Not only does the stage have to be dressed but the action and the conversation have to be dressed too; people have to greet each other, thank each other, inquire after each other, offer each other cigarettes and matches, be plausibly occupied both on stage and off it; they have to observe all the formalities of ordinary life which are quite inessential to anything except the irrelevant game of making what is going on seem "real." So much time has to be spent on superficial plausibility that it drastically reduces the time for presenting the real issues of the play. Your Elizabethan has gaily swallowed several camels before your modern has even begun to strain at his gnat.

It is clear then that the remedies of most modern poetic dramatists have been too superficial. As John Gassner says, "modern verse drama has been limited in power by the fact that it has been a more or less artificial graft on our stage"—and one might add that in many cases the stock has sent up sap that withered the shoot. The whole stock of realistic-language drama must be chopped away from that plot reserved for serious drama, and the plant regrown from seed, for three reasons.

The first is the audience's reason. I am convinced that people will not much longer continue to visit the theatre merely to listen to representations of their own inarticulacy. They come, rather, to hear expressed what they cannot express themselves, to have crystallized for them emotions that they bear about within them in solution; to escape—out of themselves, yes, but also into themselves, all by sharing emotionally in the life of the characters portrayed, which is impossible unless the language, the basic plasma of the theatre, is capable of supporting and communicating life. It is not too far-fetched to suggest that the current popularity on the stage of adaptations of radio scripts like *Under Milk Wood,* poems like *John Brown's Body,* autobiography like *Pictures in the Hallway,* novels like *Ulysses, Finnegans Wake,* and Dos Passos' *U. S. A.,* readings from Dickens, Mark Twain, Shaw, Edna Millay are all signs of the thirst of audiences for matter richer and more expressive than the contemporary drama, to its discredit, is able to provide.

The second reason is the actor's reason. He cannot bring to life characters which have no intrinsic life of their own. He is being handed the unconvertible coin of platitude, verbal and psychological, and can do no more than pass it on; he may proffer it humbly or fling it in the audience's face, it will purchase little response anyway. For poetry, in the broad sense, is the means whereby the dramatist communicates with the actor, it is the capsule in which the character the actor must embody comes to him; nothing else will survive the often arduous and changeable journey and still contain that essential variety of vitality which it is his art to embody.

Moreover, only poetry whose faculty is to say three things at once, gives him that creative opportunity of manipulating the various strands of meaning in his own way to make something that is all the more compelling for being peculiarly his own. The reproduction and illumination of the word is the center of the actor's art. It is a serious reflection that in America, where the standard of acting is generally high, the vocal tones of actors are flat and lacking in variety; the actor's principal instrument is incapable because unexercised, and most attention is devoted to the periphery of his art.

It might be added here that American critics and writers on the drama, though the most penetrating and illuminating anywhere, are singularly uncertain in their "ear." For instance, they can speak of O'Casey's style, which is rarely more than a heap of alliterative and often inapposite adjectives, in the same breath as Synge's; they can praise the cheap chintzy speeches of Marchbanks in Shaw's *Candida,* they can accept the inert, near-fetched sentimentality of Saint Joan's crucial speeches as worthy of a saint of God. These are all failures of critical "ear."

With regard to verse in the theatre, the actor should be the warmest pleader in its favor. If he speaks in prose, the ear of the audience is trained basically on the meaning, the grammar of his speech; the liberties he can take to color or emphasize anything are strictly limited. But when he is speaking verse he imposes a rhythm on the ear of the audience which, though it does not free him from conveying the sense, sets up a tension, permits an interplay of loyalty between sense and rhythm that makes his speech far more telling. Words can be given much more "air" within the binding matrix of rhythm, a sense of onward motion is established, changes of speed are more keenly felt, pauses are tauter, all kinds of subtle emphases are available which unpatterned prose cannot provide.

It follows from this that a regular and perceptibly stressed verse is the most useful in the theatre. Eliot has evolved a line, he tells us, with a varying number of syllables and three stresses divided irregularly by a caesura. It is as well he told us; one critic writing on him refers repeatedly to his "pentameter"; an actor of unusual sensitivity, known to me, played the title role in *The Elder Statesman* taking the line as a four stress one, perfectly plausibly. If the skilled go astray, how will the unskilled audience pick up the pattern? Eliot's verse form, and Fry's both miss the primary theatrical point of verse, that of imposing a ground swell, a basic rhythm.

I am far from suggesting that verse is essential to the drama. Let the practical requirements of the matter dictate the manner. The theatre has not been greatly enriched by the "I-will-now-sit-down-and-write-a-tragedy-in-terza-rima-on-some-subject-imitated-from-the-Greek" attitude. Synge's work again is adequate proof of what can be achieved without verse. Synge, however, had an uncannily perfect ear for athletic prose rhythms, some of which, elaborately formal, are worth studying. Eliot's deprecation of verse mixed with prose is once again rather aesthetic than practical; there are circumstances where a step from prose into verse may be dramatically striking. After all, the Spanish classical dramatists who used half a dozen metres in one play often achieved notable effects with changes of metre. The essential thing is the cultivation of the dramatist's ear and its unprejudiced application to his material.

This brings us to the third reason for a radical alteration in the language of drama, which is the dramatist's reason. For the language of drama is the means of communication not only between actor and audience and between dramatist and actor but between the dramatist and his characters. We are not to presume he has an absolutely clear idea of the character he is attempting to delineate, that he writes down a cold summary of what his character should say, and then whittles it into dialogue. The dramatist is like, rather, a dedicated Ahab, whose instinct it is to sense the presence of his quarry, whose skill it is to throw phrase upon phrase like harpoons after him, which plunge down slack and lifeless in the dark till at last one strikes, then another and another until the lines contain the whole strength of the prey. It is actually by means of particular words and phrases that he discovers the character, it is the authentic excitement of discovery that makes dramatic literature, and it is the embodied reenactment of that discovery that makes drama. It is not enough to throw, as it were, a whole sea onto the stage, as O'Neill does, and tell us to find our own whale. Nor is it enough to pick up scraps of what other men have already killed and cured, like all the playwrights of the cliché, who go dressed like whalers to the supermarket and come home with a ton of tins. I have spoken of the authenticity and excitement of discovery; Synge was referring to the same thing when he wrote, "On the stage one must have reality and one must have joy." Reality, or authenticity; joy, or excitement. The individual origin of every drama is a verbal process which probes, discovers, celebrates, and preserves in one action, and any theory of drama that does not look back to this origin is no more than the chattering of teeth.

Everyone in the theatre is a sharer in the same experience from dramatist to audience-member. What is it about Hamlet, Oedipus, Phèdre that grips us? It is because they are discoveries, not revelations; because Shakespeare, Sophocles, Racine wrote not merely to show us what these souls were like, but to find out.

Hence, merely external and aesthetic theories of language are not relevant or helpful. Eliot, having praised Yeats for his "purging out of poetical ornament" in his later plays, goes on to say, severely, "the course of improvement is toward greater and greater starkness." Why? Have souls all grown starker since Shakespeare's day that we need greater starkness to comprehend them? This is the realist heresy all over again. However, Hamlet, in his dying breath, indulges in poetical ornament when he says, "this fell sergeant Death is strict in his arrest." This wry, military metaphor conveys more than any starkness could, this ornament could not be purged out without purging out a part of Hamlet himself. Again, what does Shakespeare do at the peak of one of his most intense scenes, where Othello has been wrought to the desire for revenge—how does he describe the strength of that desire but in an elaborate poetical ornament:

> Like to the Pontic sea
> Whose icy current and compulsive course
> Ne'er feels retiring ebb but keeps due on
> To the Propontic and the Hellespont.

Could starkness do what this does so overwhelmingly well? Firstly, in conveying the headlong impetuosity of his desire, particularly by means of the jostling consonants in the second line; secondly, the fateful double repetition of that single syllable in the proper names; thirdly, the perspective of character it gives, sending our minds reaching back to his "travel's history," reminding us of the dimensions of that life now so fatally narrowed to revenge. If such characters are to be made known to us, it simply cannot be done by "starkness." And it is fatuous to say that people don't talk like that nowadays. Did Venetian Moors talk like that? Did Elizabethan vintners and scriveners? No, but Othello suffered like that, and people do still suffer like that and must be given voice.

Man has not changed in essence since these plays were written. Drama, however, which went indoors during the nineteenth century, has now largely descended to the cellars, while outside man is reaching for the stars. That we live in a dramatic age is obvious everywhere, except in the theatre. I suggest that the protagonists of Drama need to study again the basis of their art, which is the living word. And it is no use proclaiming "We are not Shakespeares" till we have tried and failed to be.

Tyrone Guthrie, at the end of his book, *A Life in The Theatre,* declares that drama is primarily a ritual, and likens it to Holy Communion. If that is valid then the language is the wine by which we are unified and nourished. To the outward eye today the ritual may seem complete, but what we pass about is an empty cup, a dry, unconsecrated chalice. Only when the cup is filled again will communion, communication, once more be made.

Elizabeth Burns
Conventions of Performance

ELIZABETH BURNS (1917–   ) is a British sociologist. Her book, *Theatricality: A Study of Convention in the Theatre and in Social Life* (1972), is a penetrating study of the ways that social and theatrical conventions reflect and interact with each other. Her discussion of the conventions as the rules of the game through which communication takes place is particularly helpful to our understanding of the way theatre works.

◆ . . . On all social occasions conventions are detectable in behaviour, but become explicit and even obtrusive on occasions regarded as to some extent theatrical, such as weddings, civic ceremonies, academic functions, formal conferences and receptions. On these occasions the expressiveness and persuasiveness of behaviour are stressed though the action performed or celebrated is at the same time instrumental. There is a fictive, prepared, style for an actual non-fictional content. Recognised conventions are used to express, often overexpress, solemnity at a state funeral, but the fact remains that a person has died. No conventions are essential to make this real. In fact the intention of such a performance often seems to be to stress unreality, to divert attention from the fact that the chief actor is missing. The action takes place, implicitly, at two levels.

When, however, a play is staged the social occasion is explicitly doubled. There is first the social occasion proper, the 'going to the theatre', which requires an appropriate setting, the establishment of a clearly defined social distance between actors and playgoers, appropriate mutual expectations and a common definition of the situation.

Within this social occasion occurs the realisation of the play in which fictitious characters take part in fictitious situations in a fictitious world. On one level actors and spectators see each other for what they are, disguised or undisguised, related to each other according to the demands of the occasion. On another level the spectators see the characters in the play while the actors 'in character' behave as if the spectators were invisible. Audience participation, of course, violates this convention and sets up a third type of relationship —that between characters in the play and spectators who are themselves encouraged to act 'outside themselves'—to act fictionalised characters too.

Dramatic performance is thus concerned with two distinct but related modes of interaction—interaction between performers and spectators, and interaction between the characters in the play—each making use of different sorts of convention. Between actors and spectators there is an implicit agreement that the actors will be allowed to conjure up a fictitious world, that their actions and words will be meaningful and affective (not instrumental and effective) within arbitrarily defined bounds of place, time, situation and character. This agreement underwrites the devices of exposition that enable the audience to understand the play. These conventions of which the dramatist takes account in writing the play, the producer in directing it and the actors in performing it can be described as *rhetorical.* They are the means by which the audience is persuaded to accept characters and situations whose validity is ephemeral and bound to the theatre.[1]

The second set of conventions are those which prevail for the interaction of the actors as characters in the play. They 'model' social conventions in use at a specific time and in a specific place or milieu. The modes of speech, demeanour and action that are explicit in the play have to carry conviction and imply a connection with the world of human action of which the theatre is only a part. These conventions suggest a total and external code of values and norms of conduct from which the speech and action of the play are drawn. Their function is, therefore, to *authenticate* the play.[2]

Rhetorical and authenticating conventions in the theatre bear an obviously complementary relationship to each other. The actor has to try to convince the audience rhetorically that this is the way in which he, given such a situation, at such a time, could behave and at the same time to transmit to the audience the conviction that such behaviour is taking place in a coherent, credible world and is socially authentic.[3] The two processes are, in practice, inseparable.

Rhetorical conventions rely on what Aristotle, in *The Rhetoric,* called 'the very body and substance of persuasion', the use of the *enthymeme* to play on the spectators' share in a 'stockpile of attitudes, of expectations, of scruples and conventions, of truisms and commonplaces'.[4] But in drama, as distinct from oratory, authenticating conventions are also necessary to specify the particular set of attitudes, expectations and assumptions to which the rhetoric of the performers is addressed. This adds a further dimension, as it does to all performing arts, in that new authenticating devices must be continually invented to substantiate the essentially rhetorical effort.

---

[1]In so far as ordinary social conventions are rhetorical they are represented as such on the stage 'authentically'; however, their rhetoric is directed at other characters in the play, not directly at the audience, e.g. the rhetoric of Antony's speech in *Julius Caesar* or the Inquisitor's speech in Shaw's *Saint Joan.*

[2]Inauthenticity becomes apparent in unsuccessful attempts to update productions of older plays. In the National Theatre's production of *The Dance of Death* (1968) Kurt's and Alice's passionate love-making with blouse-tearing in the drawing-room conflicted grotesquely with the rest of their correct nineteenth-century behaviour. As a result it was difficult to accept as a convention of the time Alice's command that Kurt 'kiss her foot'. Passion was implicit in the whole of the play but was surely not intended to destroy the audience's belief in the characters' strong sense of public propriety.

[3]It is to emphasise this co-operation of actors and spectators in the making of a play that Brecht says, 'It is not the play but the performance that is the real purpose of all one's efforts': *The Messingkauf Dialogues* (Methuen, 1965).

[4]E. Black, *Rhetorical Criticism* (Macmillan, 1965), p. 125.

There is, of course, an arbitrariness about distinguishing two *sets* of conventions. It is in practice extremely difficult to draw a line between the two, as between, say, the music and the libretto of an opera or even between content and form in literature or the message and the medium. What is more important is to perceive that both together, whether we regard rhetorical and authenticating conventions as two different kinds of rules or as two dimensions or aspects of convention, constitute a grammar of theatrical presentation,[5] a grammar implicit in the practical composition of drama.

For drama is not a mirror of action. It is a composition. In composing words, gestures, and deeds to form a play, dramatist and performers operate within the constraints (or generate drama according to the grammar) of both kinds of convention. Together the constraints amount to a code of rules for the transmission of specific beliefs, attitudes and feelings in terms of organised social behaviour. . . .

---

[5]The notion of implicit rules guiding the generation of utterances, which stems from Chomsky's paradigmatic revolution in linguistics, already receiving considerable attention in the social sciences and in philosophy, seems likely to provide the clue to a sizeable number of hitherto unresolved puzzles. Among other things, it bridges the gap between art as a technique and art as communication of which aestheticians have made such heavy weather; see R.G. Collingwood, *Principles of Art* (Oxford University Press, 1938), chs xi–xiv.

4

THE DRAMATIC
FORMS

◆   . . . the whole world of misfortune . . .

. . . tears of laughter . . .   . . . victims of evil deeds . . .

. . . dramas of disaster . . .   . . . struggle for

happiness . . .   . . . a time of mongrel moods . . .

. . . despair can be transcended . . .   . . . the tragic hero

is divided . . .   . . . grin and bear it . . .

. . . improbabilities of plot . . .   . . . the dark

is distilled into light . . .   . . . laughter did not come

by chance . . .   . . . exalted kind of consciousness . . .

. . . a self-understanding . . .   . . . a narrow

escape into faith . . .

Arthur Miller
The Nature of Tragedy

ARTHUR MILLER (1915–   ) has written a great deal about the nature of tragedy and the problems of writing tragedy in the contemporary world. In fact, it is next to impossible to discuss tragedy without dealing with his plays and ideas on the subject. However, the essay included here is one of his least known.

◆   There are whole libraries of books dealing with the nature of tragedy. That the subject is capable of interesting so many writers over the centuries is part proof that the idea of tragedy is constantly changing, and more, that it will never be finally defined.

In our day, however, when there seems so little time or inclination to theorize at all, certain elemental misconceptions have taken hold of both critics and readers to a point where the word has often been reduced to an epithet. A more exact appreciation of what tragedy entails can lead us all to a finer understanding of plays in general, which in turn may raise the level of our theater.

The most common confusion is that which fails to discriminate between the tragic and the pathetic. Any story, to have validity on the stage, must entail conflict. Obviously the conflict must be between people. But such a conflict is of the lowest, most elementary order; this conflict purely *between* people is all that is needed for melodrama and naturally reaches its apogee in physical violence. In fact, this kind of conflict defines melodrama.

The next rung up the ladder is the story which is not only a conflict between people, but at the same time within the minds of the combatants. When I show you why a man does what he does, I may do so melodramatically; but when I show why he almost did not do it, I am making drama.

Why is this higher? Because it more closely reflects the actual process of human action. It is quite possible to write a good melodrama without creating a single living character; in fact, melodrama becomes diffused wherever the vagaries and contradictions of real characterizations come into play. But without a living character it is not possible to create drama or tragedy. For as soon as one investigates not only why a man is acting, but what is trying to prevent him from acting—assuming one does so honestly—it becomes extremely difficult to contain the action in the forced and arbitrary form of melodrama.

Now, standing upon this element of drama we can try to reach toward tragedy. Tragedy, first of all, creates a certain order of feeling in the audience. The pathetic creates another order of feeling. Again, as with drama and melodrama, one is higher than the other. But while drama may be differentiated psychologically from melodrama—the higher entailing a conflict *within* each character—to separate tragedy from the mere pathetic is much more difficult. It is difficult because here society enters in.

Let me put it this way. When Mr. B., while walking down the street, is struck on the head by a falling piano, the newspapers call this a tragedy. In fact, of course, this is only the pathetic end of Mr. B. Not only because of the accidental nature of his death; that is elementary. It is pathetic because it merely arouses our feelings of sympathy, sadness, and possibly of identification. What the death of Mr. B. does not arouse is the tragic feeling.

To my mind the essential difference, and the precise difference, between tragedy and pathos is that tragedy brings us not only sadness, sympathy, identification and even fear; it also, unlike pathos, brings us knowledge or enlightenment.

But what sort of knowledge? In the largest sense, it is knowledge pertaining to the right way of living in the world. The manner of Mr. B.'s death was not such as to illustrate any principle of living. In short, there was no illumination of the ethical in it. And to put it all in the same breath, the reason we confuse the tragic with the pathetic, as well as why we create so few tragedies, is twofold: in the first place many of our writers have given up trying to search out the right way of living, and secondly, there is not among us any commonly accepted faith in a way of life that will give us not only material gain but satisfaction.

Our modern literature has filled itself with an attitude which implies that despite suffering, nothing important can really be learned by man that might raise him to a happier condition. The probing of the soul has taken the path of behaviorism. By this method it is sufficient for an artist simply to spell out the anatomy of disaster. Man is regarded as essentially a dumb animal moving through a preconstructed maze toward his inevitable sleep.

Such a concept of man can never reach beyond pathos, for enlightenment is impossible within it, life being regarded as an immutably disastrous fact. Tragedy, called a more exalted kind of consciousness, is so called because it makes us aware of what the character might have been. But to say or strongly imply what a man might have been requires of the author a soundly based, completely believed vision of man's great possibilities. As Aristotle said, the poet is greater than the historian because he presents not only things as they were, but foreshadows what they might have been. We forsake literature when we are content to chronicle disaster.

Tragedy, therefore, is inseparable from a certain modest hope regarding the human animal. And it is the glimpse of this brighter possibility that raises sadness out of the pathetic toward the tragic.

But, again, to take up a sad story and discover the hope that may lie buried in it, requires a most complete grasp of the characters involved. For nothing is so destructive of reality in literature as thinly motivated optimism. It is my view—or my prejudice—that when a man is seen whole and round and so characterized, when he is allowed his life on the stage over and beyond the mould and purpose of the story, hope will show its face in his, just as it does, even so dimly, in life. As the old saying has it, there is some good in the worst of us. I think that the tragedian, supposedly the saddest of citizens, can never forget this fact, and must strive always to posit a world in which that good might have been allowed to express itself instead of succumbing to the evil. I began by saying that tragedy would probably never be wholly defined. I end by offering you a definition. It is not final for me, but at least it has the virtue of keeping mere pathos out.

You are witnessing a tragedy when the characters before you are wholly and intensely realized, to the degree that your belief in their reality is all but complete. The story in which they are involved is such as to force their complete personalities to be brought to bear upon the problem, to the degree that you are able to understand not only why they are ending in sadness, but how they might have avoided their end. The demeanor, so to speak, of the story is most serious—so serious that you have been brought to the state of outright fear for the people involved, as though for yourself.

And all this, not merely so that your senses shall have been stretched and your glands stimulated, but that you may come away with the knowledge that man, by reason of his intense effort and desire, which you have just seen demonstrated, is capable of flowering on this earth.

Tragedy arises when we are in the presence of a man who has missed accomplishing his joy. But the joy must be there, the promise of the right way of life must be there. Otherwise pathos reigns, and an endless, meaningless, and essentially untrue picture of man is created—man helpless under the falling piano, man wholly lost in a universe which by its very nature is too hostile to be mastered.

In a word, tragedy is the most accurately balanced portrayal of the human being in his struggle for happiness. That is why we revere our tragedies in the highest, because they most truly portray us. And that is why tragedy must not be diminished through confusion with other modes, for it is the most perfect means we have of showing us who and what we are, and what we must be—or should strive to become.

Robert B. Heilman
Tragedy and Melodrama:
Speculations on Generic Form

ROBERT B. HEILMAN (1906–   ) has written illuminatingly on each of the major forms of drama. The essay included here was later expanded to become *Tragedy and Melodrama*. In this book Heilman discusses the crucial distinctions between these quite different yet so closely related dramatic forms.

I

◆   This essay grows out of my sense of a persistent confusion in the use of the word *tragedy*. As critics, of course, we know that we can never expect to agree on final definitions that will make possible a consistent criticism. But the discrepancies which we can never finally eliminate, even in professional usage, have got completely out of hand in popular usage. This fact is my starting point, and in this sense, literary criticism merges with social criticism. The word *tragedy* means not only plays of a certain kind but almost all kinds of painful experiences: an early death, an unexpected death by disease, a financial failure, a suicide, a murder, an automobile accident, a train accident, an airplane accident, a successful military movement by a hostile power, a sadistic act, a government error, almost any act of violence. I recall an accident in which a small plane, whose pilot had bailed out, crashed into a building; the newspaper I was then reading headlined the story, "Tragedy to Plane and Factory." This seemed to stretch the idea of tragedy pretty far. The strain was increased by the fact, which was soon revealed, that the factory was a cheese factory, for to many people cheese will not seem the likeliest of tragic materials.

What I want to explore is the possibility of finding distinctions among the host of disagreeable events lumped under the word *tragedy*. Note my word *explore*. Such criticism is not logical demonstration; it is at best a form of rhetoric. That is, it succeeds in so far as it persuades anyone else that it is useful. The most the critic can hope for is to be partially persuasive.

An experiment in making distinctions should justify itself. However, I want to note what seems to me to be an especial danger in that loose use of the word *tragedy* that penetrates our whole society. I do not think we can simply rest in our knowledge that we have wide areas of bad usage. We need to make some effort to counter bad usage. For when a word is a catchall for many meanings only loosely related, it loses character. It tends to be used only for simple or wholesale or lump meanings. In fact, we can propose it as a law of language that when one word gains several meanings, the inferior meaning will tend to force the superior meaning out of circulation: I mean that the rougher, more general, looser, or lazier meaning will win out over the more exact or precise or demanding meaning. This is Gresham's law of semantic currency. When *tragedy* means the whole world of misfortune we cannot distinguish particular misfortunes in terms of their cause, nature, and meaningfulness. We lack the words for this; what is worse, we lack the concepts. What we do not distinguish, we do not understand; I will go a step further and suggest that if experiences are not understood, there is a sense in which they are not even experienced. This confusion extends beyond verbal haziness and begins to interfere with fundamental clarity of mind and therefore, I think, with sense of reality.

II

I believe that the word *tragedy* may suitably be applied to one form of catastrophic experience, and that this can be differentiated from all others. For a start, we may use Aristotle's definition of the tragic hero as the good man who gets into trouble through some error or shortcoming for which the standard term has become the tragic flaw. This I take to be a central, irreducible truth about tragic reality.

This assumption of mine has a number of consequences. The first is that the tragic character is essentially a divided character, and I shall regularly use *divided, dividedness,* and *division* as key words. The idea of goodness and the idea of the flaw suggest different incentives and different directions, a pulling apart, though not of pathological intensity, within the personality. The division in the hero may be of different sorts. In the first place, it may reflect the kind of division that seems inseparable from human community—from the fact that, in the ordering of life, we maintain different imperatives that correspond to different and perhaps irreconcilable needs. Hamlet and Orestes, those heroes so different from each other in time and place and yet so incredibly alike in the trials that visit them, cannot avenge their fathers, the victims of evil deeds, without themselves committing evil deeds. Antigone cannot be true to family duty and love, and to religious obligation, without contravening civil law; and Creon—who in some ways is really a better tragic hero than Antigone—cannot or at least does not maintain civil order without punitive decrees that profoundly violate human feelings and sense of justice. Yet none of these heroes could refrain from the course that leads to guilt without feeling intolerably acquiescent in a public evil.

Such heroes and heroines, if I do not misread them, incorporate the dividedness of a humanity whose values, because they naturally elude the confines of formal logic, create an apparently insoluble situation. In this situation the crucial actions of heroes, though they are exacted by a powerful sense of moral obligation, nevertheless become infused with guilt. For these heroes the two counterimperatives have so much authority that no observer can say with assurance, "It would be better if Hamlet or Antigone or Cordelia had done so and so." Nor could a fully aware person, caught between injunctions that are apparently incompatible, come out of such situations without damage; he could be safe only by canceling part of his awareness. This canceling would surely threaten the common order more than the ambiguous act does. Suppose Hamlet had decided that the ghostly exhortations that he heard were simply the product of tensions within himself, that he was worrying too much, that his best step was to get adjusted to the existent order and to stop brooding about evils which he couldn't help anyway and which might well be only imaginary. Or that Orestes had decided that his father deserved his fate, or Cordelia that she might just as well follow her sisters in applepolishing an eccentric elder. Maybe these would be safe courses, at least temporarily. But what diminished persons we would have, and what a shrunken sense of reality.

Of characters caught in the Hamlet and Orestes situation we may say that they are divided between "imperatives," that is, different injunctions, each with its own validity, but apparently irreconcilable. With another type of tragic hero the division may be said to be between "imperative" and "impulse," between the moral ordinance and the unruly passion, between mandate and desire, between law and lust. Tradition and community give an ordinance, but egotism drives one away from it. Macbeth seeks power through politics, Faustus through intellect; what makes them tragic, as ordinary power-grabbers are not, is that neither of them can ever, in yielding to impulse, force out of consciousness the imperatives that he runs against. Oedipus has the same division, but with a different alignment of forces: he wants to obey the imperative but is betrayed by the riotous impulse. Finally, there is a third representative tragic dividedness—the split between impulse and impulse, which I believe to be a characteristic situation in Ibsen. Rebecca West and Rosmersholm, for instance, are divided between what I will call the impulses of the old order and those of rationalist enlightenment, in a peculiarly modern tragic situation.

I have used the term *imperative* to denote the obligation of general validity, the discipline of self that cannot be rejected without penalty, whether it is felt as divine law or moral law or civil law, or, in a less codified but no less prescriptive way, as tradition or duty or honor. Imperative reflects a communal consciousness. By *impulse* I refer to the force that originates in or is rooted in or identified with the individual personality and is of an almost biological sort; though the specific feelings that impel the individual may be of the widest occurrence in humanity, they are felt as a need, or as a satisfaction, or as an aggrandizement of the individual, in almost a bodily way. Imperative tends toward the self-abnegatory, impulse toward the self-assertive. But I do not wish to labor this distinction. I have made it, and I have suggested three basic patterns of division, as a way of trying to make concrete the idea of dividedness in the tragic hero.

There are two other consequences of the idea of tragedy as the experience of the good man with the flaw. The first of these is that division means choice: there are alternatives, and man must select one or another. This idea is so familiar that I will limit myself to this bare statement of it. The second is that choice implies consciousness: alternatives are not really alternatives, at least in the dramatic substance, if they do not in some way, however indirectly or however tardily, live in the consciousness of the hero. The drama is a lesser one—it has less range—if the hero simply does not know what it is all about or never comes to know what it is all about. Willie Loman is a hero of such limited consciousness that, for many readers, he pushes *Death of a Salesman* into a lower order of excellence. Division, finally, is not only the occasion of self-awareness or self-knowledge, but the very material of self-knowing. It is the inconsistent and the contradictory that require the studious intelligence; the unified, the coherent, the harmonious dissolve the world of alternatives and render the customary strivings of self-understanding irrelevant.

III

To sum up: *tragedy* should be used only to describe the situation in which the divided human being faces basic conflicts, perhaps rationally insoluble, of obligations and passions; makes choices, for good or for evil; errs knowingly or involuntarily; accepts consequences; comes into a new, larger awareness; suffers or dies, yet with a larger wisdom.

Now this is quite different from popular or journalistic tragedy (here we come to the social dimension of the problem): young man drives fast, hits truck that drives out in front of him, and he and his fiancée are killed. This will almost invariably be called, "Tragedy on Highway 90," and for many people this is *all* of tragedy. The death-dealing truck might be a disease or a careless engineer or a defective airplane wing or an assailant; the essence of it is the shock of unprogrammed death. This is a rather long way from the tragic pattern that we are able to discern in the practice of the Greeks and Elizabethans and at least in the intuitions of some moderns. Even in the most skillful journalism we would hardly be able to get inside the victims and see them as divided between options or struggling in a cloudy dilemma of imperative and impulse; they do not choose but are chosen; something just happens to them; consequences are mechanical, not moral; and most of all they do not grow into that deeper understanding, of themselves and of their fate, which is the dramatic heart of the experience. For in that sudden death there is little to understand; consciousness is not sharpened but is bluntly ended.

To use the term *tragedy* indiscriminately for what Oedipus does and experiences and learns, and for what happens to a car driver through his own or someone else's carelessness, I submit, is not a casual slip of the tongue or a laughable folk error, but a real confusion that can have undesirable consequences for our grasp of reality. For by our Gresham's law of semantic currency, the cheaper meaning forces out the meaning of precise value. Tragedy comes to mean *only* accidents and sudden death or anachronistic death. As a result we tend to lose touch with certain ideas that are an indispensable means of contemplating human catastrophe: the idea that calamity may come from divisions within human nature and within the ordering of life. The idea that man may choose evil. The idea that potential evil within him may overcome him despite resolution or flight. The idea that brutal events may come out of the normal logic of character. The idea that man is never safe from himself. The idea that the knowledge of such ideas is essential to the salvation of the individual and to the health of institutions. All these ideas are implicitly discarded if the word *tragedy* conveys to us only such a thing as a smashup on Highway 90. And what do we put in place of what is lost? The idea that the worst that can happen to us is an unexpected shortening of life. The idea that this cutting short is the work of causes outside ourselves. The idea that we are innocent victims. This is a fantastic loss of tools of understanding and, implicitly, an unhealthy oversimplification of reality.

Here you may want to argue that in using such a phrase as "only unhappy accidents" I am minimizing the extent, the influence, and the force of such events. Not at all. I do not deny the reality of accidents, the pain and anguish they cause, or their power to move us either in daily experience or in literary representation. I do not suppose that we can eliminate unhappy accidents, ignore them, forget them, deny their power over our actions and feelings, or discontinue making literature of them. All I am troubled by is calling them "tragedy," which I am hoping to persuade you is no trivial error. I have the greatest respect for the rare news editor who, instead of announcing "Tragedy on Highway 90," will say "Accident on Highway 90: Two Dead." There is the crux of the matter: putting experience into the right category. Now, for the category of event which is so widely called "Tragedy on Highway 90" the proper term, I suggest, is *disaster*. It is a sufficiently capacious term to include all kinds of fatal accidents, the mortal illnesses that strike (we think) ahead of time, the destructive blows of a nature not yet quite tamed, and all the murderous violence that comes directly or by ricochet from the envious, the hostile, and the mad. Its very etymology makes *disaster* an appropriate term: it implies an undoing by action of the stars, and thus it is a fitting metaphor for all the unhappinesses that seem to come from without, to have no meaningful causes, and to let us feel guiltless. From now on, then, instead of speaking of the two meanings of *tragedy*—the meaning implied in the literary examples that remain always alive, and the contemporary journalistic meaning that pervades all our speech—I shall use the terms *tragedy* and *disaster* to denote these areas of experience that may always be theoretically distinguished.

However much they may be interwoven in the concrete event, tragedy and disaster are two fundamentally different structures of experience; to confuse them will involve errors of three kinds—intellectual, emotional, moral. The intellectual error I have already described or implied: it is to seek the causes of evil always outside ourselves, to whitewash ourselves, to be always without responsibility for calamities. The loose use of the word *tragedy* also leads us to a concomitant error of feeling. For if tragedy is simply what happens to us, we are all victims; victims must be pitied; and we can soon ooze into a rich morass of self-pity. Obviously we don't want to pity ourselves, if we are well people; but the universalization of the disaster principle sneaks pity in the back door. Sometimes we can pity ourselves simply by pitying others: Othello is a case in point. Or, in glorifying the man who pities, we may reveal a desire to cuddle up under that sympathetic wing. The word *compassionate* has become a cliché of book reviewing; in our time it is almost an ultimate term of praise for a writer. It has become embarrassing. Is *compassion* the word that comes to mind when we think of Shakespeare's treatment of Lear or Sophocles' portrayal of Oedipus? Is it not rather completeness of understanding, insight into human division, a full sense of both excellence and flaw? Compare the Christopher Fry character who says, "I'm still remembering/I can give pain, and that in itself is loss/Of liberty." When we shift from feeling sorry for pain received to fear of pain given, we move from the sense of disaster toward the tragic sense.

The third error in taking disaster for tragedy is the moral one of adopting a single-standard quantitative view of life. Disaster centers in death: we are getting less life than we have coming to us. It is not necessary to quarrel with a universal disinclination to die, especially ahead of what looks like sound scheduling; but as a matter of clarity we should observe that in our day the quest for longevity is both more extensive and more passionate than it has ever been before. This appears in our obsession with disaster, the most forceful reminder of mortality. Disaster is the realm of quantity of life; tragedy, of quality of life. The inevitable fear of disaster can grow until it eliminates all issues of quality. I do not complain about fear of death, which is a fact of life; my point is only that the ending of life is not the sole imperfection of life, and that to act as though it is, is not healthful.

IV

In disaster, what happens comes from without; in tragedy, from within. In disaster, we are victims; in tragedy, we make victims, of ourselves or others. In disaster, our moral quality is secondary; in tragedy, it is primary, the very source of action.

In literature, the problem is that of distinguishing between tragedy and what I will call, for the time being, the literature of disaster, which is often called tragedy. I regard the two forms as generically different, though they look alike because they both depict suffering. The literature of disaster comprises all those pages in which we record what has been done to us by fire, famine, the sword, and unjust men; in which our role is that of Job, plagued by our own kind, by machines, and by nature. In tragedy, as an art form, we contemplate our own errors; in the literature of disaster we mark the errors of others and the imperfections of circumstance. In tragedy we act; in the literature of disaster we are acted upon.

In the literature of disaster we find victims of situations that range from very simple to very complex. Though I want to avoid little catalogues that are too neat, I will suggest that we can identify several basic types of the victims that artists have discerned—the victims of nature, the victims of society, the victims of evil individuals, and those who are victims of themselves. This last, of course, sounds very much like tragedy, and the distinction will have to be clarified later.

Since I do not have space for analysis of plays, I will have to be like the Oriental geometrician who stated a theorem, drew an illustrative figure, and substituted, for the steps of demonstration leading to a formal conclusion, simply the word *Behold!* I use Synge's *Riders to the Sea* as an example of the literature of disaster dealing with the victim of nature; this play is generally called a tragedy, but its core is pathos; we remain serene observers, sympathetic, sharing the sadness of death, but never drawn into the experience of division and of self-knowledge, for there is none. The victim of society, a familiar figure in post-Romantic sensibility, appears archetypally in Dr. Stockmann in Ibsen's *Enemy of the People*—an embarrassingly simple picture of a noble reformer done in by a crass community. Our emotional involvement here hardly approaches the adult level. The drama of disaster that deals with the victim of society is managed somewhat more complexly in Friedrich Duerrenmatt's *The Visit* (1955). In this play the townspeople, to gain a vengeful woman's gift of a billion marks, informally sentence to death and execute one of the town's leading citizens, the original seducer of the woman who gives the billion marks. Like various dramas of disaster, *The Visit* has a powerful impact because it devotes itself exclusively to demonstrating the infinitude of human venality. It gains power at the expense of depth and complication; it simply excludes any other human characteristic but vengefulness and corruptibility. It denies the division which is at the heart of tragedy; and so, I submit, it not only narrows the aesthetic experience but reduces us to shocked spectators of a crime. This is one of the two representative risks of the literature of disaster: at the popular extreme it may entice us into a stereotyped situation, ready-made for emotional wear; or, as in *The Visit*, it may lock us out of a situation by making it so eccentric that to enter it would be suicide. That, too, is always a risk of expressionist drama, to which *The Visit* belongs: in such difficulties, as well as in other matters, we realize postrealist expressionism is very much like prerealist allegory.

The victim of the politically disordered society appears in *The Diary of Anne Frank*. Here again is a drama of disaster that offers simple and easy emotional experience, pity for victims; only at one point does it approach tragedy—at the point at which Mr. Frank says, of the tensions among the hiding victims of the Nazis, "We don't need the Nazis to destroy us. We're destroying ourselves." The victim of the evil individual is found in one of the great dramas of disaster in English—Webster's *The Duchess of Malfi*, in which a charming and innocent woman is tortured and destroyed by her cruel brothers. She is not presented tragically; she does not, like great tragic heroes, "earn" her fate. Her honorable conduct simply happens to run afoul of the purposes of her vicious brothers. Lear, on the contrary, has made Goneril and

Regan efficacious in the world; they are projections of a part of his own divided nature. Lear has made his world in a way that the Duchess has not. Webster presents the evil brothers as autonomous—like a flood or holocaust that destroys. This is not to deny the existence of autonomous evil; it is simply to say that it is not the world of tragedy.

Finally, in Gorki's *Lower Depths* and O'Neill's *The Iceman Cometh* (two works with extraordinary similarities of plot and structure), we find plays that are concerned with the disaster of personality: that is, with that kind of collapse which makes the individual incapable of normal adult life. When we speak of the disaster of the self, however, we remember that the origin of the tragic situation is also within the self. At the risk of too epigrammatic a contrast we may say that the disaster of self has its origin in weakness, the tragedy of self in strength. In disaster, individuals are not up to traditional requirements; in tragedy, they are not held down by traditional requirements and eventually find themselves not up to the special rules they propose for themselves. One aesthetic leads to Mr. Zero, the other to Dr. Faustus; one character says, "Pity me," the other says, "I have sinned."

In *The Duchess of Malfi* Bosola sums up the action with the phrase "Oh this gloomy world." In *Riders to the Sea* Maurya says, ". . . there isn't anything else the sea can do to me." In *The Iceman Cometh* Larry Slade concludes, "By God, there's no hope! . . . Life is too much for me." "This gloomy world"—what is done to me—what is too much for me: this is the realm of disaster—of what happens to the victims of nature, of societal power or war, of weakness before the exigencies of life, of disillusionment, of corruption, of evil men. The realm of actual disaster that is the raw material of literary art is a large one. We do not underestimate the immediacy or anguish of that realm, or fail in sympathy with those injured or betrayed by such events, if we say, once again, that such fates are something other than tragic, and that the drama portraying such fates is not of the tragic order.

For many things that are terrible are not tragic.

V

The term *literature of disaster* which I have so far used is a cumbersome term and a limiting term. I propose, as my final point, that the literature of disaster is really a subdivision of a larger literary type. To that type I will give the term *melodrama*.

I am aware that to take *melodrama*, which in casual contemporary usage is a derogatory term designating popular machine-made entertainments, and to apply it to a wide range of literature that includes sober work and somber tones may seem capricious to the point of scandal. I hasten to deny caprice and to explain that I use melodrama as a neutral descriptive term. I use it because I believe that what we call "popular melodrama" has reduced to stereotypes and thus has trivialized the basic structural characteristics of a form that can be serious as well as silly.

Let us look first at the popular sense of *melodrama.* Its nature is suggested by phrases such as these: pursuit and capture, imprisonment and escape, false accusation, cold-blooded villain, innocence beleaguered, virtue triumphant, eternal fidelity, mysterious identity, lovers reconciled, fraudulence revealed, enemies foiled; the whole realm of adventure; the realm of mystery from the supernatural to the whodunit; the realm of vice and crime from horror to detection to reform. It is the world of shock and thrill, of what is regularly called "gripping" and "poignant." But it is rarely devoid of ideas, however flat and hackneyed these may be. In a century and a half its color has been variously revolutionary, democratic, patriotic, antitotalitarian, reformist (anti-gambling, slavery, drinking, dope addiction, etc.). The form is represented with delightful amplitude in an early example, Thomas Morton's *Speed the Plough* (1798), which, along with various popular comic effects, contains upper-class injustice, *nouveau riche* snobbery, poor man's integrity, a lover who almost gives up the poor girl for the rich one, bigamy, economic threats, secret grief, irrational enmity, mysterious identity, old villainy disclosed in a bloodcurdling confessional, a castle fire and a rescue, and garnishings of patriotic sentiment.

When we are still not free from totalitarianism it may seem blasphemous to suggest that Lillian Hellman's *Watch on the Rhine,* an anti-Nazi play of 1941, offers us, even if a little more sophisticatedly, the same fare as *Speed the Plough.* There is a simple villain-hero structure: we have no choice but to hate the Nazi sympathizer and love everyone else, and everyone else is mostly delightful Americans.

Speed the Plough and *Watch on the Rhine* both have the stock devices of entertainment popular in their day. But beneath the standardized appeals there is a basic plot form—the conflict of villains and heroes, of what we nowadays laughingly call good guys and bad guys. Yet such a pattern of action should not be dismissed as the especial property of the simple-minded. For however dull or trite or grotesque the actions of these good and bad competitors may be, the plots are simply a debased popular form of a stable central structure that appears in all times and in trivial and sober plays alike: in this structure, man is pitted against some force outside of himself—a compact enemy, a hostile group, a social pressure, a natural event, an accident, or a coincidence. This is one of the persistent fundamental structures of literature, whether it appear in a silly or meretricious form in a cinema or television thriller or be elaborated with dignity and power in *The Trojan Women* or *Romeo and Juliet.* It draws upon permanent human attitudes, some perilous and some preserving, whether we disavow these when they become ludicrous in a Western or scarcely recognize them in some extraordinary struggle into which we have been drawn by artistic skill—the story of Annapurna, *Nigger of the Narcissus, War and Peace, Richard III.*

In the structure of melodrama, I suggest, man is essentially "whole"; this key word implies neither greatness nor moral perfection, but rather an absence of the kind of inner conflict that is so significant that it *must* claim our first attention. He is not troubled by motives that would distract him from the conflict outside himself. He may, in fact, be humanly incomplete; but his incompleteness is not the issue. In tragedy, man is divided; in melodrama, he has at least a quasi wholeness against besetting problems. In tragedy, the conflict is within man; in melodrama, it is between men, or between men and things.

We can find virtually "whole" or undivided characters in Ibsen's Dr. Stockmann, fighting community greed, and Lillian Hellman's Kurt Müller, fighting against Nazis. They are created by the same conception of character that appears in popular heroes pitted against cattle rustlers, holdup men, or racketeers. I say this not to disparage but to note the neutral fact of identity of character structure. If we rarely inspect the characters of heroes, we inspect those of victims even less. We find a virtually unified nature in Synge's Maurya, whose family is cut down by the sea; in the Franks, cut down by Nazi malice; in the Duchess of Malfi, cut down by her sadistic brothers. Villains are whole characters too—for instance, Duerrenmatt's citizenry that murders for money, and the Duchess of Malfi's murderous brothers. Even the wretched characters depicted by Gorki and O'Neill have a kind of wholeness: the wholeness of half-beings really cut off from any counterimpulses that would leave them split between retreat and participation. Wholeness, in other words, is a technical structure of character and personality; it is morally neutral; in goodness or badness, strength or weakness, the protagonist is in the main free from divergent impulses.

When we speak of the structure of a form we refer not only to its system of characterization and arrangements of characters but to its dynamics, or, in other terms, the structure of its action. We have seen how the popular thriller and the serious problem play, as we usually call it, are organized alike —on some variation of the villain-hero conflict. The final problem is to see how the drama of disaster also belongs to this pattern. In all these cases we have an essentially undivided protagonist facing an outer conflict. In this kind of situation only several types of outcome are possible—victory, or defeat, or perhaps a stalemate or compromise. Here is the *key* point. Disaster and the popular happy-ending play are not different formal entities but are simply the opposite extremes of the spectrum of melodrama: at one end, man, essentially whole, is beaten down by his antagonist; at the other, also essentially whole, he comes out on top. At the one end, man is victim; at the other, victor. The nature of the conflict is the same, the central structure is the same, but the artist chooses one point of view or another. He may see man vs. nature or political forces or society or other individuals, and he may see him as lost or as triumphant; there are scores of plays doing it one way or the other. The identifying mark of the melodramatic structure is not the particular outcome of the plot, but the conception of character and the alignment of forces. This identity we can always find beneath a considerable diversity of arrangements of action.

Finally, the melodramatic organization of experience has a psychological structure. It puts us into a certain posture which we find agreeable and that within limits has a certain utility. In most general terms, what it affords is the pleasure of experiencing wholeness—not the troubling, uneasy wholeness that exists when all the divergent elements of personality remain within the field of consciousness, or the rare integration of powers that may be earned by long discipline, but the sensation of wholeness that is created when one responds with a single impulse or potential and lets this function as a surrogate for the whole personality. In this quasi wholeness he is freed from the anguish of choice and from the pain of struggling with counterimpulses that inhibit and distort his single direct "action." If there is danger he is courageous; he is not distracted by fear, expediency, or the profit motive. Or he can be serene in adversity, unhampered by self-seeking, by impatience with the frailties of others, or by doubt about ends. (Thus Kurt Müller in *Watch on the Rhine* and the stage version of Anne Frank's father: through them, melodrama affords a unity of desirable feeling—of the wisdom to bear troubles, of practical competence against evil.) One is untroubled by psychic or physical fumbling, by indecisiveness, by weak muscles or strong counterimperatives. One is under the pleasant yoke of what I will call a monopathy: that single strong feeling that excludes all others and thus renders one whole. It may be a monopathy of hope or, for that matter, a monopathy of hopelessness; a monopathy of contempt for the petty, discontent with destiny, indignation at evil doing, or castigation of the guilt of others. Even in defeat and disaster, in being overwhelmed and victimized, I am convinced, the human being is able to find certain monopathic advantages.

Melodrama, in sum, includes the whole range of conflicts undergone by characters who are presented as undivided or at least without divisions of such magnitude that they *must* be at the dramatic center; hence melodrama includes a range of actions that extend from disaster to success, from defeat to victory, and a range of effects from the strongest conviction of frustration and failure that serious art can dramatize to the most frivolous assurance of triumph that a mass-circulation writer can confect. The issue here is not the reordering of the self, but the reordering of one's relations with others, with the world of people or things; not the knowledge of self, but the maintenance of self, in its assumption of wholeness, until conflicts are won or lost. There is a continuous spectrum of possibilities from the popular play in which the hostile force is always beatable to the drama of disaster in which the hostile force is unbeatable; at one extreme we view man in his strength, at the other, in his weakness. In structure of feeling the form is monopathic.

But the tragic hero is divided; he is in some way split between different forces or motives or values. His nature is dual or even multifold; the different elements are always present and dramatically operative; they are always realities that have to be reckoned with. In structure of feeling we may call tragedy "polypathic." The monopathic concentration may actually make melodrama in some ways more overwhelming, as in *The Duchess of Malfi*, where everything enlarges the sense of ruin; but tragedy, where impulses and options are double and multifold, where we are drawn now this way and now that, exacts a very much more complex and troubling awareness. One example: the spectacle of the aged Lear in the storm is overwhelming, too. But it cannot inspire simply a monopathic pity, since we do not forget that in a sense Lear has created this storm himself. Profound pity for the victim, yes, but also acknowledgment of the paradoxical presence of justice, and sense of irony—all are present in a disturbing polypathic experience.

In melodrama, man is seen in his strength or in his weakness; in tragedy, in both his strength and his weakness at once. In melodrama, he is victorious or he is defeated; in tragedy, he experiences defeat in victory, or victory in defeat. In melodrama, man is simply guilty or simply innocent; in tragedy, his guilt and his innocence coexist. In melodrama, man's will is broken, or it conquers; in tragedy, it is tempered in the suffering that comes with, or brings about, new knowledge.

The pathological extreme of the tragic condition is schizophrenia— where normal dividedness is magnified into the split that is illness. The pathological extreme of the melodramatic condition is paranoia—in one phase, the sense of a hostile "they" who will make one their victim, and, in another phase, the sense of one's own grandeur and, implicitly, of the downfall of others. Melodrama has affinities with politics; tragedy, with religion. Pragmatic politics appears as a competition for power between good and evil; our side is "good," and the other side, "evil." In the religious view of man is a sense of his dividedness, of the co-presence of counterimpulses always striving for dominance, of the fact that throughout his life he is a dual creature with equal possibilities of coming to salvation or damnation. Melodrama leans toward the timely, tragedy toward the timeless; on the one hand we have the world of protest and problem plays; on the other, the world of meditation and myth.

So much for the efforts to pile up distinctions between two basic sets of habits and attitudes. We have described melodrama as monopathic, presenting man in defeat or victory, in guilt or innocence; as having affiliations with politics and history, drawn to the topics that change with time. We have described tragedy as polypathic, showing man's victory in defeat, his mingling of guilt and innocence; as having affiliations with religion and myth, seeking the constants that transcend change. I have meant to suggest rather than to insist. It would not be helpful to make absolute, unvarying boundary lines; in life and literature, as they exist, there are not many instances of pure types. The literary work or the human personality *leans* in one direction or the other; it rarely *plunges* toward an extreme. But one cannot judge the individual work, or the person's way of confronting reality—one cannot say that here is a melodramatic style with some moments of the tragic or that here is a tragic cast of mind that includes something of the melodramatic—without first distinguishing the theoretical poles of attraction. The test of these theoretical constructions is their helpfulness in identifying actual literary structures or in understanding the strategies of spirit that men devise to face an imperfect world.

Christopher Fry
Comedy

CHRISTOPHER FRY (1907–   ) is an English dramatist and poet. Together with
T. S. Eliot he was responsible for the revival of verse drama in England in the 1950s
(The Lady's Not for Burning, Venus Observed, A Sleep of Prisoners). Fry has also
written some marvelous essays on the drama and his discussion of comedy is one of
the best of them.

◆   A friend once told me that when he was under the influence of ether
he dreamed he was turning over the pages of a great book, in which he knew
he would find, on the last page, the meaning of life. The pages of the book
were alternately tragic and comic, and he turned page after page, his excitement growing, not only because he was approaching the answer but because
he couldn't know, until he arrived, on which side of the book the final page
would be. At last it came: the universe opened up to him in a hundred words:
and they were uproariously funny. He came back to consciousness crying with
laughter, remembering everything. He opened his lips to speak. It was then
that the great and comic answer plunged back out of his reach.

If I had to draw a picture of the person of Comedy it is so I should
like to draw it: the tears of laughter running down the face, one hand still lying
on the tragic page which so nearly contained the answer, the lips about to
frame the great revelation, only to find it had gone as disconcertingly as a chair
twitched away when we went to sit down. Comedy is an escape, not from truth
but from despair: a narrow escape into faith. It believes in a universal cause
for delight, even though knowledge of the cause is always twitched away from
under us, which leaves us to rest on our own buoyancy. In tragedy every
moment is eternity; in comedy eternity is a moment. In tragedy we suffer pain;
in comedy pain is a fool, suffered gladly.

Charles Williams once said to me—indeed it was the last thing he said
to me: he died not long after: and it was shouted from the tailboard of a
moving bus, over the heads of pedestrians and bicyclists outside the Midland
Station, Oxford—"When we're dead we shall have the sensation of having
enjoyed life altogether, whatever has happened to us." The distance between
us widened, and he leaned out into the space so that his voice should reach
me: "Even if we've been murdered, what a pleasure to have been capable of
it!"; and, having spoken the words for comedy, away he went like the revelation which almost came out of the ether.

He was not at all saying that everything is for the best in the best of
all possible worlds. He was saying—or so it seems to me—that there is an angle
of experience where the dark is distilled into light: either here or hereafter,

in or out of time: where our tragic fate finds itself with perfect pitch, and goes straight to the key which creation was composed in. And comedy senses and reaches out to this experience. It says, in effect, that, groaning as we may be, we move in the figure of a dance, and, so moving, we trace the outline of the mystery.

Laughter did not come by chance, but how or why it came is beyond comprehension, unless we think of it as a kind of perception. The human animal, beginning to feel his spiritual inches, broke in on to an unfamiliar tension of life, where laughter became inevitable. But how? Could he, in his first unlaughing condition, have contrived a comic view of life and then developed the strange ribshaking response? Or is it not more likely that when he was able to grasp the tragic nature of time he was of a stature to sense its comic nature also; and, by the experience of tragedy and the intuition of comedy, to make his difficult way? The difference between tragedy and comedy is the difference between experience and intuition. In the experience we strive against every condition of our animal life: against death, against the frustration of ambition, against the instability of human love. In the intuition we trust the arduous eccentricities we're born to, and see the oddness of a creature who has never got acclimatized to being created. Laughter inclines me to know that man is essential spirit; his body, with its functions and accidents and frustrations, is endlessly quaint and remarkable to him; and though comedy accepts our position in time, it barely accepts our posture in space.

The bridge by which we cross from tragedy to comedy and back again is precarious and narrow. We find ourselves in one or the other by the turn of a thought; a turn such as we make when we turn from speaking to listening. I know that when I set about writing a comedy the idea presents itself to me first of all as tragedy. The characters press on to the theme with all their divisions and perplexities heavy about them; they are already entered for the race to doom, and good and evil are an infernal tangle skinning the fingers that try to unravel them. If the characters were not qualified for tragedy there would be no comedy, and to some extent I have to cross the one before I can light on the other. In a century less flayed and quivering we might reach it more directly; but not now, unless every word we write is going to mock us. A bridge has to be crossed, a thought has to be turned. Somehow the characters have to unmortify themselves: to affirm life and assimilate death and preserve in joy. Their hearts must be as determined as the phoenix; what burns must also light and renew: not by a vulnerable optimism but by a hard-won maturity of delight, by the intuition of comedy, an active patience declaring the solvency of good. The Book of Job is the great reservoir of comedy. "But there is a spirit in man . . . Fair weather cometh out of the north . . . The blessing of him that was ready to perish came upon me: And I caused the widow's heart to sing for joy."

I have come, you may think, to the verge of saying that comedy is greater than tragedy. On the verge I stand and go no further. Tragedy's experience hammers against the mystery to make a breach which would admit the whole triumphant answer. Intuition has no such potential. But there are times in the state of man when comedy has a special worth, and the present is one of them: a time when the loudest faith has been faith in a trampling materialism, when literature has been thought unrealistic which did not mark and remark our poverty and doom. Joy (of a kind) has been all on the devil's side, and one of the necessities of our time is to redeem it. If not, we are in poor sort to meet the circumstances, the circumstances being the contention of death with life, which is to say evil with good, which is to say desolation with delight. Laughter may seem to be only like an exhalation of air, but out of that air we came; in the beginning we inhaled it; it is a truth, not a fantasy, a truth voluble of good which comedy stoutly maintains.

John Dennis Hurrell
A Note on Farce

JOHN DENNIS HURRELL (1924–   ) is a professor of English at the University of Minnesota and was the editor of the now defunct *Drama Survey*. For a long time "farce" was almost a dirty word in serious discussions of drama, especially in academic circles. Thanks to critics like Hurrell and Eric Bentley, we have come to rediscover that farce is one of the basic ores from which all theatre derives.

◆   Farce is one of the oldest theatrical forms, and the audience for it is almost world-wide. But criticism—and dramatic criticism is no exception—dearly loves a hierarchy, and farce, having once been relegated to the lowest level of the series headed by tragedy, has been continually taken for granted as something if not actually beneath criticism, at least beneath the need for critical discussion. Everybody knows what happens in farce: a dozen definitions in standard reference books testify to the fact that it is a "low" form of theatrical presentation, the sole object of which is to excite laughter. It is inferior in every way to "true" drama: it makes use of excessively complicated plots, improbable situations, and type characterization. It is highly unrealistic, purely ephemeral in interest, and no fit subject for serious consideration as dramatic literature.

Yet farce has enjoyed great popularity during several long periods of dramatic history; it has occupied the attention of Aristophanes, Shakespeare, Molière, and Wilde, to name but four major dramatists. It is easy to say that farce caters to a poorly educated, artistically degenerate public, but the facts do not bear this out. The farces of the Roman comedians were performed in Renaissance England by and for the university population; there is evidence to suggest that at least one early farce of Shakespeare, *The Comedy of Errors*, was designed for and appreciated by an audience of lawyers; Molière's audience was certainly not composed solely of the uneducated; and the taste for Wilde has never been a vulgar one. The taste for farce has been continuous, too, not limited to any one historical period. There has probably not been a season in London, Paris, or New York without a successful farce on the boards, new or revived, and it has been a staple of the cinema since that medium's earliest days.

Clearly there is something in the nature of farce that seems to defy its dismissal by academic critics. We all enjoy it in the theatre, yet we concur in accepting "farce" as a term of abuse. We have been made to laugh, but we feel that the laughter has not been legitimately directed. On this point there seem to exist two schools of thought. One, which gives tacit recognition to the didactic purpose of art, is fairly represented by the *Encyclopaedia Britannica's* definition of farce: "Farce is a form of the comic in dramatic art, the object of which is to excite laughter by ridiculous situations and incidents rather than by imitation with intent to ridicule, which is the province of burlesque, or by the delineation of the play of character upon character, which is that of comedy."

This attack (and almost every available definition of farce constitutes a form of attack) is double-edged. Farce is a lower form than burlesque because it has no satiric purpose, and a lower form than comedy because it relies on situation rather than character for its theatrical effects. We are left laughing, apparently, like lunatics, without cause, and after our indulgence we experience a sense of shame at our behavior. We have seen the serious business of the world (usually love, honor, and marriage) treated as though moral laws did not exist, and when the lights go up in the auditorium we are aware that for a brief spell we have not been seeking the highest. The world is a well-ordered place, thanks to our hard-won sense of morality, and we have allowed ourselves temporarily to forget this. According to this theory and its implications, then, farce exists and is enjoyed because of the dual nature of man, and for this very reason can never be openly accepted as having any relationship to that image of our morally directed lives which we keep constantly before us, especially in our art.

This leads us to the second school of thought about the legitimacy of our laughter at farce, whose views have been expressed most recently in an admirable essay by Mr. Eric Bentley.[1] His view is the Freudian one: farce permits us to look on while our repressed desires are acted out before us. The relation of farce to life is almost equivalent to that between the dream world

---

[1]Eric Bentley, "The Psychology of Farce" (introduction to *Let's Get a Divorce and other plays*, ed. Eric Bentley, 1958).

and the waking world. The improbabilities of plot do not matter, for the action of farce is purely symbolic. At the center of our society is the institution of marriage and the family, and farce is an outlet for our repressed desire to desecrate these holy places. Farce must, therefore, rest on a basis of moral society. Man is not naturally, however, a moral creature (here the two views seem to coincide) and would like to break the laws which he has created to preserve the structure of his society, and in farce this dream of freedom is fulfilled: "in farce, as in dreams, one is permitted the outrage but is spared the consequences."[2] Farce is, to use Mr. Bentley's term, a "safety valve." Neither is it an unrealistic form of art, except for distortion of "the external facts." We all have the desire to outrage our society: this is the Freudian truth, and farce adheres to it, so "to the inner experience, the farceur tries to be utterly faithful."[3]

This is perhaps the most penetrating comment on farce that has yet appeared; but while it explains the relation of farce to the inner life of man, it does little to explain its relationship to the other dramatic forms, or to drama as a reflection of man's waking life. Mr. Bentley skillfully illustrates the illegitimate nature of our laughter at farce, but he is committed, by the logic of his argument, to the precept that it *is* illegitimate. He glosses over the improbabilities of plot in farce by his theory of adherence to the truth of "inner experience." While accepting almost all of his remarks as justified comment on the *psychology* of farce, I think it is possible to suggest a theory that goes beyond this to its *philosophy*, enabling us to formulate a definition of farce that has no pejorative undertones.

Briefly, my argument is that farce, like other dramatic forms, is a comment on the human situation, and that it represents a tenable theory, expressed through its artistic form, concerning our relationships with our fellow men in the society we have created. Tragedy functions in the area of moral solutions to the problems which constantly suggest themselves to creatures conscious of a higher purpose than day to day existence: tragedy is thus highly selective, dealing with those men who are capable of, or capable of being driven to, purely moral choices. Comedy takes as its province a wider area of man's activities, concerning itself with the laws, written or unwritten, which govern men in their communities rather than those which link man with a higher force outside himself. Farce ignores both the moral and the social laws, not because it denies their existence, but because it sees an alternative to this constant reference to laws, moral or social, an alternative followed by the majority of mankind. The common denominator of farce characters is *ingenuity*, and it is on this level that in farce as in life most problems are solved. In the classic and typical situation, common to all forms of drama, of adulterous relationships, the question to be asked is not as in tragedy, "Having sinned against moral laws, how can I redeem my soul?", or

---

[2]Eric Bentley, p. xiii.
[3]*Ibid.*, p. xv.

as in comedy, "Having sinned against the sanctity of a social institution, how can I preserve my reputation?" (tragedy being, concerned with *character,* comedy with *reputation,* as Shakespeare well knew), but "Being caught in this predicament, how can I *contrive* escape or concealment, so that our world can continue smoothly and safely as it did before human weakness asserted itself?" Farce recognizes that there are alternatives to the solutions provided by tragedy and comedy, and that it is these alternatives that shape the majority of our decisions. The character in farce is barely conscious that he is a moral creature; he is always conscious that he is a thinking and devising creature.

It is in this connection that the term "lower" can be aptly applied to farce without any pejorative connotations; we are concerned with a hierarchy still, but it is a hierarchy of human abilities, moral and mental, not of dramatic types. It is, in fact, possible to speak of a "good" farce and mean considerably more than that the play in question was amusing. Farce has a particular aspect of human existence to present, and its form, far from being accidental or uneconomical, is designed specifically to present that aspect. One might argue that farce, with its temporary reversal of the well-ordered and morally-directed world, is a kind of assertion of man's continual capacity for setting his house in order through the ingenious use of his capacity to make practical, rather than ethical decisions. One sentence might sum up the action of any successful farce: a situation or a relationship gets out of hand and somehow, inefficiently perhaps but eventually successfully, it is put right.

In this respect, then, farce concerns itself with a wider area of human activity than either comedy or tragedy. It may be an accurate representation of man's suppressed inner life, as Mr. Bentley suggests, but it is also, and more obviously and intentionally, an allegory of man's outer life. I use the term "allegory" advisedly, since the relationship between the typical situation in farce and its counterpart in life is not one of imitation but of symbolization. This symbolization is not only that of the inner life, but also of the form and pattern of outer life. The common term for what I have called symbolization is, of course, "improbable situation," but this is unsatisfactory, for it does not suggest where the nature of the improbability lies. Mr. Bentley's answer to this question is prompted by his "safety valve" theory of farce. "While, certainly, the external facts are distorted, the inner experience is so wild and preposterous that it would probably be impossible to exaggerate it. To the inner experience, the farceur tries to be utterly faithful. This fact raises the question whether farce is as indirect a form of literature as it is commonly supposed to be."[4]

This statement surely avoids the question that must be asked if farce is to be regarded as a responsible form of drama: in what way are the external facts distorted? Farce is rarely completely fantastic (*i.e.,* impossible) but only improbable, and the improbability seems to me to reside, in most cases, not

---

[4]*Loc. cit.*

in the farce-situations themselves but in the fact that these situations are carried to their logical conclusions. Taken this far they are, in terms of everyday life, absurd. The actions of most farce characters are, for the duration of the play, the actions of monomaniacs. Indeed, this is one of the chief sources of dramatic unity in farce, although it is popularly assumed to lack any unity at all. For example, the practical solution to Fadinard's problem in *An Italian Straw Hat* is the finding of a hat: this is a situation which has, at the beginning, only a touch of the improbable about it. But when, as the action progresses, Fadinard is committed to this single solution, his behavior becomes absurd, simply because it constitutes reason followed beyond any possibility of compromise. This carrying of a situation to its ultimate conclusion provides the unity for the play; but it also places Fadinard, and the characters with whom he comes into contact, in other situations from which they must extricate themselves, and again the practical, or what seems to be practical, method is chosen, disaster being averted time after time until a point is reached where this kind of solution is no longer efficacious and the dramatist has only two ways open to him—morality or coincidence. Taken to this extreme the situation is, in terms of real life, absurd, distorted. But a human situation carried to such an extreme that it stands out recognizably *as* a situation, with a form and shape of its own, and not merely as a part of the irresolute, untidy, compromising flux of daily life, becomes in a sense not so much unreal as *abstract,* and so the term "allegory" seems to apply.

Another element in farce, noted by most critics, is one form or another of the "chase." The common view is summed up neatly by Leo Hughes.

> The chase has the advantage of providing suspense without at the same time distracting our attention too much from the discrete episodes. At the same time it allows the dramatist to maintain a pace too fast for the leisurely examination which the wildest flights of fancy do not readily survive. The suspense-packed movies of Mr. Hitchcock, to cite a parallel case, have exploited the advantages of fast pacing to forestall a too close scrutiny of motivation. Professor Greig has even suggested a similar benefit from the same device on a somewhat higher literary plane: our acceptance of evil in a Falstaff or a Gargantua, he believes, is earned so easily simply because the vigorousness or the furious pace does not permit us to examine the darker side of our ambivalent attitude too closely.[5]

Here again, then, the question of ambivalence, of the duality of human nature, is brought to bear on the subject of farce. But is this really necessary? The "chase," too, can be regarded as allegorical, the abstract representation of the constant forward movement of life, the tendency to solve problems not

---

[5]Leo Hughes, *A Century of English Farces* (1956), p. 25. Hughes quotes from J. Y. T. Greig, *The Psychology of Laughter and Comedy* (1923), pp. 147–149.

by contemplation of their moral significance but by ingenuity and action. Yet the example of Falstaff certainly is relevant. Falstaff's views on honor are, as most Shakespearian scholars have recognized, a corrective to Hotspur's and to Hal's. If these "nobler" characters are reminders to us that man can direct his life according to principles beyond mere survival, Falstaff is always there to show us that survival is, after all, a prerequisite without which the principles would have no point. Those who accept the view that farce has as its purpose nothing but the excitement of laughter might well ponder the essential sanity of a Falstaff in a world where the honor of nations is placed before the survival of the race. There is surely something to be said for *l'homme moyen sensuel,* the perennial hero of farce, who frequently knows that he can get along very well with his ingenuity, without recourse to morality, for he is aware that the average man must pit his wits against a world that seems always ready to collapse about his ears, and that he must do a great deal of running to stay in the same place. If farce ignores morality it is because, to be an artistically effective reflection of the life of the average man, it must do this. The writer of farce knows that morality is what we turn to when all else fails, but he is a man who has not been made cynical by this knowledge.

Our definitions of farce need not, then, be in any way pejorative or apologetic. It is not necessarily a lower form of drama simply because it portrays what, for want of a better term, we must continue to call a "lower" human faculty. It does not deny morality: it simply isolates it and leaves it for treatment in a different form. It is not comedy which has failed to come off, since it does not undertake to criticize life in any way, and constantly refuses to generalize. Where, then, does it stand in the hierarchy in relation to tragedy? The answer is simple. It stands to one side and makes the very positive and valuable statement that tragedy might not even be necessary and might, even, be a little ridiculous.

Robert W. Corrigan
Tragicomedy

ROBERT W. CORRIGAN (1927–   ) was the founder and first editor of the *Tulane Drama Review* (now *The Drama Review*). His discussion of tragicomedy, that hybrid genre which has come to be the dominant form in the modern theatre, is from his book *The World of the Theatre,* published in 1979.

> *It all comes to the same thing anyway; comic and tragic are merely two aspects of the same situation, and I have now reached the stage where I find it hard to distinguish one from the other.* —Eugène Ionesco

◆   So far we have discussed four major forms of drama. We have discovered that at the heart of each of them is the experience of some kind of pain or discord within a context of conflict. Yet each of the forms is markedly different and we have no trouble distinguishing among them.

The final form we will consider is tragicomedy. As the term suggests, it combines some of the qualities of tragedy and some of those of comedy. In tragicomedy, the serious merges with the ridiculous; helplessness is cast in a humorous vein; pain and despair are transcended or are miraculously overcome; joy and sadness become indistinguishable from one another. It is an interesting hybrid form that has dominated American and European drama since the second half of the last century.

At certain times in history, the more or less clear distinctions between the forms of drama seem to break down or to become blurred. Tragicomedy flourishes at these times. This breakdown is not due to anything that happens in the theatre but is caused by shifts in values that take place in the larger society of which the theatre is a part. In fact, we can generalize that whenever social values are in a state of radical change, distinctions between the forms of drama tend to become blurred.[1] The most striking example of this phenomenon has been in Europe and America in the past 125 years. Tragicomedy seems to thrive in a society in a state of flux.

---

[1]This was certainly the case in the second half of the fifth century B.C. in Greece and is reflected in the plays of Euripides. (*Alcestis* is a good example.) The last plays of Shakespeare *(Measure for Measure, Cymbeline, The Winter's Tale,* and *The Tempest)* and several of those by Jacobean dramatists reveal that something similar happened early in the seventeenth-century in England after the death of Queen Elizabeth I. The theatre in seventeenth-century France after Louis XIV is another instance.

Tragicomedy and Changing Values

The meaning and significance of the traditional forms of drama in any period of history depend on the existence of generally accepted standards of value within a society. Such norms make it possible to get wide agreement on what is serious and what is funny. All the forms of drama we have discussed thus far are based on this agreement. This publicly shared view of what is true provides the artist with a basis for communication. It enables the playwright to communicate emotion and attitude by simply describing incidents; it provides a storehouse of symbols with guaranteed responses; above all, it enables the playwright to construct a plot by selecting and organizing events that, because of this community of belief, are significant to the audience. The dramatist is bound more by plot than other writers are (novelists, for instance) because a play's action is first perceived by the audience through the events of the plot. The very existence of plot depends on agreement between writer and audience on what is significant in experience. All drama, if it is to communicate to an audience, depends on a shared view of what is significant in experience. Issues must really matter before we can consider any outcome tragic or comic.

Once this shared public truth is shattered and replaced with our individual private truths, all experience tends to be equally serious or equally ludicrous. This is what has happened in the last century. There is no publicly shared view of what is significant. This is the meaning of the contemporary French playwright Eugène Ionesco's statement with which we opened this discussion of tragicomedy.

Let us look at an example that illustrates what this means. The subject is the sexual seduction of a young woman. In the English theatre of the Restoration (the late seventeenth and eighteenth centuries), seduction was comic in both theme and situation. Its use as subject matter in the theatre —which was very common—reflected the commitment to dalliance, infidelity, and sexual conquest which characterized the lives of the court nobility who made up the audience of that theatre. A playwright like William Congreve (1670–1729) or William Wycherley (1640–1715) could introduce a seduction scene into one of his plays and know exactly how his audience would respond to it. They would laugh and enjoy it. His only task (no small one, to be sure) would be to do it with wit. To achieve any response other than laughter would require an elaborate manipulation of the plot and characters, since the audience's attitude toward seduction was so firmly fixed. But by the end of the eighteenth century and all through the nineteenth century, the public attitude toward seduction changed radically. The seduction of the innocent during that period was seen as a horrible catastrophe ("Poor Nell!") and as the source of personal tragedy, family dishonor, abandonment, and any number of other soul-wracking, handwringing results. Once again the public attitude, although completely different, was clearly defined and known, and a playwright could use a seduction scene (or plot) with the certainty that it would evoke a guaranteed response—shock and disapproval.

Now, what about our own times? What is the commonly shared public attitude toward seduction? Although each of us might have his or her own view on the subject—including seduction of whom by whom and what sex by what sex—we would all probably have to admit that if there is any widespread public view on the subject at all, it is "Who cares?" A playwright using this theme today has to build into the play not only the event but the ways the audience is supposed to respond to it. Even this will at best create only ambiguity, for since there is no commonly held public attitude, neither the playwright nor the members of the audience can know for certain how they will respond. We know that seduction can be harmless and even joyful. We also know that it can be the occasion of sadness, pain, outrage, and a deep sense of loss. Which one is it? Both? Neither? We can never be sure, and a world of ambiguous values is the miasma from whence tragicomedy emerges.

Tragicomedy and the Modern Theatre

Tragicomedy has thrived at various times throughout the history of the Western theatre, but without question the most significant period has been the past hundred years. Indeed, it is becoming increasingly difficult to use the terms *tragedy* and *comedy* with any precision at all. A striking characteristic of the modern drama is the way the old distinctions between the tragic and the comic (the serious and the ludicrous, the painful and the painless) have been erased. Ours has been a time of mongrel moods, and there are a number of reasons for this.

The drama's general pattern of development during this time can best be described as a gradual but steady shift away from publicly shared philosophical and social concerns toward the crises and conflicts of an individual's inner and private life. This very major change in the concerns of the theatre grew out of and reflected profound social changes in the period.

One of the dominant ideas of the modern period is the conviction that it is impossible to know what the world is really like. Before Martin Luther (1483–1546), society generally believed that there is a direct and recognizable relationship between our external actions and our innermost motivations and feelings. In rejecting a direct relationship between the outer and inner worlds, Luther began a revolution in thought that gradually made it impossible for humanity to attach any objective value to the world of experience. This insistence on such a clear-cut division between the physical and the spiritual aspects of reality had a profound effect on modern dramatists, who grew increasingly distrustful of sensory responses to the "outside" world. At the same time they tended to lose whatever belief they might have had in the truth of their own feelings and sensations. Playwrights could no longer hold a mirror up to nature, at least not with any confidence. They could only reflect their own feelings and responses to the world, knowing that these feelings and responses are inconsistent, often contradictory, and deeply personal.

One force in the nineteenth century that did much to destroy belief in an established norm of human nature and to begin this process of internalization in the theatre was the development of psychology as a field of study. Psychology has demonstrated that the distinction between rational and irrational behavior is not clear-cut, and that labelling any behavior as abnormal or inappropriate is a tremendously complicated task. Psychology has made it difficult, if not impossible, for the dramatist to present characters in a direct way. In earlier times, when it was believed there was a sharp distinction between the sane and the insane, irrational behavior was dramatically significant because it could be defined in terms of a commonly accepted standard of sane conduct. It seems clear, for instance, that in Shakespeare's presentation of them, Lear on the heath is insane while Macbeth at the witches' cauldron is not. But for the modern dramatist, deeds do not necessarily mean what they appear to mean, and in themselves they are not directly related to the characters. For example, we can never be sure why Hedda Gabler or Miss Julie acts as she does. Once a playwright believes that the meaning of every human action is relative, the dramatic events of the plot cease to have meaning in themselves. The playwright cannot count on a commonly shared view of truth to give meaning to events in a play. They take on significance only as the individual motivations of the characters are revealed. (The technique of earlier drama was just the reverse: the motivations of the characters were revealed by the events of the plot.)

While the development of psychology was a very powerful force in shaping the modern theatre, there were other factors at work as well. The industrial revolution and developing industrial technology brought incredible change to working and family life, and the speed of change made the future increasingly unpredictable. People were forced to live with uncertainty and growing isolation.

At the same time, discoveries made by nineteenth-century archeologists and the resulting interest in anthropology tended to break down existing attitudes toward human nature. Early anthropologists made it clear that human nature is not something fixed and unchanging but only a kind of behavior learned in each culture. Furthermore, by the middle of the century, democracy was finally beginning to be established both as a way of life and as a form of government. Today we tend to forget what a revolutionary idea democracy is and the shattering effects it had on the values of eighteenth- and nineteenth-century Europe. In 1835 Alexis de Tocqueville had observed in *Democracy in America:*

> Not only does democracy make every man forget his ancestors, but it hides his descendants and separates his contemporaries from him, it throws him back forever upon himself and threatens in the end to confine him entirely within the solitude of his own heart.

By the second half of the nineteenth century, every established view of God, human nature, social organization, and the physical universe was beginning to be seriously challenged, if not rejected outright.

These profound changes in values and attitudes had a tremendous influence on the nature of dramatic form. As beliefs and values crumbled and changed, the clear-cut distinctions between the established forms of drama became fuzzy. This was particularly true of the forms of tragedy and comedy. When you can't be sure what actions really mean, and when the relationship between actions and results is unclear, the serious tends to be inseparable from the ludicrous. Or you can turn this idea around, and it still comes out much the same way: the trivial can become the most effective way of communicating the serious. Either way, it is the best way to describe the vision dominant in the theatre during the past one hundred years. It is certainly the controlling vision of most of the plays of Ibsen, Strindberg, Chekhov, Pirandello, Giraudoux, Brecht, Duerrenmatt, Beckett, Ionesco, Pinter, and Albee. Even Eugene O'Neill—who had a tragic sense of life, if anyone ever did—remarked as far back as 1939 that:

> It's struck me as time goes on, how something funny, even farcical, can suddenly without apparent reason, break up into something gloomy and tragic. . . . A sort of unfair *non sequitur*, as though events, as though life, were to be manipulated just to confuse us. I think I'm aware of comedy more than I ever was before—a big kind of comedy that doesn't stay funny very long.[2]

In the modern theatre the lines of the comic mask have become indistinguishable from those of the tragic. This is the realm of tragicomedy. Probably no one embodies the spirit of this realm more fully than Gogo and Didi, the central characters of Samuel Beckett's *Waiting for Godot.* We don't know who Godot is, or why Gogo and Didi are waiting for him. By the end of the play Godot has still not come and they decide to go.

> VLADIMIR: Well? Shall we go?
> ESTRAGON: Yes, let's go.

But the last line of the play is a stage direction: *"They do not move."*[3] Gogo and Didi are two irreducible specimens of a humanity whose only capacity is to remain comically, tragically, ambiguously alive with the courage of their hallucinations as they wait for a Godot who may or may not ever come.

[2]Eugene O'Neill. Cited by Croswell Bowen. *The Curse of the Misbegotten: A Tale of the House of O'Neill.* New York: McGraw-Hill Book Co., 1959, p. 259.

[3]Samuel Beckett. *Waiting for Godot.* New York: Grove Press, 1954, p. 61.

"Hope Springs Eternal . . ."

The vision of tragicomedy is one of almost unrelieved despair. It lacks the heroism, the sense of accomplishment, and the spirit of fulfillment we discovered in tragedy. Tragedy may be painful and at times even sad, but there is something glorious and affirming in the hero's capacity to become one with his or her own fate. Tragicomedy also lacks the life-enhancing energy and the sense of triumph we associate with comedy. All the qualities of the comic world—reconciliation, change, the restoration of social order, and the celebration of new possibility—are either absent or not working.

If the vision of tragicomedy is despairing to the point of horror, why would playwrights feel compelled to choose this form? More important, why would audiences want to experience it? What healthy need could this kind of theatre fulfill? Clearly, we do not go to the theatre to witness representations of our own happiness and despair. We do not need theatre for that. Actually, the explanation is quite the reverse. Of the dramatic forms, tragicomedy is most like life itself as we live it day by day. Think about it: How often do we achieve a clear resolution to anything? We fall in love, but how often does true love last? How often is suffering ennobling or the source of wisdom? Why does success so often prove to be hollow and empty? How capable are we of really changing things? Our experience tells us that all we can do is to "grin and bear it." That is the perfect motto for tragicomedy. It expresses the way life really is with an unsparing honesty.

That brings us back to the original question: Why do we pay our hard-earned cash to spend two or three hours of our leisure time watching unhappiness and frustration when we have our fill of that in our everyday lives outside the theatre? The answer is—and this is one of the mysteries of human life—most of us never give up hope. "Hope springs eternal in the human breast!" Going to the heart of tragicomedy—beyond the despair—we find hope. Why do Beckett's Gogo and Didi keep on waiting for Godot rather than hang themselves? Why do Chekhov's three sisters go on living even as their dream of Moscow is shattered? Why does Brecht's Mother Courage, all her children dead, go trudging on? Because though their lives may be meaningless and empty, broken and sad, they never give up the hope that maybe tomorrow things will change for the better. For most of us, hope is the miracle of existence, and tragicomedy insists that we need never give up hoping. Tragicomedy may bring us pictures of despair about the meaning of existence, but it does not stop there. It celebrates the fact that despair can be transcended because of our undying capacity for hope.

> *Real hope can be found only through real despair. . . . The appeal of that comedy which is infused with gloom and ends badly, that tragedy which is shot through with a comedy that only makes the outlook still bleaker, is that it holds out to us the only kind of hope we are in a position to accept. And if this is not the hope of a Heaven in which we would live forever, it is not the less precious, perhaps, being the hope without which we cannot live from day to day.*
> —Eric Bentley, *Life of the Drama*

5

THE ACTOR
AND THE ROLE

◆   . . . tear away the masks . . .   . . . emergence
from oneself . . .   . . . digs deeper and deeper . . .
. . . technique is a means to free the artist . . .
. . . accomplish an act of the soul . . .   . . . hard work . . .
. . . physical endurance . . .   . . . there are
no formulas . . .   . . . psychological motive . . .
. . . play through the cliché . . .   . . . discern
the authentic . . .   . . . transcendental experience . . .
. . . metamorphosis . . .   . . . show . . .

Konstantin Stanislavski
The Hard Job of Being an Actor

KONSTANTIN STANISLAVSKI (1863–1938), Russian director, actor, cofounder of the Moscow Art Theatre, in his later years became the most influential teacher of acting in the Western theatre. He developed a system of exercises and techniques that would enable the actor to discover from his or her own experience the feelings and motivations of the character he or she was to play. This essay reveals Stanislavski's basic attitudes toward the art of acting.

◆   Remember that my objective is to teach you the hard work of an actor and director of plays—it is not to provide you with a pleasant pastime on the stage. There are other theatres, teachers and methods for that. The work of an actor and director, as we understand it here, is a painful process, not merely some abstract "joy of creativeness" that one hears so much empty talk about from the ignoramuses in art. Our work gives us joy when we undertake it. This is the joy of being conscious that we may, that we have the right, that we have been permitted to engage in the work we love—work to which we have dedicated our lives. And our work gives us joy when we see that having fulfilled our task, put on a performance, played a role, we have contributed something worthwhile to our audience, communicated to it something necessary, important to its life, for its development. In short I come back to the ideas of Gogol and Shchepkin about the theatre, words you have already heard many times from me and probably will hear more than once again.

Nevertheless the whole process of an actor's and director's work—including his performance—is one that requires enormous self-mastery and often also great physical endurance. This work cannot be replaced by means of general words and moods.

The thing which lies at the base of an actor's or director's creativeness is work, and not moods or any other popular slogans such as "flights," "down beats," "triumphs."

To the ordinary man in the street the most "joyous" jobs might be the dance of the prima ballerina in *Don Quixote* or *Swan Lake.* He does not know how much physical effort, concentrated attention, sheer work Madame Geltzer had to put into the preparation of her famous "pas de deux" in those ballets, or what she looks like when she is in her dressing room after the dance is over. Perspiration pours from her and in her heart she reproaches herself for any slightest shading she did not perform perfectly.

That is true of dancing. Why should it be easier in drama or comedy? Yes, the "joy of creativeness" exists and it falls to the lot of true artists after they have done a tremendous piece of work in any chosen and beloved field of work in which they reach the goals they have set themselves.

But the artist is not worth his salt who impersonates the "joy of creativeness," waves his brushes around in front of his easel, pretending he is "painting" with such "ecstasy" (that's another popular word among the modernists). He is profaning his art at such times. He is not trying to reproduce life on his canvas, life in its infinite manifestations, trying to catch the fleeting feeling or thought on the face of his model. All he is trying to do is become her lover.

The same is true of an actor on the stage. When you act as you did recently the "joy of creativeness" instead of the subject and ideas of the play, you are just flirting with the public like actor-prostitutes. Not that! Never! Leave this to the decadent artist, the futurist, cubist! The great Russian actors, painters and writers did not play fast and loose with life, rather they tried to show its revolting and its inspiring sides in order to *educate* their public.

Do not be afraid of that word in art.

I have talked at length to you on the general subject of our theatre art because I not only want you to know how to play your parts better but also to learn how to *train* yourselves to become real artists. Whatever I have achieved has been at the price of tremendous work, of years wasted in mistakes and deviations from the real line of art. I am turning over to you everything I have learned, all my experience, in order to keep you from making the same mistakes. You will have three times as much opportunity to push our art ahead if you will follow me, choose to follow the path which I point out to you.

You are a new generation, come into the theatre since the revolution. I want you to learn again in practice what is called the "Stanislavski Method." There is no "method" as yet. There are a number of propositions and exercises which I propose to actors to carry out: they are to work on themselves, train themselves to become master artists. What are the basic propositions of my "method"?

The *first* is this: There are no formulas in it on how to become a great actor, or how to play this or that part. The "method" is made up of steps towards the true creative state of an actor on the stage. When it is true it is the usual, normal state of a person in real life.

But to achieve that normal living state on stage is very difficult for an actor. In order to do it he has to be: (a) physically free, in control of free muscles; (b) his attention must be infinitely alert; (c) he must be able to listen and observe on the stage as he would in real life, that is to say to be in contact with the person playing opposite him; (d) he must believe in everything that is happening on the stage that is related to the play.

To accomplish this I shall propose a number of exercises. . . . They train these absolutely necessary qualities in actors. They shall be done every day the way a singer vocalizes or a pianist does his finger exercises.

The *second* proposition of the "method" is: A true inner creative state on the stage makes it possible for an actor to execute the actions necessary for him to take in accordance with the terms of the play, whether inner psychological actions or external, physical ones. I divide them this way arbitrarily to make it easier to explain them to you in rehearsal. Actually in each physical act there is an inner psychological motive which impels physical action, as in every psychological inner action there is also physical action, which expresses its psychic nature.

The union of these two actions results in organic action on the stage.

That action then is determined by the subject of the play, its idea, the character of a certain part and the circumstances set up by the playwright.

In order to make it easier for you as an actor to take action on the stage, put yourself first of all in the circumstances proposed by the playwright for the character you are playing. Ask yourself: what would I do *if* the same thing should happen to me as it does in the play to the character I am playing? I call *if* jokingly a "magic" word because it does so much to help an actor get into action. Having learned to take action for yourself, then determine what difference there is between your own actions and those of your character in the play. Find out all the reasons which justify the actions of your character and then act without reflecting about just where your "own" actions end and "his" begin. The one and the other will merge of their own accord if you have followed the procedure I have indicated to you.

The *third* proposition of the system: True organic action (inner-plus-external, psychological-plus-physical) is bound to give rise to sincere feelings. This is especially true if the actor can in addition find some attractive "bait," as we saw in rehearsal.

Therefore the summing up is:

A *true inner creative state* on the stage, *action* and *feeling* result in *natural life* on the stage in the form of one of the characters. It is by this means that you will come closest to what we call "metamorphosis," always providing of course that you have properly understood the play, its idea, its subject and plot, and have shaped inside yourself the character of one of the dramatis personae.

(6 October 1924)

Charles Marowitz
Acting and Being

CHARLES MAROWITZ (1934–   ) is Artistic Director of the Open Space Theatre, London's leading experimental theatre, and has directed a number of highly innovative productions of Shakespeare seen both in Europe and the United States. In his writings on acting he has been chiefly concerned with the shifting two-way relationship between the director and actor, actor and audience.

◆ Before we accept the equation that acting *is* what acting *does,* let us examine as carefully as we can precisely what it does.

The actor comes to a piece of material; a play. He experiences it as a whole, but not exactly because even as he is assimilating the entire play, he is entering into a special relationship with one part of it which is magically *his.* He comprehends the wider framework in which he will be operating but does so from the vantage-point of his role. He is already subjectifying one portion of the play while retaining comparative objectivity about the remainder.

As rehearsals begin, he digs deeper and deeper into that subjectivity. He becomes more and more immersed in his role. Theoretically, he does not lose sight of his surroundings, the objective work in which he has this subjective preoccupation, but in effect, he reduces his wider focus on the play in order to see his own contribution more clearly. During rehearsals, due to the presence of other actors and a director who is obliged to maintain a balance between all the parts (and therefore must remain as "objective" as possible), the actor is constantly nudged out of his subjectivity and forced to adjust himself to the subjectivities of others (his fellow-players) and the objective demands of the director. Nevertheless, "working on the role" means submerging himself in his own contemplations even if, eventually, he surfaces to relate these "findings" to other people. The submersion is a necessary first step.

What kind of submersion is this?

First of all, he imagines himself into his character's situation. This is done more or less unconsciously. He perceives his character's activities in a way that seems plausible to himself; the way *he* might involve himself in those activities; the way *he* might feel in those circumstances. The actor does not and cannot say: how would Joe Doakes feel about this character, because he is obliged to work from his own sensibility, instinctively relating the events in his character's life to the way they might take place if *he* were that character. In other words, he invests those parts of himself which are basic—his mind, his imagination, his will, his reason—into another personage, gradually transforming this "other personage" into himself. This is the most mysterious fusion in the entire process; the submersion of Self into Role, the delineation of Role by Self.

What next happens is a strictly mechanical process. The actor, either by rote or during rehearsal, learns his lines through repetition. This repetition becomes the main preoccupation for several weeks' time. The actor continually repeats lines, moods, emotions, situations. Frequently, this repetition is interrupted by the director or other actors, or the actor's own lack of efficiency in sustaining the repetitions, but the imperative of rehearsals is continually to restore the broken moments so that, before long, there is an unbroken series of repetitions. The actor organizes his sensibility so that it does the same thing over and over again, and he labours in order to make his organism create these repetitions as effectively as possible; that is; as involuntarily as possible. The actor endeavours to obscure the fact that he is repeating himself. He works to persuade the audience that he is doing what he is doing for the first time. So a cardinal requirement of this work is for it to appear to be *initiations* rather than repetitions of behaviour. And to do this, paradoxically, he has to concentrate not on starting anew each time, but on efficiently repeating himself.

Now we know that repetition is the key element in hypnosis. The patient, put into a receptive state, is exposed to a recurring rhythm or a regularly repeated visual image and eventually, hypnosis is induced. The actor in effect, hypnotizes himself by repetitions of his role. The fact that he is still conscious, still aware of everything going on around him on the stage and in the auditorium, does not alter the fact that his "performance" is the result of these hypnotic repetitions. When he is acting well (centred in the role), he is more intensely *into* his repetitions than when he is acting badly (centred in the auditorium). Should he wish to depart from his role, he would have to disrupt the flow of his repetitions and this would be difficult to do as *his* repetitions are coalesced with those of his other actors and embedded in the paths marked out by the director as demanded by the text. So the actor is conjoined to repeat his repetitions by the artistic régime which has been imposed upon him through rehearsals. In order to "escape", he has to get past his other actors, past the obstacles laid down by the director, and past the structure of cause-and-effect implanted by the writer. Furthermore, he has to be able to disrupt his own continuity; the self-hypnosis he has spent weeks inducing in himself.

Artaud has talked about "a theatre that induces trance, as the dances of the Dervishes induce trance". Like so many of his observations, it is an hyperbole at the root of which is a kernel of truth. A constant wave of repetitions producing a mild form of self-hypnosis is *like* the trance-state of the whirling Dervishes. The difference is that the Dervish can *give himself* to the sensations he produces through his movements and the actor instinctively holds himself back. The Dervish spins for the sake of the trance; the actor enters his trance for the sake of the spins. Nevertheless, there *is* a loss of consciousness on the actor's part—which is what engenders the alternative consciousness of the artistic creation (the role) and it is this consciously extended alternative consciousness which conveys itself to the collective consciousness of the audience.

In the course of the actor's repetitions, he has been induced to organize his inner thoughts so that they colour what he says and does. The existence of the audience is like a potent magnetic-field to the actor. It is there not only to hear his words and watch his actions, but also to read his thoughts. The phenomenon of a group of people assembled together to examine a common object is that they develop a degree of group-consciousness, even if only for an instant, which is quite beyond the individual consciousness of any single spectator. The audience divines and interprets with a psychic gift that comes into being only when they assemble as an audience. They "tune in", they "react", they "twig to"—they bring a degree of perception which "sees through" not only what artists have organized for their perceptions, but also things they have not organized; things of which they themselves are unaware. An audience's radar sees more than it is shown, and what it does not see, it can sense; and what it does not sense, it can imagine. Confronted with such elaborate scanning-devices, the actor can conceal nothing—not his talent nor his inadequacy, not his enthusiasm nor his boredom, not his presence nor his absence.

When a performance succeeds, we talk about it "getting through" to the public, being on the audience's "wave-length", and these idiomatic expressions are significant. A performance that fails to "get through" or get on to the audience's "wave-length" is one in which the electrical waves generated by the actors are not being "received" by the audience. The physical performance is unquestionably there; it is visible and apparent, but its spiritual presence (i.e. communicated sub-text) is, to all intents and purposes, non-existent. Therefore what is (or is not) "getting through" is an invisible yet palpable communication which depends on actors infiltrating some intangible barrier created by the physical presence of the audience. This barrier is, of course, the audience's awareness of the play's artifice which a successful (sub-textually communicated) performance penetrates, thereby establishing contact with the tacit information being conveyed by the actor. Having "got through", having "tuned in" to the audience's "wave-length", a kind of dialogue is suddenly made possible, but the nature of this dialogue is itself tacit. The audience comprehends what the actors are *not* saying: what is being sub-textually implied; the actors begin to play, not to the physical presence of the audience seated before them, but to the consciousness of the receptivity to which their performance is "getting through". A tacit communication arises in a framework where an overt communication is taken for granted. It soon becomes clear that this overt communication is useless without the tacit one; indeed, that it belies the other's existence; that the *apparent* attention of an assembled audience sitting quietly and listening, means nothing unless that attention has been directed to the information being tacitly conveyed.

Actor-audience contact can mean two people holding telephone receivers without any interconnecting cable. Or it can mean a one-way conversation on the false assumption that the other party is entirely engrossed. Or it can mean a nullification of communication in that one party is lying to the other and the other is not believing what he hears in any case. Or it can mean, the greatest deception of all, the belief that a dialogue is taking place simply because words are being exchanged between both parties.

An actor "addressing himself" to an audience means addressing himself to that part of the audience that comprehends his tacit intelligence, and this can be comprehended only by the existence of its counterpart in the actor; the discovery of his own tacit self which is capable of conveying the unspoken elements of which his audible and visible self is only the container.

I am not referring here to "implied behaviour" like mime, or gestures which indicate inner states, or stage-action which "carries forward the plot" and communicates narrative information to an audience, but to the quintessential centre inside the actor through which he establishes contact with an equivalent centre in the audience. On one level, this is thought-transference which is an essential part of all acting; on another, it is (what I hesitate to call) spiritual contact; that is, the establishment of communication with unseen forces which is so evident that neither the actor nor the public questions its presence.

Think for a moment with what difficulty a medium tries to establish contact with a spiritual force. There is the ritual of the séance, the darkened room, the holding of hands round the table, the group concentration, the exhortation to invisible presences to materialize or to give a sign. Whatever one's attitude to spiritualism may be, it is a matter of record that this ritual sometimes produces results—although the sceptic may deflate them and the scientist, rationalize them. The theatre works on a similar principle (social ritual, darkened room, communal presence, intense concentration, evocation of non-existent people and events) and when a performance can be said to "work", it is because it produces spiritual resonances which critics subsequently refer to using words such as "magnetism", "magic", "spell-binding" and "hypnotic".

Although spiritualism cannot serve as a metaphor for theatrical performance, the same kind of psychic energy is peculiar to both. (It is no accident that actors study Yoga, Transcendental Meditation and other "spiritual" disciplines, all of which have clear affinities to acting.) When people sense what we mean without any outward sign from us, we assume they are *psychic*. Actors are attempting to be psychic all the time. They are transmitting thoughts, experiencing desires, exerting wills, inducing states— and sending out all variety of emanations to an audience who, for their part, are psychically comprehending—or not—depending on the strength or weakness of the actor's signal. You notice that I do not say depending on the *audience's* sensitivity, or the *audience's* susceptibility to receive such messages, for I take that for granted. The arrival of the audience brings into existence one half of the psychic bargain. The other half, the actor's half, is where the real effort must be made. The audience are those people seated round the table holding hands; the actor is both the medium and the spirit through which it speaks. Bad vibrations notwithstanding, the state must be evoked by the actor. No sooner is it evoked than an audience can experience it. *Their* state-of-being is never in question; the actor's always is.

The most salient point about this psychic zone in which the actor manages to establish meaningful communication with the audience is that it cannot be entered at the last minute. The actor cannot suddenly "turn himself on" in order to "get through". It is in the labyrinths of the rehearsal period that the actor develops the interior vocabulary which will stand him in good stead at the performance—just as the audience has accumulated *its* interior cravings and potentialities before *it* enters the theatre. If the rehearsal period has amassed a wealth of sub-text on which the psyche can draw while the play is being performed, there is something to be communicated once contact is established. If the actor impudently assumes it will "be all right on the night", he is in the position of an injudicious host who invites several hundred people to a supper-party only to discover he has an empty larder. In a positive and irreversible sense, it can never be "right" on the "night" if it hasn't been *made* right during the rehearsal period. The divine bird of inspiration which may swoop down upon the performers on the première does so only if it is able to sniff out the tempting smell of provender. The rehearsal period is the time during which that provender is stored up. To assume anything else is to be a pathetic victim of the theatre's false mysticism: the notion that there is a gaggle of Muses (like unpartnered dance-hall girls) just hanging about waiting to touch the artist with genius.

The aim then is, by mental and psychic gestures, to generate spirit. But there is no such thing as spiritual evocation in and of itself. Just as there is no such thing as a "great performance" outside the context of a play. A narrative framework or a stylistic convention[1] is both the launching-pad and the recovery-vessel for all performances. If the narrative is implausible or the stylistic convention flawed, it is still possible to produce a "great performance" but only as an isolated act of skill. Henry Irving was able to transform an old blunderbuss like *The Bells* into a vehicle for himself, and throughout the history of the theatre, actors have had "vehicles" created merely to transport their personal goods. The actor of genius *can* transcend paltry material and produce "shows" of his greatness (as for instance, a great opera-singer in recital can demonstrate his or her musical skills) but the actor is integral to the play just as the singer is to the opera, and they can only realize themselves fully when the skill is being fed back to the material which stimulated it. The experience of great acting is always an experience in which an audience comprehends greatness through an understanding of things profounder than acting or production. You don't come away from a great night in the theatre preoccupied with an actor's stage-effects, but with the social, intellectual or

---

[1]Happening-structure, multi-media, an improvised scenario, etc.

spiritual repercussions those effects have produced in you. Great acting, like all great art, is a transcendental experience and not an invitation to mark scorecards. Indeed, if anyone ever desired proof positive of a mediocre experience, it would be the alacrity with which everyone proceeds to examine isolated performances.

Through the centuries, the actor has gradually altered his focal point. For the early actor, the centre was the auditorium and he emphatically directed his performance to that. Gradually, in the nineteenth and early twentieth century, he learned to draw himself in and turn his attention to his fellow players. In the mid-twentieth century, he was being exhorted to draw himself even further in and find some tremulous central point in his own nature. The excesses of the first period created the artificiality and bombast we associate with a crude and old-fashioned theatre; the excesses of the latter produced the unacceptable self-indulgence of the Method approach. It is tempting to think the truth lies somewhere in between, but it doesn't. The real focal point is neither on the stage nor in the auditorium, but in a state of consciousness which bridges the two areas. It is a plateau of sensibility in the audience which the actor reaches by climbing through himself and his material. There is no direct route, and sometimes the most circuitous paths lead him there. But unless the actor has some idea of the kind of plateau he is trying to discover, he will yo-yo between the tug of his psyche and the demands of his audience, hopelessly dividing himself trying to satisfy both. It may be no help at all to the actor to say it is a plateau where the audience and the actor's psychic energy coalesce, but that's as close a geographical location as I can provide.

Jerzy Grotowski
Statement of Principles

JERZY GROTOWSKI (1933–   ) is director of the Theatre Laboratory in Wro-
claw, Poland, and has been particularly influential in actor training in the last fifteen
years. Although greatly influenced by Stanislavski, he is primarily interested in the
actor-audience relationship. His method of training involves arduous physical exercise
as a means of giving the actor complete control of his whole being in performance.

I

◆ The rhythm of life in modern civilisation is characterised by pace,
tension, a feeling of doom, the wish to hide our personal motives and the
assumption of a variety of roles and masks in life (different ones with our
family, at work, amongst friends or in community life, etc.). We like to be
"scientific", by which we mean discursive and cerebral, since this attitude is
dictated by the course of civilisation. But we also want to pay tribute to our
biological selves, to what we might call physiological pleasures. We do not
want to be restricted in this sphere. Therefore we play a double game of
intellect and instinct, thought and emotion; we try to divide ourselves artifi-
cially into body and soul. When we try to liberate ourselves from it all we start
to shout and stamp, we convulse to the rhythm of music. In our search for
liberation we reach biological chaos. We suffer most from a lack of totality,
throwing ourselves away, squandering ourselves.

Theatre—through the actor's technique, his art in which the living
organism strives for higher motives—provides an opportunity for what could
be called integration, the discarding of masks, the revealing of the real substance: a totality of physical and mental reactions. This opportunity must be
treated in a disciplined manner, with a full awareness of the responsibilities
it involves. Here we can see the theatre's therapeutic function for people in
our present day civilisation. It is true that the actor accomplishes this act, but
he can only do so through an encounter with the spectator—intimately,
visibly, not hiding behind a cameraman, wardrobe mistress, stage designer or
make-up girl—in direct confrontation with him, and somehow "instead of"
him. The actor's act—discarding half measures, revealing, opening up, emerging from himself as opposed to closing up—is an invitation to the spectator.
This act could be compared to an act of the most deeply rooted, genuine love
between two human beings—this is just a comparison since we can only refer
to this "emergence from oneself" through analogy. This act, paradoxical and

borderline, we call a total act. In our opinion it epitomizes the actor's deepest calling.

II

Why do we sacrifice so much energy to our art? Not in order to teach others but to learn with them what our existence, our organism, our personal and unrepeatable experience have to give us; to learn to break down the barriers which surround us and to free ourselves from the breaks which hold us back, from the lies about ourselves which we manufacture daily for ourselves and for others; to destroy the limitations caused by our ignorance and lack of courage; in short, to fill the emptiness in us: to fulfil ourselves. Art is neither a state of the soul (in the sense of some extraordinary, unpredictable moment of inspiration) nor a state of man (in the sense of a profession or social function). Art is a ripening, an evolution, an uplifting which enables us to emerge from darkness into a blaze of light.

We fight then to discover, to experience the truth about ourselves; to tear away the masks behind which we hide daily. We see theatre—especially in its palpable, carnal aspect—as a place of provocation, a challenge the actor sets himself and also, indirectly, other people. Theatre only has a meaning if it allows us to transcend our stereotyped vision, our conventional feelings and customs, our standards of judgement—not just for the sake of doing so, but so that we may experience what is real and, having already given up all daily escapes and pretences, in a state of complete defenselessness unveil, give, discover ourselves. In this way—through shock, through the shudder which causes us to drop our daily masks and mannerisms—we are able, without hiding anything, to entrust ourselves to something we cannot name but in which live Eros and Charitas.

III

Art cannot be bound by the laws of common morality or any catechism. The actor, at least in part, is creator, model and creation rolled into one. He must not be shameless as that leads to exhibitionism. He must have courage, but not merely the courage to exhibit himself—a passive courage, we might say: the courage of the defenseless, the courage to reveal himself. Neither that which touches the interior sphere, nor the profound stripping bare of the self should be regarded as evil so long as in the process of preparation or in the completed work they produce an act of creation. If they do not come easily and if they are not signs of outburst but of mastership, then they are creative: they reveal and purify us **while we transcend ourselves.** Indeed, they improve us then.

For these reasons every aspect of an actor's work dealing with intimate matters should be protected from incidental remarks, indiscretions, nonchalance, idle comments and jokes. The personal realm—both spiritual and physical—must not be "swamped" by triviality, the sordidness of life and lack of tact towards oneself and others; at least not in the place of work or anywhere connected with it. This postulate sounds like an abstract moral order. It is not. It involves the very essence of the actor's calling. This calling is realized through carnality. The actor must not **illustrate** but **accomplish** an "act of the soul" by means of his own organism. Thus he is faced with two extreme alternatives: he can either sell, dishonour, his real "incarnate" self, making himself an object of artistic prostitution; or he can give himself, sanctify his real "incarnate" self.

IV

An actor can only be guided and inspired by someone who is whole-hearted in his creative activity. The producer, while guiding and inspiring the actor, must at the same time allow himself to be guided and inspired by him. It is a question of freedom, partnership, and this does not imply a lack of discipline but a respect for the autonomy of others. Respect for the actor's autonomy does not mean lawlessness, lack of demands, never ending discussions and the replacement of action by continuous streams of words. On the contrary, respect for autonomy means enormous demands, the expectation of a maximum creative effort and the most personal revelation. Understood thus, solicitude for the actor's freedom can only be born from the plenitude of the guide and not from his lack of plenitude. Such a lack implies imposition, dictatorship, superficial dressage.

V

An act of creation has nothing to do with either external comfort or conventional human civility; that is to say, working conditions in which every-body is happy. It demands a maximum of silence and a minimum of words. In this kind of creativity we discuss through proposals, actions and living organisms, not through explanations. When we finally find ourselves on the track of something difficult and often almost intangible, we have no right to lose it through frivolity and carelessness. Therefore, even during breaks after which we will be continuing with the creative process, we are obliged to observe certain natural reticences in our behaviour and even in our private affairs. This applies just as much to our own work as to the work of our partners. We must not interrupt and disorganize the work because we are hurrying to our own affairs; we must not peep, comment or make jokes about it privately. In any case, private ideas of fun have no place in the actor's calling. In our approach to creative tasks, even if the theme is a game, we must be in a state of readiness—one might even say "solemnity". Our working terminology which serves as a stimulus must not be dissociated from the work and used in a private context. Work terminology should be associated only with that which it serves.

A creative act of this quality is performed in a group, and therefore within certain limits we should restrain our creative egoism. An actor has no right to mould his partner so as to provide greater possibilities for his own performance. Nor has he the right to correct his partner unless authorized by the work leader. Intimate or drastic elements in the work of others are untouchable and should not be commented upon even in their absence. Private conflicts, quarrels, sentiments, animosities are unavoidable in any human group. It is our duty towards creation to keep them in check in so far as they might deform and wreck the work process. We are obliged to open ourselves up even towards an enemy.

VI

It has been mentioned several times already, but we can never stress and explain too often the fact that we must never exploit privately anything connected with the creative act: i.e. location, costume, props, an element from the acting score, a melodic theme or lines from the text. This rule applies to the smallest detail and there can be no exceptions. We did not make this rule simply to pay tribute to a special artistic devotion. We are not interested in grandeur and noble words, but our awareness and experience tell us that lack of strict adherence to such rules causes the actor's score to become deprived of its psychic motives and "radiance".

VII

Order and harmony in the work of each actor are essential conditions without which a creative act cannot take place. Here we demand consistency. We demand it from the actors who come to the theatre consciously to try themselves out in something extreme, a sort of challenge seeking a total response from every one of us. They come to test themselves in something very definite that reaches beyond the meaning of "theatre" and is more like an act of living and way of existence. This outline probably sounds rather vague. If we try to explain it theoretically, we might say that the theatre and acting are for us a kind of vehicle allowing us to emerge from ourselves, to fulfil ourselves. We could go into this at great length. However, anyone who stays here longer than just the trial period is perfectly aware that what we are talking about can be grasped less through grandiose words than through details, demands and the rigours of work in all its elements. The individual who disturbs the basic elements, who does not for example respect his own and the others' acting score, destroying its structure by shamming or automatic reproduction, is the very one who shakes this undefinable higher motive of our common activity. Seemingly small details form the background against which fundamental questions are decided, as for example the duty to note down elements discovered in the course of the work. We must not rely on our memory unless we feel the spontaneity of our work is being threatened, and even then we must keep a partial record. This is just as basic a rule as is strict punctuality, the thorough memorizing of the text, etc. Any form of shamming in one's work is completely inadmissible. However it does sometimes happen that an actor has to go through a scene, just outline it, in order to check its organization and the elements of his partners' actions. But even then he must follow the actions carefully, measuring himself against them, in order to comprehend their motives. This is the difference between outlining and shamming.

An actor must always be ready to join the creative act at the exact moment determined by the group. In this respect his health, physical condition and all his private affairs cease to be just his own concern. A creative act of such quality flourishes only if nourished by the living organism. Therefore we are obliged to take daily care of our bodies so we are always ready for our tasks. We must not go short of sleep for the sake of private enjoyment and then come to work tired or with a hangover. We must not come unable to concentrate. The rule here is not just one's compulsory presence in the place of work, but physical readiness to create.

VIII

Creativity, especially where acting is concerned, is boundless sincerity, yet disciplined: i.e. articulated through signs. The creator should not therefore find his material a barrier in this respect. And as the actor's material is his own body, it should be trained to obey, to be pliable, to respond passively to psychic impulses as if it did not exist during the moment of creation—by which we mean it does not offer any resistance. Spontaneity and discipline are the basic aspects of an actor's work and they require a methodical key.

Before a man decides to do something he must first work out a point of orientation and then act accordingly and in a coherent manner. This point of orientation should be quite evident to him, the result of natural convictions, prior observations and experiences in life. The basic foundations of this method constitute for our troupe this point of orientation. Our institute is geared to examining the consequences of this point of orientation. Therefore nobody who comes and stays here can claim a lack of knowledge of the troupe's methodical programme. Anyone who comes and works here and then wants to keep his distance (as regards creative consciousness) shows the wrong kind of care for his own individuality. The etymological meaning of "individuality" is "indivisibility" which means complete existence in something: individuality is the very opposite of half-heartedness. We maintain, therefore, that those who come and stay here discover in our method something deeply related to them, prepared by their lives and experiences. Since they accept this consciously, we presume that each of the participants feels obliged to train creatively and try to form his own variation inseparable from himself, his own reorientation open to risks and search. For what we here call "the method" is the very opposite of any sort of prescription.

IX

The main point then is that an actor should not try to acquire any kind of recipe or build up a "box of tricks". This is no place for collecting all sorts of means of expression. The force of gravity in our work pushes the actor towards an interior ripening which expresses itself through a willingness to break through barriers, to search for a "summit", for totality.

The actor's first duty is to grasp the fact that nobody here wants **to give** him anything; instead they plan **to take** a lot from him, to take away that to which he is usually very attached: his resistance, reticence, his inclination to hide behind masks, his half-heartedness, the obstacles his body places in the way of his creative act, his habits and even his usual "good manners".

X

Before an actor is able to achieve a total act he has to fulfil a number of requirements, some of which are so subtle, so intangible, as to be practically undefinable through words. They only become plain through practical application. It is easier, however, to define conditions under which a total act cannot be achieved and which of the actor's actions make it impossible.

This act cannot exist if the actor is more concerned with charm, personal success, applause and salary than with creation as understood in its highest form. It cannot exist if the actor conditions it according to the size of his part, his place in the performance, the day or kind of audience. There can be no total act if the actor, even away from the theatre, dissipates his creative impulse and, as we said before, sullies it, blocks it, particularly through incidental engagements of a doubtful nature or by the premeditated use of the creative act as a means to further his own career.

[Translated by Maja Buszewicz and Judy Barba]

Joseph Chaikin
The Context of Peformance

JOSEPH CHAIKIN (1935–   ), is one of America's best known and most imaginative actors. As director of the Open Theatre (which he founded in 1963) he sought
"to redefine the limits of the stage experience, or unfix them. To find ways of reaching
each other and the audience . . . To develop the ensemble." In training actors Chaikin
sought to move them away from the logical and calculated to "behavior's irrational and
more fragile qualities."

> *Art creates another universe of thought and practice against and within the
> existing one. But in contrast to the technical universe, the artistic universe is
> one of illusion, semblance,* Schein. *However, this semblance is resemblance
> to a reality, which exists as the threat and promise of the established one.*
> —Marcuse

Assumptions on Acting

◆   The context of performance—that world which the play embraces and
the mode of playing which is the entrance into that world—is different from
one play to another. Each writer posits another world (realm) and even within
the works of one writer, the worlds may be quite different. An actor, no matter
how he is prepared in one realm (world) may be quite unprepared when he
approaches another. He must enter into it with no previous knowledge so as
to discover it. An actor prepared to play in Shaw's *Saint Joan* is hardly closer
to playing in Brecht's *Saint Joan of the Stockyards* than one not prepared for
Shaw's work. It requires a whole new start, not only into Brecht's world, but
into an empathy with his intentions in that particular work. An actor can no
more proceed without empathy with the writer's struggle than with the struggle of the character whom he is to play.

Questions come up for the actor which involve a total reassessment of
everything as he moves from one play to another. What is his relationship to
the character he is playing? Is it a merging, so that the audience will believe
he is the character, or is the actor to impersonate, or is it some other relationship between actor and character?

One of the most confusing of all questions to the actor is "Who is the
audience?" Is the audience like that of a film?—A group of individual spectators, each dreaming the action in a dark room? Is the audience a number of
people who are each potential rescuers of the action which is of a drowning
civilization? Is the audience anonymous intimates who are being signaled
about their own fate by a spy who's been with the enemy? Or is the audience

a group of people wanting the relaxation of an entertainment—to be comfortably purged, fascinated, or amused? Is the audience to be addressed as fools or saints? Every performer makes some decision about the audience in his own mind: personalizing, making specific the anonymous. He makes a secret choice, in the course of events, as to "who" the audience is. When that choice is controlled, the result is entirely different. In attributing a particular quality to the audience, one invites the participation of that quality. Whom is he secretly addressing? The casting agent present in the audience? The critic who could advance his career? His parents? The ghost of Gandhi? His greatest love? Himself? The same action performed addressing each of these has in it very different messages. In other words, to whom does the actor personally dedicate his performance?

What is the reality of one actor to another while they are together on the stage? The relationship of actor to actor is inseparable from the relationship of actor to audience, and both of these questions need to be answered by the particular text performed and by decisions taken on the text by the actors. These problems must be consciously considered by the actor in order to avoid letting these relationships fall into an unexamined pattern.

The theatre is different from the film in that those who attend and those who perform are all present. This is the single most important distinction. It is with this distinction that the actor needs to come to terms.

A List of Assumptions

"Does it require deep intuition to comprehend that man's ideas, views and conception, in one word, man's consciousness, changes with every change in the conditions of his material existence in his social relations and his social life?"

—(Marx & Engels, 1848)

All entertainment becomes instructive. It instructs the sensibility. It needn't give information in order to instruct. In fact, the information can more easily be neglected than the ambiance of the entertainment.

All acting is an example of human action, including that which takes place on the stage. The modes of expression in behavior give us examples of human realms.

The ultimate value in acting on a stage is to see heroism. The ultimate value of even a temporary community of people—that of the audience and actors—*is to confront our own morality.*

Technique is a means to free the artist. The technique which frees the artist for one realm of reality may draw him no closer to another than an artist who has never been free for any. The accomplishment of the set of tasks for the playing of a family comedy is of no use to the actors whose tasks are performing political theatre or theatre of dream. The actor must be able to play the material with full understanding—not just play himself. Of course an actor's tool is himself, but his use of himself is informed by all the same things that inform his mind and body—his observations, his struggles, his nightmares, his prison, his clichés—him as a citizen of his times and society.

Just as good manners very often keep in check the violence in a situation, confining behavior on the stage to the simple social reality keeps concealed all that which is bewildering. Bewilderment is one of the fundamental common denominators.

Shock: We live in a constant state of astonishment which we must ward off by screening out much of what bombards us and focusing on a negotiable position. An actor must in some sense be in contact with his own sense of astonishment. Reality is not a fixed state. The word "reality" comes from the Latin *"RAS"* which means—that which we can fathom.

Process

When beginning work in a particular realm, the first problem is to be able to mark off the area of belief that the company is projecting itself into. Even when it is clear and agreed on by the company involved, it is easier to imagine than to act. One way an actor can find to play that which he understands, but which isn't in the field of immediate social behavior, is to play through the cliché. This may very well come out first for an actor, but if he censors it, he may always stay behind it. If he plays the cliché out, it's more possible that he will go beyond it.

With the inundation of advertising and platitudes, an actor must be able to discern the authentic from the popular. What we know takes on a more and more separate life in the imagination, and what we act takes on a smaller and smaller repertoire of responses. In order to release action which is in the imagination, but cut off from the behavior, one has to go through a process. That process must be discovered by each actor for himself. For example, Stanislavsky developed a process through which the actor would have a reliable technique for the use of himself in relation to a role. However, according to the actor's vision, the process is altered. The aesthetic remakes the process. One can learn steps which have been taken by other people, but they apply to the other people, and the steps must be completely reexamined for each company and each actor. We can get clues from others, but our own culture and sensibility and aesthetic will lead us into a totally new kind of expression, unless we simply imitate both the process and the findings of another.

As for the disciplines of movement and voice, the actor must carefully choose. Particular mannerisms go along with the particular kind of movement discipline. Modern dance, acrobatics, yoga, etc.—each have associations that are not separated from the particular discipline. The same is true of the voice. The actor must discern what kinds of expressions he wants to release. The focus is acting with all the implications of behavior and "real life" and the formalizing of this rather than the borrowing of an already developed formalized process that is unrelated. Acting is the expression using the personality in all its manifestations. If it doesn't seem possible to develop one's own system of related disciplines, an actor should study another only to the point where he can still depart from it.

The Situation

Most of the time when we learn about acting, it is in relation to naturalistic situations. In our lives we are all involved in situations and we often identify ourselves to ourselves in terms of the situation we are in. Yet, if you move to a foreign town where, as a stranger, you have no particular interest in the existing circumstances, it isn't long before you become quite involved with the currents and stakes with which the townspeople are involved. The same is true of a new job, new friends, etc. Situations enclose us like caves and become the walls and ceilings of our concerns. When we first learn about acting, we learn how to find out what really matters to the character we are playing. We say, "If I have been starving for one week without a morsel of food while lost in the woods and I suddenly come upon an apple tree full of ripe apples, how would that be?" Then the actor imagines for himself this set of circumstances and comes to experience the kinds of sensations that might follow. He puts himself in the shoes of the starving man. Where he has no particular empathy with the man, he substitutes imaginary circumstances of his own that would bring the part alive for him.

In the work of Brecht, the ordinary is set against the strange: and an actor giving a sensitive account of the starving man's plight, without being sensitive to Brecht's plight as a particular poet rather than a reporter, would tilt the emphasis and obscure his intentions. Here, the event of the playing and of the actor-audience relationship forms its own situation for the actor to respond to and play within. For situations of the mind, which deal not with the actual but with the imaginary, the actor would have to know the circumstances of the dream (which I will call the situations of the mind). He must ask himself of his relationship to the dreamer, without narrowing the circumstances to that same kind of logic which limits the perception of actual "reality." Only when he is awake to the whole event of the piece, rather than just his part, and his interest in what is told in the piece is immediate, rather than substituted, can his work be organized to each performing situation. What he learns is how to live through the situation each time, instead of simply repeating the results. If he simply repeats his findings and plays the result, his performance is without the most essential acting dimension—that of being there and inhabiting the play as it's performed.

The actor is a collaborative artist informed and influenced by all those people whose efforts are also involved in the event which he performs. In rehearsal, he exposes himself to the elements which together form the event. In performance he is awake after a process of discovery. The situation, if it is a dream, requires different responses by the actor than the kind of rage and delight of the actual, even when the dream may be a retelling of an experience that has also been actual. But always to limit responses to those which are understandable in the realm of the actual is to diminish the actor's possible choices to the same few which he permits himself at other times, and to limit the possible stage behavior to the existing laws of society.

The actor must come to a connection with the material as a person is connected with his environment. When he performs, he plays the material rather than himself. He should be like a singer who sings the song, rather than singing his voice, which one often hears.

There is that theatre which concerns itself with what we already know and that theatre which explores what we don't clearly know. The choice an acting company and the actors within it make is whether they will follow the interpretations of human action which the times and society give or follow a kind of inner speculation.

I have a notion that what attracts people to the theatre is a kind of despair. We despair with life as it is lived, so we try to alter it through a model form. We present what we think is possible according to what is possible in the imagination rather than what is socially possible.

Perhaps the ultimate in acting through an exploration of behavior is to show not so much another kind of society, but rather another kind of man.

The teacher of the actor is like the teacher of small children who looks for the right steps for the particular student, and when the student is about to make his discovery, the teacher must disappear. If the teacher looks for his own satisfaction of having brought the student to the point of discovery, the student does not fully discover.

My own studies as an actor have introduced me to many teachers and their techniques, and I have sought to learn about all those teachers I couldn't study with personally whose work grabbed me. Peter Brook said once, of improvisation, that it opens a door which, until that point, has been shut, and once it is opened, one finds oneself in a vast place where all there is to do is waltz around and around the same space. I think there is much improvisation which does that. Among those teachers with whom I studied I found the Theatre Games of Viola Spolin, with whom I took four classes and had two conversations, to be the most initially freeing but ultimately confining. The exercises of Nola Chilton, who was an early teacher of mine, opened an enormous area within a psychological approach. From Mira Rostova I found the subtlety of invisible intentions which criss-cross each other all the time made visible. But beyond that invaluable perception I found her system to be a very narrow study. I have studied and been exposed to many other influences which I've repudiated or incorporated. There has been no single influence which was greater than the dialogues I had with Judith Malina and Julian Beck. None of this involved exercises, acting, specific techniques—because for the time that I was a member of the Living Theatre they did not inquire into real stage behavior or ritual. But they were free of all the aspirations and assumptions of established theatre, and therefore did not need to structure their inquiry according to the banal goals. Most recently, the biggest influence on me has been the company of people with whom I've been working, and their ideas and gestalts.

I think that each step of the acting requires the actor to return to a conscious awareness of what he is doing. Still, most of the creative work is done in that dream life between thinking and fantasy, and requires sometimes that the actor rest, and let the image move itself in his mind.

The realm of a situation dictates the kind of responses, and because at this time we have so much separated our actions from our impulses, renamed our acts and committed ourselves to a servitude of denial, replacing what we feel we need with what is recommended, we must not close the possibilities of behavior in the theatre to correspond with the international office etiquette. We should keep it open to the vast range of understanding. One has to be able to imagine an alternative realm of behavior expression in order to play it. The spectator will feel that what is true on the stage is what most represents himself—that realm which he most identifies with as his "real life" and perhaps that one which he most inhabits. But at the same time, the realm played recommends a "reality" that he may adapt.

Everything we do changes us a little, even when we purport to be indifferent to what we've done. And what we witness, we also do.

The mask which an actor wears is apt to become his face.—PLATO

Ronald Hayman
The Actor's Motives

RONALD HAYMAN (1932–   ) is one of England's best-known critics. He has written voluminously on all aspects of the theatre and drama. In this essay, he probes one of the most important but seldom asked questions related to the actor's art: "Why do actors act?" While there are no simple answers to this question, in pointing to the (usually unconscious) identity needs that prompt actors to act, Hayman raises some central issues pertaining to the theatre.

I exist only through those who are nothing apart from the being they have through me. —Genet

◆   Acting and playing—the words are synonymous, and the word *actor* did not come into common use until the end of the sixteenth century. The word *player* had been used since the middle of the fifteenth. What actors do when they are working is what children do when they are playing: they dress up, slip into other identities, mimic other people's ways of talking and moving, all the time wanting to be watched, and feeling more confident, more real, than when they are merely being themselves. The pleasures of acting are usually more apparent in a bad performance than in a good one. There are actors whose relish for self-assertion is blatant. They listen to their own voices, as if the auditorium had an echo. They occupy stage-space like a liberating army. They dunk each gesture in the nectar of the audience's silent attentiveness. For the good actor, too, there is pleasure in controlling the reaction of a large number of people, but there is also a possibility of being buoyed up, stimulated by their concentration to a higher level of creativity. And when this happens it feels very much like an upward escape from the confines of the everyday personality. Aldous Huxley would have called it a form of self-transcendence.

Dr. D. W. Winnicott, a paediatrician who became a psychoanalyst, has suggested that for the adult, as for the child, it is only in playing that the individual can be creative and use the whole personality. If this is true, it would follow that there are far too few situations in our social life in which creative play is possible for adults, and this would help to explain why so many people, so different from each other in type, talent and background, are constantly and persistently struggling to join a profession which is already overcrowded. It is not a cohesive profession. The word 'actor' is indiscriminately applied to people involved in a range of fairly diverse activities from street theatre to television commercials, from summer seasons on the Isle of Wight to two-year contracts with the Royal Shakespeare Company. The life of an actor who stays for three years at the repertory in Stoke-on-Trent is totally unlike the life of an actor in London whose agent gets him a succession of brief but highly paid jobs in films and television, with only a very occasional foray into the theatre when he can afford it. Working on the so-called 'Fringe' is a very different experience from working in the established theatre. And all this is to make no mention of the differences between being a star and being a small-part actor who is usually out of work.

While there are some actors who become addicted to high salaries, money is not usually a prime consideration. . . . As an executive of American Equity put it, 'An actor is the only human being who will work for nothing, if you let him.' He will put up with long periods of unemployment, and long periods of waiting around in theatres, rehearsal-rooms, film-sets and cramped, shabby, ill-equipped dressing-rooms. He is also working with no prospect of a pension. The fact that so many actors tolerate such very daunting professional conditions indicates an extremely powerful drive to go on working in the theatre, a drive which has never properly been explained. . . .

. . . Most actors do not themselves understand why it is so important to them to be actors. If asked they will reply disarmingly, 'There's nothing else I could do.' But there is more to it than this. Psychoanalysts like Winnicott and Ronald Laing have shed so much light on identity delusions that it may be worth considering whether there is any underground connection between the actor and the schizophrenic. While the actor is not under the delusion that he is really Galileo or Julius Caesar, there may be unconscious processes at work which have little to do with schizophrenia but which can be understood better in the context of what has been discovered about it.

In *The Divided Self*[1] Laing describes the life of the schizophrenic as being torn between two contradictory desires: to reveal himself and to conceal himself. The sensation of being an object of other people's observation—whether based on fact or illusion—is a source of both pleasure and pain. The schizophrenic feels that he is more exposed and vulnerable than other people: their gaze is dangerous to him because it could penetrate to the core of his inner self. At the same time he feels isolated. Desperation at not occupying the first place in anyone's affections can lead to paranoiac delusions of persecution. An illusion of the enmity of all others is preferred to the realisation that they are indifferent.

The schizophrenic feels unreal, precariously differentiated from the rest of the world, uncertain of his identity. At the same time as dreading relationships with other people, who may rob him of his autonomy, he needs them because without them he has no sense of his own reality. 'I am only a response to other people,' one of Laing's patients said. 'I have no identity of my own.'

Against this background, exhibitionism can be seen as a desperate bid for attention. It seems possible to show oneself off at the same as holding one's real self back, to exhibit the body while inhibiting what goes on inside the mind. Or, as Laing puts it in *The Self and Others,*[2] 'The exhibitionist who shows off his body, or a part of the body, or some highly prized function or skill, may be despairingly trying to overcome that isolation and loneliness which tend to haunt the man who feels his "real" or "true" self has never been disclosed to, and/or confirmed by others.'

This splitting of what feels like the real self from what feels like the unreal self is characteristic of schizophrenic behaviour. Another patient of Laing's felt 'as though somebody was trying to rise up inside and was trying to get out of me'. This is very much like what the actor feels when the character seems to be taking over. The split, for the schizophrenic, can come to feel like a separation between the self and the body. The real self is held back so much that it comes to feel disembodied, while the body becomes the centre of what Winnicott calls 'the false self'. The disembodied self is then withdrawn from contact with other people, confined to purely mental activity, while the body feels as though it is capable of acting independently, without compromising the integrity of the real self. It is only the body that is exhibiting itself or dressing up in women's clothes or pretending to be Napoleon. The real self remains detached, elusive, uncommitted, and the schizophrenic may well be priding himself on the absolute honesty he is maintaining in communing with it. The persona assumed by the false self is an amalgam of part-selves,

---

[1]Tavistock, 1960.
[2]Tavistock, 1961.

collected from different sources and undeveloped or only partially developed. Deliberate mimicry of other people's ways of walking and talking is a form of defence against the impression that one's own existence is unreal. By resembling other people one can participate in their reality. The alternative is to behave so outrageously that they will be embarrassed or offended. If the effect you produce on them is real you must be real too. It is only their indifference which is intolerable.

So the desire for reciprocity in relationships with other people has been first subordinated and then sacrificed to the compulsion to get through to them, at whatever cost, to be certain that they are receptive to what is being transmitted. But to expose oneself to what they might want to transmit would be too dangerous: it could lead to a dependence on them in a way they might exploit. Underneath all this, of course, is a loss of faith in one's own capacity to give or to receive love. Other people are made into an audience and whatever is going out to them is given out by the false self, so the real self is safe.

Anyone who has worn a mask, whether as an actor or at a fancy dress party, can understand something of the relief that the schizophrenic experiences when, without realising that he is acting, he assumes a false self. The face reflected in the looking glass is someone else's; the feelings behind the eyes are still one's own, but different. The iceberg has shifted, and something that was laboriously submerged has floated effortlessly to the surface. There is a new freedom, a release from the self-imposed restrictions that have become too familiar to be observable, an almost intoxicated sensation of privileged irresponsibility. Self-confidence mounts to the point where it seems almost possible to do anything and get away with it. Physically the mask is restricting: voice and movements need to conform to the new persona. But this sense of being circumscribed by someone else's physical characteristics is precisely what produces the feeling of liberation. There is no reason to be shy. If you go too far it will be this other person, not yourself, who has to take the rap.

This is only an intensification of what the actor always feels when he is 'in character'. Wearing make-up and a costume can be almost like wearing a mask, and without wearing either, the actor can still have the feeling that he is and is not himself, that some of the puppet strings are in somebody else's hands. He is concealing himself behind the character but simultaneously revealing more of himself than he could normally reveal in his off-stage life. There may be things about himself that he dislikes—physical characteristics, personality traits. These can be made to disappear. When Alec Guinness started to work in the theatre in the early thirties, he had to play a lot of character parts. 'And I suppose I got into that sort of habit. And it amused me. And I was very happy to disguise myself. I was always rather embarrassed with me, personally, so to speak. I didn't quite know what all that was about and I was glad to go into a thin cardboard disguise. Later I tried to make it a bit rounder.'[3]

The actor can enjoy the fact of being observed by other people but without letting their gaze penetrate to what he thinks of as the weak spots in his private identity. He is palpably making an impact on an audience. If he cannot hear its reaction to him he can at least sense it. Other people are reaffirming the reality of his existence and showing their attitude towards him, but, hiding behind the shell of an *alter ego,* he does not have to reveal his attitude towards them. He may think they are a rotten audience compared with last night's, but this will not show in his behaviour. The controlling intelligence remains detached, uncommitted, while the voice and the body do what the character has to do.

No one will be able to judge how much satisfaction the real self is getting from dressing up in a fine costume and putting make-up on and impressing an audience. Nor will anyone know what went on in the actor's mind when he was auditioning for the part or how much gratification he felt at being wanted for it. He may have been waiting in suspense for a cast list to go up on a notice board, announcing whether he was to have a big part or a minute cameo, to appear as a romantic juvenile or a coachman with bad breath. However shy he is in his private life, however much reassurance he needs about the management's or the director's regard for him, the audience will never find out. The time and the space that he fills in the play have been carved out for him by other people. It will be the production, not his own self-assertiveness, that will push him into the foreground; the only rebuffs he can receive on stage are rebuffs for the character he is playing. The relationship with the audience is the only one that cannot be predetermined, and this cannot possibly be reciprocal. Nor was there ever less danger of rebuff from that quarter than in England today, when audiences hardly ever show any displeasure at a bad performance. So he may appear three times as self-possessed as he ever does in private.

Consider a young Wagnerian soprano. She may be plump and nervous. The week before she makes her début as Isolde it may seem terrifying that she had to make a huge audience accept her as a romantic heroine; on the actual night it feels as though she is being carried along by the music and the movements she has rehearsed. There is a tiny corner of her mind in which she is excited by the sense of being in control of a voice that is exciting the audience, but it feels more as if her voice and her body are being controlled by something bigger than herself which is making her feel and seem bigger than she is, or as though she is handing herself over to something which is using her as its medium. If the thought suddenly struck her in the middle of a high C how dependent the whole performance was on her own willpower, her throat muscles might contract so much that the sound would be strangled.

---

[3]Interview in *The Times,* 7 August 1971.

And in fact her willpower is not involved at all in any conquest of new territory: the space she is to occupy has been mapped out for her in advance. All she has to do is fill it out. The analogy is not totally misleading: the actor has no orchestra to buoy him up, but for him too the territorial battles have already been won, the script is a score which has been developed in rehearsal into a series of interdependencies involving not just the cast but the people operating the lighting board and the sound effects. The actor's responsibility to everyone whose performance slots in with his own is not merely a pressure that weighs him down, it also holds him up, provides him with a sense of duty that distracts him from the functioning of his own willpower, just as a soldier shooting at the enemy can be distracted by a sense of duty and loyalty to his fellow-soldiers from any private desire to kill a man.

This is not to suggest that the aggressions involved in acting are murderous or that actors, any more than the rest of us, are potential schizophrenics, or that they are incapable of reciprocal emotional relationships. But obviously the libidinal discharge they can achieve through performance is profoundly satisfying, and obviously there is an element of exhibitionism in it, together perhaps with a bigger appetite for admiration than can be satisfied privately. There is also, probably, an element of voyeurism, as Edmund Bergler has suggested[4]: the actor is narcissistically peeping at himself through the audience's approving eyes.

The actor's actions are also effective only in appearance. There are no real bullets in the revolver, no desire to kill in the duel or seduce in the love scene. The display of virility is an end in itself. The actor is choosing to realise himself by making himself into an object of other people's observation, and in Sartre's terms[5] this is more passive than active, more female than male. Not everyone today would accept this conventional equation of activity with the male principle and passivity with the female. There is also a danger that this approach to the actor's unconscious reasons for wanting to act could be abused by the people who jump all too readily at any opportunity to tell you that theatre is essentially camp, acting essentially a homosexual pursuit, that only 'queers' enjoy making up their faces and dressing up in showy costumes.

It would be hard though to find any indications of effeminacy or homosexuality in the dances out of which drama originated. They seem to have been primarily acts of dedication to the invisible powers that were believed to control the workings of nature. As the dancer gave himself up to the spirit, the gods became a felt presence in the rites. In Bacchic revels, for instance, they were believed to participate personally, joining in the orgies of drinking and sexuality. With the normal human restraints thrown aside, the divine and the animal elements could enter in. This objective of self-abandonment is less remote from modern acting than it sounds. Nineteenth-century romantic actors believed themselves to be at their best only when in a state

---

[4]*Psychiatric Quarterly Supplement* XXIII, 1949.
[5]See Sartre's *Saint Genet.* W. H. Allen, 1963.

of 'frenzy' and when 'inspired'. Sarah Bernhardt said that the actor should 'forget himself and divest himself of his proper attributes in order to attain those of the part . . . Hamlet's frenzy will make the spectators shudder if he really believes he is Hamlet'. Today we no longer want 'frenzy', but the word *inspiration* is still used, and there is even an explicit suggestion of its divine source in the phrase that old actors still use for moments of apparent self-transcendence: 'The god descends,' they say. The assumption is that the performance reaches the heights only when the actor partially loses control of himself, abandons himself to something external which is waiting to take possession of him.

But of course it is not really external; it has been inside him all the time, waiting to get out. The relevance of Euripides' play *The Bacchae* and of the appeal it still has will be obvious. In forbidding the worship of Dionysus, the austere King Pentheus is inhibiting a part of his nature at the same time as inflicting repressive laws on his subjects. Dionysus himself, disguised as a priest, encourages Pentheus to dress in female clothes so that he can spy on the women who are breaking the law by worshipping the god on Mount Cithaeron. But then the god drives his worshippers into a frenzy. The disguised king is mistaken for a lion and torn to pieces by the women who are led on by his own mother, Agave. He had denied part of the nature she gave him.

But is there any relevance in the behaviour of the psychotic who puts on female clothes and tries to mimic female behaviour in order to protect himself from the woman that he feels is there inside him, struggling to get out? His schizophrenic subterfuge is to put on an act of submitting to her as a defence against really having to submit.

One possible cause of schizophrenia is parental treatment of a baby as if it were of the opposite sex. The father and especially the mother, having had two sons already, badly want the third child to be a girl and they damage his psyche for life by handling him, talking to him and dealing with him physically as if he actually were a girl. The growing child, confused but eager to please, tries to adapt himself to what seems to be required of him. Already he is playing a role. Perhaps he will grow up to be an actor. One of our greatest living actors started life in this way. Or perhaps he will grow up to be neurotic, or even psychotic. Dr Winnicott describes[6] how he helped one of his patients by talking to him as if he were a girl. The man, who was married and had two children, was eventually able to reply, 'I could never have said "I am a girl" But you said it and you have spoken to both parts of me.'

One of the qualities that the neurotic and the artist have in common, then, can be described as a feeling of having more parts to the self than can safely be brought into play in the normal relationships that society permits. While a man who is mentally ill may have a distorted notion of what is safe,

---

[6]In *Playing and Reality*.

society can also be sick and do a lot of distorting. In England industrialisation produced a social morality which is still with us. The spirit of Mr Gradgrind and Mr Podsnap is not dead. The virtues of early rising and regular hours for work are still religiously cultivated, and one attraction of a theatrical career is the refuge it offers from a nine-to-five day of boring repetitive work.

In the twentieth century, as in the sixteenth, Puritanism flourishes more in some climates than in others. In the Mediterranean countries the regime of office and factory work breeds less Puritanic values than in England, while the church, which is more theatrical than ours—not only in its rituals but in its colours, costumes and décors—bulks larger in the community's life. Both the professional theatre and the amateur are correspondingly less active, but there are more outlets for histrionic impulses in everyday life. A conversation in a shop or a café is patently more demonstrative and more physical: there is more movement of the body and of the adrenalin inside it. Africans are still more extrovert and uninhibited in their natural speech and movement. When the Zulu version of *Macbeth* was brought to the Aldwych in 1972, the director had to tone down behavior which was quite unexaggerated, because to an English audience it would have looked too theatrical.

Mechanisation of a society also tends to make song and dance less available as means of self-expression. We listen to records instead of performing, whereas Zulus break into song or dance spontaneously and unselfconsciously both individually and in groups. In many of the less industrialised areas of Europe song and dance arise more naturally than they do here. There are still folk singing and dancing which belong to a tradition that goes back almost as far as the Greek tragedies and tell us something about the way their choruses may have been a formalised theatrical coefficient of the singing and dancing that went on spontaneously in Greek society. In our society, there is relatively little ritual and theatre in everyday life. The aggressions which, in a primitive society, each adult male could release in a series of activities like hunting, fishing and fighting, or in ritual dances that represented fights, can hardly ever be released except vicariously, in watching football matches, for instance. And industrial society inevitably casts most of its members in roles which engage only a fraction of their potential. The endemic fear of automation is pathetic: men are fearful of losing jobs which could be done better by machines. There are still societies where it would be inaccurate to suggest that the adult, like the child, can be creative and use the whole of his personality only when he is playing. But if it is true of England, it must be the basic reason so many thousands of would-be actors feel that, riddled as it is with unemployment, the profession still provides the best available life.

6

THE PLAYWRIGHT
AND THE SCRIPT

◆ . . . pretending a fragment of life . . .
. . . laws of narration . . .   . . . create the word . . .
. . . dark journeys . . .   . . . structure is action . . .
. . . order out of chaos . . .   . . . words becoming flesh . . .
. . . this is what happened . . .   . . . lives by
conventions . . .   . . . suffering hero . . .
. . . represents a world . . .   . . . nature of festival . . .
. . . the least needed person . . .   . . . my words . . .

Thornton Wilder
Some Thoughts on Playwriting

THORNTON WILDER (1897–1975) was not a prolific playwright, but his work played an important role in shaping the modern theatre. Many European writers, in particular, have acknowledged their debt to him. Wilder also wrote several interesting essays on the nature of theatre. The one included here is the best known of them. In it he sets forth some of the basic principles which govern dramatic art.

◆ Four fundamental conditions of the drama separate it from the other arts. Each of these conditions has its advantages and disadvantages, each requires a particular aptitude from the dramatist, and from each there are a number of instructive consequences to be derived. These conditions are:
1. The theatre is an art which reposes upon the work of many collaborators;
2. It is addressed to the group-mind;
3. It is based upon a pretense and its very nature calls out a multiplication of pretenses;
4. Its action takes place in a perpetual present time.

I. The Theatre Is an Art Which Reposes Upon the Work of Many Collaborators

We have been accustomed to think that a work of art is by definition the product of one governing selecting will.

A landscape by Cézanne consists of thousands of brushstrokes each commanded by one mind. *Paradise Lost* and *Pride and Prejudice,* even in cheap frayed copies, bear the immediate and exclusive message of one intelligence.

It is true that in musical performance we meet with intervening executants, but the element of intervention is slight compared to that which takes place in drama. Illustrations:

1. One of the finest productions of *The Merchant of Venice* in our time showed Sir Henry Irving as Shylock, a noble, wronged and indignant being, of such stature that the Merchants of Venice dwindled before him into irresponsible schoolboys. He was confronted in court by a gracious, even queenly, Portia, Miss Ellen Terry. At the Odéon in Paris, however, Gémier played Shylock as a vengeful and hysterical buffoon, confronted in court by a Portia who was a *gamine* from the Paris streets with a lawyer's quill three feet long over her ear; at the close of the trial scene Shylock was driven

screaming about the auditorium, behind the spectators' back and onto the stage again, in a wild Elizabethan revel. Yet for all their divergences both were admirable productions of the play.

2. If there were ever a play in which fidelity to the author's requirements were essential in the representation of the principal role, it would seem to be Ibsen's *Hedda Gabler,* for the play is primarily an exposition of her character. Ibsen's directions read: "Enter from the left Hedda Gabler. She is a woman of twenty-nine. Her face and figure show great refinement and distinction. Her complexion is pale and opaque. Her steel-gray eyes express an unruffled calm. Her hair is an attractive medium brown, but is not particularly abundant; and she is dressed in a flowing loose-fitting morning gown." I once saw Eleonora Duse in this role. She was a woman of sixty and made no effort to conceal it. Her complexion was pale and transparent. Her hair was white, and she was dressed in a gown that suggested some medieval empress in mourning. And the performance was very fine.

One may well ask: why write for the theatre at all? Why not work in the novel where such deviations from one's intentions cannot take place?

There are two answers:

1. The theatre presents certain vitalities of its own so inviting and stimulating that the writer is willing to receive them in compensation for this inevitable variation from an exact image.

2. The dramatist through working in the theatre gradually learns not merely to take account of the presence of the collaborators, but to derive advantage from them; and he learns, above all, to organize the play in such a way that its strength lies not in appearances beyond his control, but in the succession of events and in the unfolding of an idea, in narration.

The gathered audience sits in a darkened room, one end of which is lighted. The nature of the transaction at which it is gazing is a succession of events illustrating a general idea—the stirring of the idea; the gradual feeding out of information; the shock and countershock of circumstances; the flow of action; the interruption of action; the moments of allusion to earlier events; the preparation of surprise, dread, or delight—all that is the author's and his alone.

For reasons to be discussed later—the expectancy of the group-mind, the problem of time on the stage, the absence of the narrator, the element of pretense—the theatre carries the art of narration to a higher power than the novel or the epic poem. The theatre is unfolding action and in the disposition of events the authors may exercise a governance so complete that the distortions effected by the physical appearance of actors, by the fancies of scene painters and the misunderstandings of directors, fall into relative insignificance. It is just because the theatre is an art of many collaborators, with the constant danger of grave misinterpretation, that the dramatist learns to turn his attention to the laws of narration, its logic and its deep necessity of presenting a unifying idea stronger than its mere collection of happenings. The dramatist must be by instinct a storyteller.

There is something mysterious about the endowment of the storyteller. Some very great writers possessed very little of it, and some others, lightly esteemed, possessed it in so large a measure that their books survive down the ages, to the confusion of severer critics. Alexandre Dumas had it to an extraordinary degree, while Melville, for all his splendid quality, had it barely sufficiently to raise his work from the realm of nonfiction. It springs, not, as some have said, from an aversion to general ideas, but from an instinctive coupling of idea and illustration; the idea, for a born storyteller, can only be expressed imbedded in its circumstantial illustration. The myth, the parable, the fable are the fountainhead of all fiction and in them is seen most clearly the didactic, moralizing employment of a story. Modern taste shrinks from emphasizing the central idea that hides behind the fiction, but it exists there nevertheless, supplying the unity to fantasizing, and offering a justification to what otherwise we would repudiate as mere arbitrary contrivance, pretentious lying, or individualistic emotional association spinning. For all their magnificent intellectual endowment, George Meredith and George Eliot were not born storytellers; they chose fiction as the vehicle for their reflections, and the passing of time is revealing their error in that choice. Jane Austen was pure storyteller and her works are outlasting those of apparently more formidable rivals. The theatre is more exacting than the novel in regard to this faculty, and its presence constitutes a force which compensates the dramatist for the deviations which are introduced into his work by the presence of his collaborators.

The chief of these collaborators are the actors.

The actor's gift is a combination of three separate faculties or endowments. Their presence to a high degree in any one person is extremely rare, although the ambition to possess them is common. Those who rise to the height of the profession represent a selection and a struggle for survival in one of the most difficult and cruel of the artistic activities. The three endowments that compose the gift are observation, imagination, and physical co-ordination.

1. An observant and analyzing eye for all modes of behavior about it, for dress and manner, and for the signs of thought and emotion in one's self and in others.

2. The strength of imagination and memory whereby the actor may, at the indication in the author's text, explore his store of observations and represent the details of appearance and the intensity of the emotions—joy, fear, surprise, grief, love, and hatred, and through imagination extend them to intenser degrees and to differing characterizations.

3. A physical co-ordination whereby the force of these inner realizations may be communicated to voice, face and body.

An actor must *know* the appearances and the mental states; he must *apply* his knowledge to the role; and he must physically *express* his knowledge. Moreover, his concentration must be so great that he can effect this representation under conditions of peculiar difficulty—in abrupt transition from the nonimaginative conditions behind the stage; and in the presence of fellow-actors who may be momentarily destroying the reality of the action.

A dramatist prepares the characterization of his personages in such a way that it will take advantage of the actor's gift.

Characterization in a novel is presented by the author's dogmatic assertion that the personage was such, and by an analysis of the personage with generally an account of his or her past. Since, in the drama, this is replaced by the actual presence of the personage before us and since there is no occasion for the intervening all-knowing author to instruct us as to his or her inner nature, a far greater share is given in a play to (1) highly characteristic utterances and (2) concrete occasions in which the character defines itself under action and (3) conscious preparation of the text whereby the actor may build upon the suggestions in the role according to his own abilities.

Characterization in a play is like a blank check which the dramatist accords to the actor for him to fill in—not entirely blank, for a number of indications of individuality are already there, but to a far less definite and absolute degree than in the novel.

The dramatist's principal interest being the movement of the story, he is willing to resign the more detailed aspects of characterization to the actor and is often rewarded beyond his expectation.

The sleepwalking scene from *Macbeth* is a highly compressed selection of words whereby despair and remorse rise to the surface of indirect confession. It is to be assumed that had Shakespeare lived to see what the genius of Sarah Siddons could pour into the scene from that combination of observation, self-knowledge, imagination, and representational skill, even he might have exclaimed, "I never knew I wrote so well!"

II. The Theatre Is an Art Addressed to a Group-Mind

Painting, sculpture, and the literature of the book are certainly solitary experiences; and it is likely that most people would agree that the audience seated shoulder to shoulder in a concert hall is not an essential element in musical enjoyment.

But a play presupposes a crowd. The reasons for this go deeper than (1) the economic necessity for the support of the play and (2) the fact that the temperament of actors is proverbially dependent on group attention.

It rests on the fact that (1) the pretense, the fiction on the stage would fall to pieces and absurdity without the support accorded to it by a crowd, and (2) the excitement induced by pretending a fragment of life is such that it partakes of ritual and festival, and requires a throng.

Similarly the fiction that royal personages are of a mysteriously different nature from other people requires audiences, levees, and processions for its maintenance. Since the beginnings of society, satirists have occupied themselves with the descriptions of kings and queens in their intimacy and delighted in showing how the prerogatives of royalty become absurd when the crowd is not present to extend to them the enhancement of an imaginative awe.

The theatre partakes of the nature of festival. Life imitated is life raised to a higher power. In the case of comedy, the vitality of these pretended surprises, deceptions, and the *contretemps* becomes so lively that before a spectator, solitary or regarding himself as solitary, the structure of so much even would inevitably expose the artificiality of the attempt and ring hollow and unjustified; and in the case of tragedy, the accumulation of woe and apprehension would soon fall short of conviction. All actors know the disturbing sensation of playing before a handful of spectators at a dress rehearsal or performance where only their interest in pure craftsmanship can barely sustain them. During the last rehearsals the phrase is often heard: "This play is hungry for an audience."

Since the theatre is directed to a group-mind, a number of consequences follow:

1. A group-mind presupposes, if not a lowering of standards, a broadening of the fields of interest. The other arts may presuppose an audience of connoisseurs trained in leisure and capable of being interested in certain rarefied aspects of life. The dramatist may be prevented from exhibiting, for example, detailed representations of certain moments in history that require specialized knowledge in the audience, or psychological states in the personages which are of insufficient general interest to evoke self-identification in the majority. In the Second Part of Goethe's *Faust* there are long passages dealing with the theory of paper money. The exposition of the nature of misanthropy (so much more drastic than Molière's) in Shakespeare's *Timon of Athens* has never been a success. The dramatist accepts this limitation in subject matter and realizes that the group-mind imposes upon him the necessity of treating material understandable by the larger number.

2. It is the presence of the group-mind that brings another requirement to the theatre—forward movement.

Maeterlinck said that there was more drama in the spectacle of an old man seated by a table than in the majority of plays offered to the public. He was juggling with the various meanings in the word "drama." In the sense whereby drama means the intensified concentration of life's diversity and significance he may well have been right; if he meant drama as a theatrical representation before an audience he was wrong. Drama on the stage is inseparable from forward movement, from action.

Many attempts have been made to present Plato's dialogues, Gobineau's fine series of dialogues, *La Renaissance,* and the *Imaginary Conversations* of Landor; but without success. Through some ingredient in the group-mind, and through the sheer weight of anticipation involved in the dressing up and the assumption of fictional roles, an action is required, and an action that is more than a mere progress in argumentation and debate.

III. The Theatre Is a World of Pretense

It lives by conventions: a convention is an agreed-upon falsehood, a permitted lie.

Illustrations: Consider at the first performance of the *Medea,* the passage where Medea meditates the murder of her children. An anecdote from antiquity tells us that the audience was so moved by this passage that considerable disturbance took place.

The following conventions were involved:

1. Medea was played by a man.
2. He wore a large mask on his face. In the lip of the mask was an acoustical device for projecting the voice. On his feet he wore shoes with soles and heels half a foot high.
3. His costume was so designed that it conveyed to the audience, by convention: woman of royal birth and Oriental origin.
4. The passage was in metric speech. All poetry is an "agreed-upon-falsehood" in regard to speech.
5. The lines were sung in a kind of recitative. All opera involves this "permitted lie" in regard to speech.

Modern taste would say that the passage would convey very much greater pathos if a woman "like Medea" had delivered it—with an uncovered face that exhibited all the emotions she was undergoing. For the Greeks, however, there was no pretense that Medea was on the stage. The mask, the costume, the mode of declamation, were a series of signs which the spectator interpreted and reassembled in his own mind. Medea was being re-created within the imagination of each of the spectators.

The history of the theatre shows us that in its greatest ages the stage employed the greatest number of conventions. The stage is fundamental pretense and it thrives on the acceptance of that fact and in the multiplication of additional pretenses. When it tries to assert that the personages in the action "really are," really inhabit such and such rooms, really suffer such and such emotions, it loses rather than gains credibility. The modern world is inclined to laugh condescendingly at the fact that in the plays of Racine and Corneille the gods and heroes of antiquity were dressed like the courtiers under Louis XIV; that in the Elizabethan age scenery was replaced by placards notifying the audience of the location; and that a whip in the hand and a jogging motion of the body indicated that a man was on horseback in the Chinese theatre; these devices did not spring from naïveté, however, but from the vitality of the public imagination in those days and from an instinctive feeling as to where the essential and where the inessential lay in drama.

The convention has two functions:

1. It provokes the collaborative activity of the spectator's imagination; and
2. It raises the action from the specific to the general.

This second aspect is of even greater importance than the first.

If Juliet is represented as a girl "very like Juliet"—it was not merely a deference to contemporary prejudices that assigned this role to a boy in the Elizabethan age—moving about in a "real" house with marble staircases, rugs, lamps, and furniture, the impression is irresistibly conveyed that these events happened to this one girl, in one place, at one moment in time. When the play is staged as Shakespeare intended it, the bareness of the stage releases the events from the particular and the experience of Juliet partakes of that of all girls in love, in every time, place and language.

The stage continually strains to tell this generalized truth and it is the element of pretense that reinforces it. Out of the lie, the pretense, of the theatre proceeds a truth more compelling than the novel can attain, for the novel by its own laws is constrained to tell of an action that "once happened" —"once upon a time."

IV. The Action on the Stage Takes Place in a Perpetual Present Time

Novels are written in the past tense. The characters in them, it is true, are represented as living moment by moment their present time, but the constant running commentary of the novelist ("Tess slowly descended into the valley"; "Anna Karenina laughed") inevitably conveys to the reader the fact that these events are long since past and over.

The novel is a past reported in the present. On the stage it is always now. This confers upon the action an increased vitality which the novelist longs in vain to incorporate into his work.

This condition in the theatre brings with it another important element:

In the theatre we are not aware of the intervening storyteller. The speeches arise from the characters in an apparently pure spontaneity.

A play is what takes place.

A novel is what one person tells us took place.

A play visibly represents pure existing. A novel is what one mind, claiming omniscience, asserts to have existed.

Many dramatists have regretted this absence of the narrator from the stage, with his point of view, his powers of analyzing the behavior of the characters, his ability to interfere and supply further facts about the past, about simultaneous actions not visible on the stage, and above *all* his function of pointing the moral and emphasizing the significance of the action. In some periods of the theatre he has been present as chorus, or prologue and epilogue or as *raisonneur*. But surely this absence constitutes an additional force to the form, as well as an additional tax upon the writer's skill. It is the task of the dramatist so to co-ordinate his play, through the selection of episodes and speeches, that though he is himself not visible, his point of view and his governing intention will impose themselves on the spectator's attention, not as dogmatic assertion or motto, but as self-evident truth and inevitable deduction.

Imaginative narration—the invention of souls and destinies—is to the philosopher an all but indefensible activity.

Its justification lies in the fact that the communication of ideas from one mind to another inevitably reaches the point where exposition passes into illustration, into parable, metaphor, allegory, and myth.

It is no accident that when Plato arrived at the height of his argument and attempted to convey a theory of knowledge and a theory of the structure of man's nature he passed over into story telling, into the myths of the Cave and the Charioteer; and that the great religious teachers have constantly had recourse to the parable as a means of imparting their deepest intuitions.

The theatre offers to imaginative narration its highest possibilities. It has many pitfalls and its very vitality betrays it into service as mere diversion and the enhancement of insignificant matter; but it is well to remember that it was the theatre that rose to the highest place during those epochs that aftertime has chosen to call "great ages" and that the Athens of Pericles and the reigns of Elizabeth, Philip II, and Louis XIV were also the ages that gave to the world the greatest dramas it has known.

John Whiting
Writing for Actors

JOHN WHITING (1917–1963), the English playwright, is best known for his disturbing play, *The Devils.* Several years after his death a collection of his writings on the theatre *(The Art of the Dramatist)* was published, from which this essay is taken. In it he stresses the point that in the process of writing a play the dramatist must keep in mind that he or she is first and foremost writing for actors and not readers, audiences, or critics.

◆ The art of writing for actors has fallen into disrepute. The idea that plays are written bearing in mind that they are to be performed appears to disturb many people nowadays. It is easy to understand how this state of affairs has come about. No form lends itself more easily to the meretricious and the cheap than the theatre. No other art can provide such immediate and extensive, although ephemeral, gratification to the practitioners. There have been those—and their names often rank very high in theatrical history—who have used the theatre and the credulity of large crowds to practise what, in the end, proved to be nothing more than the tricks practised by the experienced on the innocent. A conjurer at a children's party does much the same.

Throughout the history of the theatre this kind of magic can be found. The most guilty men were usually actors; often they were what are called 'great actors'. They achieved much of this sleight-of-hand by the commission of dramatic works to their own dictation or by the mutilation and perversion of existing plays. In this way many great moments of theatre were achieved, but the play went limping off to take refuge between the covers of a book. The excuse for these virtuoso players is not difficult to find. Authors have, during the past hundred and fifty years, provided actors with everything to act except plays. They were given for performance epic poems, political and sociological pamphlets, religious tracts, novels and newspaper reports. Because of this the best actors, who are animals with a strong sense of self-preservation and considerable ingenuity, put together, usually without benefit of so commonplace an object as a book of words, a number of well-dressed and surprising situations which found considerable favour with the innocent. This was very poor art but extremely good business.

We live in a less credulous and, theatrically, more scrupulous age. The measure of a great actor is no longer what he can achieve in prescribed circumstances but what he can achieve with the full weight of the author's intention. There remains, however, much doubt even today. Is the rabbit from the hat alive or is it stuffed? Influenced by this, it is natural that any play of today which *seems* to have been primarily written for actors should be regarded with suspicion. (It is not only natural, it is right: every work of art should be approached with extreme suspicion.) Natural, also, that it should be carefully examined to see that it is not merely an excuse for virtuosity—for fine voices, beautiful clothes and settings and a dazzling, ingenious lighting plot. It must always be remembered that workers in the theatre possess enough technical trickery to deceive even the very discerning. It must also be remembered that never before has it been so scrupulously used. On this basis it is interesting to examine the relation between the dramatic author—who is not, contrary to general opinion, a technical trick—and his actors.

The actor's art provides the dramatist with an instrument of great range. So great, indeed, that only a fool would attempt to employ it without due consideration and seriousness. For the actor's power lies not in his voice, his face or his mind, but in his humanity. Only in the theatre can we call upon men as men to interpret and communicate. That communication can be achieved with great sympathy by an actor lacking, as it does, the bonds of academicism. It is strange the actor's art should be deplored because of its transience. Surely the emotional, the moving quality of the actor's performance is that it is gone into the past as irrevocably as any human action, that it possesses a mortality of its own.

The actor's concern is to achieve, not a truth, but a rightness. There is no constant in human behaviour and it is with human behaviour the actor deals.

To perfect this rightness is the job of the actor. Clothes, make-up, movement, even the words of the part are subsidiary equipment. From whatever point the actor may approach a part, however much he may change his appearance, the part he plays will have firm foundation in the actor's personality as a man. Once he has identified the character of the part with his own personality the words, moves and idiosyncracies fall naturally into place. There is no necessity to memorise them in the usual sense of the word—a common misconception—for after a period of rehearsal there is no conscious effort to remember what is said or done and when. Such things come from the rightness of the performance.

The degree of greatness in a performance depends on the power of identification which springs in sympathy from the individual personality of the player. This plans an ideal performance in the mind which, in fact, may never be given either in rehearsal or before an audience; yet, from this ideal can be taken the performance for the theatre. Delacroix expresses this vividly: 'He (the actor) makes tracings, so to speak, of the original idea.' The similarity and detail of these tracings will determine the fineness of subsequent performances.

An actor will expect from a new play not that it should be merely a book of words containing a narrative in dramatic form, but that it should provide a stimulus to his imagination. It is at this point that the author and his actors first come together.

What else must the author have prepared to bring about this fusion? From the director's and actor's points of view he must have prepared a blueprint, a coldly technical document. This may suggest the subordination of the writer in the theatre as a creator. There is an old argument as to whether the direction and performance of a play is interpretive or creative. The question can be answered: the writing, directing, designing and acting of a play are each creative in their own part to the whole. More important, surely, is that they are interdependent. It is an author's vanity to claim creation because he is the mere starting-point. His play would be no play if it remained words on paper.

The modern play is not a work of literature. Unfortunately, it is often considered and criticised as such not only from the printed page but from performance. It is not unusual to find critics who are capable of translating words spoken by an actor back into the written word, and on that written word they make their judgment. This is understandable. Performances in a theatre are difficult to judge dispassionately—at least, they should be difficult to judge —and the printed word has stability. Nevertheless, it is a mistake to judge plays in such a way. Acquaintance with the text is admirable, though rare, but criticism should be confined to performance.

The concern, therefore, is not with 'good prose' or with 'good verse' in the accepted sense. The structure is action and the action is controlled and formed by dialogue. The action must never become subordinated to the dialogue. In the modern play, which is attempting to achieve a greater unity of time and place, much difficulty can be experienced in carrying forward narrative. More difficulty, for example, than would be experienced in a play of such structure as the Elizabethan dramatists who were not generally attempting unity of time or place. This allows for a considerable complexity of plot as in certain plays by Shakespeare. It would be impossible and not in the least desirable to attempt such goings-on in a modern two or three act play.

It has been attempted in recent years in historical plays usually with lamentable results.

The shaping of prose dialogue determines the style. This does not mean the characteristic idiom of the dialogue but the use of voices to achieve dramatic form. Not what is said or how it is said but *when*. For example, the exact placing of unbroken passages for a single voice or dialogue in half-speeches for two or more voices perhaps speaking together. By this method it is possible to control from within the text of the play the speed and exact rhythm which are usually imposed by the director. Also, in this form, the play can be 'read' from the printed page without regard to theme, or in this case sense, in very much the same way as a musical score. The actor can then see the dramatic shape of an individual part within a scene and not be forced to rely on an intuitive sense which is sometimes false and leads to distortion.

The basic, the unalterable factor of drama is the moment 'when'; the moment of happening which is contained in the action. The dramatist must concern himself with this moment of action and not leave it, as so often happens, to be imposed by the director or players. In other words, the dramatist must create what is done and *when,* and not only the words to be spoken. During the past years much critical enquiry has taken place to determine a style of play-writing. Almost without exception this enquiry has dealt with the form of the spoken word. Yet this is not the starting point. There is no unhappier sight in the world than an actor at rehearsal searching for the motive of the words he is given to speak. There is an old and, alas, only half-humorous dictum of the theatre: never pay any attention to the author's stage directions. Those directions, however, are the author's first means of communication with his actors. They must never be mechanical directions— where to move, how to sit. Nor must they presume to instruct—to be said 'angrily', 'sadly', 'bitterly'. They must augment the words to be spoken. They are a guide-line of motive and action throughout the individual parts and, when translated into action in performance, as much part of the play as the spoken word.

All this is a plea for a greater discipline and exactness in the transcription for action. Perhaps it will be wise to work towards a script which is only comprehensible to the theatre worker and remains nonsense to the layman. It is interesting to speculate on the harm done to the play in the theatre by the fact that it is expected the text should be readable by the non-expert. Other forms—the film, television, radio—have begun to devise a method of transcription for their actors which is far from readable in any pleasurable sense yet admirably suits the demands for translation into performance. The theatre, however, remains tied to an outmoded convention. Every other factor in the theatre—playing, designing, staging, lighting—has developed with the age. The text of the play alone remains unchanged, an archaism.

In rehearsal the author's contact with the actors is through the director of the play. In this relation there must be, of course, considerable sympathy and respect. From the moment a play is in the hands of a director the technical resources for translation to performance are brought into action. At this point it is often considered that the author's job is finished. Very often at this time the author hides himself. He should not do this. The author is as much a worker *in* the theatre as directors, designers, actors and the rest. He cannot deliver a play and then sit back with no further participation. At the stage of the first rehearsal his work is not half done. The position of an author at rehearsals is certainly not an enviable one. It calls for a high degree of tact and great consideration of actor's problems, for it is here the play becomes a work of collaboration and, as in all works of collaboration, there must necessarily be considerable adjustment. A slavish and literal representation of the printed play by the director and actors is as wrong as misrepresentation for the sake of virtuosity. These problems arise because the direction and acting of a play in the modern idiom is, in detail, a thing of inspiration and improvisation in the moment of rehearsal. Only the very broad and, of necessity, practical details of production can be laid down before rehearsal. The creation of the play, the intangible substances, the magic, the poetry and mood are drawn from the text sometimes by so prosaic a method as trial and error during rehearsal. Indeed, rehearsals are not the time spent to get everything right but to get everything wrong. Such methods can prove most difficult for an author. There is the constant necessity for adjustment in detail while the structure and essence of the play must be retained. It is vital that the limits of this adjustment should be previously laid down between the author and director; limits not only within the play as a whole but within its units, the individual characters and scenes. An example of this adjustment is that an actor may, by imagination in his performance, make certain words unnecessary. The emotional content of a scene may crowd out the necessity for the spoken word. The lines, therefore, are well deleted. There should be no deletion, however, without replacement by another factor—emotional or visual, perhaps—otherwise the overall structure of the play is affected.

This formal structure is the poetry of drama. Given this, anything is possible to the actor. From it he can build in a disciplined and poetic way. Without it he will retreat into naturalism, and instead of acting he will behave.

The theatre in this day has an opportunity to become an art in its own right. In the past twenty-five years much dead wood from theatrical convention has been taken over by the cinema. In the same way television is going to relieve the cinema of many elements it can well do without, leaving it a freer and purer form.

A time has been reached when the terms of theatre and of dramatic art generally need to be redefined. Dramatists of today suffer from a set of values derived from every artistic form under the sun. The body of the theatre is immensely, wonderfully healthy; the mind wanders a little at the moment but only from indecision, not from a permanent derangement. If the value of the theatre as an independent art can be assessed, and that art practised by writers, it may be possible to talk about the modern play in the same sense as modern music and modern painting.

Peter Shaffer
The Cannibal Theatre

PETER SHAFFER (1926–   ), in his essay "The Cannibal Theatre", has described as well as anyone the way in which actors gradually assimilate and then transform the playwright's script through the rehearsal process. The author of such plays as *Equus* and *The Royal Hunt of the Sun* stresses the fact that until this process is completed, theatre does not occur.

◆ I shall always remember my first encounter with actors, probably because it so disappointed and depressed me. It occurred in a B.B.C. studio at the rehearsal of my first play, a piece for radio. That day was certainly the most exciting of my life up till then: the acceptance of the play (after many rejections of plays and ideas for plays); the invitation to attend rehearsal; a Sunday journey to London into the peeling, cracked, almost defeated shabbiness (1947 shabbiness) of Marylebone. I remember a long corridor, red lights on and off, and then the vast studio itself and the control room into which I was ushered in a flurry of half-rising figures, whispered greetings, and uncompleted handshakes. The actors were grouped around the microphone, out in the middle of the floor. I listened, and suddenly a huge wave of joy bashed over my head: the sound, the first irrecapturable sound of my words being spoken by professionals! My words! For five minutes they made no sense; the surf of pleasure pounded inside me. Then, when this hurricane of self-approbation was over, I began to listen critically. They weren't very good lines, but at least I had selected them from all possible combinations, and that thought gave me an encouraging sense of my own existence. More, it gave me a curious sense of proprietorship in the actors, a vain, childlike, rather thrilling emotion. It was soon to be dispelled.

At the lunch interval I was introduced to this cast I mentally owned. Nervously I went with them to a pub nearby, all exposure and anxious amiability. They asked me what I'd like to drink; I said beer. That was our whole conversation. Thereafter nobody said anything to me at all. For the rest of the hour the actors talked shop among themselves, workaday shop with all the unromantic trivia of the true professional. Finally they returned to work, briskly performed my play, and walked off together, forgetting even to say good night. Suddenly it was all over. I found myself in the subway, feeling injured and disappointed. It was my first taste of that deep sense of rejection which nonacting playwrights feel around actors. They went their way, I went mine; they together, I alone.

This is always how it is, at least on the surface. Actors, no matter how solipsistically mad they are, live in a fraternity, an indissoluble Order. They take vows to join it, largely unspoken; they feel safe with other members of it, even though they often resent them: behind their most irresponsible displays is the awareness of a Calling. Though here, of course, as elsewhere, few are chosen.

My first reaction was one of annoyance, concealing envy. It must be so good to belong, to be sustained by the professional warmth, the intimacy, the pattern of dressing-room life, and the inalienable duty to play, whatever happens. I have never lost this envy, although when I tell an actor so he rarely believes it. For his part, the actor is made nervous by authors; as often as he can he retreats behind a screen of simple-mindedness ("I'm just the actor") which is only partly sincere. If you say to an actor, "How do you remember all those lines?" he will spit in your eye; but that same actor will say to an author, or wonderingly imply, turning on him the half-mocking, half-impressed blue eye of theatrical innocence, "However do you think of it all? I wish I were clever like that!" Now, behind all this banter, and behind even the deep yearnings to belong, or to be "clever like that," is a deep, grave antagonism which cannot be eradicated. Between actors and playwrights exists, at best, a violent, desperate, irrefragable relation which makes reconciliation in a conventional sense impossible between them, and even undesirable. It is perhaps the most profoundly loving, because the most urgently needful, of all relations—that between hungry beings and their prey.

Over the years my simple view of actors, as a jolly company of people to be wistfully envied, changed and deepened as I came to see their exclusiveness and their ultimate indifference to writers as something infinitely more profound than mere trade unionism. What I had first observed as a fraternity was also in fact a primitive tribe, with which I was intimately and terribly connected—over which, indeed, for a short spell, and with the inevitable penalty, I had to rule.

The rehearsal of a serious play is an elaborate and quietly awful ceremony of fertilization; a ritual, despite its frequent appearance of disorganization and its very real air of friendliness, of sacrifice and rebirth. At the beginning, the playwright is accepted as God-King; he is felt to contain some truth without which the players cannot live. He is treated with deference, consulted, danced before. He speaks, or his interpreter speaks for him, and is eagerly obeyed.

For a spell the tribe, still weak and undernourished, moves at his nod; he sits enthroned in the secrets they require, assured, assuring, needed. Then, gradually the actors gain strength—his strength: they learn his words, his secrets; they cut off his hair. They take away everything he has, at first tentatively, and then boldly, with increasing assurance. They catch his quick sentences and acquire his speed; they subdue his big speeches and take away his gravity; they tear out his jokes and leave him humorless or imperceptive. They must invade him entirely and search for their nourishment in his darkness; they need his potency, and do not rest—cannot rest—until they have it. *For the actor dies between roles, and comes to work seeking his spring.* It is not an accident that we speak of the theatrical "season." Under that trivial word you may see primal planting, the earth wetted with lifeblood, the shoots emerging, thickening, talling, harvested, and eaten: a corn of text, and words becoming flesh.

It is an awesome thing for a playwright to watch good modern actors who have played his parts for a year on the stage become suddenly obliged, say for a new production somewhere else, to take up the actual scripts again and do a reading of the play. They stumble and slur, they look resentfully at the lines, they are surprised and at times quite thrown by minute alterations between the original typescript and what they have been saying for months. They are made uneasy by the printed page, by the return of flesh to word. (Re-productions of plays with the same cast in another city can never be easy; they represent a reversal of the order of nature. How does one resurrect the dismembered body of an author, or turn back the process of ingestion, except by vomiting?) Actors will tell you, and tell you rightly, that they can do nothing until they have thrown away the text—until, that is, *they have thrown away you,* until there does not survive a single punctuation mark to remind them of your vanished power, or a word remaining undissolved in their blood streams.

And when this happens, you feel your death. You are the least needed person in the theater; you are totally superfluous. The actors go on stage and forget you; they even forget they had to memorize your words. They must do this. The parts, all parts of the parts, the very private parts, are theirs now. You may have brought John into the world, but like a mother who learns about her children from everyone else, you must accept the fact that John has become Mr. A., the actor, and that with a dazzling arrogance which you cannot but acknowledge, he can truly say: "I (John) don't feel it like that," "I would never do that," and even, when your rewrites are disputed, "I would never say that." When the actor comes to say this last, the sacrifice is really complete, there is nothing left of the author at all.

Of course, the playwright doesn't merely accept this role; he needs and demands it. He also seeks rebirth, and the only way for him to achieve it is to be liberated from his old play, to have the obsessional demon who first beat it from the cover of his unrest haled out of his body in the fullness of performance. The actor is the playwright's exorcist.

But the actor, too, needs freeing. He also lives in isolation and needs to be released, through the harness of a text, from intensity of feeling unyoked to purpose. Thus each of these incomplete beings is living in the other and released by the other, as in an inevitable love affair. Unease must remain, for the writer, quite simply, writes; and this hard process of setting down is never really acknowledged by the actor, who to be true to himself must believe that the words are born in his living throat without any intermediary process. Paper, for the actor, is a commodity which does not exist; for the author, it is the focus of his reverence. Still, each is united to the other with a true force, without which none of this ritual, this loosing of carnivores, would be tolerable.

I have noted that actors are a fraternity and take vows. In England, certainly, they are regarded with extreme suspicion. Something deep in the conforming heart is distrubed by the thought of the actor's nonattachment to homes and steady visits to offices. And something is also puzzled and offended by a certain indifference in him to social reality, political iniquity, world danger—a seeming frivolity he shares with priests. Our attitude toward actors is always uneasy; though we are hardly aware of it, and actors themselves do not understand it, we treat them with the same half-scornful, half-flattering wariness which we would show to priests of some incomprehensible but rather awesome cult. Which is certainly the right way to regard them.

What is their article of faith? It is simple and immense. Every man contains in himself the history of man. No man is an island; he isn't even a continent: he is, viewed rightly, the world. Therefore, no pattern of behavior should be incomprehensible to us, and no feeling in another inaccessible to us. We fail in our sympathy over and over again, because of our preconceptions and our unexercised imaginations, and because our hearts shrink in the effort to present to the world an image of ourselves.

The actor is not concerned with this at all; in his dual nature he can succeed where we fail, and in a real sense succeed (as in all art) *for us*. He has therefore an almost divine function in society, for to survive as a true speaker for us he must find in himself what most of us deny is there—the experience of the race. He must refuse in himself the pressured right we claim to prejudice; he must take on all lonelinesses and fears, relish confidence where he himself has none, enjoy many kinds of jokes, though he himself has but one sense of humor. Ideally, no hunger is too acute, no perversion too obscure for him to live it out imaginatively, and to do this he must set aside, as a barrier, all personal condemnation. The moral purpose of actors, which is the exorcism not only of playwrights but of society, can be accomplished only by slaying the mortal enemy of truth, preconception.

And in the same degree the playwright does likewise. This is where we meet, on moral ground. We both sense what charge is laid upon us, what dark journeys have to be made in the way of business, descents into Nibelheim to gratify Wotan. The encyclopedic imagination which is necessary to the actor is needed as urgently by the playwright; he must list from within himself an inventory of authentic emotions enough to furnish all the mansions of the blessed and unblessed. Many actors fail—I don't mean technical failure— because of their inability to meet these demands in full or because they don't even realize unconsciously that the demands are being made, which means that they are bad actors. The strictures of good actors on bad actors are harsher than in any other profession, for this reason: to a dedicated player, a bad piece of acting is a betrayal, and a bad actor is a whisky priest. And most playwrights fail for the same reason. Both are moral agents.

One last thought: the playwright has an added duty, specifically to the actor. He has an obligation to write good parts. Without them, despite what theatrical fans say, the actor can do very little. What good is it to own the Tarnhelm, if all you are asked to do is turn yourself into a frog? There is no excuse under heaven for creating people whose sole reason for living is to hear a pistol shot, to say the carriage is without, to announce Lady Bore's arrival, to hold a spear or a Martini. These parts are betrayals. I would be truly ashamed if an actor told me a part of mine wasn't, in the real sense, big enough —even though, as often as not, the actor will prove to be foolish enough to have counted the lines and not the heartbeats of the part.

So, on this frail bridge of obligation, the baker can meet the starving boy: he offers him homemade bread; the boy snatches it and waves him impatiently away. The baker goes, dismissed, knowing that in a little while the boy will be hungry again and will wander the streets hollow-eyed, seeking his shop, praying there will be something in it worth eating.

And that is the prayer of the playwright too: to be full again.

Harold Pinter
The Writer in the Theatre

HAROLD PINTER (1930–   ) is the best-known English dramatist writing today. Since 1957 he has been writing powerful and puzzling plays that have been challenging to both actors and audiences. Over the past two decades, he has given interviews and written occasionally about the nature of his work. The piece included here is one of the least known of these. It is a speech he gave in Hamburg, Germany in 1970 when he accepted the prestigious Shakespeare Prize for his two plays *Landscape* and *Silence*.

◆ . . . Once, many years ago, I found myself engaged uneasily in a public discussion on the theatre. Someone asked me what my work was 'about.' I replied with no thought at all and merely to frustrate this line of enquiry: 'The weasel under the cocktail cabinet.' That was a great mistake. Over the years I have seen that remark quoted in a number of learned columns. It has now seemingly acquired a profound significance, and is seen to be a highly relevant and meaningful observation about my own work. But for me the remark meant precisely nothing. Such are the dangers of speaking in public.

In what way can one talk about one's work? I'm a writer, not a critic. When I use the word work I mean work. I regard myself as nothing more than a working man.

I am moved by the fact that the selection committee for the Shakespeare Prize has judged my work, in the context of this award, as worthy of it, but it's impossible for me to understand the reasons that led them to their decision. I'm at the other end of the telescope. The language used, the opinions given, the approvals and objections engendered by one's work happen in a sense outside one's actual experience of it, since the core of that experience consists in writing the stuff. I have a particular relationship with the words I put down on paper and the characters which emerge from them which no-one else can share with me. And perhaps that's why I remain bewildered by praise and really quite indifferent to insult. Praise and insult refer to someone called Pinter. I don't know the man they're talking about. I know the plays, but in a totally different way, in a quite private way.

If I am to talk at all I prefer to talk practically about practical matters, but that's no more than a pious hope, since one invariably slips into theorising, almost without noticing it. And I distrust theory. In whatever capacity I have worked in the theatre, and apart from writing, I have done quite a bit of acting and a certain amount of directing for the stage, I have found that theory, as such, has never been helpful; either to myself, or, I have noticed, to few of my colleagues. The best sort of collaborative working relationship in the theatre, in my view, consists in a kind of stumbling erratic shorthand, through which facts are lost, collided with, fumbled, found again. One excellent director I know has never been known to complete a sentence. He has such instinctive surety and almost subliminal powers of communication that the actors respond to his words before he has said them.

I don't want to imply that I am counselling lack of intelligence as a working aid. On the contrary, I am referring to an intelligence brought to bear on practical and relevant matters, on matters which are active and alive and specific, an intelligence working with others to find the legitimate and therefore compulsory facts and make them concrete for us on the stage. A rehearsal period which consists of philosophical discourse or political treatise does not get the curtain up at eight o'clock.

I have referred to facts, by which I mean theatrical facts. It is true to say that theatrical facts do not easily disclose their secrets, and it is very easy, when they prove stubborn, to distort them, to make them into something else, or to pretend they never existed. This happens more often in the theatre than we care to recognize and is proof either of incompetence or fundamental contempt for the work in hand.

I believe myself that when a writer looks at the blank of the word he has not yet written, or when actors and directors arrive at a given moment on stage, there is only one proper thing that can take place at that moment, and that that thing, that gesture, that word on the page, must alone be found, and once found, scrupulously protected. I think I am talking about necessary shape, both as regards a play and its production.

If there is, as I believe, a necessary, an obligatory shape which a play demands of its writer, then I have never been able to achieve it myself. I have always finished the last draft of a play with a mixture of feelings: relief, disbelief, exhilaration, and a certainty that if I could only wring the play's neck once more it might yield once more to me, that I could get it better, that I could get the better of it, perhaps. But that's impossible. You create the word and in a certain way the word, in finding its own life, stares you out, is obdurate, and more often than not defeats you. You create the characters and they prove to be very tough. They observe you, their writer, warily. It may sound absurd, but I believe I am speaking the truth when I say that I have suffered two kinds of pain through my characters. I have witnessed *their* pain when I am in the act of distorting them, of falsifying them, and I have witnessed their contempt. I have suffered pain when I have been unable to get to the quick of them, when they wilfully elude me, when they withdraw into the shadows. And there's a third and rarer pain. That is when the right word, or the right act jolts them or stills them into their proper life. When that happens the pain is worth having. When that happens I am ready to take them into the nearest bar and buy drinks all round. And I hope they would forgive me my trespasses against them and do the same for me. But there is no question that quite a conflict takes place between the writer and his characters and on the whole I would say the characters are the winners. And that's as it should be, I think. Where a writer sets out a blueprint for his characters, and keeps them rigidly to it, where they do not at any time upset his applecart, where he has mastered them, he has also killed them, or rather terminated their birth, and he has a dead play on his hands.

Sometimes, the director says to me in rehearsal: 'Why does she say this?' I reply: 'Wait a minute, let me look at the text.' I do so, and perhaps I say: 'Doesn't she say this because he said *that*, two pages ago?' Or I say: 'Because that's what she feels.' Or: 'Because she feels something else, and therefore says that.' Or: 'I haven't the faintest idea. But somehow we have to find out.' Sometimes I learn quite a lot from rehearsals.

I have been very fortunate, in my life, in the people I've worked with, and my association with Peter Hall and the Royal Shakespeare Company has, particularly, been greatly satisfying. Peter Hall and I, working together, have found that the image must be pursued with the greatest vigilance, calmly, and once found, must be sharpened, graded, accurately focused and maintained, and that the key word is economy, economy of movement and gesture, of emotion and its expression, both the internal and the external in specific and exact relation to each other, so that there is no wastage and no mess. These are hardly revolutionary conclusions, but I hope no less worthy of restatement for that.

I may appear to be laying too heavy an emphasis on method and technique as opposed to content, but this is not in fact the case. I am not suggesting that the disciplines to which I have been referring be imposed upon the action in terms of a device, or as a formal convenience. What is made evident before us on the stage can clearly only be made fully evident where the content of the scene has been defined. But I do not understand this definition as one arrived at through the intellect, but a definition made by the actors, using quite a different system. In other words, if I now bring various criteria to bear upon a production, these are not intellectual concepts but facts forged through experience of active participation with good actors and, I hope, a living text.

What am I writing about? Not the weasel under the cocktail cabinet.

I am not concerned with making general statements. I am not interested in theatre used simply as a means of self-expression on the part of the people engaged in it. I find in so much group theatre, under the sweat and assault and noise, nothing but valueless generalizations, naive and quite unfruitful.

I can sum up none of my plays. I can describe none of them, except to say: That is what happened. That is what they said. That is what they did.

I am aware, sometimes, of an insistence in my mind. Images, characters, insisting upon being written. You can pour a drink, make a telephone call or run round the park, and sometimes succeed in suffocating them. You know they're going to make your life hell. But at other times they're unavoidable and you're compelled to try to do them some kind of justice. And while it may be hell, it's certainly for me the best kind of hell to be in. . . .

Friedrich Duerrenmatt
Problems of the Theatre

FRIEDRICH DUERRENMATT (1921–   ) is a Swiss playwright, novelist, short-story writer, and dramatic theorist. He has been a prolific playwright, but is best known in America for *The Visit of the Old Lady.* In 1955 he published a long monograph, *Problems of the Theatre,* in which he discusses the challenges facing the playwright in the "Age of the Atom Bomb." It is generally regarded as one of the major works of dramatic theory written in our times. The piece included here is an excerpt from that essay.

◆ . . . In theories of the drama a difference is made between a tragic hero, the hero of tragedy, and a comic hero, the hero of comedy. The qualities a tragic hero must possess are well known. He must be capable of rousing our sympathy. His guilt and his innocence, his virtues and his vices must be mixed in the most pleasant and yet exact manner, and administered in doses according to well-defined rules. If, for example, I make my tragic hero an evil man, then I must endow him with a portion of intellect equal to his malevolence. As a result of this rule, the most sympathetic stage character in German literature has turned out to be the devil. The role of the hero in the play has not changed. The only thing that has changed is the social position of the character who awakens our sympathy.

In ancient tragedy and in Shakespeare the hero belongs to the highest class in society, to the nobility. The spectators watch a suffering, acting, raving hero who occupies a social position far higher than their own. This continues still to impress audiences today.

Then when Lessing and Schiller introduced the bourgeois drama, the audience saw itself as the suffering hero on the stage. But the evolution of the hero continued. Buechner's Woyzeck is a primitive proletarian who represents far less socially than the average spectator. But it is precisely in this extreme form of human existence, in this last, most miserable form, that the audience is to see the human being also, indeed itself.

And finally we might mention Pirandello, who was the first, as far as I know, to render the hero, the character on the stage, immaterial and transparent just as Wilder did the dramatic place. The audience watching this sort of presentation attends, as it were, its own dissection, its own psychoanalysis, and the stage becomes man's internal milieu, the inner space of the world.

Of course, the theatre has never dealt only with kings and generals; in comedy the hero has always been the peasant, the beggar, the ordinary citizen —but this was always in comedy. Nowhere in Shakespeare do we find a comic king; in his day a ruler could appear as a bloody monster but never as a fool. In Shakespeare the courtiers, the artisans, the working people are comic. Hence, in the evolution of the tragic hero we see a trend towards comedy. Analogously the fool becomes more and more of a tragic figure. This fact is by no means without significance. The hero of a play not only propels an action on, he not only suffers a certain fate, but he also represents a world. Therefore we have to ask ourselves how we should present our own questionable world and with what sort of heroes. We have to ask ourselves how the mirrors which catch and reflect this world should be ground and set.

Can our present-day world, to ask a concrete question, be represented by Schiller's dramatic art? Some writers claim it can be, since Schiller still holds audiences in his grip. To be sure, in art everything is possible when the art is right. But the question is if an art valid for its time could possibly be so even for our day. Art can never be repeated. If it were repeatable, it would be foolish not just to write according to the rules of Schiller.

Schiller wrote as he did because the world in which he lived could still be mirrored in the world his writing created, a world he could build as a historian. But just barely. For was not Napoleon perhaps the last hero in the old sense? The world today as it appears to us could hardly be encompassed in the form of the historical drama as Schiller wrote it, for the reason alone that we no longer have any tragic heroes, but only vast tragedies staged by world butchers and produced by slaughtering machines. Hitler and Stalin can not be made into Wallensteins. Their power is so enormous that they themselves are no more than incidental, corporeal and easily replaceable expressions of this power; and the misfortune associated with the former and to a considerable extent also with the latter is too vast, too complex, too horrible, too mechanical and usually simply too devoid of all sense. Wallenstein's power can still be envisioned; power as we know it today can only be seen in its smallest part for, like an iceberg, the largest part is submerged in anonymity and abstraction. Schiller's drama presupposes a world that the eye can take in, that takes for granted genuine actions of state, just as Greek tragedy did. For only what the eye can take in can be made visible in art. The state today, however, can not be envisioned for it is anonymous and bureaucratic; and not only in Moscow and Washington, but also in Berne. Actions of state today have become *post-hoc* satyric dramas which follow the tragedies executed in secret earlier. True representatives of our world are missing; the tragic heroes are nameless. Any small-time crook, petty government official or policeman better represents our world than a senator or president. Today art can only embrace the victims, if it can reach men at all; it can no longer come close to the mighty. Creon's secretaries close Antigone's case. The state has lost its physical reality, and just as physics can now only cope with the world in mathematical formulas, so the state can only be expressed in statistics. Power today becomes visible, material only when it explodes as in the atom bomb, in this marvelous mushroom which rises and spreads immaculate as the sun and in which mass murder and beauty have become one. The atom bomb can not be reproduced artistically since it is mass-produced. In its face all of man's art that would recreate it must fail, since it is itself a creation of man. Two mirrors which reflect one another remain empty.

But the task of art, insofar as art can have a task at all, and hence also the task of drama today, is to create something concrete, something that has form. This can be accomplished best by comedy. Tragedy, the strictest genre in art, presupposes a formed world. Comedy—in so far as it is not just satire of a particular society as in Molière—supposes an unformed world, a world being made and turned upside down, a world about to fold like ours. Tragedy overcomes distance; it can make myths originating in times immemorial seem like the present to the Athenians. But comedy creates distance; the attempt of the Athenians to gain a foothold in Sicily is translated by comedy into the birds undertaking to create their own empire before which the gods and men will have to capitulate. How comedy works can be seen in the most primitive kind of joke, in the dirty story, which, though it is of very dubious value, I bring up only because it is the best illustration of what I mean by creating distance. The subject of the dirty story is the purely sexual, which because it is purely sexual, is formless and without objective distance. To be given form the purely sexual is transmuted, as I have already mentioned, into the dirty joke. Therefore this type of joke is a kind of original comedy, a transposition of the sexual onto the plane of the comical. In this way it is possible, today in a society dominated by John Doe, to talk in an accepted way about the purely sexual. In the dirty story it becomes clear that the comical exists in forming what is formless, in creating order out of chaos.

The means by which comedy creates distance is the conceit. Tragedy is without conceit. Hence there are few tragedies whose subjects were invented. By this I do not mean to imply that the ancient tragedians lacked inventive ideas of the sort that are written today, but the marvel of their art was that they had no need of these inventions, of conceits. That makes all the difference. Aristophanes, on the other hand, lives by conceits. The stuff of his plays is not myths but inventions, which take place not in the past but the present. They drop into their world like bomb shells which, by throwing up huge craters of dirt, change the present into the comic and thus scatter the dirt for everyone to see. This, of course, does not mean that drama today can only be comical. Tragedy and comedy are but formal concepts, dramatic attitudes, figments of the esthetic imagination which can embrace one and the same thing. Only the conditions under which each is created are different, and these conditions have their basis only in small part in art.

Tragedy presupposes guilt, despair, moderation, lucidity, vision, a sense of responsibility. In the Punch-and-Judy show of our century, in this back-sliding of the white race, there are no more guilty and also, no responsible men. It is always, "We couldn't help it" and "We didn't really want that to happen." And indeed, things happen without anyone in particular being responsible for them. Everything is dragged along and everyone gets caught somewhere in the sweep of events. We are all collectively guilty, collectively bogged down in the sins of our fathers and of our forefathers. We are the offspring of children. That is our misfortune, but not our guilt: guilt can exist only as a personal achievement, as a religious deed. Comedy alone is suitable for us. Our world has led to the grotesque as well as to the atom bomb, and so it is a world like that of Hieronymus Bosch whose apocalyptic paintings are also grotesque. But the grotesque is only a way of expressing in a tangible manner, of making us perceive physically the paradoxical, the form of the unformed, the face of a world without face; and just as in our thinking today we seem to be unable to do without the concept of the paradox, so also in art, and in our world which at times seems still to exist only because the atom bomb exists: out of fear of the bomb.

But the tragic is still possible even if pure tragedy is not. We can achieve the tragic out of comedy. We can bring it forth as a frightening moment, as an abyss that opens suddenly; indeed many of Shakespeare's tragedies are already really comedies out of which the tragic arises.

After all this the conclusion might easily be drawn that comedy is the expression of despair, but this conclusion is not inevitable. To be sure, whoever realizes the senselessness, the hopelessness of this world might well despair, but this despair is not a result of this world. Rather it is an answer given by an individual to this world; another answer would be not to despair, would be an individual's decision to endure this world in which we live like Gulliver among the giants. He also achieves distance, he also steps back a pace or two who takes measure of his opponent, who prepares himself to fight his opponent or to escape him. It is still possible to show man as a courageous being.

In truth this is a principal concern of mine. The blind man, Romulus, Uebelohe, Akki, are all men of courage. The lost world order is restored within them; the universal escapes my grasp. I refuse to find the universal in a doctrine. The universal for me is chaos. The world (hence the stage which represents this world) is for me something monstrous, a riddle of misfortunes which must be accepted but before which one must not capitulate. The world is far bigger than any man, and perforce threatens him constantly. If one could but stand outside the world, it would no longer be threatening. But I have neither the right nor the ability to be an outsider to this world. To find solace in poetry can also be all too cheap; it is more honest to retain one's human point of view. Brecht's thesis, that the world is an accident, which he developed in his *Street Scene* where he shows how this accident happened, may yield—as it in fact did—some magnificent theatre; but he did it by concealing most of the evidence! Brecht's thinking is inexorable, because inexorably there are many things he will not think about.

And lastly it is through the conceit, through comedy that the anonymous audience becomes possible as an audience, becomes a reality to be counted on, and also, one to be taken into account. The conceit easily transforms the crowd of theatre-goers into a mass which can be attacked, deceived, outsmarted into listening to things it would otherwise not so readily listen to. Comedy is a mousetrap in which the public is easily caught and in which it will get caught over and over again. Tragedy, on the other hand, predicated a true community, a kind of community whose existence in our day is but an embarrassing fiction. . . .

7

THE DIRECTOR AND THE PLAY

◆　　 . . . guides a group . . .　　 . . . exchange
of ideas . . .　　 . . . expert observer . . .　　 . . . spent hours
in rehearsal . . .　　 . . . pressures of time . . .
　 . . blocking . . .　　 . . . backbone . . .
　 . . . vocal interpretation . . .　　 . . . live people talking
to live people . . .　　 . . . exhaustive knowledge . . .
　 . . . without pushing . . .　　 . . . delicate balance . . .
　 . . . results . . .　　 . . . an outsider . . .

Tyrone Guthrie
An Audience of One

TYRONE GUTHRIE (1900–1971) was one of the great directors of this century. As director of the Old Vic in England and the creator of the Stratford Shakespeare Festival in Canada and the Guthrie Theatre in Minneapolis, he has left an indelible mark on the theatre of both continents. He also wrote a great deal about the theatre and his life in it. This essay—one of his best—is a transcript of the talk he gave in 1952.

◆   Producing a play clearly requires the coordinated efforts of many people, and the producer* is no more than the coordinator. His work may, and I think should, have creative functions, but not always. The important thing is gathering together the different pieces and welding many disparate elements into one complete unity, which is never, of course, fully achieved in artistic matters.

The work of the producer can be analyzed—indeed has been analyzed —in many different ways. I propose to deal with it under two headings: firstly, the producer in relation to the script of the play, that is to say the raw material of his work; and secondly, the producer in relation to actors and staff, that is animate collaborators.

It seems to me that the producer's business, when faced either with a new script or with being asked to revive a classic or an old play, is first of all to decide what it is about. Clearly, that is not entirely simple. To take an obvious instance, who is really going to give the final word as to what *Hamlet* is about? As we all know, more books have been written about *Hamlet* than almost any other topic under the sun. I am told that, as far as biographies are concerned, the three champions about whom the most has been written are Jesus Christ, Hamlet and Napoleon Bonaparte, in that order. *Hamlet* is an obviously difficult case in which to decide what the play is about, but take a nice simple little play called *Charley's Aunt.* What is that about? It is just a question of telling the story, or is it a question of finding a meaning to the story? Are Charley's "Aunt" and all those jolly undergraduates symbols of this or that, or are they to be taken at face value? Is the thing to be—as I have seen it done in Scandinavia—a serious study of English university life, or is it just to be made as funny as possible? Personally, I think the latter; but before you can make it funny you have got to decide why it is funny, what is funny about it, and what the joke is, which is quite a tricky little problem.

I think very often the lighter the play is the more it is composed of thistledown and little else, the more difficult it is to pin down. One has often

---

*In England the stage director is customarily referred to as "the producer." [Editor]

seen little tiny plays absolutely slain by the great mechanism brought to bear on their own interpretation. An obvious case in point is *Così Fan Tutte.* I do not know whether anyone has seen a satisfactory performance of that. I have seen it a great many times, but it always seems to me that a great many steam hammers in human form are assembled to crack a little jewelled acorn.

With regard to what the script is about, the last person who, in my opinion, should be consulted, even if he is alive or around, is the author. If the author is a wise man, he will admit straight away that he does not know what it is about, unless it is a very perfunctory work indeed. If it is just a little piece of journalism on the minor problems of psychoanalysis, then he probably will know all too well what it is about. But if it has the potentialities of being an important work of art, I am perfectly convinced he will not have the faintest idea of what he has really written. He will probably know what he thinks he has written, but that will be the least important part of it. Were it possible to find out, I would lay any money that Shakespeare had only the vaguest idea of what he was writing when he wrote *Hamlet;* that the major part of the meaning of it eluded him because it proceeded from the subconscious. A great work of art is like an iceberg in that ninety per cent of it is below the surface of consciousness. Therefore, in my opinion, the more important the work of art, the less the author will know what he has written.

I had the great privilege and pleasure to know the late James Bridie extremely well. I worked with him often, but he would never even discuss what his plays were about. He would say, "How should I know? I am the last person you should ask. I am only the author. I have written an armature, inside which, possibly, are the deepest ideas which have never quite formulated themselves in my consciousness. If, as I hope and believe, I am a poet, there will be something in these, but I am the last person to know what it is."

The producer has to decide what he thinks the play is about, and of course I am largely joking when I say that he does not really take the author seriously. Naturally he does, but not as to the deeper, the inner and the over-and-above, the between and through, meaning of the lines. If somebody does not decide at an early stage what the play is about, obviously the casting will be made for the wrong reasons. Ideally, a play should be cast because the actors chosen are people that somebody—be it the producer or be it the manager—thinks will express the play best. In fact, in the exigencies of commercial production and the exigencies of practical affairs, all too often plays are cast because somebody thinks that Mr. X will help to sell the beastly thing, and Mr. X happens to be living with Miss Y so she is a cinch for the leading lady, and all sorts of vulgar and extraneous considerations of that kind which really have nothing whatever to do with art but everything in the world to do with the practical business of putting on a play. I cannot sufficiently differentiate between the two, but seeing that we are speaking in these almost hallowed precincts I am going to try to behave as though we were in an ideal atmosphere and plays were cast solely with artistic considerations in view, or at all events very much in the foreground with practical things far away in the background.

In theory, the artistic way to cast a play is to decide who, of the available actors, seems to be the most like the principal part in the script that we are given, and who would best understand the thing. Let me qualify that. It is not entirely a question of who is the most like the principal character, because very often the last thing that an actor does well is to portray a character that is like himself as one conceives him to be in private life. Very many actors do their best work when they are hiding from themselves behind a mass of hair and make-up and fantasy, when they present something entirely unlike their real selves.

One must think which of the available actors would seem to give the best interpretation of a given part. That is why, at a very early stage, the whole business of producing a play has to move into conference. It is, in my opinion, very unwise for the leading actor not to work step by step from the very earliest stages with the three or four people with whom he is going to collaborate most closely: the manager, or whoever is responsible for the budgetary financial side of the production, the leading actors, and certainly the designer, the man who is ultimately going to be responsible for the pictorial look of the thing. All their work should grow together and should, I think, be the result of a productive exchange of ideas.

Therefore, it is clearly necessary that, if the thing is going to work well, they should be people who can to some extent speak one another's language, who can exchange ideas, who can admit themselves to be wrong without red faces in the company of the others, and so on. So that, long before the thing gets to the stage of rehearsal and parts being read or movements made, there should have been a quite extensive exchange of ideas about the look of the thing, about the sound of the thing, about the shape of the thing in predominantly musical and choreographic terms.

To elaborate that a little, the performance of a play is clearly analogous to the performance of a symphonic piece of music. By the time the play is ready, if it is properly rehearsed, the diverse voices, the group of people who are playing the thing, will have found a music for their parts. Why acting, in my opinion, is so much more interesting than opera singing is that the actors invent the music of their parts to a very great extent. In an operatic score, the composer's intention is made extraordinarily clear. The rhythm, the inflection, the loudness and softness, the pitch and the pace at which the idea is to be conveyed, are all clearly defined in the score. Almost the only creative piece of work left to the conductor and the singers is the color, because so far no form of notation has been found for musical color. The actor has to find nearly all those things for himself. Supposing you are an actor who is playing Hamlet. "To be, or not to be: that is the question: whether 'tis nobler in the mind to suffer . . ."—those infinitely familiar lines. You have to find the inflection, that is to say the tune, to which they are sung or spoken, the pitch, the pace, the rhythm and the color. That is, in fact, very highly creative.

Parallel with the creation of the actor must, I think, come the coordination of the producer. Supposing two of us are playing a scene, and one has decided that the scene must be played lightly and forcibly, and the other person takes a different view of the scene and feels that it must be managed in a very dark and very black way with long pauses. It is the business of the producer to coordinate the two without necessarily making either man feel that he has been a fool or stupid. It is a point of view which way the scene should be taken, and somebody has to be the chairman, somebody has to decide. That is really in most cases what the producer is.

I know there is an idea abroad, largely cultivated in popular fiction, about the theater and films, that the producer is a very dominant person who goes around doing a lot of ordering about, saying, "Stand here, stand there, copy me, do it this way, do it that way." Of course, with experienced and accomplished actors that would be complete nonsense. Imagine my saying to Dame Edith Evans, "Do it this way, dear, copy me."

The performance of a play should be able to be observed by any-body who knows it well just like a graph, like a patient's temperature chart, like a graph of the sales statistics of a firm or anything else. One should be able to see the peaks and the hollows, and it should be possible to delineate the shape of each scene in a graph, which helps to make the scene more intelligible, which helps to make it illuminate the scene preceding it and the scene following it, which helps it to contrast, and at the same time to blend with the neighboring scenes; and, while each little scene should have a graph, similarly a graph of the whole act should arise from that.

Now on to the second main heading about production.

First of all, and very briefly, there is the question of organization, discipline and that kind of thing. If the company is any good and if the producer is any good, that is simply a matter of general convenience. I do not think the producer has any difficulty over discipline provided the rehearsals are not boring, and provided they are kept moving not at the pace of the very slowest person present but at a fairly decent tempo.

Then comes the question of coaching. How far is a producer to coach the interpretation? How much is he to say to the actors, "Do it this way"? I do not think one can give a complete answer to that. If you are taking the first production that has ever been done by the dramatic society attached to the Little Pifflington Women's Institute, you will probably have to do a great deal of coaching and coaxing to break down the self-conscious giggling of people who are quite unaccustomed to impersonation and pretending to be someone they are not. But if you have a good professional cast the amount of coaching you have to do is very small.

I do not think one should be at all afraid of saying to actors in a quite dogmatic way, "Play this scene sitting on the sofa, and if you are not comfort-able let me know later on, but don't decide until we have done it once or twice. Later on, maybe you would feel like getting up halfway through and going to the window." Otherwise, if the actor is allowed to grope it out too much for himself, there is a waste of time, and the dominant personalities start bullying the milder, more unselfish and cooperative ones, which is what we have to be on the lookout for.

Then comes what I have tried to indicate is very much the main business of the producer, the work of coordination from the departments inwards.

Clearly, the coordinating of an idea, so far as it is concerned with visual matters, lies to a considerable degree in the hands of the person responsible for the lighting. Here, as elsewhere, I feel there should be the minimum of dogmatism. A good designer will have been working from quite an early stage in collaboration with the leading actors. Actors on the whole are sensible people about their clothes. Most actors have not at all a vain idea of their own appearance, but a very realistic appreciation of their good points and bad points, and they can be very helpful to a designer in suggesting things like the length of their coats or the width of their sleeves. If an actor says, "I want a long sleeve because I think I can do something with it," that should be taken very seriously; and, in my opinion, an actor should never be forced to wear a dress he does not like, unless it is for economic or disciplinary reasons. You could not expect people to feel free, unself-conscious and at ease on the stage in dresses they feel to be unsuitable.

Where I think the producer's work of coordination requires the greatest amount of time and care spent upon it is in the vocal interpretation of the play. As I have already tried to indicate, the performance of a play is, on a smaller scale, a performance of a musical work. The script is, as it were, sung, because speaking and singing are, after all, the same process. Although I am speaking now and not singing, I am uttering a definable tune all the time. Every syllable I utter is on a certain pitch and a musician could say precisely where it was. Every sentence that I phrase is consciously phrased in a certain rhythm. The pauses, although I am not conscious of it, are expressing an instinctive need to pause, not merely to breathe, but for clarity and various other interpretative purposes. This is even more pronounced in the performance of a play, where all that has been most carefully thought out in terms of pace, rhythm, pitch, volume and all the rest of it, to make a certain expressive effect. That is particularly where the coordinating hand of the producer is required, joining up the various songs that are being sung and making them into a unit; and similarly, joining up the various patterns that are being danced, because even in the simplest realistic comedy, in the most ordinary kind of realistic set—the actors have to move, and their movements have to tot up to some kind of choreographic design which expresses the play, which has some meaning over and above the common-sense position in which one would pour tea or put sugar into it. For long stretches of the play the positions have to be guided not at all by anything that is afoot. Of course, it is mere journalism to think that plays are concerned with action. They are not. Plays in the cinema may be, but in the theater the action is a tiny point.

In almost every play for the stage, there is scarcely any action. The movements of the play are almost all concerned with the expression of ideas and not of action. If there is action, it is very short-lived and very brief. The choreography is much more concerned with the subtle delineation of emotions by the way people are placed, with the subtle changes of emphasis by putting people into the brighter light or taking them out of it, by having them face the audience or turn their backs, by putting them in the center or near the side. It is all very much more delicate and allusive than simply getting them into common-sense positions to perform certain actions.

Finally, I should like to discuss what to me is the most interesting part of the job, the blending of intuition with technique. If I may elaborate those terms, by intuition I mean the expression of a creative idea that comes straight from the subconscious, that is not arrived at by a process of ratiocination at all. It is my experience that all the best ideas in art just arrive, and it is absolutely no good concentrating on them and hoping for the best. The great thing is to relax and just trust that the Holy Ghost will arrive and the idea will appear. The sought idea is nearly always, in my opinion, the beta plus idea. The alpha plus idea arrives from literally God knows where. Prayer and fasting can no doubt help, but concentration and ratiocination are, I think, only a hindrance. And yet I think no artist worth his salt will feel he can rely on inspiration. Inspiration must be backed up by a very cast-iron technique.

It is the case that as one gets older one's technique, if one is an industrious and intelligent person, tends to become better; but there is also the danger that it becomes a little slick. I think not only artists, but anybody engaged in any activity must feel the same thing. The record begins to get worn, and we slip too easily into old grooves, the same association of ideas comes back too readily and easily. I notice with my own work in the theater —and I have been at it now for nearly thirty years—that I have to check myself all the time from slipping into certain very obvious and, to me now, rather dull choreographic mannerisms. I instinctively think, "Oh, obviously the right place is so-and-so, and the right way to group this is such-and-such." Then I think, why do I think that? And usually the only reason is that one has done it that way a good many times before. That is obviously frightfully dangerous in any creative work. It is the negation of creation; it is just falling back onto habit.

Yet there are certain very valuable things about experience and about technique. It is now comparatively easy for me, in late middle age, to establish a good relation with actors. They think because I have been at it for a long time that I know something about it, and they are readier to take suggestions from me now than they were twenty-five years ago when I was a beginner, though I am inclined to think that most of the suggestions are duller ones. Twenty-five years ago, intuition functioned oftener and more readily. That is, I think, one of the very difficult paradoxes about production.

Clearly, for practical reasons, it is very difficult to put the highly intuitive, gifted youngster in charge of a responsible production. He will make too many mistakes. He will be too dependent on the things that experience and authority bring easily from the older people. Also, it is difficult for the senior actors. It requires enormous tact, both on the part of the young producer and the old actor, to be helpful to one another. Yet the young producer is precisely what the experienced actor with a cast-iron technique—and consequently a great many mannerisms, too many clichés and short cuts—needs. He needs a very bright, sharp, critical young person of twenty-five to say, "No, Sir X, don't do it that way. You have been doing it that way for twenty-five years and it has been fine for twenty-five years, but that is just the reason for not doing it that way now." Well, you can see that unless that is done with supreme tact it is all too easy for Sir X or Dame Y to cast down their script and summon their Rolls-Royce.

I should like to conclude by telling a little anecdote which was told to me by a distinguished producer now resident in this country, who began life in Czechoslovakia and early in his career went to Germany. He soon got quite a good position while still in his early twenties in one of the German provincial theaters. He was a fine-looking young fellow and very "castable" in hero parts, and the management of the theater sent him to see Reinhardt, then at the very apex of his celebrity and power in Berlin. My friend was still young enough to be madly thrilled, not only with the great opportunity of meeting this god and the possible advancement that it might produce, but with such childish and naïve, but extremely natural, things as the overnight journey in a first-class sleeper and all that kind of thing. All that was a terrific thrill, and he described very touchingly how he enjoyed it. He arrived in Berlin on a delicious crisp autumn morning, and went to the theater at which Reinhardt was working, the Grosses Schauspielhaus. He described the grand chandeliers, the polished floors, the gentlemen in livery who collected him at the door, how he swept up the marble staircase, along a passage with portraits of eminent people all down the side, through a less important door in the side of the passage, down some stairs with no polish and carpets at all, through a very squalid little passage, round various corners, and across a courtyard, until he came to a room really more like a kitchen. He said at first the only things he could see were the long windows all down one side with the sun streaming in. Then, as he began to get accustomed to that, he saw a group of rather drab-looking actors rehearsing at one end. Then he suddenly saw that one of these actors was somebody whose face had been familiar to him all his life, a great star of Germany, and I think he had that experience which anybody has who suddenly comes face-to-face with a very familiar face that he has seen illustrated, whether politician, film star, or anybody else. You suddenly think, "How small they are! I thought they were much bigger." He was busy taking all this in and thinking what a small person this gentleman was whom he had always thought so great when suddenly, at the end of the room, he saw a very unimportant-looking gentleman sitting on the kitchen table swinging his legs and looking at his hands. It was Reinhardt. He thought, "Now the great moment has come and I shall hear Socrates pour out words of wisdom and technical advice to these people. Eminent they may be, but they will not be above getting a little tip or two from Reinhardt." But nothing happened.

Then he thought, "Well, they must be so bad that he is going to give them a hell of a slating at any minute. There will be a few glorious minutes when high-powered abuse will pour from the golden lips and the boys down there will get very hot under the collar." Nothing happened, and nothing continued to happen for quite a long time until the actors came to the end of a scene. Then there was a short pause, not a rudely long pause at all, but *quite* a pause, and my friend was agog with excitement to know what would be said. Reinhardt just looked up and said, "Thanks very much. Now can we go back to the maid's entrance?" That, or something like it, went on through the whole morning, and he said that, far from it being a dull rehearsal, it was clearly—he was artist enough to perceive it—an immensely constructive rehearsal, and he began to think why it was, because nothing was being said, no instructions were given, no abuse poured forth and no praise. He analyzed it this way, and the more I think of it the more profoundly convinced I am that he is right, that Reinhardt was performing the one really creative function of the producer, which is to be at rehearsal a highly receptive, highly concentrated, highly critical sounding-board for the performance, an audience of one. He is not the drill sergeant, not the schoolmaster, and he does not sweep in with a lot of verbiage and "Stand here and do it this way, darling, and move the right hand not the left." He is simply receiving the thing, transmuting it, and giving it back. When you come down to analyzing what the creative part of acting is, it is the giving of impressions to the audience and then, on the part of the actor, the taking back of their impressions and doing something about them. The best simile that I can make is that the actor throws a thread, as it were, out into the house which, if the house is receptive, it will catch. Then it is the actor's business to hold that thread taut and to keep a varying and consequently interesting pressure on it, so that it is really pulled in moments of tension and allowed to go as slack as possible in moments of relaxation, but never so slack that it falls and cannot be pulled up again. The producer at rehearsals can be that audience. He can perform that function, and if he is a good producer he will perform it better than the average audience; he will be more intelligently critical and alive, and the rehearsals will not be dreary learning of routine; they will be a creative act that is ultimately going to be a performance.

That is why, in my opinion, the analogy between the producer and the conductor holds good. A *good* conductor is a man with a fine technique of the stick. He has a clear beat and an expressive beat, and is an interesting chap for the audience to watch. He can bring one section in with a fine gesture and blot another out. He knows his score, and so on, but it is all interesting showmanship. But the *great* conductor does not require any of those things. He can have a terrible beat and look like nothing on earth, but if he is a great conductor every man in the orchestra will give, under his baton, not only a better performance than he would under another conductor, but a better performance than he knew he could give. That is not got out of them by instruction; it is a process of psychic evocation. Precisely the same thing holds good for the producer of a play. His function at its best is one of psychic evocation, and it is performed almost entirely unconsciously. Certain conscious tricks can come in the way or aid the process, but this evocative thing comes from God knows where. It is completely unconscious. Nobody knows when it is working, and nobody knows why it is working. Some people, and only the very best, have it; others do not. I could not answer why or wherefore, but I am just convinced that that is so.

Peter Hall
Is the Beginning the Word?

PETER HALL (1930–   ) is the Artistic Director of the British National Theatre. (He succeeded Laurence Olivier in 1973.) Prior to that, he was largely responsible for making the Royal Shakespeare Company one of the preeminent ensembles in the contemporary theatre. His little-known essay, which is included here, is a condensed version of the Herbert Read Lecture, which he delivered in London in 1971.

◆ My title is a puzzle, an enigma; my proposition is a question: is the beginning the word in the theatre? Does it begin with the word? In the beginning was the word is the basis of our religion; is the beginning of the theatre the word?

Let me propose a children's party. The entertainer, the conjurer, the uncle who's been engaged by the family to do their work, is making the children happy. He asks each child to sing, to dance, to recite, to tell a story. One by one these five or six-year-olds get up. They chant quickly, nervously through to the end. Will they remember 'Baa baa black sheep, have you any wool?' Perhaps they get it wrong; they sit down. Then one stands up and begins to recite, 'Twinkle, twinkle little star, how I wonder what you are,' and a silence falls on the room. Not just a silence among those five-year-olds, a silence among the adults. Is he an actor? No, he's a five-year-old child. Why is everybody silent? Why are they (as we say in the theatre) held? For me, I am held because the child is wondering what that star is—really wondering. And there is a moment in the room where the proverbial pin can be heard dropping. At the end of the experience we all applaud wildly. Wasn't he marvellous? But the child is in touch with something which he is communicating to us. Later on his parents arrive to collect him; he is asked to do it again. Now he can't. He stands up and he does it, but that contact, that moment, that strange instant of something communicating has disappeared.

Think of a group of actors doing an improvisation. They're trying to find the reality of death—or love, or happiness, or something very obvious, like the need for food. They improvize words, they improvize actions, they take from each other, they begin to understand each other. Their fellow actors watch them, breathless. If it is working, if it is happening, no one wants it to stop. You are in touch with something, something that can be found nowhere else. Then the actors need to repeat it. Difficult. How can you repeat? Ever? How can you repeat?

I'll take you quickly to another scene—a rehearsal in a play I was doing. The whole point of one character was that she was a very sad, lonely woman. But she was also entirely articulate, entirely self-possessed. Inside, shy and alone; outside, possessed, sophisticated, totally in control. The actress was defeated because in no way could she show the inner life of this character, without destroying the outside. We improvized. Then she improvized by speaking the text of the play but by allowing her inner feelings to show. She played half an act sobbing her heart out. It was so dreadful that all of us thought, we must stop this. Can we do this to another human being? She is actually suffering. The woman was heartbroken, the tears were pouring, she was saying the lines of the text which by now were nonsense. They were nothing, because her actual emotions were contradicting them. She was possessed by an emotion which she felt deeply. Had we stopped—and this is one of the terrifying things about being a director—I believe she would never have been able to play the part. Because she went to the end and released the emotion, ever after that loneliness, that misery has been in her performance; disguised, but inside her heart. Communication again—an emotional communication. Something strange passing between the actors who want to say, 'It's only a play—stop.' But it was marvellous, because she was demonstrating that in that moment the most serious thing in the world is a play, when a play is deep and real and actual.

One last scene. Think of a difficult speech—a very difficult speech, the Ulysses speech on order in *Troilus and Cressida*—the great set piece about degree, the form of nature, the form of man, the ladder from the lowest beasts up to God. I defy any one of you, however intelligent, to pick up the text, read that speech through once, put the book down and then tell me its argument. It is metaphysical, clotted, elaborate, hair-splitting—very difficult. But an actor who may not have the greatest intellect in the world off the stage, but who understands that speech, can make you—the audience—understand in utter clarity what that speech is about. Now that is an intellectual argument; it is not emotional. But an audience will be held, will understand why. Again, there is some mysterious communication.

Rare Moments of Telepathy

I am trying to define something which defies analysis. It is something so alive, so precious, so tender that we only meet it in living performance between live actor and live audience. It is telepathic, mysterious. It is why we endure miserable evenings in the theatre; because one night we may get this —a direct, complete communication. I suspect it is why the theatre remains a superstitious craft, a superstitious profession, one with its own mystique, its own sense of the mysterious. We still wish each other 'good luck' in the theatre with a fervour and a desperation that you won't find anywhere else in this materialistic age. We still talk about a good house. The audience helped us, therefore we could do it. We still know when we hold the audience—and, indeed, when the audience holds us.

Now some people in the theatre would say that this is all a question of social commitment, others would say it is all a question of craft, or that it's art or that it's genius. Some would say it's *true*—it's the truth. But *is* the theatre truth? No: in that sense, the theatre is not true. It is clear that theatre is a game of make-believe—a willing suspension of disbelief on both sides of the division between actor and audience. But each generation finds its new actors true. The old rhetoric is gone—the new actors are much truer, much more natural. Each decade a new generation of actors found more true? What is true? Is it real? Are we actually representing death, passion, agony, the mad cruelty of farce? No, we're not. So may I simply use the word 'theatre.' Because 'theatre' will do to express what the child reciting did to the room. 'Theatre' will do to describe why the Ulysses speech is clear—intellectually understood. It is pure communication. It is the most difficult thing to create, but it is always recognizable.

Is it the text? Is it the scenery? Is it the actors? Is it the backroom boy, the director? It can't be the text always, can it? We know that Irving was a great actor who spent his life doing a lot of rotten plays. We know his greatest success in communication was in *The Bells*, a text which doesn't stand up at all. We know that throughout history we can recall moments where the actor triumphed, but triumphed in terms of this 'theatre,' this communication, this instinct. We will never get the same thrill out of a piece of scenery, or a stage effect, or a trick. Any trick is exciting for two seconds. After two seconds you ask how? Then you ask why? If you know why, you may be moved. But it can never be done again. Scenery is not what the theatre is about. An actor standing on a stage can make a stage anywhere—with nothing. If he has a good text, it is that much easier.

This instant of theatre belongs to an instant of time. It is an art which has life for its material. It uses life—living people, living audience, living actors. And it deals with human actions, and they are infinite, as you are infinite. And here we come to the difficulty of creating theatre, of making rules for theatre, or judging theatre. Two men are so different that comparisons are impossible. If you ask an actor to walk across a stage with a motive, and then you ask another actor to walk across a stage with the same motive, the nature of that life is entirely different because they are two separate people. Unless each of them is imitating the way they *think* an actor should move as he walks across a stage—in which case they are both dead and impersonal and un-released.

Death-Blows to Communication

I think a director's main function is to be the man who sits there and judges the quality of the life, judges whether it is alive, particular, unique— or whether it is a cliché, tired, usual, that which is accepted. The important thing about the theatre is that a performance cannot and, indeed, must not survive. It is of now—of tonight, of this minute. It is a communication in which the audience of tonight is as important as the performer of tonight. As it is done it vanishes. And if it has worked then we want it to happen again. We want to repeat it. But if we repeat it, it is dead. You cannot repeat, you can only recreate, re-live. And in that sense the theatre is totally self-destructive: it wants to do it again and it can't. The audience is different, the actor on Tuesday is different to the way he was on Monday. I think the whole history of the theatre can be defined as a series of attempts to define and recapture and set these moments of truth, these moments of telepathy, these moments of actual 'theatre.' It was a way once of reaching religion. Religious ritual, the fullness of the religious experience, helped the theatre to find its communication and helped religion to find its celebration. That is gone for us. It is one of the languages that we are seeking and looking for again now.

As soon as a ballet is created (and when I speak of the theatre tonight I want to range wide, because I don't believe that theatre is actors and text alone. Theatre is many things.) As soon as a ballet is created, then, with a group of dancers and a choreographer expressing something at this moment, someone wants to notate the steps and pass them on to another group of dancers and then try to make it live again. Unfortunately, only on rare occasions does the choreographer remake it for other people, only very rarely is it handed down in living terms. Many theatres have died, as I believe at this moment the Berliner Ensemble—one of the greatest theatres of our century —is dying by the strong desire to carry on doing things the way they were. We have only one similar example really in this country; if you go to Gilbert and Sullivan done by the D'Oyly Carte, you can see what a great director W. S. Gilbert was—just. But it means nothing to us at all. It's amiable, enjoyable and very secure if you are a member of the Gilbert and Sullivan Club, but it is not in actual fact an experience.

And opera is perhaps the worst illustration through history of the perils of attempting to freeze and fix and make a test, make something rigid, make something which is repeatable. I am fascinated by Baroque opera, by seventeenth century opera, because we know it was free, flexible. We know that it was a libretto and a vocal line and a base line, and that the performers and the musicians, given the situation, made up the thing as we would rehearse a play. The instrumentalists orchestrated with the composer because of the needs of the scene. We know that it took forever. We know that it was uncommercial. We know that it had to be written down if it was to be commercially repeated, and we know as a consequence that the freedom of Monteverdi and of Cavalli and the Venetian opera led straight to the relatively formalized opera of the eighteenth century, where the freedom and a deal of emotion has gone, because they had to repeat. French's Acting Edition of eighteenth century opera.

The Writer as Inspirer

One easy way of preserving a piece of theatre is to write it down, whether it be in notes or in movements or in words. Write it down. If you improvize, write the words down, make the actors learn the words, make them then try to act the words. Something that could be done by the stage manager, or the director, the manager. Perhaps one day there is a man who is so inspired by what is going on that he writes something which is inspired—by what the actors have been doing—and then he becomes a playwright. Or perhaps the reverse procedure occurs. Perhaps he dreams a theatre dream in the privacy of his own room, writes it, and hands it to the actors and says, 'Embody that. Make that work. Make that true.' But if a play is written down it can march on into the future—a poor misleading thing perhaps, but a blueprint. Just a sketch of what the thing is—but it can go on. Gradually over the years theatre becomes literature. A score, a text, a beginning—that which must be observed or abused. The writer becomes the leader because he gives the theatre a tenuous and fragile hold on the future. He is in fact the imaginer. Now I begin to take positions which I don't really want to take, because the essence of the theatre to me is so changeable, so contradictory, so ambiguous and so pragmatic, that if I propose a writer's theatre tonight I wish to have the absolute right to propose something else tomorrow. Because the theatre must not deal in dogma and it must not deal in extremes; it is in a state of constant uneasy balance, of tension between the varying factors.

The playwright has been a great advantage to the actor. The stage belongs to the actor. But the actor needs a playwright to give him artistic security. First of all, the writer is the better imaginer. However brilliant a group of actors improvizing, however sacred and strange that moment of communication which comes on a group or an individual, they are unlikely to have the sensibility of Shakespeare or of Chekhov. They are unlikely to have the power to condense, to economize, to focus. That is the province of the great writer. And a great writer therefore inspires the actor, the theatre and the audience. He gives us form, he gives us economy. We know as actors, as people in the theatre, that it is never enough to feel passionately or even to feel truly—you need form. I may feel passionate in my emotions for two hours, but you the spectators will have got the message in two minutes, and if I indulge the feeling, you will be bored.

The writer can give us that focus. But he can also give us the plain potency of words. And I think this is a great danger—which is why I ask the question tonight. I believe that words are the most potent thing in the theatre and that is both a good thing and a thoroughly bad thing. Words define silence in the theatre. There is no silence without words. In opera there is no silence without music. In ballet there is no action without stillness. Words define, then, in the verbal theatre. They define action. Nothing happens on the stage in clear terms unless it is prepared for in some way by that which is said.

But I would then propose that words are the beginning in a verbal theatre, not the end. I believe that verbal poetry is the least poetic thing about a truly poetic theatre—the least. If you have a Shakespearian text and are faced with the responsibility of embodying that on the stage, it is not enough to understand it, it is not enough to like it, it is not enough to have your imagination engaged. Can you actually embody that text so that it is *alive?* Can you actually present that to the audience? Just the thought of presenting *King Lear*—which we all have a private vision of, a private experience of— the responsibility of putting *that* on the stage. You cannot reach out to those riches without those words, and you certainly cannot deny those words. But everything else—the way the play lives, the way the play is set, the way the play is acted, the way the play looks—has to measure up to that vast poetic object.

So we will welcome the writer in as our leader and our inspirer, but it is an awful thing for people in the theatre if we accept his text as literature. And I believe the greater the writer, the greater the challenge, the greater the danger. There is a school that you all know well, that believes that all you have to do with a great play is to speak it purely, simply, to allow it, as they say, to speak for itself. I've never heard a play speak. You may have your version of the play when you read it in the silence of your own home. I may have mine. But as soon as we take that play down and cast it, and decide that in 1971 we should do it, we shall try to embody it, it is something else—transitory, of now, and only of now. The appalling thing about this is that if you believe that the words of a play are all that matters, which many scholars do (many Shakespearians can read into a play private conceptions and thoughts without the discomfort of an experience which may challenge their assumptions), then you get into the dead world of convention which threatens this pure theatre every second of the day. It is true that an audience, once it loves the text above all else, makes assumptions about the form which prevent it listening and prevent it experiencing.

Theatre Conventions as Barriers

I know from bitter experience that most audiences at Shakespeare don't listen. Providing the Shakespearian noise is proceeding equably and easily, they are perfectly lulled and perfectly satisfied. It is, indeed, possible to talk complete nonsense in a Shakespeare production without anybody in the audience noticing. I've seen it happen again and again and again—providing the noise is correct. But once come on and make a noise which is different to the one which has been expected, and everybody listens and is appalled, infuriated or excited—it depends on your reaction. Indeed, it is often worse in the world of opera where we very carefully perform texts of operas in languages and situations which the audience cannot understand. It avoids the danger of understanding them. Opera audiences tend to like the form rather than the meaning. Actually, the average audience that wants an evening's entertainment in the West End has a similar liking for form. If you think about it, it is not strange—there's no difference in strangeness between me pretending that a little box-set here is a room, when it quite clearly isn't, and me walking on with a placard saying, 'This is a room.' It is a question of the convention which is accepted and allowed.

Audiences of enthusiasts, of buffs, actually resent communication. They resent passion, they resent disturbance—it upsets the club in some curious way. Opera lovers like to hear opera, they don't like to think what it's about. Shakespeare lovers like to *hear* Shakespeare. They are a little bit disturbed if the play's meaning is revealed. They go to observe the form, and that is death. And it encourages actors and singers to rely on technique and not to embody the text, not to embody the word.

Actors lead naked and uncomfortable lives. It is a marvellous profession, but it's a very difficult one, difficult to do honestly. Because to walk on-stage each night and expose yourself in truth, to try and actually reach this naked communication, is a tiring and nerve-racking business. Much easier to know what 'goes,' what works. Much easier to know: 'I speak quickly. I do this. This is how I'm loved. . . . I can speak verse. I can sing an aria.' Much easier to rely on technique, which is a kind of acrobatic skill—nothing more—and is applauded accordingly. This is not life. To speak Shakespeare's verse correctly is a skill. To sing Mozart correctly, if you are blessed with a voice, is a skill. But a skill is not enough—that's not what I'm talking about. That's not 'theatre.' In fact, the reliance on the text can mean a refusal in the actor's imagination to take the next step, because he feels all right if he's doing it well and he's making the expected noises. In fact, my definition of a star—which as a word is imprecise and fairly hateful—would be a performer who transcends technique so that he reveals his own human complexity through his technique. Now I can be moved by an ice-skater who reveals his human complexity by his skill at ice-skating, by a ballet dancer, by a singer, by an actor. It is that revelation of self—the telepathy again, the communication.

A Text to Trigger Off Responses

My main concern is to make a distinction between *theatre,* which is pure—although it occurs rarely—and *theatricality,* which is technique, trick, custom, that which is easily accepted. A text does not have an absolute meaning—cannot have an absolute meaning. It can trigger off responses in an actor and in an audience which are contradictory and ambiguous. Does the playwright know all the meaning? In my experience not. Certainly not. And why should he? Does a poet know in intellectual terms what he has actually written? It depends who's asking him the question. It depends who's making the proposition or what it means to him. There is no ultimate meaning. One of my closest working relationships is with Harold Pinter. If you say to him, 'What does it mean?' he says, 'What does it say?' And that's not an evasion —that's a truth about the theatre. 'What does it say? I've written it—what does it say to you? You actors—what will you do with it? What does it say? What information does it give you? How will you convey that to an audience?'

All great theatre writing is compressed. It is dense and highly personal. In some sense, it is all poetry. Each time a new dramatist arrives, he is found, like the new actors, more actual. 'Well, Chekhov is more naturalistic. Ibsen is more naturalistic.' Thirty years later they say, 'Chekhov was a poet you know. Ibsen was a poet.' Samuel Beckett arrives—quickly we shove him into a category called 'Theatre of the Absurd.' We hope we have categorized him: he writes colloquial speech. But wait a minute. Twenty years later, he's a poet. He has his own voice, his own precision. And he does. But those particularities are the challenge to the actor: he can rapidly evolve a new dead technique. It is just as bad to play Beckett or Pinter only with technique as it is Shakespeare. You can't do any of them without technique, but technique is not enough. You have to reveal yourself, in order to endorse the author.

Nothing is valid in the theatre unless it illuminates what you are trying to communicate to the audience. There can be no dogma—no method—ever. So I will not define what comes first. Sometimes it's a writer, sometimes it's an actor. Always it's a place—that I know. Always it's live people talking to live people. Always there is a two-way emotion. Perhaps there's a story, perhaps there's a mood. Perhaps there's a conflict. Perhaps there's a character (although I would put a character rather low on the list because we don't go into a theatre to be reassured that the actors we see appearing are not actors but characters. This is the whole wastefulness of over-naturalistic playing—it tells you lots of things about a character that you don't need to know.) So the theatre is ambiguous, and as changeable as the people who make it and the people who listen to it. And it changes from performance to performance because of the circumstances that we're all living in.

Is it true the better the writer the better the evening? I wouldn't say so. I would much sooner go to the production of *1789* that was recently seen in London by the *Théâtre du Soleil*, which has a text which is undisciplined, messy, long, making its points in a very unsubtle way, than an evening of pure Shakespeare, well spoken by a series of talking heads which did not embody it in any way whatsoever.

A Starting Point for Actors

The theatre now is reflecting—which is why there are so many questions abroad—the problems that we have in society. Many theatre people don't want a writer at this moment. And there are a lot of directors who don't want directors, who take the quite false position of saying, 'This play is created by the commune and I am not the director—I'm just a fellow.' Yet without them the play would not have happened. Theatre cannot be created without somewhere or other the individual act of anarchy of the leader. He doesn't have to be called a director, but he has to be a leader. It illustrates the crisis of the theatre that we are trying to move into new forms, new fields, by maintaining that we mustn't have dictatorship of anything—of the word, the actor, or the director. And four hundred years of mounting concern with the text, with the playwright and his literary values, have made a lot of people very suspicious. They feel that those who say, 'The text is enough are not recognizing that the text encourages cliché in actor and audience. It encourages a routine response in both. The text is old, pure, holy, probably studied at school. So the reaction is, 'Away with the text—improvize—be true—be true to yourself.' Sometimes they are then faced with the agony of speaking the text, having been true to themselves. It is difficult to do both. If you have got a text to speak, you will have to improvize on the basis of the information, the responses, which the text has given you. You have actually to start from the text, if your task is to use a text.

Out of these ferments will come a new kind of raw material which new writers will be able to use. They will concentrate it, they will purify it, they will hand it back to us. And we will perform it. And very quickly we shall have killed it by making it technical, routine, conventional, repetitious. And the process of action and re-action will go on and on and on and on while there is theatre and while there is time.

Danger of Hiding behind Words

The theatre is finally the actor—must be. Even if he's a dull actor, he is a man, and a man is a very complex organism. The dullest man can give you something. If that actor can be committed to thoughts, to emotions, to opinions, to attitudes, inspired by a writer and helped by a director, he must reach near these moments of telepathy. I demand that he will be good at his craft, that he will be able to speak verse, that he will be able to use his body in any way that is necessary—that is only right and proper. Like a pianist being able to play the piano—no more, no less. And he must improve this craft. But he must commit all of himself as a person into the experience of the theatre, into the work. And it therefore follows that it is as dangerous for an actor to hide behind words as for an audience to hide behind words, behind stock responses.

The relationship between the living writer and those who play is sometimes uneasy. The actor, to some degree, suspects the writer as much as the writer suspects the actor. The writer may not feel that the full embodiment of his text is really necessary; most writers can't help thinking somewhere inside them the text is enough—get my text right and it will work. But it doesn't. I've spoken already of Harold Pinter. People think that a Pinter play works if you observe his pauses. It doesn't. It's what's *in* the pauses that matters. It's the embodiment of those pauses, trying to find out why they are there and how we can use them, that's what actually matters. And each time we go out to do a play, we are trying to find the play. And that is not the text: it is all the text suggests. For that any means can be used. There is actually only one criterion: does it work? There is no such thing as stylistic purity in the theatre. There is a style for a production if it works—then it's pure to itself. And in our day and age, finding the play and keeping the intricate system of checks and balances has devolved more and more on the director.

The director is somebody who has to find a way he doesn't know. He guides a group of people down a difficult path: and doesn't even know whether it exists. The director has to discover as much as the actors, because if he doesn't he is hiding behind his technique as the actors are hiding behind theirs. It's easy enough for a director to say, 'This is the way the play should be done and this is how you should do it. This is where you should stand and this is how you should speak the text.' Dead again—dead. It won't achieve the life I'm talking about. So with each group of people at any given place and any different time, you set out to find a play. Maybe you start with a text, maybe you don't, but you set out to find a play which you know of, and it is there, different every time. If it has a text, you can't stop at the text. If it has a text you can't betray the text—by which I mean it's no use speaking blank verse as if it were prose, in the interests of twentieth century reality. It doesn't work. It's no good speaking ironic prose as if it were heightened rhetorical verse. It doesn't work.

So the director must always ask questions. He must challenge his cast to consider the problems with him. 'Is the beginning the word? What is the word? How do you speak? Why do you speak? What does speech mean?' Nothing must be accepted, nothing rejected. You can't rely on the sanctity of the text and you certainly can't rely on the sanctity of improvization or of political commitment, or being a commune, or being a propaganda theatre, or being a poetic theatre, or being a ritualistic theatre, or being a 'cruel' theatre. All these things are slight swings in this perpetual action and reaction of the theatre. They are none of them guarantees of art.

We are always told that directors must be true to the author. How can you be true? True to what? You can only be responsible for seeing that the play should live. But it should live within its own definitions. Sometimes it's impossible to do that. But how can you, at this moment in time, do Greek tragedy within its own definitions? The dialogue between the audience and the actor is gone, it is dead. You have to find different equivalents. Some different form of making the dialogue happen.

There is no philosopher's stone. There is no Stanislavsky, no Marxist theory of art, no People's Theatre, no aristocratic entertainment, which will actually ensure that we will produce theatre. And we can never be sure of words. There is only life.

For every production, there has to be a finding. The true way for a play to be born is for a group of actors to meet together with a leader. If it has a text, it has to be studied, openly, critically. If there is no text, a scenario has to be established. The work of finding goes on together. Then, and not until then, should the play be designed. Then they should rehearse it and rehearse it, then bring it to the point of preview, show it to an audience, understand if the audience understands or not, and then go back to work again. That is the right way to make communication. It almost never happens.

Jean Vilar
Murder of the Director

JEAN VILAR (1912–1970), as noted earlier, was the founder of the Théâtre National Populaire. His book, *The Tradition of the Theatre,* which has never been published in its entirety in English, is one of the major documents of the modern theatre. It is filled with wise observations concerning the role of the director. The chapter included here is one of the better-known sections of the book.

1

◆ The following notes concern only a particular technique of theatrical art, that of transposing a written work from the imaginary realm of reading to the concrete realm of the stage. To look for anything more than "means of interpretation" in these often deliberately cryptic lines would be vain.

When so many theories, *ars poetica* and metaphysics have been made up about this art, it is perhaps necessary that one advance, as a preliminary, a few artisan's considerations.

2

One can never read the play often enough. Actors never read it often enough. They think they understand the play when they follow the plot more or less clearly—a fundamental error.

Sticking my neck out, I would point out that in general, directors underrate the professional intelligence of actors. They are asked to be bodies only, animated pawns on the director's chessboard. The play once read by the director, read a second time *à l'italienne,* the actors are thrust onto the stage. What is the result?

Subjected too early to the demands of physical presence and action, the actors fall back on their habitual, conventional reactions, and develop their characters conventionally and arbitrarily, before their professional intelligence and their sensibilities can grasp the director's intention. Whence, so many hack performances!

For there are hack performances in the most sensitive actor, just as a writer will produce hack work when he hurries or is hurried. How many actors, including some of the best, have murmured to us for twenty years in the same voice, with the same bearing and gestures, with the same emotional quality, in the most diametrically opposed roles!

Hence the necessity for many reading rehearsals: about a third of the total number. At least. Manuscript in hand, seat firmly planted on a chair, body in repose. Thus the deepest sensibilities will gradually pitch themselves to the desired note, as the actor comes to understand, or feel, the new character that is to become himself.

3

All characters must be *composed.* All good actors are necessarily *composers.* All roles are the result of *composition.*

4

The composition of a character is the work of creation which, alone, assimilates the actor's craft to the artist's; for composing a character implies selection, observation, research, inspiration, and discipline.

5

The actor selects within and around himself.

Around himself, because nature presents to his eyes the most various and distinct models, for his observation; one might almost say, for his contemplation.

Within himself, because if, on the one hand, the actor cannot sufficiently observe the life teeming around him, neither can he sufficiently expose his sensibilities to contact with it.

In short, the actor must be able to retain in his visual memory the human types that strike his attention, as also the sympathetic (or sensory) memory of his own wounds and moral suffering. He must know how to use this memory and, better yet, cultivate it.

6

In blocking, the point is to simplify and pare down. Contrary to the usual practice, the idea is not to *exploit* space, but to forget or ignore it.

For a production to have its full power of suggestion, it is not necessary that a so-called scene of action should be "busy" (with acrobatics, fisticuffs, brawling and other "realistic" or "symbolic" activity). One or two gestures, and the text, suffice; provided both are "right"

7

The work of blocking and physical characterization should be fairly quickly completed by good professional actors: say fifteen rehearsals out of forty.

8

An actor's—or a director's—talent does not necessarily lie in the variety and strength of his powers (which are a relatively unimportant gift of Providence), but above all in the refining of his powers, the severity of his selectivity, in his voluntary self-impoverishment.

9

Music-hall theatre: a great actor, a splendid costume, a striking decor, music brimming with genius, strong-colored lighting.

10

No actor worthy of the name imposes himself on the text; he serves it. Humbly. Let the electrician, musician, and designer, accordingly, be even more humble than this "right interpreter."

11 Character and Actor

The script carefully studied and the characters "felt" in all their ramifications, in the course of the fifteen or twenty reading rehearsals, the director begins the bland work of blocking, completes it, and finds himself at once in a renewed struggle with those slippery monsters, the characters. The actors know it well, for character and actor are two separate entities. For long days, the first eludes the second with infernal ease. The worst thing to do at this stage is to try to fight the demon, to force him to your will. If you wish him to come and meekly enter into your body and soul, forget him. The director's role, as expert observer of this pursuit by osmosis, is to inspire the actor with confidence, to convince him that he has, in the very expressive phrase, "found" or "rediscovered" his character. It is by no means naive to state that at a certain point in the development of a character, this confidence is all. It is by non-violence, by confidence in his ultimate conquest of the elusive monster, that the actor finally triumphs.

12

The scenic artist must realize the designer's sketches. Alternatively, there should be a designer-carpenter, right hand of the director, with full powers over the stage: a man of taste, devoted to his work and cultured. A hard trade.

13 Of Costume

In theatre, the hood sometimes makes the monk.

14 What Must Be Done?

The work of production must include a written analysis of the play. The director must write it, and not despise the thankless job. The drafting of such an analysis compels the director to a clear and exhaustive knowledge of the play.

15

Question: Can one interpret something one doesn't understand?

16 Coda to "What Must Be Done?"

How may playwrights would be incapable of giving you a precise analysis of their play! of its plot, even!

17

A director who cannot detach himself from his work during the final rehearsals is only a mediocre craftsman, however much it might seem that this is the very point at which he should be most intensely involved in it. Failing this detachment, the director blinds himself—the worst possible error. Such poor fools forget that the theatre is play, in which inspiration and child-like wonder are more important than sweat and tantrums.

It is true that such detachment is so difficult to achieve at the right time that it is not surprising to find that few directors either desire or achieve it.

18

A quality fully as important to the actor in the right practice of his art as sensitivity and instinct, is the spirit of *finesse* (for a definition, see Pascal, who opposes it to the spirit of geometry). Without this quality, his work will only present a riot of anarchic expressions.

19

The actor is not a machine. This is a truism that needs to be shouted in people's ears. The actor is neither pawn nor robot. The director must assume from the start that his players have all the necessary talent.

20 Intermission

"The idleness of an artist is work, and his work, repose." Signed, Balzac.

21

There is no technique of interpretation, but only practices, *techniques* (plural). Personal experience is all, and personal empiricism.

22

For the director, every actor is a special case. From this follows the requirement that he know every member of his cast well. Know his work, of course, but even more his *person*, up to the threshold of his inner life, and perhaps even beyond.

23 Director and Actor

Where the actor is concerned, the director's art is one of suggestion. He does not impose, he suggests. Above all, he must not be brutal. The "soul of an actor" is not an idle phrase: even more than the "soul of a poet," it is a continuing necessity. One does not win a creature's soul by brutalising it, and the actor's soul is more necessary to the work of theatre than his sensitivity.

24 Of Simplicity

Three references:
a. Shakespeare-Hamlet: "Speak the speech, I pray you, as I pronounced it to you, trippingly on the tongue; but if you mouth it . . . I had as lief the town-crier spoke my lines . . . Be not too tame neither, but let your own discretion be your tutor . . . etc.", and all the rest of this famous passage.
b. Molière: *The Versailles Impromptu.*
c. Talmá-Lekain: "Lekain guarded against that hunger for applause that torments most actors and leads them into frequent error; he wished to please only the discriminating members of the audience. He rejected all theatrical fakery, aiming to produce a genuine effect by avoiding all "effects" . . . He *practiced a right economy of movement and gesture, deeming this an essential part of the art, since their multiplication detracts from dignity of bearing.*" (Talma)

25

A production must be reduced to its simplest—and most difficult—expression: the stage action or, more precisely, the acting. Hence, the stage must not be turned into a crossroads of all the arts, major and minor (painting, architecture, electromania, musicomania, mechanics, etc.).

The designer must be put in his place, which is to solve the sightline problems of masking and teasers and to see to the construction of such set and hand properties as are strictly necessary to the action on stage.[1]

The immoderate use of projectors, floodlights and arc lamps should be left to the music-hall and the circus.

Music should be used only for overtures and scene bridges, and otherwise only when the script explicitly calls for music off, a song, or a musical interlude.

In short, all effects should be eliminated which are extraneous to the pure and Spartan laws of the stage, and the production reduced to the physical and moral action of the players.

[*Translated by Christopher Kotschnig*]

Carl Weber
Brecht As Director

CARL WEBER (1933–   ) was one of Brecht's proteges and served as an assistant director at the Berliner Ensemble while Brecht was alive and for some time after his death. Weber now lives in this country. In addition to directing, he also is head of the directing program at New York University. In 1967 he gave this lecture in which he described Brecht's methods of working with the actors of the Ensemble.

◆   Much has been written about Brecht in this country, some—though not enough—of his theoretical writings have been translated, and most of his plays have been published in English. From all of this, people quite naturally get the idea that Brecht was primarily a poet and playwright. But, although this is true, in order to understand Brecht the playwright one ought to know Brecht as a man of practical theatre—as a director. Brecht's influence on the theatre of his time stems mainly from the productions he created at the Berliner Ensemble; Germany's theatre has changed totally since he did his exemplary work during the early and mid-fifties in East Berlin. The new movement in England—The Royal Court, Peter Brook and Peter Hall, Kenneth Tynan, to mention a few names only—would probably have been

---

[1]His chief task being to find the single *keynote of the set,* if set there must be. (J.V.)

vastly different if the Berliner Ensemble had not presented his work in London in 1956, and again in the sixties, and Giorgio Strehler in Italy and Roger Planchon in France have been deeply influenced by what, and how, Brecht created in Berlin. Though Brecht had worked for the theatre nearly all his life, as a critic first, then as a playwright and director, it was not until 1949 that he found a permanent place for his experiments, a company, and later a building, which he could form into the ideal instrument for his ideas, a theatre which was a laboratory, a place for investigation, analysis, and construction of models.

When Brecht returned to Europe after his war-time stay in the United States, the East German authorities offered to let him direct a production of *Mother Courage* with his wife, Helene Weigel, in the lead; for the first time in 15 years he had a chance to demonstrate the theories he had been fighting for all his life, in Germany and elsewhere. The production opened in 1949, at the Deutsches Theatre, Berlin, and was the turning point of German theatre history, perhaps in this century—surely at least since Reinhardt. The critics—who had almost unanimously condemned Brecht's work in the years before 1933—did a somersault, and the production was a great success. I went to see it as a young man coming from the university at Heidelberg; it remains the greatest theatre experience of my life. It is hard now to describe exactly what was so unique, since I since have come to know the production so well, from acting in it and restaging it in 1954. One thing: it was the first time I had ever seen people on the stage behave like real human beings; there was not a trace of "acting" in that performance, though the technical brilliance and perfection of every moment was stunning. The economy of the set, of every prop used, was absolutely overwhelming to one who had seen until then only run-of-the-mill—and sometimes the best—German theatre. And it was astonishing how the idea of the play was brought across without pushing, without hammering it into the audience. All this was above and beyond the superb individual performances of Weigel and the rest of the company.

I decided that I had to work with Brecht, but it was not until 1952 that the Ensemble had a vacant position for an assistant director. I went to a dramaturg of the company, Peter Palitzsch, and asked how to apply to Brecht. He answered that Brecht didn't like to interview people and the best thing was to submit a piece about one of the Ensemble's productions—not a review, just a description of what the actors did, why, and whether it worked. I went to see *Puntila* several times, wrote about two of its scenes, and sent it to Brecht. After a while, I called Brecht's secretary and said, "Shall I come, or is it so bad there's no point?" The answer was, "How can you make him read anything? He doesn't read very much." But I convinced her to try again to bring the piece to Brecht's attention. I called after two weeks, and she said, "Well, we've lost it." Disaster! I didn't have a copy: but they found it again. Then three more weeks went by, and I phoned again, and she said that Brecht had read the piece and wanted to see me.

The next morning, there he was in his cap. I was very embarrassed and shy, and right away he became even shyer than I. He said, "Yes, you are . . . Yes, I have read . . ." There was a long pause. I didn't know what to say and he just looked at me. Then finally he said, "I have to go to rehearsal. Why don't you go to our business office and talk to Weigel about your contract?" And off he went.

I asked at the office if I could watch a rehearsal, and they told me that anyone who had a legitimate interest could watch rehearsals unless Brecht, as happened rarely, thought an actor was extremely nervous—even then he would work with that actor separately, but the rest of the rehearsal would be kept open. He wanted actors to get used to spectators, to get laughs, to be in contact with the people down there as early in the process as possible, to work *with* an audience. At that time they were rehearsing the *Urfaust,* which Goethe wrote when he was about 25, decades before he did the final version of *Faust.* Brecht preferred the *Urfaust* for several reasons. It is written in *Knittelvers,* a verse which is unrhythmic or of changeable rhythm, and rhymes either not at all or very forcefully. It was used in the farces and mystery plays of the late Middle Ages and early Renaissance; also, it is the language of German Punch and Judy shows. *Faust* itself, however great, is the play of an old man, with a detached view of society and of the individual—the *Urfaust* is a *Sturm und Drang* work with a young, aggressive approach to the world. In its treatment of the love story, it is remarkably close to the way Brecht wrote in *Baal* and *Drums in the Night.*

I walked into the rehearsal and it was obvious that they were taking a break. Brecht was sitting in a chair smoking a cigar, the director of the production, Egon Monk, and two or three assistants were sitting with him, some of the actors were on stage and some were standing around Brecht, joking, making funny movements and laughing about them. Then one actor went up on the stage and tried about 30 ways of falling from a table. They talked a little about the *Urfaust-*scene "In Auerbachs Keller" (Mephisto brings Faust into an inn where drunken students enjoy themselves with dirty jokes and silly songs). Another actor tried the table, the results were compared, with a lot of laughing and a lot more horse-play. This went on and on, and someone ate a sandwich, and I thought, my god this is a long break. So I sat naively and waited, and just before Monk said, "Well, now we are finished, let's go home," I realized that this *was* rehearsal. And it was typical of the loose way Brecht often worked, of his experimental approach and of the teamwork the Ensemble was used to. Whatever ideas he brought to rehearsal he tried out, threw away, tried something else; sometimes 40 versions of one scene were tried, once in a while only two. Even when a production had opened, and been reviewed, he re-worked parts of it, re-rehearsed it, changed the blocking. The actors also took an experimental attitude. They would suggest a way of doing something, and if they started to explain it, Brecht would say that he wanted no discussions in rehearsal—it would have to be tried. Of course, his whole view of the world was that it was changeable and the people in it were changing; every solution was only a starting point for a new, better, different solution.

All this was—of course—not just for love of experiment. Brecht was mainly concerned with the play as the telling of a story to an audience, clearly, beautifully, and entertainingly. If he found that in an almost completed production one certain part was opaque or boring, he cut it. I have never seen anyone cut a script as mercilessly as Brecht cut his own. Brecht had another important ability: if he had worked at a scene, and then dropped it for a week, he could come back and look at it as if he never seen it before. I remember a scene from the third act of *Caucasian Chalk Circle,* when Grusha, with her adopted child and her brother Lawrentij, arrives at the house of the dying peasant whom she is forced to marry. The scene hadn't been done for about three weeks (the play was rehearsed for eight months); he came back to it, and we all thought it was going rather well when suddenly Brecht yelled, "Stop!" He asked what the actor playing Lawrentij, who was walking across the room, was doing. Well, we answered, there's a good reason; he has to be over there for his next line, you blocked it this way. Brecht denied this angrily, saying there was no reason for such a move. "But his next line asks for it." "What line?" he barked. The actor said the line. "But that's impossible, I couldn't have written that!" We had to show him in the book that he had indeed written it, and he was furious—at us. But he rewrote the scene. He had looked at it as if it were by someone else, from a play he'd never heard of before, which he was judging as a spectator, and it failed.

The initial preparation of a play usually took about half a year, while it was discussed, and adapted (if it was a translation). The set was developed on paper and as a model during that period, as were the costumes. Then, when Brecht went into rehearsal, it could take three to four months to block the play. This blocking involved the working out of a considerable number of details. To Brecht, blocking was the backbone of the production; ideally, he thought, the blocking should be able to tell the main story of the play—and its contradictions—by itself, so that a person watching through a glass wall, unable to hear what was being said, would be able to understand the main elements and conflicts of the story. To work out blocking this clear takes an enormous amount of time; he would try out every thinkable possibility—and if a scene didn't seem to work in dress rehearsal, the first thing reworked would be the blocking.

After the basic blocking was finished, we started to work on the acting detail; by this time the actors knew their lines completely, and could play around with them freely. The most meticulous attention was paid to the smallest gesture. Sometimes it took an hour to work out whether an actor should pick up a tool one way or another. Particular attention was devoted to all details of physical labor. A man's work forms his habits, his attitudes, his physical behavior down to the smallest movement, a fact usually neglected by the stage. Brecht spent hours in rehearsal exploring how Galileo would handle a telescope and an apple, how the kitchenmaid Grusha would pick up a waterbottle or a baby, how the young soldier Eilif would drink at his General's table, etc. Often paintings or other pictorial documents of the play's period were brought into rehearsal for the study of movements and gestures. Brecht's favorite painters were Breughel and Bosch: their paintings told "stories" (not in the sense of the veristic 19th-century school, of course), their people were stamped by their lives and occupations, their vices and beliefs. The influence of pictures he had seen often could be felt in Brecht's work; certain moments of the blocking, as well as character-images, were derived from paintings or photos.

Each moment had to be examined: for the characters' situation, for the story's situation, for the actions going on around the character. When all these details had been brought to a certain point, not of completion, but of diminished possibilities, Brecht would have the first run-through. This might be six months after the actors started work on the play, six months of working on blocking, single beats, and small units of scenes. The first run-through was usually a disaster—it was impossible for the actors to pull things together so fast. But this was just what Brecht was waiting for; in the second and third run-throughs, a rhythm began to appear, and all the mistakes made so far emerged clearly. So then Brecht broke the whole thing down again into short beats and small units, and reworked every part that had been unsuccessful. After the second break-down of the play, the final period of rehearsal usually came. This included run-throughs—but interrupted by frequent reworking of scenes and details. A week or more was given to the technical rehearsals. Lighting a show sometimes took five days alone, and extras were used for walking through all the motions, so the actors wouldn't waste their time and energy. During dress rehearsals, details were constantly changed or developed further, including the blocking and quite often even the text. I remember first nights, when actors would find a little note from Brecht on their dressing-room tables, wishing them good luck and asking them to say a new line in scene X instead of one Brecht had decided to cut, because audience reactions in dress-rehearsals had indicated that the former line didn't work the way Brecht intended it.

After the last dress rehearsal Brecht always did an exercise, which he called the "marking" or "indicating" rehearsal: the actors, not in costumes, but on the set, had to walk quickly through all the actions of the show, quoting the text very rapidly, without any effort at acting, but keeping the rhythm, the pauses, etc., intact. The effect—if you were sitting far back in the house— was very much like an early silent movie: you saw people moving and gesturing very quickly, but you couldn't hear the words or get any kind of emotions, except the most obvious ones. This proved to be an extremely helpful device; it made the actors relax, helped them to memorize every physical detail and gave them a keen sense for the show's rhythmic pattern.

Finally first night came, which in fact was a preview with audience, after which rehearsals were used to change the production according to audience reactions. After five to eight previews, the official "opening" with press and invited guests took place. Brecht introduced these previews to Germany, probably drawing on his American and English experiences. In the beginning, the German critics strongly rejected this procedure; now other theatres have followed Brecht's example. After the opening, work on the production didn't stop. The director—or one of his assistants—watched every performance, and whenever changes or a reworking were felt necessary, rehearsals were scheduled.

This sounds like a monumentally laborious process, and to some extent it was. But it took place in an atmosphere of humor, ease with experimentation, relaxation. Actors (and directors) new at the Ensemble were usually very tense, and tried to get results right away—as they must when they have only a few weeks rehearsal time. Brecht would tell them, "Fast results are always to be regarded with suspicion. The first solution is usually not a good solution. Not enough thinking goes into it. Instinct is a very dubious guide, especially for directors."

Brecht regarded design as of the highest importance, and had worked out his methods of handling it with his friend Caspar Neher. When Neher designed a play for him, he started with little sketches depicting the important story situations—sometimes he arrived at a kind of comic strip of the entire play. He began with people, sketching the characters in relation to a given situation, and thus visualizing the blocking. When he and Brecht were satisfied with the sketches, they started to develop a set. For Brecht, for Neher when he worked with Brecht, for Otto and von Appen, who worked with Brecht in the fifties, the set was primarily a space where actors tell a certain story to the audience. The first step was to give the actor the space and architectural elements he needed; the next was to work out the set so it by itself would tell the audience enough about the play's story and conflicts, its period, social relations, etc.; the last step was to make it beautiful.

Whatever is called the "style" of Brechtian productions was always something arrived at during the last phase of production. Brecht never began with a preconceived stylistic idea, even something so "basic" as whether the production should be "period," "naturalistic," or whatever silly labels theatre convention usually pins on plays. He began with a long exploration of the intricate social relationships of the characters and the behavior resulting from them. Their psychology was not left out, but was developed from the social relations. The designer watched, working out his ideas as Brecht rehearsed. Twice I saw about 75% of a completed set—and the finished costumes that went with it—thrown away after the first dress rehearsal, because although it was beautiful it did not tell the audience what Brecht and von Appen wanted. An enormous amount of money was poured into these experiments, but certainly not wasted. One of Brecht's favorite proverbs—"The proof of the pudding is in the eating"—was always applied to his theatre work.

From the time Brecht began directing in Munich in the twenties, until the end, he liked to have people around him when he directed. He asked everyone he trusted to come to rehearsal and constantly asked their opinions;

he controlled his work through their reactions. In the fifties, his productions were always team-work, and he constantly used all the people connected with a production—assistants, designer, musicians (Eisler was at many rehearsals). Brecht asked the Ensemble's technicians to attend dress-rehearsals, and afterwards sought their opinions. I remember the last rehearsals of *Katzgraben* (a play by the contemporary East German novelist and playwright Erwin Strittmatter, which Brecht produced in 1953), to which Brecht had invited a group of children between 10 and 14. He spent two hours with them after rehearsal to find out what they understood and what not, trying to pin down the reasons. The discussion's result was a reworking of many scenes to achieve more clarity, a higher quality of "telling the story." Brecht believed strongly in the unspoiled and unprejudiced observation of children. They possessed the naive and poetic quality of thought he felt so important for the theatre.

In the Ensemble, Brecht decided that the young directors should co-direct—two or even three of them as directors of the same standing. This worked well. The directors would arrive at a basic concept on which they could agree before going into rehearsal. But in actual rehearsal, beautiful things would come out of the tension between different minds working on the same problems—better solutions than any one of the directors could have arrived at on his own. In fact, many productions before and most productions after his death were directed this way. For instance: *Playboy of the Western World* by Synge (Palitzsch/Wekwerth), *The Day of the Great Scholar Wu* (Palitzsch-/Weber), *Optimistic Tragedy* by Wishnewski (Palitzsch/Wekwerth), *The Private Life of the Master Race* by Brecht (Bellag/Palitzsch/Weber), *Arturo Ui* by Brecht (Palitzsch/Wekwerth), *Coriolanus* by Brecht/Shakespeare (Tenschert/Wekwerth), *Little Mahagonny* by Brecht (Karge/Langhoff).

Brecht never cared how his actors worked. He didn't tell them to go home and do this or that, or to go behind the set and concentrate. He didn't give a damn about the mechanics they used, he just cared about results. Brecht respected actors and was extremely patient with them; he often used their suggestions. During breaks, he would listen sometimes to rather obvious nonsense from the actors, wanting them not to feel uncomfortable with him, wanting to gain their confidence in all matters. He himself could probably have become a great actor. He could be a marvelous clown; sometimes the actors would provoke him to demonstrate something, for the sheer joy of watching him. He did not prod the actors to ape what he had demonstrated, but rather would exaggerate enough so that while they saw exactly what he wanted, they were never tempted to copy him.

It is interesting to compare the way in which I saw Brecht direct actors with what's reported by Leon Feuchtwanger's wife (who was there) about his first directing. When Brecht was 24, and his play *Drums in the Night* was being rehearsed in Münich, the director found to his surprise that the young author was coming to rehearsals, interrupting him, yelling at the actors, and demonstrating how they should do things. Pretty soon Brecht had almost taken over the entire production, and the director—a mature man—was practically his assistant. As usual in the German theatre of that time, the rehearsal period was short, somewhat under three weeks, but by the last week the actors, some of whom were quite prominent, were trying very hard to do what Brecht wanted them to. Basically, he was attempting to wean them from the pompous, overambitious typical German manner of the time, to bring them back to a realistic treatment of the lines. Mrs. Feuchtwanger's report is of great interest. That very young man, who came to attend rehearsals of his first play, kept yelling at the actors that what they offered was shit. When I met him in his fifties, mellowed perhaps, but not the least weakened in his determination, he was still busy cleaning the stage (and all art) of the "sweet lies" which keep man from recognizing the world as it is. Brecht tried to present in his theatre a real view of the world, no goldplated images of false heroes, no "revealing" photos of rabbits, busy nibbling cabbage and humping their mates, of whatever sex. Doubt in man-made gods, doubt in man-made rules, doubt in whatever man is told to accept was proclaimed on his stage. And a profound insight into man's weakness and longing to conform, an insight, by the way, which was not without understanding, and even compassion.

Brecht used his theatre as a laboratory, to experiment with plays and players. Human behavior, human attitudes, human weakness—everything was explored and investigated, to be exposed finally to a public which often enough refused to recognize its image in this very clear, but sometimes perhaps too well-framed, mirror. The realistic treatment of the lines, which Brecht demanded from his first hour in the theatre to the last, was more than a theatreman's protest against the theatre's degraded conventions. For him, the stage was a model of the world—the world we all have to live in.

Alan Schneider
I Can't Go On, I'll Go On

ALAN SCHNEIDER (1917–   ), Russian-born, American director, is best known
for directing the plays of Beckett and Albee. However, the range of his work is much
wider than that. He has also had a wide influence as a teacher. He was the director
of the Julliard School of Drama and is currently the head of the directing program at
the University of California in San Diego. This essay originally appeared in *Theatre
4: The American Theatre 1970–71.*

◆ Of my fifty or so productions of all sorts directed in the New York
theatre, on Broadway and off, 'successful' or less than so, except to my inner
eye, in over fifteen years since I was foolish or foolhardy enough to stray
northward from the pleasanter corners of the Arena Stage in Washington,
only a bare handful—and I have to search for the fingers—have not turned
out to be total agonies of one kind or another from beginning to end; the
special agonies in each case always unexpected and surprisingly unique. Nor
do I feel especially accursed in this regard. My best friends tell me the same
story: Tommy Ewell once mentioned to me casually that the only show he'd
ever not had his total agonies in had closed in Philadelphia. And recently, I
noticed that Gerald Hiken, a fine young director-actor and ex-associate of
mine, who has withdrawn himself completely from the 'formula and noise' of
New York for a kind of communal touring existence in California, confessed
in the drama pages of the Sunday *New York Times* that in his nine years and
twenty-two shows, he had hated rehearsing nineteen of them. To reverse one
of Mr. Beckett's cheerier lines, it's an unreasonable percentage. But a normal
one. That is to say, despair is normal in our work: it's the nature of the
beastliness. Only, recently, despair like the smog has been reaching abnormal
levels.

Some time ago, I was sent a script to read by a young playwright
unknown to me. Not having my home address, he sent it to me c/o Executive
Office, Sheridan Square Playhouse, where my off-Broadway *Godot* had been
playing for eight months—with four or five complete reversals of each of the
roles, constant administrative and artistic crises of every sort, even occasional
difficulties with such psychological matters as the state of the plumbing and
the efficiency of the air conditioning (not to mention lesser matters, like the
roof leaking), and total suspension of royalties to playwright, director and
designer because of declining grosses (the theatre owners, the company manager and the press agent, of course, being more essential to the production,
continued to get paid); and most recently not a single understudy, because the
management, even though it was making a fortune with another production

at the same time, refused to add to the weekly outlay. Can you picture a stage manager going on to play the blind Pozzo—holding a book? Ours did one evening.

The sender of that script, besides being a playwright of some promise, was clearly a romantic idealist and therefore to be cherished. For the Sheridan Square Playhouse not only has no office space of any kind, executive or otherwise, it has barely enough space to contain and costume the actors. Dressing-rooms off-Broadway, and sometimes even on Broadway, are considered to be luxuries not necessities; ask Kate Reid what would have happened in hers at the Longacre if she took a deep breath while a visitor was present. Nor have I ever had any kind of office in a New York theatre (the new regional playhouses sometimes offer some version of such an amenity, in those cases where the Artistic Director has been able to sneak them into the plans while the architect was dozing); although producers sometimes have offices of their own where, while the casting or the reading of scripts took place, I have occasionally been allowed a desk drawer (if not an entire desk) and a telephone (so long as I made no long-distance calls).

The Bottom of the Ladder

The ordinary director, far from being the star of the American theatre, is, like the playwright, the actor, the assistant stage manager, and for that matter everyone else—except possibly the doorman—an outsider, picked for this one occasion and discarded afterwards. Although the director is, perhaps, more defenceless and vulnerable than the others. It is the director, first of all, who waits all alone somewhere to be asked by someone—with an office—to read a play. A playwright, after all, has a typewriter to keep him company. Nor can the director even audition to show how good he is, as can the actor—although I'm not sure actually which condition is to be the more avidly sought. Anyhow, what's clear is that the director has to wait for an opportunity to direct which can come only after someone has seen him direct, a fairly vicious sort of circle. Also, he tends to get offered only the kind of play that he's just done. My first production in New York was an ordinary family comedy: all I got offered after that was a series of ordinary family comedies. When I wanted to do *Anastasia*, the producer resisted because she thought all I could do was comedy. (I had rarely done comedy before coming to New York.) After *Anastasia*, I got only melodramas or plays with scenes for two women. And so on. Because I've done so many small cast elliptical plays lately (especially Beckett and Albee) most producers assume that I would be terror-stricken with more than four people in the cast. Actually, I would be delighted for a change.

In addition, very few persons with power in the theatre are qualified to differentiate between talent and success. So the director knows that he can only succeed by being successful, not just by doing good work. Therefore, he is doomed to be nervous about not being successful, a synonym for being unemployed. So he either repeats what he's been successful at for as long as possible, usually becoming less successful as he goes along. Or getting more successful, which may turn out to be even worse because he stops being good. Or he remains cautiously inactive for as long as he can survive, always recalling his last success as though it had been yesterday—or becomes dangerously over-active, the danger coming from the theatre's inevitable law of averages and its constant yen for new names and models. That's why our successful directors immediately turn to films.

If and when the director ever gets into rehearsal, he is always the convenient party to blame for whatever mysterious (or not so mysterious) plagues afflict the enterprise. Jehovah, as I recall, sent only ten plagues; but the theatrical gods, being much more imaginative, can afflict a production on its way to Broadway (or even to off-Broadway because plagues, being infectious, have now spread below Fourteenth Street) with hundreds: Nerves, Uncertainty, Tension, Intrigue, Emotions, Egos, Irrationality, Madness, Terror, Hysteria, among others. For instance, the leading lady, after two days rehearsal, calls her agent (who also happens to be the director's agent but the leading lady's salary is much higher so that the agent tends to side with her) to complain that the director has placed her co-star centre stage eleven times in the first act and her stage centre only seven times. If this artistic imbalance is not corrected immediately (regardless of what the text might suggest) she insists on getting another director with greater mathematical ability. Or, the leading man, whose personal draw while slightly above nil happens to be responsible for whatever theatre parties have been sold, even though he has no talent for doing anything but exploiting his personal idiosyncrasies, decides that the director's insistence on dealing with text or motivations is inhibiting his artistic flow—and refuses to go on rehearsing. Or a super-star, who has been eating out of the director's hand for three weeks and lavishing kisses and gold tie-clasps on him as a token of her undying devotion, gets told by her fourth husband at the first run-through that the director is actually engaged in a diabolical plot to destroy her effectiveness and sex appeal; she immediately calls in her previous director to direct her scenes—and the two directors, hers and theirs, spend the next two weeks passing each other silently in the darkened auditorium.

The director, who is in the meantime supposed to be concentrating on higher aesthetic goals related to the demands of the play, or setting a tone and style for the production, or advancing the art of the theatre, usually spends most of his waking (and sleeping) time during the three-and-a-half weeks of rehearsal (seven out of eight hours, though it usually turns out to be five or six because actors get tired in the afternoon) trying to keep that delicate balance among all the forces involved: to mediate between producer and playwright about the cuts, to spar for status with the stars, to soothe the ruffled egos of almost everyone, including the walk-ons, to be all things to all elements, in effect serving as an unlicensed but very much needed psychoanalyst without portfolio, and worrying a lot. I once directed a show in which the leading man kept wandering into my kitchen before dawn each day wearing various combinations of bedraggled pyjamas and bathrobe, for a cup of coffee and a handhold all the weeks we were trying-out, out of town. I wanted to sleep so that I could face what he was doing at rehearsals; he wanted to talk so that we wouldn't be able to rehearse.

Out of Town Opening

Then, finally and unavoidably, you open and those critics out of town tell you the show isn't ready—which is the only reason you went to Baltimore or Philadelphia in the first place. Or if you open in New York to previews and the word-of-mouth turns out to be awful, which is obviously what often happens, of course it's the director's fault. We should have gone to Baltimore but the director didn't want to leave his wife alone, for various reasons. The director hasn't been able to get the playwright to rework that second act scene, or he's gotten him to rework it and it was better before. The possibilities are infinite.

Or the word-of-mouth by some miracle is not bad or even good, which turns out to be equally if not obviously a problem, because everyone tends to get over-confident, and the performances start to deteriorate. Or an agent or a brother-in-law comes in and tells one of the actors that he's going to be a big star on this one no matter what happens to the show—and then that particular actor becomes impossible to deal with. And so on. Everything that's possible suddenly becomes necessary.

The idea that rehearsals of all plays should have a fixed limit of what amounts in practice to be 20 to 24 days (that is allowing one day off each week for everyone to worry and shop for groceries), with a maximum of four weeks —five in cases of certain special magnitude—although it's Actors' Equity and not the director who defines that magnitude—is ridiculous enough; after all, some plays might need more and some might subsist or even be improved with less. (*Virginia Woolf,* incidentally, was rehearsed for only two weeks and two days, plus ten previews, because one of its performers was unavailable until a certain date, while our theatre had to be taken and paid for as of another date.) What is even more frustrating is the stupidity of not being able to rehearse with either the setting or the properties without incurring exorbitant stage-hand expenses, which means that you don't get to use the props. This stupidity is compounded by the allowable presence of rehearsal props (like paper cups for real cups and wooden sticks for swords), some of which tend to be very similar to the real props, depending upon the cooperativeness and ingenuity —and convenience—of the prop man, who is usually a genial fellow, extremely anxious to please. So you wind up using a real telephone as the frying pan, and a real frying pan as the telephone. But woe betide you if you use the real phone as a real phone because then you'll have to put on a full crew. Or, if you are in Baltimore and trying to rehearse in the second setting of a three-set play, you will wind up rehearsing in the lobby while that second-act setting remains tantalizingly within reach but light years away from use.

Pressures of Time

Eventually, as it must to all directors, there comes a day at the end of all those weeks when 'they' have to move the physical setting in. Furniture, chosen and viewed at various hurried times and in various underlit places, doesn't always fit together (but then neither do the actors, who have had to be assembled and auditioned separately because of Equity regulations). Never mind, you are too busy reeling from the blows of the technical confusions to make changes now. Later maybe, 'we'll see.' And without anyone but the director knowing it, you wind up getting used to what you started out with. Is there ever time to try something else, to sample other possibilities or hopes, even to change the wallpaper a bit because in spite of what the designer said, it does tend to stand out? You've read somewhere about how the Berliner Ensemble once discovered that its masks or costumes or something were all wrong on *Arturo Ui*, and started all over again; does that ever happen in our capitalist/materialist society? It doesn't to me, although I've heard tales whispered of sets entirely redone, costumes altered, even money spent. Oh, yes, I remember that on *Virginia Woolf* we actually got another sofa because the one we had was much too large. But the change brought on a major crisis and was only resolved, as I remember, by one of the producers buying the offending sofa for his own personal use at the price we had paid for it. Obviously, a very astute gentleman and a fine producer.

Nor is there ever enough time within those portions of the one or two days allotted to technical rehearsals in which to do more than make sure everything is nailed down and rendered roughly usable by the actors—and then to get on to the lighting. 'We'll improve things later'; although 'later' rarely if ever comes. And the lighting is, of course, not finished in those two days, just sketched in—partly because the equipment, temporary and rented and hastily thrown together is left over from another century, and partly because lighting is always done while everyone wanders about the stage except the actors. Just as sound levels are always tested while someone is doing some hammering. The idea theoretically is that lights will continue to be refined all during the previews or out of town performances; although in practice, since lighting rehearsals require the presence and cost of complete crews, you rarely if ever get them again. So that whatever improvements or changes are to be made, have to be 'winged,' that is sneaked in *ad lib*, improvised, thrown in hurriedly at odd moments such as the period between 'half hour' and curtain. As with every other part of the production process, ends become subverted by means, changed drastically in order to accommodate the means, and eventually entirely lost or forgotten—except later in retrospect.

First Night Critics

And then, in spite of everything, the day comes, the play opens; and the Herculean labours of weeks or months or even years (the playwright's) rest on the throw of an unmarked but nevertheless loaded (in more ways than one) set of dice: the critics. You never know, not even five minutes beforehand, what they are going to say except that they'll tend to miss the most important things and concentrate on what is unimportant. You do know that if it's a serious play, which is what I tend to direct, all that has to happen is for whoever is reviewing for *The New York Times* that week to turn his critical thumb slightly downwards—or even not to be energetic enough in turning it upwards—and the closing notice will be visible by the end of the week, if not tomorrow. You also know, by experience, that a play at which preview audiences have roared for weeks doesn't get more than a few scattered chuckles opening night because the orchestra floor is jammed with working press all too busy judging and writing down things in the dark to laugh—and the following morning the director gets blamed for not having a sense of humour. Worse almost, you know that a play which has got a reasonably warm response though nothing special during previews will, once the rave notices saying 'delicious hit comedy' are out, get gales of laughter and applause on every funny line, including one like 'Good morning, so there you are.' I once got reviewed on the sound of the radiator pipes clanging backstage; the pipes got better notices than the play, which happened to be Beckett's *Endgame*. You know that any resemblance between success in this system and quality is generally purely coincidental. My best work as a director has usually run a couple of weeks— see *Play* and *The Lover* and *Entertaining Mr. Sloane* and one or two others.

Other little quirks along the way, professional aberrations rarely written about in the Sunday drama sections:

> *The basic problem of filling the day while you're not working, or rather working harder looking for work. Working in an absolute vacuum. Waiting for that* Godot *of a play to come along. What do you do while you're waiting? How do you fill in the day, the month, the year?*

> *The profusion of actors and the impossibility each time of getting the actors you need. If life is a brief flash between twin eternities of darkness, the actor's life consists of a brief appearance between being unknown and becoming unavailable. (Dustin Hoffman, Stacy Keach, Paul Benedict, and a host of others.)*

> *Good unemployed actors turning down perfectly good but smallish roles for reasons of career status—to make their living in television soap operas or commercials. Then they complain that there is no work, or that the British actors are taking all the parts. I recall Glenn Anders, one of the greatest of them all, almost seventy at the time, taking a small part after some 50 or 60 actors had been offered it, and making it into the high spot of the production.*

The arguments over billing: I've never alienated or lost an actor because of salary disagreements but often over the location and size of his name —or his dressing room or his place in the curtain call.

The pressure on everybody and everything to be 'successful' at all costs, always bigger and better than the last time. Always sensational, socko, terrific. Why hasn't Edward Albee, for example, the right to come up with a good play once in a while instead of a great one?

Those smelly dirty stage-door alleys, the dust and airlessness onstage under the glare of that monster work-light. (Why do actors complain about everything else to their union but that!) The theatre, that 'dwelling place of wonder' is often not only a pigsty but an untended urinal.

The long dark tunnel you enter the moment you start on rehearsals; all the director does is work with the actors eight hours a day, spend the rest of the day rewriting, re-casting, re-arguing, begging, dying, gulping down some food, and sleeping once in a while. How much more productive if there were time to think or walk or listen to music or visit an art gallery or read a book. Why not a four-hour rehearsal day spread over a longer period of time?

Finally, a small matter but galling: we never take real production photographs of our plays, so that posterity—or our European friends—never get to see a proper record of the performance the way our audiences saw it. In order to meet various deadlines set by management or the publicity department, we always have to take the photos before the sets and props and costumes are ready; we improvize and shoot, and there it is forever. And we always choose what we shoot and how we shoot it not because it looks interesting or tells us something about the show but because it suits the topographical or typographical requirements of the New York Daily News. *I have marvellous production photographs of every show I've ever done outside of New York—and practically nothing from Broadway except a bunch of glossy closeups.*

Brutish Life in the Theatre

The real evil in the way we work is ultimately psychological rather than physical. Our lives in the theatre are, in Hobbes' words, 'nasty, brutish, short.' But what we lack most is that which might be called a sense of being involved within some purpose or process that extends beyond our own personal needs and ambitions, of being part of a larger theatre community. Not just having lunch together at Sardi's to be noticed or envied. Not only having greater opportunity to be involved with the same people, actors and staff, over and over again in productions, as the British do; most directors, after all, hate our system of one-shots enough constantly to seek out the people they know; but the feeling that we are all part of one organism, whose health and well-being depends on all of us. We know how to compete but not how to co-operate.

Too Big and Sprawling

Maybe it's just that the New York theatre, like the city itself, is just too big and sprawling, too individualistic and selfish. Maybe it's just so hard for each of us that there is no time or space to consider somebody else. There are dozens of first-rate theatre artists with whom I have never been associated or even met; many of those I have met are interested in me only when I am successful or in the public eye. Nor is it easy to meet other theatre people if you are not at the moment involved with them professionally, nor to hang on to their company after the show has closed. One is constantly meeting new people and forgetting old ones with whom one has been working very closely. If I am sufficiently interested in a play or a production to see it before its official opening, I have to hide in a corner because anyone who sees me there automatically assumes I'm 'taking over' the production. If I come after a show has been running a while, the inevitable response is that I'm probably there to steal an actor—or a piece of business. Motives are always distrusted, I know. Several times, well known directors of the motion picture versions of plays I did on the stage came to see the stage performances over and over again, and took notes. They never even bothered to write me a note to thank me. As my union informs me sadly, stage business is not yet copyrighted.

Were I to see a show and afterwards write a friendly but critical letter to the director in order to help him, as say Arnold Wesker did once after he saw Peter Brook's version of *US*, in preview—because he liked it but thought Brook had missed some essential elements—ulterior motives of some kind would immediately be ascribed. I've had directors even get nervous at Workshop sessions when they saw me going up to the playwright of the evening to congratulate him on his work. And so it goes. We're all in it only for ourselves. No one understands, as did that marvellous man, George Devine of the Royal Court, that after we do indeed get rid of our desire to exhibit ourselves, the creation of 'conditions in theatre' is the only thing worth doing. But not enough people really believe that or care. In our theatres, as on the streets outside, we are all too busy fighting and hating, pushing and shoving, ever to look at each other and remember that we all live in the same place and are one.

And of course we are beginning to see that there is another way, to see the possibility of this old worn-out pattern of selfishness and hostility vanishing from our lives. Mostly, it is the younger people who see this, but then there are many ways of being young. Both spontaneously and with great deliberation; from dissatisfaction as well as from positive faith that sees theatre as always greater than the sum of its individual sections or parts, a variety of new kinds of theatre is emerging. 'Ensembles' of one kind or another, 'free theatres,' collectives, 'street theatres,' new theatre places and new theatre ideas. Some of them are already known: La Mama is ten years old, the Open Theatre and the Public Theatre and the Negro Ensemble Company only a few years younger. Others, some not so well known: the Chelsea Theatre Centre in Brooklyn, the Company Theatre in Los Angeles, El Teatro Campesino, the New Lafayette. They are all striving through their own special techniques and feelings to find a better way of people coming together and creating the experience and excitement of theatre together. Some of them will fail and disappear, some of them are already succeeding and becoming subject to the very pressures and corruptions they have been struggling against. But their reasons for existing are very much there and steadily intensifying.

What is clear is that we are all dissatisfied. Not only directors but almost everyone in the theatre, with the possible exception of the hacks and the business men who happen to have a hit going for them at the moment. We have only two choices, that of leaving the theatre—which a great many of us are contemplating doing at the moment, either for the groves of Academe or the graves of Hollywood—or that of making the theatre over in some grander and less self-seeking image.

In the meantime, we go on.

8

THE DESIGNER AND THEATRICAL SPACE

◆   . . . an artist of occasions . . .   . . . House of
Dreams . . .   . . . arrives at a vision . . .
. . . three dimensional space . . .   . . . associative
value of light . . .   . . . visual statement . . .
. . . drama of the body . . .   . . . make a show
with clothes . . .   . . . illusion of reality . . .
. . . catch the eye . . .   . . . organic production process . . .
. . . visual interpreter . . .   . . . bathed in the
moving lights . . .   . . . open space . . .

Robert Edmond Jones
To a Young Stage Designer

ROBERT EDMOND JONES (1887–1954) was the first American scene designer to achieve international renown. In fact, his settings for *The Man Who Married a Dumb Wife* (1915) are generally considered the beginnings of modern stage design in the U.S.A. In 1941 Jones wrote a wise book entitled *The Dramatic Imagination.* The chapter included here is still thought to be an unrivaled expression of what is involved with the designer's art.

> *Beauty is the purgation of superfluities.* —Michelangelo

> *Behind the words and movements, imperturbable, withdrawn, slumbered a strange smoldering power.* —Henry Brocken

◆ A stage designer is, in a very real sense, a jack-of-all trades. He can make blueprints and murals and patterns and lightplots. He can design fireplaces and bodices and bridges and wigs. He understands architecture, but is not an architect: can paint a portrait, but is not a painter: creates costumes, but is not a couturier. Although he is able to call upon any or all of these varied gifts at will, he is not concerned with any one of them to the exclusion of the others, nor is he interested in any one of them for its own sake. These talents are only the tools of his trade. His real calling is something quite different. He is *an artist of occasions.*

Every play—or rather, every performance of a play—is an occasion, and this occasion has its own characteristic quality, its own atmosphere, so to speak. It is the task of the stage designer to enhance and intensify this characteristic quality by every means in his power. The mastery of this special art demands not only a mastery of many diverse techniques but a temperament that is peculiarly sensitive to the atmosphere of a given occasion, just as the temperament of a musician is peculiarly sensitive to the characteristic qualities of a musical composition. Stage designers, like musicians, are born and not made. One is aware of atmospheres or one isn't, just as one has a musical ear or one hasn't.

A stage setting has no independent life of its own. Its emphasis is directed toward the performance. In the absence of the actor it does not exist. Strange as it may seem, this simple and fundamental principle of stage design still seems to be widely misunderstood. How often in critics' reviews one comes upon the phrase "the settings were gorgeous!" Such a statement, of course, can mean only one thing, that no one concerned with producing the drama has thought of it as an organic whole. I quote from a review recently published in one of our leading newspapers, "Of all the sets of the season, the only true scenic surprise was . . ." The only true scenic surprise, indeed! Every stage designer worth his salt outgrew the idea of scenic surprises years ago. If the critics only knew how easy it is to make a scenic surprise in the theatre! Take two turntables, a great deal of—But no. Why give away the formula? It is not surprise that is wanted from the audience; it is delighted and trusting acceptance. The surprise inherent in a stage setting is only a part of the greater surprise inherent in the event itself.

And yet a stage setting holds a curious kind of suspense. Go, for instance, into an ordinary empty drawing-room as it exists normally. There is no particular suspense about this room. It is just—empty. Now imagine the same drawing-room arranged and decorated for a particular function—a Christmas party for children, let us say. It is not completed as a room, now, until the children are in it. And if we wish to visualize for ourselves how important a part the sense of expectancy plays in such a room, let us imagine that there is a storm and that the children cannot come. A scene on the stage is filled with the same feeling of expectancy. It is like a mixture of chemical elements held in solution. The actor adds the one element that releases the hidden energy of the whole. Meanwhile, wanting the actor, the various elements which go to make up the setting remain suspended, as it were, in an indefinable tension. To create this suspense, this tension, is the essence of the problem of stage designing.

The designer must strive to achieve in his settings what I can only call a high potential. The walls, the furniture, the properties are only the facts of a setting, only the outline. The truth is in everything but these objects, in the space they enclose, in the intense vibration they create. They are fused into a kind of embodied impulse. When the curtain rises we feel a frenzy of excitement focused like a burning-glass upon the stage. Everything on the stage becomes a part of the life of the instant. The play becomes a part of the life of the instant. The terrible and wonderful dynamic of the theatre pours over the footlights.

A strange, paradoxical calling, to work always behind and around, to bring into being a powerful non-being. How far removed it all is from the sense of display! One is reminded of the portraits of the Spanish noblemen painted by El Greco in the Prado in Madrid, whose faces, as Arthur Symons said, are all nerves, distinguished nerves, quieted by an effort. What a phrase for stage designers to remember! *Quieted by an effort. . . .*

It is to the credit of our designers that they have almost made a fetish of abnegation. But let me remark parenthetically that it is sometimes difficult to go into the background when there is nothing in front of you. These pages are hardly the place in which to perpetuate the centuries-old squabble between playwrights and stage designers begun by peevish old Ben Jonson, who scolded Inigo Jones so roundly for daring to make his productions beautiful and exciting to look at. This kind of petty jealousy makes sorry reading even when recorded in verse by the great Ben himself. It is enough to say that the jealousy still persists and is as corroding in the twentieth century as it was in the seventeenth. The error lies in our conception of the theatre as something set aside for talents that are purely literary. As if the experience of the theatre had only to do with words! Our playwrights need to learn that plays are wrought, not written. There is something to be said in the theatre in terms of form and color and light that can be said in no other way.

The designer must learn to sense the atmosphere of a play with unusual clearness and exactness. He must actually live in it for a time, immerse himself in it, be baptized by it. This process is by no means so easy as it seems. We are all too apt to substitute ingenuity for clairvoyance. The temptation to invent is always present. I was once asked to be one of the judges of a competition of stage designs held by the Department of Drama of one of our well-known universities. All the designers had made sketches for the same play. The setting was the interior of a peasant hut on the west coast of Ireland. It turned out that these twenty or thirty young designers had mastered the technique of using dimmers and sliding stages and projected scenery. They had also acquired a considerable amount of information concerning the latest European developments of stagecraft. Their drawings were full of constructivism from Russia, every kind of modernism. They were compilations of everything that had been said and done in the world of scenery in the last twenty years. But not one of the designers had sensed the atmosphere of the particular play in question.

I recalled for them my memory of the setting for the same play as produced by the Abbey Theatre on its first visit to America. This setting was very simple, far simpler and far less self-conscious than any of their designs. Neutral-tinted walls, a fireplace, a door, a window, a table, a few chairs, the red homespun skirts and bare feet of the peasant girls. A fisher's net, perhaps. Nothing more. But through the little window at the back one saw a sky of enchantment. All the poetry of Ireland shone in that little square of light, moody, haunting, full of dreams, calling us to follow on. . . . By this one gesture of excelling simplicity the setting was enlarged into the region of great theatre art.

Now here is a strange thing, I said to the designers. If we can succeed in seeing the essential quality of a play others will see it, too. We know the truth when we see it, Emerson said, from opinion, as we know that we are awake when we are awake. For example: you have never been in Heaven, and you have never seen an angel. But if someone produces a play about angels whose scenes are laid in Heaven you will know at a glance whether his work is right or wrong. Some curious intuition will tell you. The sense of recognition is the highest experience the theatre can give. As we work we must seek not for self-expression or for performance for its own sake, but only to establish the dramatist's intention, knowing that when we have succeeded in doing so audiences will say to themselves, not, This is beautiful, This is charming, This is splendid, but—This is true. This is the way it is. So it is, and not otherwise.

. . . There is nothing esoteric in the search for truth in the theatre. On the contrary, it is a part of the honest everyday life of the theatre.

The energy of a particular play, its emotional content, its aura, so to speak, has its own definite physical dimensions. It extends just so far in space and no farther. The walls of the setting must be placed at precisely this point. If the setting is larger than it should be, the audience gets a feeling of meagerness and hollowness; if smaller, a feeling of confusion and pressure. It is often very difficult to adjust the physical limits of a setting to its emotional limitations. But great plays exist outside the categories of dimension. Their bounty is as boundless as the air. Accordingly we need not think of a stage-setting, in a larger sense, as a matter of establishing space relations. Great plays have nothing to do with space. The setting for a great play is no more subject to the laws of space composition than music is. We may put aside once and for all the idea of a stage-setting as a glorified show-window in which actors are to be exhibited and think of it instead as a kind of symphonic accompaniment or obbligato to the play, as evocative and intangible as music itself. Indeed, music may play a more important role than we now realize in the scenic evocations of the future.

In the last analysis the designing of stage scenery is not the problem of an architect or a painter or a sculptor or even a musician, but of a poet. By a poet I do not mean, of course, an artist who is concerned only with the writing of verse. I am speaking of the poetic attitude. The recognized poet, Stedman says, is one who gives voice in expressive language to the common thought and feeling which lie deeper than ordinary speech. I will give you a very simple illustration. Here is a fragment of ordinary speech, a paraphrase of part of Hamlet's soliloquy, *To be or not to be:* I wish I were dead! I wish I could go to sleep and never wake up! But I'm afraid of what might happen afterward. Do people dream after they are dead? . . . But Hamlet does not express himself in this way. He says, *To die, to sleep; to sleep, perchance to dream: ay, there's the rub; for in that sleep of death what dreams may come,* . . . Here are two ways of saying the same thing. The first is prose. The second is poetry. Both of them are true. But Shakespeare's way—the poetic way— is somehow deeper and higher and truer and more universal. In this sense we may fairly speak of the art of stage designing as poetic, in that it seeks to give expression to the essential quality of a play rather than to its outward characteristics.

Some time ago one of the younger stage designers was working with me on the scenes of an historical play. In the course of the production we had to design a tapestry, which was to be decorated with figures of heraldic lions. I sent him to the library to hunt up old documents. He came back presently with many sketches, copies of originals. They were all interesting enough, but somehow they were not right. They lacked something that professionals call "good theatre." They were not *theatrical.* They were accurate and—lifeless.

I said as much to the designer. "Well, what shall we do about it?" he asked me. "We have got to stop copying," I said. "We must try something else. We must put our imaginations to work. Let us think now. Not about what this heraldic lion ought to look like, but what the design meant in the past, in the Middle Ages.

"Perhaps Richard, the Lion-Heart, carried this very device emblazoned on his banner, as he marched across Europe on his way to the Holy Land. Richard, the Lion-Heart, *Coeur de Lion . . .* what memories of childhood this name conjures up, what images of chivalry! Knights in armor, enchanted castles, magic casements, perilous seas, oriflammes, gonfalons. Hear the great battle-cries! See the banners floating through the smoke! *Coeur de Lion, the Crusader, with his singing page Blondel. . . . Do* you remember Blondel's song, the song he sang for three long years while he sought his master in prison? 'O Richard, O mon Roi! L'univers t'abandonne! . . .'

"And now your imagination is free to wander, if you will allow it to do so, among the great names of romance. Richard, the Lion-Heart, King Arthur, Sir Percival and the mystery of the Holy Grail, the Song of Roland, the magic sword, Durandal, Tristan and Isolde, the love-potion, the chant of the Cornish sailors, the ship with the black sail; the Lady Nicolette of whom Aucassin said, *Beau venir et bel aller,* lovely when you come, lovely when you go; the demoiselle Aude, who died for love; the Lady Christabel; the Ancient Mariner with the Albatross hung about his neck; the Cid, Charlemagne, Barbarossa, the Tartar, Kubla Khan, who decreed the pleasure-dome in Xanadu, in the poem Coleridge heard in a dream. . . . And there are the legendary cities, too, Carcassonne, Granada, Torcello; Samarkand, the Blue City, with its façades of turquoise and lapis lazuli; Carthage, Isfahan, Trebizond; and there are the places which have never existed outside a poet's imagination—Hy Brasil, Brocéliande, the Land of Luthany, the region Elenore, the Isle of Avalon, *where falls not hail, or rain, or any snow, where ever King Arthur lyeth sleeping as in peace. . . .* And there is the winged Lion of St. Mark in Venice with the device set forth fairly beneath it, *Pax Tibi, Marce, Evangelista Meus;* and there are the mounted knights in the windows of Chartres, riding on, riding on toward Our Lady as she bends above the high altar in her glory of rose.

"These images of romance have come to our minds—all of them—out of this one little symbol of the heraldic lion. They are dear to us. They can never fade from our hearts.

"Let your fancy dwell and move among them in a kind of revery. Now in this mood, with these images bright in your mind, draw your figure of the lion once more.

"This new drawing is different. Instead of imitating, describing what the artists of the Middle Ages thought a lion looked like, it summons up an image of medieval romance. Perhaps without knowing it I have stumbled on a definition of art in the theatre; all art in the theatre should be, not descriptive, but evocative. Not a description, but an evocation. A bad actor describes a character; he explains it. He expounds it. A good actor evokes a character. He summons it up. He reveals it to us. . . . This drawing is evocative. Something about it brings back memories of medieval love-songs and crusades and high adventures. People will look at it without knowing why. In this drawing of a lion—only a detail in a magnificent, elaborate setting—there will be a quality which will attract them and disturb them and haunt them and make them dream. Your feeling is in it. Your interest is in it. You have triumphed over the mechanics of the theatre and for the time being you have become a poet."

The poetic conception of stage design bears little relation to the accepted convention of realistic scenery in the theatre. As a matter of fact it is quite the opposite. Truth in the theatre, as the masters of the theatre have always known, stands above and beyond mere accuracy to fact. In the theatre the actual thing is never the exciting thing. Unless life is turned into art on the stage it stops being alive and goes dead.

So much for the realistic theatre. *The artist should omit the details, the prose of nature and give us only the spirit and splendor.* When we put a star in a sky, for example, it is not just a star in a sky, but a "supernal messenger, excellently bright." This is purely a question of our point of view. A star is, after all, only an electric light. The point is, how the audience will see it, what images it will call to mind. We read of Madame Pitoeff's Ophelia that in the Mad Scene she handled the roses and the rosemary and the rue as if she were in a Paradise of flowers. We must bring into the immediate life of the theatre —"the two hours' traffic of our stage"—images of a larger life. The stage we inhabit is a chamber of the House of Dreams. Our work on this stage is to suggest the immanence of a visionary world all about us. In this world Hamlet dwells, and Oedipus, and great Juno, known by her immortal gait, and the three witches on the blasted heath. We must learn by a deliberate effort of the will to walk in these enchanted regions. We must imagine ourselves into their vastness.

Here is the secret of the flame that burns in the work of the great artists of the theatre. They seem so much more aware than we are, and so much more awake, and so much more alive that they make us feel that what we call living is not living at all, but a kind of sleep. Their knowledge, their wealth of emotion, their wonder, their elation, their swift clear seeing surrounds every occasion with a crowd of values that enriches it beyond anything which we, in our happy satisfaction, had ever imagined. In their hands it becomes not only a thing of beauty but a thing of power. And we see it all—beauty and power alike—as part of the life of the theatre.

Ming Cho Lee
What Does a Scenic Designer Do?

MING CHO LEE (1930–   ) is one of America's most versatile scene designers. At home in opera, dance, television, as well as theatre, his work ranges from the sumptuously elegant to the expressively spare. In this edited transcription of an interview, Lee discusses the basic craft and the day by day procedures of his profession. Like all good designers, he knows that the mastery of craft inevitably stretches the limits of the designer's art.

◆   Designers may not be necessary to a production, but the act of making visual choices, in other words, design, has to be done. There's no way you can get away from it. Even using a theatre without any set is designing because someone has made that choice, realizing that the play will happen in that room. To choose what kind of room, to choose what kind of background, to choose what should be revealed on the empty stage, is designing. That can be done by a director, that can be done by a collaboration between the director and designers, that can be done by the director and the janitor, or the janitor can just do it and you can come in and stage the play. But you cannot avoid it because people do go to a play with their eyes open. They do look at things. The actors have to perform within a physical environment of some kind. And therefore you cannot ignore the fact that you have to make choices. And to make choices in order for this play or this author or this Shakespeare to ultimately become a theatrical event, that area of decision, of organization, is what the designers do.

We are the people who are responsible for the whole visual counterpart of a piece of work that is not visual. We are the visual interpreters. We, as designers, happen to be trained because we know how to draw or we know how to build models, or we are trained to read something and somehow, emotionally or whatever, get a visual imagery—and translate that visual imagery into a physical reality that's called the production. The director is trained to do something else, and it's with the collaboration between the director and the designers that design is done. That's why I say that I don't care who does it, you can't avoid it.

Aside from what is given in raw material, whether it's an old play or a new play or an old opera or a new opera or ballet, no one has a concrete idea about exactly how this work should be done. A director reads a play or listens to a piece of music and reacts by saying 'I think the emotional value is such, I think the metaphor of the play is this, I think the play is about this.' With that, there are many ways to approach it, and the designer is someone who translates that kind of guidance into visual terms. It's a process of evolving.

Usually designers get the director's feelings first. Sometimes a designer talks about his or her feelings about the work. Usually it's give and take, but it is the director who is going to make sure that the actors and the singers and everything becomes a unified whole. The director's feelings are sometime paramount. Unless you can work along his approach, or his sense of the work, then perhaps you shouldn't do that play. Quite often there are many ways of looking at a piece of work, and if you see what he (the director) is saying, and you find it a possibility, then you go along with him. Sometimes his feeling may not be that certain so it's a combination of the two.

Very few designers do a lot of drawings before talking to the director. Usually, if you do drawings, you will be very apologetic about it, explaining 'I read this play and I can't help but feel that it looks a certain way.' Occasionally the director will do some drawings, and will also be very apologetic, saying 'I can't help but feel it's that way, but don't take it literally,' and so forth. Essentially it's a matter of how the director and the designer make their feelings about a non-visual piece of work as clear as possible, so that there isn't a mishap or misunderstanding in the process of evolving toward a total production.

It's not like seeing through someone else's eyes. Let's take HAMLET. The director can talk about an emotional value in HAMLET, for instance. I did a HAMLET at the Arena Stage for Liviu Ciulei. He is also an excellent designer. He felt that HAMLET is about the end of a kingdom, and that true monarchies did not exist around the Renaissance, so that essentially it's a play that has to be set during the end of the Age of Kings. He felt that he understood the end of the 19th century better than the Renaissance or pre-Renaissance. He also felt that he would like to approach the play with a very specific human behavior, rather than the typical Renaissance posturing, the typical Shakespearean reading of the famous lines, and so forth. He wondered whether we should shift the period to the end of the 19th century, since he considered that WWI was about to happen, and that it was the end of a period. But he was worried that when you shift periods, sometimes Shakespeare rebels. For me it was quite clear that it would be a wonderful way to try it. He said he was thinking that it should happen on an island, and so I did some drawings. I took the stage floor out and, using the pit, built an island. Before I knew it I was designing the underground and I felt that the top of the floor, the island, would be very, very sophisticated, a very polished, black, shiny floor, but underneath would be all the bricks, vaulting, and so forth. It's all the corruption underneath and what goes on above is all posturing attitude. We looked at pictures of various people of the period, we bought books from Germany and Austria, and eventually we evolved the set. It's like trying to see together rather than trying to see someone else's vision, because someone else's vision is never that clear. The designer only, ultimately, arrives at a vision by thinking about it, doing some drawings, and letting the director react. Sometimes it's through drawings that you begin to evolve the idea and you begin to find the reason that it's that way.

The whole theatre world is essentially an act of collaboration. It's not somebody trying to sell somebody else an idea, someone else trying to impose an idea. Sometimes imposition happens, but still it is really a collaboration evolved into a concrete physical item from something that's non-physical, non-visual to begin with.

Designers work in different ways, but usually we will read the play and have our first meeting with the director. Various people react differently. Some people will read the play simply like an audience, some people—after reading the play—may gather general research materials or pictures or things that somehow reflect the play. Then we will sit down and talk about everyone's feelings. Certain choices are made. Do you think it's a realistic play that has to be approached realistically, or do you think that the director thinks that it is not a realistic play, that it should be presented in a Brechtian, epic theatre way, or a presentational way where the audience will know that the actors are actors, they are not trying to see through the fourth wall, and so forth? Certain decisions are made, or at least guidelines are given. Certain physical limitations or physical necessities of the actors need to be talked about. Sometimes some designers will ask what the basic material of the play feels like—is it full of wallpaper, or is it metal structure, or wooden structure, is it really all masonry; how do you feel the physical environment is, or do you feel that it is everything just thrown together to give a statement of Paris or whatever?

Then, after that meeting, if the designer feels that he has enough information and the director feels that the talk has been wonderful, then the designer will start drawing. And then the next step is the designer and the director agreeing on something and the designer will usually make more rough sketches and then we get together again. The director will react to the rough sketches and sometimes pick out a specific approach. The designer will refine that approach. Sometimes it's a dead end and he will leave it alone and push some other approach. Hopefully, by the second or third meeting something feels right to a point where there's a little elevation in the ground plan and so forth. At that step if it seems right, then quite often we will start making a rough model. We draw it and then we make models so that instead of just looking at drawings we can begin to deal with things in three-dimensions in space and three-dimensional reality. We may paint the model, we may finish the model, we may make a bigger model if we have time, and if that is approved by the director, if the director feels he can live with it, he can see how he can start rehearsing with it.

And if the producer likes it and the playwright likes it, then what happens is that we will do our draftings very much like an architect's drawing with everything that we want to show. We don't put in how to build it, but we include things like paneling, the painting on the wall, the chips, everything as clearly as we know how. We will also have estimates from the commercial scenic suppliers. They will come in, get the drawings, and give the producer a price. Then the haggling starts. Perhaps this is too expensive and we have to adjust it. Finally, the shop takes over and builds it and paints it, and the designer will supervise it. When the director starts rehearsing, the designer will try to get the right props with the help of prop men. Ultimately the set gets into the theatre and you see if everything fits together.

At some point, early in the game, the set and costume designer and director usually have to meet so that their approach is similar. And after there are some drawings and sketches and especially models, the lighting designer should come in. It's very difficult for a lighting designer to get in when the idea is not yet formed. The lighting design can only begin when the physical, visual statement has been formulated.

The designer is always in the peculiar position of being the person who spends money not on other people, but on lumber and metal, and people tend to resent that. The designer is always in the middle because they are dealing with the creative group, the director, the playwright, the costume designers, the actors, of which they are a part. But they must also be able to make themselves very clear to the technical craftsmen, and they must also deal directly with the businessmen because the designer's crew is spending money. That's why I don't enjoy working with commercial theatre.

I find institutional theatre much easier to work with because, first of all, the purpose of producing is different. They produce because if they don't produce they will die as an institution. And the reason they want to produce is not only to survive, but also because each production is some kind of renewal, and they have something to say about that play otherwise they wouldn't choose to do it. Commercially, the whole motive of why you're doing it gets confused. Some want to make a pot of money, some want to have something to say, but you need the people who make the pot of money to support the ones who want to say it. The motives get all confused. I find it very straining. Half the time you're really a manipulator, a manager, rather than a designer. It's things like hassels with producers that begin to take the joy out of designing for the commercial stage. Designing for the Met, designing for the Arena Stage, working for Joe Papp, even though the money isn't the best, means that you can feel like you're working as a designer instead of trying to avoid being a victim.

Shakespeare is a joy to do because the visual statement is bigger. It goes beyond the actuality and you get to deal with the very heart of a person while also dealing with the large scale of a time and a period. You can put a whole city on stage—or the statement of it—but in a lot of musical comedy you almost have to reduce that statement, you have to trivialize it, which is not as enjoyable. I have done almost all of Shakespeare. I would love to do another MERCHANT OF VENICE. There are plays in which you can always find new things, something new to say, because they are so rich and hold so many layers of reality. As you grow older you find new perceptions, and those are the works that I don't mind doing four or five times. HAMLET is one of those plays. Quite often when a show or a design is finished, you may have something specific you're not happy with or you feel that you've made the wrong choice, or that something went wrong in the collaboration. I tend to simply say, OK, it's not the best experience, and then get on to something else rather than stew about it.

Adolphe Appia
Light and Space

ADOLPHE APPIA (1862–1928) was a Swiss artist who for many years worked as a designer with Richard Wagner at Bayreuth. His writings on production proved to be revolutionary. Appia's underlying premise was that light should be the guiding principle of all design. He thought of light as an actor in the performance and believed that light alone could be the unifying force among the many contradictory elements of production.

◆ For some years now dramatic art has been in a process of change. Naturalism on the one hand, Wagnerianism on the other, have violently displaced the old landmarks. Certain things which, twenty years ago, were not "of the theater" (to use an absurdly hallowed expression) have almost become commonplace. This has resulted in some confusion: we no longer know to which type a given play belongs; and the fondness we have for foreign productions fails to give us guidance.

This would not, however, create serious difficulties if our stages adapted themselves to every new effort. Unfortunately, this is not the case. The author with his manuscript—or the composer with his score—may be in agreement with the actors; but once on the stage, in the blaze of the footlights, the new idea slips back into its old framework—and our directors ruthlessly cut anything that goes beyond that.

Many assert that it cannot be otherwise, that the conventions of scene design are rigid, etc. I say just the opposite. And in the following pages I have tried to formulate the basic elements of staging which, instead of paralyzing and stifling dramatic art, will not only be faithful to it but will also be a source of inexhaustible suggestion for the playwright and his interpreters.

I trust that the reader will bear with me during this difficult résumé.

Our modern staging is entirely the slave of painting—the painting of sets—which purports to give us the illusion of reality. But this illusion is itself an illusion, because the physical presence of the actor contradicts it. In fact, the principle of the illusion achieved by painting on vertical pieces of canvas ("flats") and that of the illusion achieved by the plastic, living body of the actor are in contradiction. So it is not by developing in isolation the play of these two kinds of illusions—as is done on all our stages—that we shall obtain an integrated and artistic performance.

Let us therefore examine modern stagecraft from these two points of view in turn.

It is impossible to set up on our stages real trees, real houses, etc.; besides, that would hardly be desirable. Hence we feel that we must *imi-*

tate reality as faithfully as possible. But to render things plastically is difficult, often impossible, and in any case very expensive. That forces us, it would seem, to reduce the number of things represented. Our directors, however, are of a different mind. They consider that the stage set must represent anything they want it to; consequently, what cannot be rendered plastically must be painted. Undoubtedly, painting allows one to show the audience a countless number of things. Thus it seems to give to staging a much-sought freedom; so our directors stop right there. But the basic principle of painting is to reduce everything to a flat surface. How then can it fill a three-dimensional space—the stage? Without any attempt to solve the problem, the directors have decided to cut up the painting and to set up these "cut-outs" on the floor of the stage. It means therefore giving up any attempt to paint the lower part of the stage picture; if it is a landscape, for example, the top will be a dome of forest scenery; to the right and left there will be trees; at the rear there will be a horizon and a sky— and at the bottom, the floor of the stage! This painting, which was supposed to represent everything, is forced from the very outset to renounce representing the ground; because the illusory forms it depicts must be presented to us vertically, and *there is no possible relationship* between the vertical flats of the set and the stage floor (or the more or less horizontal canvas covering it). That is why our scene designers cushion the base of the flats.

So the ground cannot be reproduced by painting. But that is precisely where the actor moves! Our directors have forgotten the actor: they want to produce a *Hamlet* without Hamlet! Are they willing to sacrifice a bit of the dead painting in favor of the living, moving body of the actor? Never! They would rather give up the theater! But since it is nonetheless necessary to take into account this quite living body, painting consents to place itself here and there at the actor's disposition. At times it even grows generous, although by so doing it looks quite ridiculous; at other times, however, when it has refused to yield a single inch, it is the actor who becomes ridiculous. The antagonism is complete.

We have begun with painting. Now let us see what direction the problem would take if we began with the actor, with the plastic, moving human body, seen solely from the point of view of its effect on the stage— as we have done with stage setting.

An object becomes plastic for our eyes only by the light that strikes it—and its plasticity cannot be artistically produced except by an artistic use of light. That is self-evident. So much for form. The movement of the human body requires obstacles in order to express itself; all artists know that the beauty of the body's movements depends on the variety of the points of support afforded by the ground and other objects. The actor's mobility cannot therefore be improved artistically except by an integrated relationship with other objects and the ground.

Hence the two basic conditions for an artistic presentation of the human body on the stage are: lighting that brings out its plasticity, and a harmonizing with the setting which brings out its attitudes and movements. Here we are a long way from painting indeed!

Dominated by painted sets, the *décor* sacrifices the actor and, more than that, as we have seen, a good deal of its pictorial effect, since it must cut up the painting. This is contrary to the essential principle of the art of painting. Moreover, the stage floor cannot share in the illusion offered by the flats. But what would happen if we subordinated it to the actor!

First of all, we would make lighting free again! As a matter of fact, under the domination of the painted set, the lighting is completely absorbed by the *décor*. The things represented on the flats must be *seen:* so lights are lit and shadows are painted. . . . Alas! It is from this kind of lighting that the actor must take what he can get! Under such conditions it cannot be a question either of true lighting or of any plastic effect whatever! Lighting in itself is an element the effects of which are limitless; once it is freed, it becomes for us what the palette is for the painter. All the color combinations become possible. By simple or complex searchlights, stationary or moving, by partial obstruction, by different degrees of transparency, etc., we can achieve infinite modulations. Lighting thus gives us a means of externalizing in some way most of the colors and forms that painting freezes on the canvas and of distributing them dynamically in space. The actor no longer walks *in front of* painted lights and shadows; he is immersed in an atmosphere *that is destined for him.* Artists will be quick to grasp the scope of such a reform.[1]

Now comes the crucial point: the plasticity in the *décor* necessary for the actor's harmony of attitudes and movements. Painting has gained the upper hand on our stages, replacing everything that could not be realized plastically, and it has done this with the sole aim of giving the illusion of reality.

But are the images it piles up thus on the vertical flats indispensable? Not at all: there is not one play that needs even a hundredth part of them. For note this well: these images are not living, they are *indicated* on the canvas like a kind of hieroglyphic language. They *signify* only the things they purport to represent—and all the more so because they cannot enter into real, organic contact with the actor.

The plasticity required by the actor aims at an entirely different effect: the human body does not seek to produce the illusion of reality *since it is itself reality!* What it demands of the *décor* is simply to set in relief this reality. This results inevitably in a shift in the aim of the stage set: in the one case it is the real appearance of *objects* that is sought; in the other, it is the highest possible degree of reality of the human body.

Since these two principles are technically opposed, it is a question of choosing one or the other. Is it to be the accumulation of dead images and

---

[1] A well-known artist in Paris, Mariano Fortuny, has invented a completely new system of lighting, based on the properties of *reflected light.* The results have been extraordinarily successful —and this far-reaching invention will bring about a radical transformation in staging in all the theaters . . . in favor of lighting.

decorative richness on the vertical flats, or is it to be the spectacle of the human being in all its plastic and mobile manifestations?

Can there be any possible hesitation in our answer? Let us ask ourselves what we are looking for in the theater. We have beautiful painting elsewhere, and fortunately not cut up. Photography allows us to sit in our armchair and view the whole world; literature evokes the most fascinating pictures in our imagination; and very few people are so devoid of feeling that they are not able from time to time to contemplate a beautiful sight in nature. We come to the theater in order to witness a dramatic *action.* It is the presence of the characters on the stage that motivates this action; without the characters there is no action. So it is the actor who is the essential factor in staging; it is he whom we come to *see,* it is from him that we expect the emotion, and it is for this emotion that we have come. Hence it is above all a question of basing our staging on the actor's presence. To do this, we must free staging of everything that is in contradiction with the actor's presence.

This, then, is the way we must frankly pose the technical problem.

Some may object that this problem has at times been rather successfully solved on several of our Paris stages—at the Théâtre Antoine, for example, or elsewhere. No doubt; but why has this always happened with the same type of plays and settings? How would those directors go about staging *Troilus and Cressida* or *The Tempest, The Ring of the Nibelung* or *Parsifal?* (At the Grand Guignol Théâtre, they are adept at showing us a concierge's lodging; but what happens, for example, when they want to depict a garden?)

Our staging has two distinct sources: opera and the spoken drama. Up to now, with very few exceptions, opera singers have been considered glorified machines for singing, and the painted set has been the outstanding feature of the spectacle. Hence its impressive development. The evolution of the spoken play has been different: the actor of necessity comes first, since without him there is no play; and if the director occasionally feels that he has to borrow some of the trappings of opera, he does so prudently and without losing sight of the actor. (Let the reader compare in his memory the decorative effect of such a lavish play production as *Theodora* with that of any opera.) Yet the principle of stage illusion remains the same for the spoken play as for the opera, and it is that principle which is the most seriously violated. Besides, dramatists are well acquainted with two or three combinations in which modern staging can achieve a little illusion despite the presence of the actor; and so they never venture beyond them.

During the last few years, however, things have changed. With the Wagnerian music-dramas, opera has come closer to the spoken play, and the latter (apart from the plays of naturalism) has sought to overcome its former limitations, to come nearer to the music-drama. Then, strangely enough, it turns out that our staging no longer fits the needs of either the one or the other! The ostentatious display that opera makes of painting no longer has anything to do with a Wagner score (the Wagnerian directors, at Bayreuth and elsewhere, do not yet seem to realize this); and the monotony of the settings in the spoken drama no longer satisfies the sharpened insight of the dramatists. Everyone feels the need of a reform, but the power of inertia keeps us in the same old rut.

In such a situation theories are useful, but they do not lead far. We must come directly to grips with stage design and, little by little, transform it.

The simplest method perhaps would be to take one of our plays exactly as it is, *already completely set,* and to see what could be done with its staging if it were based on the principle elaborated above. Of course we would have to choose carefully a play written especially for modern staging, or an opera that adapts itself perfectly to it. The *décors* in our traditional theaters are of no help to us. On the contrary, we must choose a dramatic work whose requirements obviously do not jibe with our present-day means: a play by Maeterlinck, or some other play of the same type, or even a Wagnerian music-drama. The latter is preferable because music, by definitely delimiting the duration and intensity of the emotion, can be a valuable guide. Besides, the sacrifice of illusion would be less conspicuous in a Wagnerian music-drama than in a spoken play. We shall then see everything in the fixed set which runs counter to our efforts; we shall be forced to make concessions that are quite revealing. The question of lighting will concern us first of all: on this point we will have an example of the tyranny of painted flats; and we shall understand—no longer theoretically but in a thoroughly concrete manner—that immense harm still being done to the actor and, by him, to the dramatist.

No doubt that would only be a modest effort; but it is extremely difficult to accomplish such a reform all at once, because it is as much a question of reforming the audience's taste as it is of transforming our staging. Moreover, the results of material and technical work *on ground that is already familiar* are perhaps surer than those arising from a radical reform.

Take, for example, the second act of *Siegfried.* How are we to represent a forest on the stage? First of all, let us be clear as to the following: is it *a forest* with characters, or rather *characters* in a forest? We are at the theater to witness a dramatic action. Something takes place in this forest which apparently cannot be expressed by painting. Here then is our point of departure: So and So does this and that, says this and that, in a forest. To design our set we do not have to try to visualize a forest; but we must depict in detailed and logical sequence everything that takes place in this forest. Hence perfect knowledge of the score is indispensable, and the director's source of inspiration is thus completely different: his eyes must remain *riveted on the characters.* Then if he thinks of the forest, it will be as a kind of special atmosphere surrounding and hovering above the actors—an atmosphere which he can grasp only *in its relation* to the living, moving actors from whom he must not avert his eyes. At no point in his conception, therefore, will the stage picture remain a lifeless arrangement of painting; it will always be alive. In that way the staging becomes the creation of a stage picture in its time-flow. Instead of starting with a painted set ordered by somebody or other from somebody else, with the actor then getting along as best he can with shoddy props, we start with the actor. It is his art we wish to highlight and for which we are ready to sacrifice everything. It will be: Siegfried here and Siegfried there— and never: the tree for Siegfried, the road for Siegfried. I repeat: we no longer seek to give the illusion of *a forest* but that of *a man* in the atmosphere of a forest. Reality here is a man, alongside whom no other illusion matters. Everything this man touches must be part of his destiny—everything else must help create the appropriate atmosphere around him. And if we look away from Siegfried for a moment and raise our eyes, the stage picture does not of necessity have to give us an illusion: the way it is arranged has *only* Siegfried in mind; and when a slight rustling of the trees in the forest attracts Siegfried's attention, we the spectators *will look at Siegfried* bathed in the moving lights and shadows; we will not look at parts of the *décor* set in motion by backstage manipulation.

Scenic illusion is the living presence of the actor.

The setting for this act, as it is now presented to us on stages through-out the world, fails woefully to live up to our conditions. We must simplify it a great deal, give up lighting the painted flats as is now the rule, institute a complete reform in the arrangement of the stage floor and, above all, provide for our lighting by installing a wealth of electrical equipment regulated in great detail. The footlights—that astonishing monstrosity—will hardly be used. Let us add that most of this work of re-creation will be with the characters, and the production will not be finally set until after several rehearsals with the orchestra (indispensable conditions which may now seem exorbitant yet are elementary!).

An attempt along these lines cannot fail to teach us the course to follow in transforming our rigid and conventional staging into living, flexible, and artistic material, suitable for any dramatic creation whatever. We shall even be surprised that we have so long neglected so important a branch of art and have consigned it, as unworthy of our personal attention, to men who are not artists.

As far as staging is concerned, our aesthetic feeling is still in a state of paralysis. A person who would not tolerate in his own apartment an object that was not of the most exquisite taste, finds it quite natural to buy a high-priced seat in a hall that is ugly and built in defiance of good sense, and to sit there for a couple of hours watching a play alongside which the worst chromos from an antique dealer are delicate works of art.

Methods of staging, like methods in the other arts, are based on forms, light, and colors. These three elements are at our disposal; consequently we can use them in the theater, as elsewhere, in an artistic manner. Up to now it was felt that staging should achieve the highest possible degree of illusion —and it is this principle (an unaesthetic principle if ever there was one!) that has paralyzed our efforts. I have endeavored to show in these pages that the art of scene design must be based on the only *reality* worthy of the theater: the human body. We have seen the first and elementary consequences of this reform.

The subject is a difficult and complex one, particularly in view of the misunderstandings surrounding it and the bad habits we have formed from frequenting present-day plays. To be thoroughly convincing, I would have to develop this idea a good deal further. I would have to discuss the brand-new task that is incumbent on the actor; the influence that a flexible and artistic scene design would inevitably exert on the dramatist; the stylizing power of music on a stage production; the changes that will be required in building new stages, new theaters, etc. It is impossible for me to do that here;[2] but perhaps the reader will have found in my aesthetic desire something approaching his own. In that case, it will be easy for him to continue this work by himself.

[*Translated by Joseph M. Bernstein*]

Anne Hollander
Costume

ANNE HOLLANDER (1930–   ) is an art historian with a special interest in costume history and design. Her *Seeing Through Clothes* (1978) is a remarkable book which demonstrates the reciprocity between clothes as depicted in art and the fashions which govern what people wear. Theatrical costume is a part of that interaction; a section of her chapter on costume is included here.

◆ Theatrical events have altered much through time since their religious beginnings, and they have passed through some of the same metamorphoses undergone by representational art. But images in art may be made up of anything, whereas theatrical events require human beings; and human beings have the need to be dressed—not just covered but invested appropriately according to the circumstances. Since theater requires human bodies behaving in front of a human audience, all productions, no matter how abstract or fantastic, must be based on the inescapable drama of the body, a drama that is produced by the identification each beholder cannot help feeling with the performers, his empathy with their gestures and poses. Costume that conceals, stylizes, or dehumanizes the body still cannot eradicate that essential physical accord between actor and audience.

---

[2]I have published a complete study of the subject in Germany with the publishing house of Bruckmann in Munich. The volume, illustrated with sketches, is called: *Die Musik und die Inscenierung.*

The particular mode in which a theatrical event pretends to be a representation of real life determines how its characters may seem properly—that is, "realistically"—clothed. Of primary importance is how its representational method relates to language. The performance of dance, for example, seems to require that the costume fulfill a visual function different from that required by poetic drama, though both may be using the same thematic material in somewhat the same way. When the characters utter no sounds, their clothes obviously speak more loudly, in a way that is closely related to similar messages delivered by the static clothed figures in pictorial art. When theatrical personages sing, they must be especially dressed for that lengthened and intensified kind of drama. Such differences depend much less on the physical necessities of dancing, acting, and singing than they do on the different visual needs of the three audiences. When performers do all three, as in modern musical comedy, a carefully synthesized mode of dress seems necessary if they are not to look ridiculous. They must be stylized and simplified for the abstract activities of song and dance, and still remain believable during straight dramatic scenes. On the modern stage a character representing a poor medieval peasant in a play, a ballet, or an opera cannot be dressed in the same costume for these different modes, even if the convention of "realism" is observed in each.

The costumes worn by extras automatically convey more than the principal actors' or singers' costumes do, since they are performing a purely visual function. Audiences for naturalistic drama, classical or modern, will accept the most minimally conceived costumes on the chief actors, who can convey all the significant atmosphere by their speech and movement. Hamlet can wear anything; so can Gertrude; the only restrictions on their dress might be that no jarring symbolic elements be superadded. But extras in *Hamlet*, particularly if they are not expected to behave dramatically, must wear carefully conceived clothes, which may be a lot more elaborate than the ones on the chief actors. This difference can itself have a spectacular dramatic effect as long as the extras can effectively act the part of people properly wearing those clothes. If they cannot, and are insentient bodies, the fancy garments of extras will look ludicrous.

In ritual and emblematic rather than dramatic productions, such as masques and pageants, principals, whether they talk or sing, must wear appropriately significant garments, since the medium is visual and the theme ideal. The costumes *are* the drama, the characters are known by what they wear, and any accompanying words support the clothes instead of the other way around. Ballet, which finally emerged from such earlier forms of theater, could do away with all language and eventually with all mime, but not with costume, until choreography itself could more and more arrive at the condition of music.

In what exactly does the appropriate significance of any costume lie? What is a "good" costume? Has the concept changed at all, and is the standard different for different stage mediums? Obviously, yes. Dressing up meaningfully to perform a rite is as old an institution as religion itself. But not only do cultural habits change; the relations between them also change. Modern performance now draws on a storehouse of historical conventions for utterance and movement, as well as on the independently developed traditions of representational art. More than speech and gesture, the clothes suitable for any kind of theater cannot escape visual conventions, established by art. They are what enable us to perceive and to judge costume correctly, to understand what a clothed figure on the stage is supposed to look like.

This is not to say that stage costumes have no well-developed visual conventions of their own. These have flourished, particularly in any mode of theater that has been produced according to a rigid formula for several generations and that owes its success to this very fact—Western movies and classical opera, for example. The clothes become part of the formula, visually satisfying only if they conform to certain expectations. To depart in the direction of greater realism or in the other direction, of more abstract, imaginative conceptions, will seem to violate the character even if an unorthodox costume makes him look more visually pleasing, more historically correct, or even more natural. But at certain moments, revolution and innovation in conventional stage dress, usually created by and associated with the success of a certain performer, become established and eventually create new formulas themselves.

The history of theatrical costume shows that the first purpose of dressing for theatrical events is to catch the eye with something unusual. This aim has never substantially changed, despite the ever-broadening range of theatrical purposes. The kind of serious domestic drama created for film, for example, which purports to reflect real life at close range, nevertheless offers ordinary clothes whose common look has been magnified and distorted out of proportion, simply by their appearance as costume. Ordinary clothes automatically become extraordinary on the stage or screen. The frame around the events invites intensified attention to what is being worn; we know it is there intentionally even though it represents something worn casually, and so it has the ancient status of dramatic costume.

This same intense perception of clothes, however, as they are being worn in the magnified circumstances of cinematic life, also has the opposite effect—that of making ordinary dress seem dramatic because it resembles what is worn in the movies. It is there that the true influence of movies on fashion operates. It is an influence on perception, one that may have some similarity to the way garments worn at public theatrical events in the Renaissance—civic processions, essentially, which marked festivals year after year in the streets and squares of European towns—were perceived. Such Renaissance street festivals were in fact moving pictures in which both spectators and performers saw themselves sharing, both dressed to see and be seen, two groups of ordinary people in festive clothes made more extraordinary by ceremonial circumstances. Modern film audiences see extraordinary stars in ordinary clothes like their own; but the glow of the stars, and of the screen, transforms both sets of plain garments into extraordinary clothes. Movies, like Renaissance spectacles, make art out of life.

Since the seventeenth century most theater has been produced by professionals for nonparticipating spectators, but the ritual origins of theater have never been lost. The theatrical impulse to dress up and participate in special occasions has deeply affected people's lives. The wearing of special clothing in the sight of other people has in fact often been arranged to constitute a complete theatrical event in itself. To make a show with clothes, without the demands of song or dance or spoken text, is a way of permitting ordinary citizens to be spectacular performers without any talent whatsoever. Physical beauty is not necessary, either. A simple public procession of specially dressed-up ordinary people is one of the oldest kinds of shows in the world; it has probably continued to exist because it never fails to satisfy both those who watch and those who walk.

Clothes for such events in the past had a function quite separate from dress in either stylized popular comedy or religious drama, in which costume had a symbolic importance and was necessary, not to intensify the action, but to illustrate it with the full complement of visual meaning. Costumes for popular comedy or religious drama might even signify the action itself if they were seen out of context—Pierrot's suit, for example. This kind of dress is more properly called dramatic than theatrical costume; and the distinction is important, especially in modern theater, in which these two kinds of costumes may be used to dress different characters in the same show or may even be combined in one costume. Drama requires action in significant sequence, some representation of events; theater may produce the whole show at once, so that vision and movement and sound are synchronically significant. Although theatrically dressed figures may move about—march or dance or gesture appropriately—they are essentially still; that is, they are symbolic figures who happen to move, not characters undergoing experience.

In society, where dress has always had a degree of unacknowledged theatrical and dramatic importance, the performers are usually in competition, not cooperation. Consequently a good deal of anxiety is mixed with the theatrical satisfactions of a social occasion in gala dress. To see and be seen, measuring and being measured on the same standard, is very demanding, although it has its own perilous charm; and one of the most satisfying ways of combining these pleasures was clearly achieved by the festival-theatrical events of the Middle Ages and the Renaissance. At the civic procession of the fifteenth century, whether secular or religious, some people in gala clothes could look at others dressed up in remarkable costumes (or vestments), and all in one setting. The clear light of day illumined both at once and so kept a balance between them rather than an opposition. Audience and participants were mutually visible. No distancing mechanism, such as that of the later illusionistic theater, kept them apart in different modes of being, to make each group seem ridiculous to the other out of context. Moreover, in the fifteenth century, which was the high point of this kind of participatory theater, the means of confirming this unified reciprocal vision of costumed performers and dressed-up spectators was pictorial art—also then at a high point in its history.

Renaissance paintings have always been remarkable for the way the clothes worn in them are made to look. Clothes for citizens of earth and heaven, for men and angels alike, are elegantly and realistically presented together. They combine in a pictorial harmony so perfect that the modern eye can believe that the clothes all conform to current fashion. Robes for ancient saints and coats for modern dukes, though different in design, look as if they were fitted by the same tailor, whether in Bruges or in Florence. And the apparent living reality of celestial garments is matched by the apparent unworldly perfection of rich people's festive dress. But, in fact, both are representations of the kind of costume—rich clothes worn by spectators and rich trappings worn by participants—that was a regular ornament of public life itself.

The unified presentation of these different clothes reflects the unified perception of them possible at the time, when a single visual standard prevailed for both dress and dress-up. The privately produced entertainments of the nobility in the fifteenth century were done outdoors and were not exclusive. Nobles were visually accessible, even at play, to the general urban public. Moreover, their entertainments were no more sumptuous than the festival processions produced at the expense of the towns, to honor the entry of rulers, which everyone also saw. And they were certainly no more sumptuous than the religious drama, which by that time had reached a peak of gaudy display.

Theater in the different parts of Europe in the fifteenth century, like serious public art, developed many different styles; but in general most of it was very rich, glittering, elaborate, and colorful, and also open to the general public for free, outdoors in daylight. Furthermore, nobles, courtiers, and members of rich families not only rode and marched publicly in theatrical dress but danced, sang, and performed roles in theatrical shows, all in the public view. The poor man in the street, although he might have had little to eat and too much work, was certainly not visually starved. Indeed his eye could rest—from time to time—on the most sophisticated artistic productions of the age, whether live in the form of lavish public entertainments or represented on panels and frescoes in churches. If he were a craftsman or an artisan, he might have a part in the building of festival architecture or the construction of splendid theatrical garments, all as beautifully conceived as the pictorial masterpieces over altars—and sometimes by the same artists.

Thus one form of popular art, specially intended for the people at large, was embodied in aristocratic and ecclesiastical display of the utmost elegance. It was not a tawdry version fit for the debased sensibilities of groundlings but the best that could possibly be produced at the time. This high standard was evident not only in Italy but also in Northern Europe, despite vast differences in the themes and styles of theatrical display. Dramatic art, of course, had both vulgar and lofty versions. Terence was performed for the learned, and smutty farce enlivened the street theaters, for which the costumes were significant rather than magnificent. But beauty in dress, a magnificence that included sophistication of design and embellishment rather than mere idiotic glitter, was something for which everyone (at least in towns) could acquire the highest visual standards.

A personal identification with such standards, furthermore, must have been possible. People could see themselves participating in pageantry and looking like figures in the greatest paintings of the time. Citizens could believe themselves becomingly and beautifully, even if modestly, dressed—costumed, in fact—by virtue of their very participation in a tradition in which painting might be frozen theatrical festival, and a festival a living work of art. Both blended clothes and theatrical costume into a single pictorial harmony, and so the public consciousness of dress as costume was perpetually reinforced by art. It must have resulted, rather generally, in the sense of being a visual object, a kind of perpetual representation of a clothed figure, and no less satisfactory to look at than a saint or a king in a jeweled robe. The reciprocal visual action of art and theater in the fifteenth century could give the public the chance to see itself participating in the visual arts through dress. Today, we have a similar phenomenon in effect through the movies, though we don't have Ghirlandaio and Bellini.

It is interesting that the *tableaux vivants* that were set up along the routes of various processions included both dressed dummies and living figures. The success of this device depends on the audience's acceptance of pictorial art as an exact recorder of visual fact: a person and an effigy could both stand in for characters in an altarpiece, since both were considered as lifelike as a painting and a painting as lifelike as they. The artistic authority of dress, made possible by this unity between public spectacle and public art, was destined to become fragmented and specialized in the sixteenth century and to remain so until the twentieth. Perhaps photography and film have revived some of the visual harmony between art, theater, and life for the general awareness of clothes. The intervening history of European stage clothes, not only for serious spectacle and lofty drama but for fun—smut, satire, dancing, and mime— shows how costume was both linked to and separated from dress in art and dress in the world. . . .

Jerry Rojo
Some Principles and Concepts of Environmental Design

JERRY ROJO (1935–   ) was an obscure young designer working in a college drama department, when he began to work with Richard Schechner's Performance Group in New York City. The problem of transforming the Performance Garage into a theatrical environment posed bold challenges to him as a designer. He responded with results that are described in this essay.

◆ The majority of concepts developed by a theatre artist over the course of a career should have little practical meaning for anyone other than himself. Let me begin by stating that I resist the idea of presenting a set of abstract rules or axioms that presume to outline universal ways of theatre. It has been said that any theatre artist is a criminal who ultimately adheres to no established laws or methods; indeed he destroys, then creates anew in each venture. The strongest work evolves from an individual artist who possesses a private unique vision about what he does. He spends a lifetime in pursuit of that vision (someone said it takes ten years of work before anybody knows what he is doing) and each work consists of *ways of doing* or *concepts*. For the artist, concepts exist on three levels: a way of doing life, a way of doing theatre, film, TV, etc., and a way of doing a specific work or project. There is a certain unity of transactions among these three levels, but in a relative way it is possible only to examine the concepts around a specific work. It seems to me that only if each work is dealt with on its own terms can we come to know about it in a meaningful way. For me each theatre assignment consists of a continuum of problems to be solved in view of some vision. Rather than attempting to catalogue "truths" about environmental theatre I prefer to talk about specific projects, the theory and concepts out of which they grew.

Perhaps it would be worthwhile to define environmental theatre as I understand it and as it is reflected in my own work. Environmental theatre in the broadest sense has come to mean for me an organic production process in which an ensemble of performers, writers, designers, directors, and technicians participate on a regular basis in the formation of the piece through workshops and rehearsals. The ensemble may itself compose the text or *mise en scene* as in the Performance Group's *Commune;* an ensemble may perform the work of a writer not connected to the group as in Shaliko's production of Ibsen's *Ghosts;* or a writer may be in residence with the ensemble as in Jean-Claude van Itallie's collaboration with The Open Theatre's *The Serpent.* In the idea of the *mise en scene,* or living action in time and space, the environmentalist begins with the notion that the production will both develop from, and totally inhabit, a given space; and that, for the performer and audience, time, space, and materials exist as what they are and only for their intrinsic value. All aesthetic problems are solved in terms of actual time, space, and materials with little consideration given to solutions that suggest illusion, pretense, or imitation.

In the more traditional theatre experience, the production is appreciated from outside, in a world especially created for the relatively passive observer. In the environmental experience, on the other hand, appreciation generates from within by virtue of shared activity. Each environmental production creates a sense of total involvement on the part of the audience and performer. There is a sense of the immediate in which the principle "suspension of disbelief" does not apply. With the notion "suspension of disbelief" the audience is asked to believe that an artificial event is actually happening as it is *acted;* whereas in environmental theatre the audience believes the event is actually happening because it is *performed* and there is no question of make-believe. Also important to the environmentalist is the notion that environmental theatre places heavy emphasis on physicalization rather than verbalization. In addition to the shared activity between audience and performer in traversing complex space, there is a new awareness of the performers' potential in physicalization. The environmental theatre space encourages dramatic action and activity that is in the form of "signs" and body language. Some words about kinds of space. The title of this book is *Theatres, Spaces, Environments.* In effect, for the purpose of this book, the three terms are synonymous. The orthodox physical theatre arrangement has the audience in fixed relationship to a stage area because the stagehouse is used to create illusion and spectacle, and the distancing is necessary for these effects. Also, the bifurcated space of auditorium, stage, lobby are each designed for autonomous functions. In the environmental theatre there is a tendency to unify these areas or at least arrange them so that the spaces seem to transform one into the other. The facilities in an environmental theatre are utilitarian in purpose, in that they help change space relationships and serve to augment performer activity. Therefore, with each production the entire complex is transformed in appearance or feeling to suit the needs of the particular piece. Thus the theatre, space, and environment are one and the same and change for each production.

Many of these theatres developed from existing spaces such as churches, gymnasiums, and halls and are referred to as "open space" theatres. They are without fixed seating, accommodating no more than a few hundred people and are fitted out with rudimentary lighting and rigging. The Performing Garage is an example of such a converted space. Formerly a metal stamping factory in an industrial district of New York City, The Performing Garage consists of a room with no fixed seats, 50' long, 35' wide, and 19' high. A new environment is constructed in the room for each new production. The room contains a simple and flexible lighting system, consisting of a metal gridiron which covers the entire ceiling and from which lighting instruments are suspended; outlets for plugging instruments are located throughout the room; and there is a very simple lighting control board with six dimmers, and a total capacity of 15,000 watts.

It is becoming increasingly common for regional, university, and commercial theatre complexes to include—along with more conventional proscenium and thrust stage theatres—an "open space" theatre on the order of The Performing Garage for environmental or other experimental productions. The most recent theatres (sometimes called "black box theatres") are no longer improvised rooms developed out of existing spaces, but completely new structures designed with environmental principles in mind.

Variations from the usual "open space" environmental design are represented by new theatres at Sarah Lawrence College near New York City and at the University of Connecticut. The theatres are built according to a concept which I have called "fixed environments theatre." In this concept the attempt is to provide a *permanent* environment used for all productions, consisting of varied levels, companionways, and stairs, used both by audience and actors. Here, as in the "open space" concept, where the environment changes with each production, there is no fixed seating. Rather, different parts of the "fixed or permanent environment" are used for both audience seating areas and acting areas during each new production. Spectators may sit on edge of platforms, or on movable benches, or they may "float" freely from one part of the theatre to another depending on the dictates of the production.

While the fixed environmental theatre seems to contradict the principle of a new organic space for each production, in practice there is no inconsistency. I have directed a number of pieces in the UConn Mobius Theatre and have found that while the disposition of areas is physically fixed there is a psychic difference for each space within the environment depending on how it is used. The inherent neutrality of the overall space is open for reinterpretation with each production. Also, we have in some more conventional productions effectively added scenic elements to the environment—changing the appearance.

The scope of the environmental designer's responsibility extends to organizing the total space, selecting materials, determining construction techniques, and considering the associational and intrinsic value of each aspect of design. The traditional bifurcated space of lobby, stage, technical areas, backstage, and auditorium are, in this kind of theatre, no longer considered to be immutable, but are subject to organization and reorganization according to a particular production concept. Traditionally, spatial arrangements are imposed on a production, as in theatres with fixed seating. The environmentalist, however, feels that aesthetic considerations should determine movement and actor-audience arrangements.

Typically the environmental designer's impulse begins with architectural and engineering considerations because he has to serve a new kind of physically oriented actor-director, an actively participating audience, and a concept that views space, time and action in terms of an immediate living experience. Therefore, the designer is concerned with the total disposition of space and its related problems—not only problems of production, but also those involved with building codes, safety, comfort, public services, and the peculiar engineering and construction difficulties that arise when a whole complex of theatre experiences is placed under one roof. Thus, in the environmental production, the interaction and negotiation between performers and audience requires a sharing of facilities which implies not so much stage design but architecture. In essence, the designer becomes a hybrid architect-designer who conceives of a totally new theatre for each production.

One fundamental concept that shapes the environmental theatre production is that it is usually approached using the principle of unity of time, place, and action. And the immediacy of this concept suggests that environmental theatre productions are experienced organically from *within* the total space. In the space, the performers and audience members perceive and interact with the piece in individual ways. Traditionally, the audience experiences the production safely at a distance, as if it were part of a puzzle which must be put into the correct place if the director's intentions are to be correctly realized. In environmental theatre, however, each audience member, in his own way, works with and is integrated into the production. The same is true for the actors, whose function in the space is more active than that of the spectator but essentially similar.

The function of lighting in environmental theatre illustrates how a production is experienced from within. When the audience is separated from the production, as in the proscenium theatre or the cinema, the lighting is designed to provide a more or less two-dimensional, picture-frame unifying effect. The concept is based on the idea of composing pictures that move with time. In such cases, the lighting exists as a kind of layered effect; that is, on top of the performer and in between the audience and performer. Traditionally, light is used to affect the brain through eye sensation. Environmental theatre lighting, however, engages other senses as well. One can approach light, retreat from it, feel light, even smell it. Environmental theatre lighting is not used to create unity, balance, rhythm, and the like, through pictorial organization; it is used as *activity* within a constantly changing and fugitive space in a living theatre situation.

An example is the use of light in The Manhattan Project's production of *Endgame*. The environment consisted of a hexagonal-shaped performing area that is about 26′ in diameter; the audience was seated around the six-sided arena, on two levels; these levels were divided into stall-like cubicles that accommodated two to four people; a companionway behind the stalls allowed the audience access into their cubicles. Separating the audience members from performers was a 12′ high wire screen which, when lighted properly, prevented the performer from seeing the audience but allowed the audience to clearly see the actors. The screen also prevented the audience from seeing the mass of audience members on the opposite side of the playing area. The "wall" of light and the stall-like cubicles for the audience served in an active way to allow each spectator to "tune in" or "tune out" at will, and privately, the content of the production. Further, the use of light provided insulation for the audience who viewed the production as if they were witness to the activities of a scabrous and repugnant group of inmates from some madhouse. On the other hand, the performer could interact with the "wall-of-light cage" effect of the environment because it served to augment the feeling of human isolation important to their performance. The four characters of the play are the last of humanity engaged in an end-game just before the void sets in. For them the lighted screen/cage became a real barrier to the cosmic void beyond. Throughout this production the lighting was generated in a concrete way from *within* and interacted with the audience and performer.

In Shaliko's production of *Ghosts* at the Public Theatre in New York, the lighting, props and spatial arrangement all worked to generate internal activity for audience/performer. To encourage an historical environmental reality for audience/performer there was an authentic use of props and light. The lighting was created by using period practical electric light fixtures (1910) to achieve a natural incandescent light. And the performers were directed to actually control the illumination for the play. The audience was set in clusters around the room on various levels to suggest the rooms and walls of an Edwardian mansion.

It is interesting to note that environmental designs are not readily translated into pictorial renderings that depict mood or idea. This is because these productions exist in concepts which rely on transactions among audience, performer, text, time and space; and are therefore, only perceived internally during production.

Another concept at work in environmental theatre is the use of production elements that originate from non-matrixed or abstract exploration. Most theatrical use of props, space, costume, and light derives from historical or common usage sources. That is, there is a matrix or common information of how something is used. A chair historically is designed to be occupied in a certain logical manner. The non-matrixed use of a chair may find it turned into, say, a costume and thus may be worn instead of sat in. This non-matrixed or alogical use of a prop does not try to imitate the use of a prop as seen in society, but represents an attempt to use props as agents for discovery through accident, chance and intuition. Using a non-matrixed approach to production provides an open-ended use of elements around us.

An example of a non-matrixed use of a costume-prop is seen in *The Big Enchilada*, an adaptation of *Ubu Roi*, staged in the Mobius Theatre at the University of Connecticut. One of the performers playing an Ubu-like military tyrant used a Kodak Instamatic flash camera as a "weapon," and part of his costume was made up of a Mexican-bandit-crossed-bullet-belt. Instead of bullets he carried an arsenal of flash cubes. The camera-flashing motif used throughout the production helped to establish the performer's character relationship to Watergate activities, Madison Avenue public relations, and the military complex, in one fell swoop.

In the same production a performer playing a ghostlike seductress performed a ballet nude with flashlights strapped to her wrists. Delivering fragments of Shakespearean ghost dialogue she danced among the audience with only the light from the flashlights reflecting off her body and the space around her. As in this production, lighting effects used in performance are generally discovered in process of workshops and rehearsal rather than being logically preconceived at the outset. In effect, such "unnatural" non-matrixed use of light is an act of confrontation or transgression because the unnatural effect initiates a trauma that ultimately draws attention to itself. Here one thinks of Brecht's concept of alienation and Grotowski's idea of transgression.

The environmentalist is preoccupied with extracting and exploiting the intrinsic qualities of materials and space. From this sensitivity to the nuances of the characteristics of materials there develops an entire logic based on the associative and connotative value of things around us. For example, a performer may choose to use the warming quality of light—the simple fact that the temperature is higher inside the light than outside—or he may select the crisp edge of a sharp-focused ellipsoidal spotlight to delineate territory. In such a pragmatic approach there is an attempt to exploit the salient features of the lighting equipment and the possibilities offered by light itself. In environmental theatre there is an emphatic move away from using materials to create illusion, promote deception, or theatrical surprises, to instead accepting material in an unaltered or undisguised manner. This practical approach to materials suggests that materials have their own psychic energy and which exists by itself and not only for the production as is the tradition. In this case, actors are trained to negotiate with and develop private associations with materials. Using lighting as an example, it is not unique to environmental theatre to employ the intrinsic and associative value of light since historical plays such as *Othello, The Three Sisters,* and the work of such practitioners as Brecht, Meyerhold, Craig, and Appia all suggest strong use of the associative value of light. When, in the second act of *The Three Sisters,* Natasha carries a candle light alone she is foreshadowing her takeover of the household. The playwright clearly intends that light and power are to be associated. It must be noted, however, that historically this use of light often was relegated, like sub-text, to a position of relative minor importance in order to maintain the rigors of realism or to make the play conform to some other stylistic mode. By comparison, in the environmental theatre *mise en scene* the use of associative values of materials is presented openly and conspicuously. In the production of *Baal Games,* an adaptation of Brecht's *Baal* performed by the Mobius Ensemble at the University of Connecticut, the actor playing Ekart was associating with images of sun, clouds, air and light. Consequently this light-complected, blond-haired actor in white clothing did much of his performing in proximity to light and high places. For example, he may be seen casting shadows on the other performers or bathing in light as if to take on energy from it. The Performance Group's production of *Mother Courage* utilized an extensive system of ropes and block and tackle as a metaphor for the use of the wagon. Instead of using a literal wagon of merchandise, Mother Courage and her children were often fettered to the myriad of ropes and pulleys and were free to associate with being tied down or manipulated. In environmental theatre, the actor necessarily uses elements of *mise en scene* for motivational and associative purposes in ways and means not found in other forms of theatre.

Traditionally young designers are taught to be jacks of all trades. They are taught to be capable of a range of design styles and problems—musicals, box sets, scene painting, decor, portrait painting, electronics, props, etc. As Moliere pointed out, "one who masters all, masters none." I feel there should be a deep art and art appreciation training, and subsequent study in theatre history and styles. However, soon a selective elimination process should take place. One in which the designer begins to focus and become committed to a style of work. Taking a cue from painters and sculptors—who spend long periods of their life exploring specific problems—the stage designer needs not to see himself in servitude to every play and project that comes along, but accept only those that foster some vision and discovery.

9

AUDIENCES AND CRITICS

◆ . . . nearly all strangers . . . . . . spiritual perception . . . . . . willingness to submit . . . . . . communicating the play . . . . . . amazing phenomenon . . . . . . useless activity . . . . . . I like it . . . . . . power to destroy . . . . . . enhances our understanding . . . . . . necessary evil . . . . . . it is all pretense . . . . . . make something for fun . . . . . . expression of personal opinion . . . . . . thunderous applause . . .

Elmer Rice
The Audience

ELMER RICE (1892–1967) was a playwright and an occasional director who was active in the American theatre for nearly fifty years. In 1957 he gave a year-long course of lectures in New York City, which were later published in book form as *The Living Theatre*. His chapter on audiences reveals the on-going struggle that always exists between the performers and those in the audience. Theatre artists have always had ambivalent feelings about audiences; they are both a fatal threat and a source of triumph.

◆ Of all the factors that contribute to a complete theatrical performance, none is more necessary or important than the audience. For the dramatist has not succeeded in communicating the play he has created until an audience has assembled for the purpose of viewing it. The mere presence of an audience in a theatre is convincing evidence not only of the attractive power of enacted drama, but of the astonishing and unique human capacity for deliberate and voluntary self-discipline. Every time I go to see a play, I am struck afresh by the amount of social organization that is involved in the performance. Even passing over the construction and maintenance of the building itself, we find in the pattern of the production an amazing complex of personal relationships and co-ordinated skills. The more easily the performance flows, the more, we may be sure, it depends upon the split-second timing, the nicely balanced give-and-take and the unity of purpose of dramatist, actors, director, designer and technicians.

The audience is an even more amazing phenomenon. After all, the theatre workers are pursuing their chosen careers, and often their livelihood depends upon the success of their efforts. They have special reasons, therefore, for concentration of their energies and for submission to discipline. But the members of an audience are under no such compulsion. For the most part, they are drawn to the theatre by nothing stronger than a desire for entertainment, using that word in its broadest sense. The reader picks up his book and puts it down at will, wherever he happens to be. The art lover wanders into the gallery at almost any hour of the day, and stays as long as he chooses. Further, the reader takes his pleasures in solitude; for the art lover a companion or two suffices.

Not so the theatregoer. At a very specific time, he must take himself, at considerable expense and often at great physical inconvenience, to a specific place, to join a gathering of five hundred or a thousand fellow-theatregoers, nearly all strangers to him, and linked to him only by momentary similarity of purpose and willingness to submit to immobile captivity for the "two hours' traffic of our stage." Apart from this unity of purpose, the audience is almost certainly a heterogeneous assemblage indeed, composed of individuals varying widely in age, occupation, religion, race, education, intelligence and taste. The coming together of this motley gathering is both accidental and purposeful; ordinarily, neither its exact composition nor its exact response to the performance is predictable.

Yet this crowd, like any crowd, takes on an identity and a character of its own, which is not wholly like that of any of its component members. In certain respects everybody in the audience will react in the same way. For example, if the theatre is overheated, if the seats are too uncomfortable, if the actors are only half audible or half visible, nobody will enjoy the play, no matter what its merits. But in quite another category is the operation of the mores, those indefinable but very real criteria that somehow express the collective sense of what is fitting to be seen and heard in public. Obviously, there is a vast difference between private and public behavior; and people will be outraged to hear in a theatre the use of language and the mention of subjects which may be conversational commonplaces at their dinner tables. When Clyde Fitch's play *The City* was posthumously produced, the general opinion was that it was not one of his best. Yet people flocked to see it apparently for the shock value of hearing "God damn" spoken for the first time on the New York stage. At much less trouble and expense, they could have stood at any street corner and heard far stronger language used by the passers-by. Marc Connelly and I once speculated on what the audience reaction would be to a play in which the characters discussed their physical disabilities and hygienic problems in the manner familiar to the readers of advertisements in the mass-circulation magazines designed for "home" consumption.

Again, the moral judgments and intellectual concepts of the audience are likely to vary greatly from those of its individual members. An audience is almost certain to react hostilely to a character who is guilty of dishonesty, cruelty, non-comic drunkenness or non-comic marital infidelity, even though many of its members may not be entirely guiltless of one or more of these offenses. On the other hand, a *comic* treatment will evoke laughter even from those who have had painful experiences. Patriotic, pious and moral platitudes and clichés are often greeted in the theatre with approval and even applause by persons who would reject them in cold type or in private conversation. On the other hand, an audience may respond to poetic beauty or spiritual perception that is far above the general level of feeling or even of comprehension. Of course, the appeal of the theatre is primarily emotional rather than intellectual and the effect of a play is to increase sensitivity and to blunt the power of judgment. Theatregoers who read a play after seeing it often wonder why they were moved to laughter or to tears, or why they accepted situations or ideas that will not bear examination. (Sometimes they discover points that they missed in the theatre; but that is likely to be due to inattentiveness or to an inadequate performance.)

For me the most fascinating thing about an audience has always been the kind of gyroscopic balance it maintains between objectivity and participation. A play is most effective when the performance creates an illusion of reality so strong that it enables the audience to identify itself in some way with the characters and to share their joys, sorrows and perplexities. Yet this "voluntary suspension of disbelief" is never so complete that it destroys the audience's awareness that it is all pretense. It knows that the walls of the elegant salon are painted canvas, that the liquor that flows so freely is cold tea, that grandfather's beard is held in place with spirit gum, that the baby carried so tenderly is only a doll, that the falling snow is torn paper, that the lethal gun is loaded with blank cartridges, that the dead hero will arise in a moment to take his curtain call, and that the beautiful weeping heroine who kneels beside him has just divorced her third husband. Stated in these terms, the whole business of the theatre seems ridiculous. Yet it is not so, and the audience is only too glad to give itself up to the enjoyment of what it knows to be only make-believe. In fact, that is the very purpose for which it has come to the theatre. There is nothing more amazing than to see an audience that has been torn to shreds by the enactment of an emotional scene burst into thunderous applause the moment it is over, thus expressing acknowledgment of the skill of the actors, and perhaps of the dramatist, who have aroused it to this high pitch of excitement.

One of the best ways to judge the effect of a performance is to sit in a stage box, with one's back to the stage, and watch the audience. The changing expression of the faces and the movement of the bodies are a clear index to how the play is being received. "Sitting on the edges of their seats" is a literal description of audience behavior in moments of tension, and while "rolling in the aisles" is certainly figurative, it suggests the contortions of people who are in the throes of uncontrollable laughter. Smiles, tears, clenched hands, wide eyes all reflect the changing moods induced by the stage proceedings. Sexual allusions sometimes produce disapproving looks, sometimes self-conscious giggles or smirks; telling lines prompt an interchange of knowing looks between companions; and tender scenes are conducive to hand-holding. If there are coughs, yawns and restless squirmings you may be certain that the interest is slackening and that, for one reason or another, the contact between stage and auditorium has been broken. In fact, the nonrespiratory cough is an almost infallible danger signal: an attentive spectator does not cough.

Audiences are singularly obtuse about some things, singularly observant about others. Important information must usually be conveyed two or three times before it is fully grasped, as most dramatists are well aware. Yet frequently an audience will anticipate the point of a joke or the significance of a situation (as actors say: "They're way ahead of us") and after a performance or two, lines that were carefully written and rehearsed are eliminated. Incredible happenings are sometimes readily accepted, while trivial flaws are instantly detected. I once saw an actor—obviously an understudy pressed into service at the last moment—read his entire part from various documents that he kept bringing forth. It was not until the last act that the audience became aware of what was going on. In *Counsellor-at-Law* there is a climactic scene near the end of the play which hinges on a telephone call. On the morning after the first preview at least twenty people called up to say that Paul Muni had dialed only six times instead of the required seven. No reader is very much disturbed by typographical errors or even the omission or repetition of a word. But very often an actor's mispronunciation of a word or the substitution of an incorrect one will break the mood of the audience or even produce a titter. A smudged collar, a protruding slip or a lipstick smear may provide a focus of attention that is fatally distracting. Actors almost invariably check their zippers before making an entrance. And any accident in the audience itself will destroy the spell: an explosive sneeze, an ill-timed guffaw, a drunken altercation, to say nothing of people suddenly bolting out of their seats and up the aisle, or having epileptic fits—not infrequent occurrences.

It is this element of audience participation and this constant interplay across the footlights—figuratively speaking, for footlights are almost obsolete —that keep the theatre boiling and give each performance a touch of adventuresomeness. For no two performances of any play are ever exactly alike. Audiences vary with the season, the weather, the day of the week, the day's news. Any actor will tell you that Monday audiences are usually quiet; that Saturday-night audiences are relaxed and out for a good time; that Wednesday matinee audiences do not respond to humor but adore all the little homey touches; that benefit audiences are hard to please; that Sunday-night audiences are impervious to subtleties; and so on. These generalizations are undoubtedly a little too broad, but they are based upon long experience. And anyone who stands backstage during a performance is almost certain to hear an actor say, as he comes off: "They're laughing at anything tonight," or "They're sitting on their hands out there." Many times I have seen an actress almost in tears because she did not get the accustomed round of applause on her exit. The longer a play runs, the less perceptive is the audience. The reason is clear: the first audiences consist mainly of seasoned theatregoers, who are sophisticated and "theatre-wise" and therefore quick on the uptake. Audiences in which "out-of-towners" predominate are quite different from audiences of New Yorkers. If a play is a great success the audience is often "sold" on it well in advance. An actor in a great hit said to me: "You know, we used to wait for that first big laugh about two minutes after my entrance. Well, by the third week they began laughing the minute I came on. By the second month they laughed when the curtain went up. And after that, they were laughing as they came down the aisles to their seats." On the other hand, an audience may be oversold, and theatregoers who have waited months to see a play may find themselves disappointed in watching a tired performance, or hearing lines that have lost their luster through familiarity.

For the actor, as for any interpretive artist, the immediate response of the audience is of paramount importance. He has direct personal contact with it, in a way that no creative artist who does not also happen to be a performer can. His performance is necessarily ephemeral, forever wasted if it is not appreciated at the moment of execution. This is not to say that he finds no satisfaction in the characterization itself, which at its best demands the employment of imagination and many skills. But we have seen that for any artist expression is not enough; there must be communication too. And for the actor true communication exists only when he stands physically in the presence of an audience and wrests recognition from it by the display of his talents. That is why there are very few actors who do not prefer the stage to the television or motion-picture screen. Broadcasting and the movies may offer more security and greater financial rewards, but acting for a camera can never be the same as acting for an audience. Besides, a filmed performance is frozen and unalterable, whereas a stage performance is always fluid and vibrant, slightly modulated at each repetition to attune it to the mood of the audience, and having its minor defects, like the small irregularities that distinguish a bit of handicraft work from the smooth cold flawlessness of a factory job.

The dramatist, of course, has no such personal communion with the audience. When the curtain rises, he must depend upon the actors—and all his other associates in the production—to reveal what he has created. If he happens to be in the theatre during a performance he can see and hear for himself how his work is being presented and how it is being received. He is elated when the play is going well, disheartened when it is going badly. But the fact that it is going at all represents the accomplishment of what he desired from the beginning: the communication to others of what he had expressed. The communication may be incomplete because of faulty expression, of feeble interpretation or of imperfect apprehension. But, for better or worse, he must have an audience. If there can be no drama without a theatre, then certainly there can be no theatre without an audience. The audience then is more than a mere passive recipient. In a vital, living theatre, the role of the audience is functional and creative.

Eric Bentley
Theatre and Therapy

ERIC BENTLEY (1916–   ) as critic, translator, editor, and playwright has been
for the past thirty years one of the theatre's most powerful and influential voices. He
has brought back the old into the repertoire and he has encouraged that which was
genuinely new. The essay included here is not one of his better-known ones, but it is
especially significant because it discusses what happens in the theatre when the lines
between art and life become blurred or break down altogether.

◆ For better or for worse, the principal event of the 1968–1969 theatre
season was the visit to New York of the Living Theatre. Of their offering, they
made a kind of take-it-or-leave-it proposition. I was one of those who "left it,"
but not in the sense that I left off thinking about it. What I propose to pursue
here is the question: What has all the talk of the Living Theatre and kindred
theatres really been about?

There is no one correct answer but a central topic has certainly been
"audience involvement." The Living Theatre was trying to change the character of the theatrical event. They wanted to move the audience onto the stage.
They wanted to exercise a therapeutic influence. On the audience, of course;
but also, as they proclaimed, on themselves: the audience was to help cure
them. I asked myself when had I heard something of the sort before. The
whole conception seemed to be one of group therapy, rather than theatre as
previously conceived, but had not one celebrated group therapist already
effected a merger of these two, and, in his system, was the actor not indeed
the patient, and did not the audience assist in treating him?

The therapist was Jacob Levy Moreno; his name was in the Manhattan
phone book, and I had no difficulty getting myself invited to attend the
group-therapy sessions of the Moreno Institute on West Seventy-eighth
Street. Meanwhile I was seeing various shows around town that claimed to be
doing something special with audience participation, and/or trying to give
theatre a push toward therapy. I saw *The Concept, The Serpent, Dionysus in
69. . . .* Even the current nudism proved relevant. Insofar as it was more than
a pursuit of a quick buck, it was an affirmation of the body, the health of the
body, and was related to "nude therapy," sensitivity training, encounter
groups, etc. I visited some of these groups and also saw *Hair, The Sound of
a Different Drum, We'd Rather Switch, Geese, Che, Oh! Calcutta!,* and so on.
Of the theatres, I think the Play-house of the Ridiculous and the Ridiculous
Theatrical Company were probably the most cathartic, being founded on the
deepest rejection of The American Way, and inspired with the cockiest faith
that they can get along without imitating that form of life. But gradually I

found myself seeing shows less and Moreno's "psychodramas" more. If one wanted theapy in the theatre, why not go the whole hog? At the Moreno Institute, therapy was the acknowledged and sole aim in view, yet the sessions there were emotionally affecting and intellectually interesting to a much greater degree than the New York theatres. What more did I want?

For the moment, nothing. And I concluded that, rather than attempt any sort of survey of the new trend in theatre,[1] I would simply try to explain what is at stake. Should drama be psychodrama? Is psychodramatic therapy the same as dramatic art? Are certain mergers called for? Or are certain separations—certain firm distinctions—in order? If we could attain to a degree of clarity on these matters, "current trends on and off Broadway" would be child's play.

Since it was psychodrama that prompted this approach and underpins the reasoning that follows, it will be as well to state in advance just what a psychodramatic session is. Perhaps a hundred people are placed on three sides of a platform. The platform itself has steps on all sides, is in this sense an "open stage." A patient, here called a protagonist, presents himself for a psychodramatic performance. A director-psychiatrist talks with him briefly, to find out what he sees as his problem, and what scenes from his life might be enacted. A scene being chosen, the roles of others taking part in it are played either by trained assistants or by anyone else present who might volunteer. What and how they are to play is briefly explained to them by the protagonist and director. If they then seem too far wide of the mark, the protagonist may reject them. But in each session, successful scenes do develop, "success" here being measured by the degree of spontaneity attained: if the protagonist does not "warm up" to his role, he cannot play it in its vital fullness.

Generalizations about the course of psychodramatic sessions are hazardous, since one session differs widely from another, but a typical line of development would be from relatively trivial scenes with friends in the recent past to serious and crucial scenes with parents in the more distant past. It will often happen that a protagonist will have an illumination, or at least a surprise, in one of these later scenes. He may suddenly realize that where he had seen only love there was also hate, or vice versa, in one of his main relationships. And here the stress should be on the word "realize," for it is likely to be a powerful emotional experience: a given insight is borne in upon a person in the midst of a very lively distress. The distress has opened the channels of communication. It may also have reached a kind of climax. The patient may, for the time being, feel cleaned out. The director now ends the play-acting and asks the audience to share common experience with the protagonist. The point is not to elicit interpretations but to discover what chords were touched in the onlookers, what degree of therapy was in it all for them.

---

[1]As I had been invited to do by *Playboy*. When the present "comment" was submitted to them, they declined to print it.

I

Dramatic art and psychodramatic therapy have a common source in the fact that life itself is dramatic. In other words, life is not a shapeless stuff which is given form only by a dramatist or clinician. Human life, like the rest of nature, has been shaped, indeed so markedly that this shaping has always been the leading argument for the existence of God. As the beauty of leaves or seashells is attributed to God the Creator, so the shape of events, large or small, is attributed to God the Dramatist: life, as Dante classically stated it, is a divine comedy. The idea that "all the world's a stage/And all the men and women merely players," is not a clever improvisation casually tossed off by Shakespeare's cynic Jaques, it was written on the wall of Shakespeare's theatre, the Globe, in a language older than English: *Totus mundus facit histrionem.* To speak of life, as many modern psychiatrists do, as role-playing is only to make a new phrase, not to advance a new idea.

I shall return later to role-playing and would only at this point call attention to the positive side of the pattern. The negative side is all too familiar: it is that people are often hypocritical—use a role to pretend to be better than they are and deceive other people. It is curious how the phrase "play-acting" has come to be a slur: it implies insincerity. Yet the commonplaces I have cited imply that one has no alternative to play-acting. The choice is only between one role and another. And this is precisely the positive side of the idea: that we do have a choice, that life does offer us alternatives, that one's will is free within whatever limits, and the end is not yet determined. Life is not merely going through the motions, it is an adventure: which is often all that people mean by calling it dramatic.

What else might they mean? In the vernacular, these days, "dramatic" means little more than thrilling, and if it also means "spectacular" the sense of an actual theatrical spectacle is probably not intended. Dramatist and psychodramatist give the term "dramatic" a much more elaborate interpretation. Just as they see more roles to role-playing than Jaques' seven, they break down the "stage" which "all the world" is said to be into various departments. Given that there are roles to play, how are they played? A full answer to this question would be by way of a description of myriad different roles and relationships. A short answer, aiming at providing a basic scheme, might run somewhat as follows.

A role is properly and fully played by being brought into living contact with another role played by another actor. The "full" playing of the role implies that living contact is made, that if "I" am playing one role, "I" feel that the other role is a "Thou" and not an "It." (I am using terminology that most people will associate with Martin Buber, though J.L. Moreno has long thought along these lines too.) Buber's point has been that the modern person reacts to others as an It, and so forestalls communication. "I," too, become an It, if the other is an It. Neurosis walls us off from each other. That's modern life.

Now drama does not depict a utopia in which neurosis is absent, but, with an exception to be noted in a minute, it is utopian to the extent that it normally, not exceptionally, shows human beings in living contact with each other, shows couples who are "I" and "Thou" to each other. It may be living hatred that communicates, as in Strindberg's *Father,* or love, as in *Romeo and Juliet,* but that there *is* direct and lively communication is not only obvious, it is what interests us, it is what we want from theatre. Could it be said, then, that life is not dramatic in this respect, only theatre is? Perhaps. But the point is that this is a norm, not just for our theatregoing, but for our living. The "I" and "Thou" relationship is present enough in actual life for us to want to see more of it, and when we do see it in the theatre, our attitude need not be, "but that's because theatre is not life" but rather "this is what is trying to happen in life if only we would let it." For art need not be regarded as a more abundant life, but unreal. It can be regarded as an attempt by the life force (or what have you) to make our real life more abundant.

If life does afford real I/Thou relationships, and also, which is crucial, holds out the hope of ever more successful I/Thou relationships, drama can, for its part, portray the failure to achieve such relationships. But how could this possibly prove dramatic? Wouldn't the absence of live contact kill the stage action stone dead? It would—if nothing else is added. Drama character-ized by a mere absence of emotion is dead. Suppose, however, the absence of emotion, of flow, is the very point? That, you say, is ridiculous. Then, I reply, the way to give it life is to give it ridiculous life. The dramatic form which regularly presents people who are out of contact with each other is the art of comedy, whose mode is ridicule. The role-playing in *The Importance of Being Earnest* is all a game of pretending to have living I/Thou relationships— friend to friend, parent to child, man to woman—when such relationships are not in the cards. Again, when we say comedy presents types, not individuals, we might just as well say it presents individuals who cannot make contact with other individuals because of a crust of nonindividual class characteristics. This is not a *man,* Molière or Shaw is forcing us to say, it is a *doctor.*

The question whether tragedy or comedy is closer to life becomes rather a snarled one. Tragedy presents us in our emotional fullness; it has, therefore, more of life in it. Comedy presents our customary failure to live that way and, in presenting less of life, gives a more characteristic version of it. As for I/Thou relationships, if they are per se dramatic, then we may say that life aspires to the condition of drama.

Does the I/Thou relationship, granted that it includes role-playing, amount to drama? If we would be inclined to say yes, that is because we have taken ourselves for granted. *We* are watching the "I" and the "Thou." We are their audience, and from their viewpoint a "They." Theatre is this com-pleted circuit: an "I" and a "Thou" on stage and a "They" out front. Which is a very radical, if schematic, version of the rudiments of living: *I* relate to *you,* while *they* watch. I, Romeo, relate to you, Juliet, while the other Mon-tagues and Capulets watch. This example, if extreme, serves to remind us how much those watchful eyes modify the I/Thou experience. We live out our lives in full view of other people. We do not live in a world of our own. We live in "their" world. How much tragedy, both of life and literature, lurks in that formula!

II

This, at any rate, is the image of life which psychodrama has appropriated: an "I," talking on stage to a "Thou," in front of a "They." By that token, psychodrama may be said to resemble life or even to be a slice (many slices) of it. Visitors are surprised how close it comes to the real thing. And its watchword is spontaneity. Nonetheless, psychodrama has to depart from life in a number of ways, notably:

(1) The "I" is not presented in a sheer, naked, literal state but buttressed, clothed, supplemented by another person. When the protagonist, at a psychodramatic session, is found to be reluctant, silent, overdefensive, another person is asked to play his double and to come forward with exactly those responses which the protagonist is holding back. Thus to take a crude instance, in the matter of ambivalence, if the protagonist keeps saying, "I *love* my mother," and clamming up, the double will say, "I hate her guts." This is as different from life as can be, since help is being given precisely where it was, perhaps disastrously, lacking. (The double can of course guess wrong, but this fact will probably emerge from what the protagonist then says and does. In any case, there is nothing definitive in a possibly false suggestion. The situation remains open.)

(2) The "Thou" is rendered in more or less the form not of life but of drama, namely: impersonation. Any partner the protagonist's story requires is enacted either by a trained assistant or by a member of the audience at the session in question. Since this is a "stranger" to the protagonist, the difference, for him, from the real thing is very great indeed. Often it is necessary for the protagonist to reject outright what the player of such a role says. Sometimes he has to have him replaced. "My father just wouldn't react that way."

But—and this is what matters—some degree of I/Thou relationship is generally worked out before a session is over. Indeed what needs calling attention to is not the difficulty of reaching a degree of direct communication under the conditions of a psychodramatic session but the fact that life is outdone by psychodrama in this respect, somewhat as it is by dramatic art, though not by as much. It must be galling, for example, for a parent to learn how his child enters into rapport with a substitute parent far more readily than with the real one, but a moment's thought explains this: the "objection" is precisely to the real parent, and the "false" one is the real one minus the objection. Hence psychodrama is not "naturalistic," is not a duplication of actuality but, in the most relevant way, an improvement on it in exactly the same way as nonnaturalistic art is, for nonnaturalistic art is actuality not merely reproduced, but interpreted normatively, which means: to a certain extent transformed. Psychodrama and drama have in common a thrust toward human *liberation*.

To take up a single example. When a person fails to communicate with his nearest and dearest, he is apt to reach the extreme conclusion: "If I cannot reach them, I can reach no one." Actually, it is only they whom he cannot reach. The rest of the human race is more accessible. And psychodrama is not an argument to this effect but the living proof written in letters of emotion upon a person's whole nervous system: the kind of proof even philosophers don't easily reject when it's their own nervous system that is responding.

The form taken by scenes created in psychodramatic sessions stands, correspondingly, at a remove from actuality. The patient-protagonist is not encouraged to rack his brains for accuracy in reporting, as when someone tries to be very honest and self-disciplined in telling the police what occurred on a given occasion. What he does, after reminding himself as vividly as possible of the actual moment and location, is to let go and *throw* himself into the situation with a lack of reservation that at the time he hadn't actually achieved. Thus what is "brought back" from that actual happening is, in one sense, more than was there in the first place—more than was *known* to be there, more than actually emerged. Which is, of course, the reason for going to all the trouble. Mere rehash is a waste of energy for the rehasher, as well as being a great bore for those who have to listen. But I shall leave further comment on the psychology of recapitulation till later. The point here is that the "Thou" who is less, in that he may be a mere stranger, is also more, in that he is really a "Thou" where the nonstrangers were not.

(3) A third way in which psychodrama deviates from life is in making use of a director. There are few who feel, these days, that the drama of their lives is directed by God. That was hard to believe with any constancy at any time; today, if there is a God at all, He is an absentee landlord, a director on perpetual sick leave abandoning the actors to their own resources. Jacob Moreno, though, always wanted to play God, and the modern age obviously placed no special obstacles in his path. He modestly called himself—or any of his standbys—directors; but they preside over the psychodramatic sessions in fairly godlike fashion.

In psychodramatic sessions, the director intervenes in several ways. In the beginning, he elicits the information on the basis of which a first scene is set up. He then *interrupts* whenever it seems to him the drama is (a) repeating itself, (b) wandering off, or (c) petering out. Since anyone could easily be wrong on any of these three matters, it is clear that considerable shrewdness is called for, not to mention knowledge. Interruption is, in any event, a very dynamic factor in itself, as some playwrights (e.g., Brecht) have known. It gives a jolt, which can be salutary or disastrous according to the moment when it occurs.

Interruption is the director's chief negative act. But he does something positive, too, and usually right after the interruption: he *suggests* an alternative path. Having stopped the patient-protagonist from pursuing one course, he propels him into another. Again, the possibility of error is considerable, but again much can be expected from knowledge and know-how. And again, errors need not be final. On the contrary, given the patient's set of mind, they will probably be exposed rather soon. A dead end is a dead end, and is seen to be so by patient and/or audience.

In one sense, then, the director is *not* called on to be God and always right, but only to be resourceful and always quick. The right moment to reach a stop or institute a change passes fast. The director must have instantaneous reactions that indicate immediate conclusions such as: "This is when a double is needed," "We must go straight to the scene just suggested in the dialogue," "Let's reverse roles here."

Reversal of roles, incidentally, is one of the chief devices of psychodrama, and perhaps one of the most efficacious. At a word from the director, the protagonist plays the "other fellow" in the scene. Thus "I" is forced to see and feel out the situation from the viewpoint of "Thou." Which is not only morally edifying but generally illuminating and specifically therapeutic. Our whole failure as human beings can be found in the failure to take in the reality of the other person. But merely knowing this doesn't help. Psychodrama can help by the *work* involved in "I"'s playing seriously at being "Thou."

In a sense, too, the director is not outside the psychodrama, but inside it. His is a voice that the patient sorely lacked the *first time around;* which was why seemingly fatal mistakes were made. *This time,* on stage, the voice speaks, like that of another double. *Next time,* if all goes well, the voice will be that of a double successfully internalized: it will be the patient's own voice. It is a "He" that becomes a "Thou" and that ends up as an "I."

Obviously the most important single instrument in psychodramatic therapy is the director, and this is not just saying that the director is the psychiatrist: it is saying that he has to possess the specific talents required by the situations that arise on the psychodramatic stage.

(4) If the "I" and "Thou" of life are modified in the psychodramatic theatre, so is the "They." The "They" of life is by definition general and amateur. The "They" of psychodrama is specialized and professional. At Dr. Moreno's public demonstrations the audience consists partly of those who see themselves as possible patients, partly of students of psychodrama. Any third element—such as the scoffers or the visitor who finds himself there by accident—is minor. So we are limited to people with a pre-established involvement, a curiosity that is really keen because it comes from need or greed.

It is perhaps seldom realized that in all theatrical situations there is a specific, understood relationship between actor and spectator, a kind of unwritten contract between the two. And it is probably just as seldom realized that the contract holds for only one type of theatre, while other types make other contracts. Thus what an expense-account executive at a Broadway show is buying from the actor is different from what, say, the Athenian people were buying from their festival players, which in turn was different from what Louis

XIV had contracted for with Molière, and so on. A clear difference in aim, not to mention relationships outside the theatre, produces a clear difference in the actor/spectator relationship.

Such relationships, insofar as the facts are before us, can be examined in such terms as the degree of passivity (or its opposite) on the audience side. Lack of passivity can show itself in what I have just called need or greed: a felt need for what the spectacle intended to convey, an eagerness to know and in some sense possess it. At one extreme, audiences are both bored and bossy. "Entertain me," they say with a patronizing yawn. The actors are their slaves, their jesters, and will get whipped if they failed to be funny: what sharper whip than economic boycott? At the other end of the scale, the performer is looked up to: much is expected of him. The spectator is humble: it is he who hopes to profit by the exchange. The psychodramatic audience inclines to this other end of the scale, and its humility, combined as it is with neurotic involvement and intellectual curiosity, will show itself largely in the form of sympathy and human understanding.

It is not the audience's attitude in itself that is interesting but the way it functions in the reciprocal actor/spectator relationship. And it is necessary here to anticipate somewhat and say that one of the chief differences between drama and psychodrama is this: while drama is judged, fairly enough, by the effect the actor has on the audience, in psychodrama the highest priority goes to the effect the audience has on the actor. This effect, like that of the director's interventions, is by way of *propulsion.* The audience's sympathy oils the wheels; the audience's eager curiosity speeds things along. The whole occasion is a form of *public confession.* There is relief, and therefore pleasure, in such confession. The person who takes over much pleasure in it is called exhibitionistic. But if a degree of exhibitionism is normal, so is a degree of shyness. The presence of an audience makes it harder to be frank. Psychodrama addresses itself to this shyness and asks that it be tackled, not avoided, as it largely is by psychoanalysis.

(5) A psychodramatic session differs from another two hours of living in that it is *literally* theatre while life is theatre only metaphorically speaking. I mean, to begin with, that there is a stage and that otherwise there is only an auditorium. This organization of space is so ruthlessly selective that most of the detail of actuality is omitted. To say the world is a stage is one thing. To represent the doings of this world *on* and *by* a stage is another. The physique of the psychodramatic theatre bears no resemblance to the world-in-general and not too close a resemblance to the world-in-particular. A scene in a garden will be redone without the garden. A scene about a man as a child will be redone without a child—the physical presence of a child—on stage. Conversely, the physical characteristics of *theatre*—a floor of a certain type, steps, suggestive bits of furniture, the spectator's seats arranged in a certain pattern, the rows of faces above the seats—have a quality (reality, atmosphere) of their own which contributes to the character of psychodrama as a whole.

The sheer physical nature of a theatre does more to determine the nature of the whole theatrical event than has commonly been appreciated, except by recent writers on environmental theatre who have gone to the opposite extreme. Yet, if we turn now to the psychodramatic event as a whole, there is one feature more decisive than environment, and that is—it is so obvious, one could forget to notice—re-enactment itself. Such and such was done in life: it will now be acted. Or, to return to the premise of role-playing, such and such was enacted in life: it will now be re-enacted. The first thing the director does is to ask the patient to *show* (instead of narrating) what once happened. Psychodrama is not life but recapitulation of life, living life over a second time, having your cake and eating it.

And this, which is indeed the key idea of psychiatry as we know it, can properly be the cue for a comparison of psychoanalysis with psychodrama. It was Freud who encouraged us to believe that, if anything at all could be done about our mental illnesses, it would be by going back to the time of their origin and reliving it. *The first time around,* we retreated at a certain point or stood still. The hope which therapy holds out is that, returning to this exact spot, we can *this time* make the needed advance from it. It is a repetition with a difference: an innovation, a nonrepetition.

All life is repetitious. There is the salutary and needed repetition by which good habits are formed. There is the baleful repetition by which bad habits are formed. There is the endless repetition of therapy sessions before the point is reached when any positive result is attained. Then, in the midst of repetition itself, the breakthrough. A paradox, if you will, and yet one which seems built into the process of living. Even love-making is all repetition—of words, of caresses, of body movement—until the breakthrough of orgasm. Scientists report similarly of the breakthrough into discovery; artistic performers of the breakthrough from the repetition of the rehearsal into performance.

As for bad habits, by innumerable repetitions an undesired action has become a habit. The habit is to be broken by yet another repetition, the repetition of perhaps the earliest performance, the original act, which is then *not* repeated, even once. It now leads when it should have led in the first place. In order to be freed from the old captivity one re-enters it one last time.

Now psychoanalytic therapy is itself psychodramatic—up to a point. At one time, certainly, it specialized in the search for the early traumatic scene which was re-enacted, with the patient playing his childhood self and the analyst, for example, the hated father. Freud's first great discovery in the therapeutic sessions themselves was that the analyst did become father, mother, etc., in other words, that the patient assigned him roles—the main roles in his personal drama. Such *transference* was the key to the whole patient/doctor transaction, and therapy came about through the pain the patient endured in reliving the old troubles. If the patient fought back, he could hope to work through neurotic darkness into light.

It is unfortunately impossible to make any survey of the results of Freudian therapy and compare them with the results of any other therapy. One can only assert the a priori likelihood that one person might get more help from one form of therapy, another person from another. One can also point to what for many patients would be an unnecessary limitation in Freudian procedure. Freud in his day had to be much concerned with what one might term the sanctity of the confessional. His patients would never have "got it out" had anyone but the doctor been listening. Even at that they needed further encouragement by the device of the couch. You lie down and avoid looking the doctor in the eye. So in a way you are alone and can get into a reverie and say things you couldn't say into anyone's face. Freud preserves his patients both from the "Thou" and the "They." The patients' efforts to convert the analyst into a "Thou" are stoutly resisted. They are seen only as interference with the intention of making the latter a receptacle for roles not truly his, a ghost. "Look," the analyst must always be imagined as saying, "you have attributed to *me* all these characteristics of your father, but that's *your* problem."

Whatever help may be provided by such constantly re-enacted dramas of disenchantment, it may plausibly be maintained that there is often much to be gained by a contrary procedure: introducing the "Thou" by way of an actor and the "They" by way of an audience and letting the analyst emerge into daylight as a director. That the director can then be accused of pushing things too much is inevitable, but this risk may be worth taking, and there are self-corrective elements, as noted above. The "Thou" of the psychodramatic stage is neither the actual "Thou" nor a duplicate, but if he is a poor substitute in some ways, he is superior (as also noted) in others. The slow pain of free association, in conjunction with transference, produces certain realizations and has doubtless been curative on some occasions in some degree. But no patient is overly satisfied with the results, and that alone is justification for other methods than this Freudian one. And, as against transference, there is much to be said for engaging the other fellow, if not in his own person, at least in flesh-and-blood form. This encounter too inflicts a degree of salutary pain. And very painful indeed (as well as the opposite) is the presence of onlookers: something one has to face in life, something it may be needful to face in therapy. Many of us suffer specifically from fear of the others, and it may be doubted if psychoanalysis tackles this fear boldly enough. Many fear the flesh-and-blood actuality of the "Thou." It is often just this fear that makes a potential "Thou" into an actual "It." Here again, why not take the bull by the horns? There has been in the Freudian tradition itself a certain vestige of the Judaeo-Christian hatred of the body. In this respect Karl Kraus may have hit the mark when he said, "Psychoanalysis is the disease of which it purports to be the cure." And after all, Dr. Moreno is not the only one to ask if Freud hadn't overweighted things on the mental side in reaction against the physiological emphasis of nineteenth-century medicine. If today we talk in psychosomatic terms, by that token the somatic element is half of the whole. Is it not just as reasonable to get at the spirit through the body as vice versa? But these queries go beyond my topic, which is—to summarize this section—that, while there is drama as between couch and chair in the dimly lit office, there is an ampler drama when "I" meets "Thou" upon a stage in the presence of a director and an audience.

III

If psychodramatic therapy is at a remove from life, dramatic art is at two removes from it, for while the protagonist of psychodrama is "spontaneous" and presents himself, the protagonist in a play is held to a script on the basis of which he presents someone else.

If we see these two rearrangements of life—psychodrama and drama —as running in competition with each other, which one do we regard as the winner? It depends wholly on our own angle of vision. The psychodramatist inevitably looks with horror upon the written text. Dr. Moreno contemptuously terms it a "cultural conserve," and sees it exclusively as a hindrance to spontaneity, the highest value in his philosophy. From the viewpoint of therapy, I believe his point is well taken. Here there is nothing but advantage in improvisation. The protagonist is a patient, and only his life matters. I have remarked that even the audience in psychodrama exists for the sake of the protagonist, not vice versa, as in drama. The dialogue, a fortiori is all his. Even the director is not an author but at best a sort of film-editor. Nor are there any prescribed forms of dialogue or character, as with the *commedia dell'arte,* which the psychodramatic "actor" must follow. Improvisation in any art— *commedia dell'arte* or a jazz combo—is free only within narrow limits. By comparison, psychodrama offers its protagonist freedom indeed!

It is obviously possible that "confinement" within the rules of an art may become a neurotic problem for a given individual. Dr. Moreno reports that this was the case with John Barrymore. This actor was sick (literally) of playing Shakespeare: he wanted, he needed, to play Barrymore. Of course, one thing one would need to know to make anything of this example would be whether psychodramatic therapy, if diligently pursued, would have cured Barrymore of alcoholism and of whatever else ailed him. That he wanted to play himself only proves him human: every infant wants the same. But I am prepared to grant that subjection to a written role may have compounded rather than solved this particular man's problems. No written role was ever intended to solve such problems anyway.

Spontaneity, as Dr. Moreno sees it, is a very useful, even an inspiring idea. I would define it as one of the forms of human freedom, a subjective form, in that it is a psychological, not a political, one. It is a matter of how one feels. A spontaneous man feels free. He feels disburdened of all the inhibitions and evasions and shynesses which normally hold him back from fully feeling what he could and would otherwise feel. If this is correct by way of definition, I would add that, like other forms of freedom, spontaneity operates within limits—within an iron ring of unfreedom, of unspontaneity. A completely free and spontaneous man would not only feel what he wants to feel but say what he wants to say—which would abolish politeness and saddle him with libel suits, to say the least. He would also do what he wants to—which would interfere grossly with the freedom of others. Life, then, has to set bounds to spontaneity. Indeed, some neurotic problems derive from such limits. Psychodrama moves the boundary posts out a little; but it doesn't throw them away.

What the psychodramatists have worked on, and worked for, is one particular kind of spontaneity which we may call solidification of the present moment. The neurotic's trouble is seen as the disintegration of the present: all is diffused into memories of the past and fantasies of the future. This entails great instability in the whole emotional system and, since joy is of the present, an incapacity for enjoyment: life is stale, flat and unprofitable. To re-create the present tense, to create spontaneity, is to bring a person back to life, it is to enable him to experience life in its fullness. For, as Blake put it,

> He who catches the joy as it flies
> Lives in eternity's sunrise.

If all this makes it sound as if the purpose of psychodrama were to stimulate to momentary pleasure I should go on to say, first, that this is no contemptible purpose but, second, that no one has claimed that a single achievement of that sort is a cure for any mental illness. Nor am I retracting the statement that psychodrama, like psychoanalysis, is painful: both therapies believe in possible progress through pain to pleasure. The difference between the two therapies, in regard to past and present, is that the Freudians keep constantly in mind the persistence of ancient hurts into the present and until recently have tried to refer the patient back just as constantly to the trauma of long ago, whereas the psychodramatist has always worked gradually back from the present. This labor, and not the discovery of trauma, is what "works through" the trouble: its pain, and not the vestigial pain of the trauma itself, is what the psychoanalyst assumes to be therapeutic. He begins "spontaneously" (i.e., as spontaneously as possible) in the present; works back to the obstacles, the rigidities, the nonspontaneities; only to help the patient back to the present; if he is lucky, with a true spontaneity.

Such a conception of spontaneity has in its favor that it is unpretentious. Its normal field of vision is a restricted one. Envisaged (initially at least) is not a whole life, a whole civilization, remade. In the clinical situation faced by the individual, doctor and patient can concentrate upon moment-to-moment experience. (If an invalid is still breathing, his breath will becloud a mirror.) Much psychiatry goes astray by overextending the field of vision: asking so many questions that there can be no coherent, compact answers. In psychodrama the question can usually be limited to: Is the patient's soul still breathing? Can this man warm up to an encounter with another man? Can he feel? Will his limbs go along with his feelings? Can he blush? Shout? Whisper? Kiss? Embrace? It is useful not to have to ask if a man is this or that type of neurotic, but instead: Is he in shape to survive as a human being among other human beings? Can he face the suffering? Can he experience the joy?

Limits are placed on spontaneity in life; in psychodrama; and in dramatic art. To the psychodramatic therapist the limits placed on spontaneity by art seem particularly threatening because, indeed, to impose a script and a role on someone would be to nip their psychodrama in the bud. This and the fact that psychodrama itself throws up scenes with considerable strength as dramatic *art* have encouraged Dr. Moreno to view the two activities as competitive and to feel that, in this competition, psychodrama wins. Actually, there is no competition. The problem, if it is a problem, is only that this therapy and this art overlap, and if chunks of a psychodramatic session are art, pure theatre could in some ways be therapeutic. More useful than taking sides, it seems to me, would be an attempt to sort things out a little.

To maintain flatly that theatre itself is or should be therapeutic will only lead us to the conclusion that it has less to offer than other therapies. If one had a serious mental illness, no amount of theatregoing in even the greatest of theatres could be expected to help very much. Dr. Sophocles and Dr. Shakespeare would find themselves hopelessly unable to compete with Drs. Smith and Jones on Central Park West, neither of whom has ever laid claim to genius.

This is not to say that the notion of a *connection* between drama and therapy, between all the arts and therapy, is ill founded, only that it has been exaggerated, often by a kind of literal-mindedness. Take the most famous notion in the whole field: catharsis. There is a certain agreement, now, among scholars that the word should be taken as a medical term, that it signifies a purge, and not a moral purification as scholars used to think. Even so, there remains much to say, and chiefly that the word was pounced upon by psychiatrists of the 1890s and applied to a much lengthier and deeper process than any that a visit to a theatre could elicit. The word now described what happened in five years of psychoanalysis. Which, I would say, effectively takes it out of dramatic criticism altogether.

Was Aristotle wrong? Did he exaggerate? Did he mean something else? I doubt that a great pother is called for. After all, Aristotle said very little about catharsis, but the accepted modern interpretation of the word does apply to many works of art, provided we can forget psychiatry for a moment and remember art for quite a few moments. Is it the case that a psychiatric session provides a thoroughgoing catharsis, whereas a play provides an inadequate one? To be sure, patients have often been known to vomit after a session; the theatre could seldom achieve such a result even if it tried.

What is needed, perhaps, is not that we judge art as therapy but that we distinguish one kind of therapy from another. Society needs therapy on two different scales. In the case of individual breakdowns, something more drastic than art—any art—is needed: that's why we have psychiatrists. But these complete breakdowns do not exhaust the list of psychic ill that flesh is heir to. At present, it is true, the others are just let go, if not actually encouraged, because they serve this or that sinister interest. Mother Nature does what she can. Many mental illnesses arise, take their course, and are gone, like physical illnesses. As Freud noted, there are even happy therapeutic accidents. But by and large, mental illness is left to flourish, is *encouraged* to flourish, as physical illness was in the Middle Ages. Which means both that individual special therapy is needed by more and more people and that whole societies can be described as sick in something more than a metaphorical sense.

Now the arts are helpless in the face of such serious maladies. They can only help counteract such tendencies when other forces are doing so on a much larger scale than art itself: in other words when the situation is not as bad as all that. The Greeks viewed the arts as just a part of the good life, and the arts do need a good life to be part of, even if it's a good life that is beset by bad life. In such a context it makes sense to speak of a poet's "healing power" and even of the "corrective effect" of comedy. Poetry could not heal, and comedy could not correct, if things had gone more than just so far, *and not even then on their own.* But if there exists a real civilization, then, just as there are cures effected by nature, and others by lucky circumstances, so one could speak of the arts, too, as therapeutic, alongside other therapeutic agencies of a nonclinical sort. If it is a mistake to see art as standing alone, when it is in fact part of a common effort, a common culture, so it is a mistake to see art as therapy alone, when in fact, as we are all aware, it is other things as well.

What is the total function of art? That might seem too large a question to pose here, especially as there has never been any agreement on the answer. Yet there is no getting any further till the question *is* posed, and it is possible that the disagreements are not relevant. Suppose we just forge ahead.[2]

The function of art, say some, is to please. The function of art, say others, is to instruct. But what if being pleased is itself instructive? What if being instructed is itself a pleasure? The artistic impulse is the impulse to make something for fun. Why is it fun to make something?

The human creature has destructive urges. Little children wish to kill their parents. But destructive wishes trouble the conscience. We would like to atone for the sin of "thought crime." We would make restitution. We would repair the crockery we have broken, and restore it to its owner. The toy that a child willfully breaks but then guiltily repairs—or better still, replaces—and returns to its owner is perhaps the prototype of artwork. What arouses that "pity and terror" of which Aristotle spoke? Destruction and the resultant disorder. The tragic artwork is the poet's restoration of order and restitution for wrong. And his audience receives it as such. I offer these sentences only as thoughts that might help us understand the actual effect of tragedy, which

---

[2]Not, of course, alone. In the following paragraphs I am drawing upon Shaw's Preface to *Misalliance* and two articles by the Scottish psychoanalyst, W. R. D. Fairbairn, "Prolegomena to a Psychology of Art" and "The Ultimate Basis of Aesthetic Experience," which appeared in volumes 28 and 29, respectively, of the *British Journal of Psychology.*

is in part a healing effect, not indeed in the outright sense that tragedy would cure a case of epilepsy or schizophrenia, but in the sense that it springs from a need to feel that one can make good one's destructions. Without such feelings, I suggest, one would go mad. I am not saying nothing but tragedy, or nothing but art, can provide them. I *am* saying that art, that tragedy, can provide them.

If the therapeutic element is only part of a whole, what is the whole? I'd suggest that the best name for the whole is *education,* though you may prefer, at one pole, *child-rearing* or, at the other, *culture.* I mean that art is the pabulum of the people, and that they should be nourished by it from childhood on: this (along with other contributions) makes a culture, makes up the spiritual life of a civilized community. The function of art is to educate, but to say so is not to plump for a didactic type of art: rather, for the idea that art per se is didactic, whereas what is called didactic art tends to fail to be didactic, fails actually to teach because it is boring and therefore soporific. It is because art is *fun* that it can succeed in being didactic, for there is no true teaching except in eagerness, amusement, delight, inspiration.

On the one side, then, all the deadly hate and destructiveness; on the other, the desire to make restitution by creating something for fun. Such restitution is therapeutic, among other things, not to the extent that it alone can clear up the acute sicknesses of either individuals or societies, but on a smaller scale which is nevertheless not all that small and which, in any case, is without time limit. Once there is a good society, even a society good enough to earn the name of civilization not chronically sick, art will join with Mother Nature and with Happy Accident, as also with other branches of culture, to attend to the psychopathology of everyday life, neutralizing many minor toxins, killing many small germs. Which is but a modern and clinical way of restating the ancient belief that art is part of the good life.

Returning to the idea of spontaneity: if all spontaneity is a little unspontaneous too, as I believe, one can certainly find in art—and specifically in theatre—a kind of spontaneity. And indeed a true theatre person is one who craves this type of spontaneity. John Barrymore's problem, as I see it, was that he didn't want to be a theatre person, even though he had the talent for it: which is like being allergic to your own hormones.

Let me try to describe the spontaneity of an actor in a play. On the face of it he has surrendered it to the playwright: Barrymore mustn't be Barrymore, he must be Hamlet. But consider what really happens—from the first rehearsal on. At the first rehearsal, the actor hasn't yet built his characterization, so presumably what he brings along is himself and nothing but himself, and no script ever made an actor feel inhibited about this. As rehearsals progress a little, he comes into contact with his colleagues on stage. Maybe a little electricity is generated. He's attracted by the leading lady. He hates his male partner. Or vice versa. The electricity, in any case, is not between characters, it is between actors. Now the fondest hope of any professional actor (as of his director) is that the electricity generated in rehearsals will be preserved in the performance. That, to a large extent, is what rehearsals are for. Is such electricity a form of byplay, an additional stage effect like background noise? Just the opposite. Properly handled, it does not damage or distort the characterization itself, but is combined with it. Quite a trick! The characterization is to be what the author wanted: that, to be sure, is a principle of drama that there is no getting around. But the actor still meets the eye of another actor, not of a character, which is to say that both actors are still present: their own bodies and all that two human beings have that is not body. And they continue to use all of this, in live contact, as "I" and "Thou."

Should they fail to maintain the contact, could we say, "The actor having now withdrawn his own personality, what is left must be the character"? By no means: when the actors seem dead, as now they would, the characters would never be born. In other words, the life of the stage is a dual life, and through one of these two lives the principle of spontaneity enters, and is indeed essential: that the character may *seem* to have a spontaneous existence, the actor must *actually* have a spontaneous existence. The pulling-off of this "trick"—it is of course much more—is perhaps the main task to which the actor addresses himself. Other things are important. There has to be a characterization to animate. But unless the actor animates it, a characterization has no theatrical value whatever. Conversely, if an actor comes on stage as his spontaneous self, and throws characterization to the winds, we may possibly get something of *psycho*dramatic interest—but even this not really, because the other actors won't relate to it properly, nor will we ourselves relate to it properly: it isn't what we "paid our money for." Whether we know it or not, we have different criteria for dramatic art, different expectations. Barrymore was finally ruined precisely by playing himself instead of the stage character. Life is life. Therapy is therapy. Drama is drama. All afford some freedoms, some opportunities for spontaneity, but, in all, freedom and spontaneity are very strictly circumscribed, so that the acceptance of the circumscription is as necessary an attitude to human beings as love of freedom. Freedom, says Engels, is the recognition of necessity. Goethe says, *"In der Beschraenking zeigt sich erst der Meister"*—"only in his confrontation of limits does a master show his mettle." This is another way of saying: we marvel that spontaneity exists at all; and we marvel how much spontaneity can be created by masters of living; of therapy; or of art.

(1969)

Alfred Emmet
A Short View of Dramatic Criticism

ALFRED EMMET (1908–   ) is the founder of the Questor's Theatre in Ealing. Largely through his efforts, it has been England's leading amateur theatre since 1933. This essay was first published in 1947 and was reprinted in 1973 by the fine British magazine *Theatre Quarterly*. Emmet points to the unique differences between theatre criticism and other forms of art criticism, and his arguments are instructive.

◆ It is difficult to find anyone who has a good word to say for the *Dramatic Critic*. At best he is regarded as a necessary evil, to be appeased if possible. At worst, as a parasite, battening on the theatre for his own nourishment, and contributing nothing thereto.

Nor is it easy to find general agreement as to what the true function of a *Dramatic Critic* is. Indeed, that is at the root of the trouble. Not only do the critics disagree among themselves as to what their job is, but the manager, the playwright, the actor, the producer, the member of the audience, even the editor, all make different demands on the critic which are not easily reconciled.

Much has been written about the function of criticism, from Aristotle onwards. Anatole France, who somewhat dogmatically declared that there was no such thing as objective criticism, describes it as 'the adventures of a soul among masterpieces.' For him, the critic's function is to write of himself *à propos* of say Shakespeare or Goethe. This is what A. B. Walkley described as 'impressionist' criticism. The critic, he says, asks himself, 'Do I really like this work? Does it please me?' If it does, then he cannot explain his pleasure to others unless he explains himself, so he is committed to an analysis of self —he narrates the 'adventures of his soul.'

Now this is a very convenient philosophy for dramatic critics, especially for those who are more interested in themselves than in the theatre. It is an invaluable defence against those who attack the *Critic* for not writing objectively, for not writing constructively, for not writing responsibly, for not fulfilling some one or other of the myriad demands made upon him from various quarters. 'That's not my job,' he says, quoting Anatole France with a display of great erudition (but overlooking the fact that Anatole France was not writing about dramatic criticism at all). 'I am writing about the adventures of my soul, and of course I am captain of my soul. I voyage where I wish and take orders from none.' A *Very Eminent Critic* implied with some show of indignation that he was a *Dramatic Critic*, not a theatrical plumber. But your plumber is not to be sneezed at—he knows his trade.

Nevertheless, the critic's attitude is difficult to answer, unless his premise can be upset. Of course there is some truth in Anatole France's dictum, but when applied to dramatic criticism, it is surely an over-statement. And because he has wrapped the truth in an outstandingly imaginative and colourful phrase, it is the more successfully hidden. None would deny that criticism, in part at least, must be an expression of personal opinion, and the whole must be coloured by the personality of the writer. But it does not follow that this is a good thing. It is inevitable, but not necessarily desirable. Because the critic must unavoidably write in some degree of himself, or at least from a personal viewpoint, it does not follow that his function is to write primarily about himself, or even that it is permissible for him to emphasize the personal aspect in his writing. Because there is some water in beer, it is not an *et sequitur* that the best beer has no hops.

It is sometimes advanced as an argument in favour of the purely personal school of criticism, that no two persons' opinions are the same. If that were entirely so, it would mean that all criticism as such is quite valueless. The truth is that while it is unlikely that any two persons' opinions will be exactly the same, it is likely that they will have points in common.

The *Critic* then must give his personal opinions—no other opinion is worth anything. Inevitably in doing so he is giving something of himself. He cannot help his opinions, and, for those, he is responsible to no one but himself. But in writing his criticism, he cannot include every opinion that he formed on each aspect of the show. He has to select. And in selecting the particular opinions for inclusion in his article, he can help himself. That is what his will directs. For that he is responsible. At that point he must recognize his responsibility. To whom? Or to what? We will examine that later.

It is no defence therefore for a critic accused of writing an ill-balanced or irresponsible criticism to say, 'Criticism is a matter of personal opinion, and those are my opinions.' One is entitled to ask, 'Why do you express those particular opinions and not others. Why do you address yourself only to such and such aspect of the performance and ignore others? What motives had you in selecting from all the opinions you formed just these particular ones to put into your article?'

It is one of Stanislavsky's principles of acting that a player should always be clear as to his objective in each scene, both his near objective and his more distant objective, and he must find his true objective. In just the same way, the *Dramatic Critic* must be clear about his objective. If his objective is to write about himself, to reveal his own ego, his notices may be very interesting; they may be very entertaining; they may even be very instructive; but they will not be *Dramatic Criticism.* But if his objective is truly to serve the theatre, it is good (and indeed unavoidable) that there should be something of himself in his writing.

'It is the function of criticism,' (again, I quote Walkley) 'not to inculcate methods, but to appraise results; to examine the thing done, not the way to do it.' On the face of it, an incontrovertible statement—but see where it leads us if pursued too far. This is the defence of every *Critic* when he is told he is not constructive (unless he takes the even more dogmatic attitude that there is 'no such thing as constructive criticism'). But the *Critic* wilfully misunderstands.

> *I do not like thee, Dr. Fell,*
> *The reason why I cannot tell,*

may be a true appraisal of the joint efforts of the Almighty and the worthy doctor; it may be a genuine expression of a personal opinion; but it is hardly valid as a piece of criticism, because it is not reasoned. What the critic refuses to see is that all *reasoned* criticism is constructive. It should be the function of criticism, not merely to appraise results, but to discuss them in a reasoned way. And to discuss them intelligently, it is necessary to lift the curtain to some extent, to go in some measure behind the finished result and examine how that result was produced.

Now that is not to say the *Critic* should lay down how, in his opinion, the thing ought to have been done—that is to go too far. But it does imply that he should be knowledgeable about the technical and artistic processes that go to make the particular art form he is judging. The *Dramatic Critic* who understands, for instance, the nature of acting, is better able to discuss the effect of an actor's performance. If he appreciates the function of the director, he can more intelligently discuss his work.

Another aspect of criticism which Walkley is at pains to emphasize, while he himself points out the dangers of it, is that criticism is of itself an art, a form of the art of literature. 'A criticism is a picture with its own laws of perspective and composition and "values," and the play which furnishes the subject for this picture has more often than not to be "humoured" a little, stretched here and squeezed there, in order to fit into the design. The salient points in the pattern of the play may not suit the salient points in the pattern of the criticism. . . . The critic must have his "general idea", his leading theme. . . . This general idea, however legitimately it may have been derived from the play criticized, will very likely get exaggerated. . . .' Clearly, if pursued too far, there is here another dangerous heresy. The *Dramatic Critic* is a writer, and, as such, he has to express himself, he has to convey his thoughts, his impressions, his ideas. He must, therefore, be something of an artist in his own right.

But the point again is, what is his objective? At the point where he has to choose, where he has to select the ideas to which he is going to give expression, where does his duty lie? Towards his own literary art-form? Or towards the theatre? Is it more important for him to achieve a neatly-rounded literary composition, or to discuss an aspect of the performance he has seen which may be of significance or importance to the theatre, even if it does not fit into the preconceived pattern of his piece of writing?

Much of what has been written about the theory of criticism is concerned primarily with *Literary Criticism*—criticism of the art of literature—

and it is too easily assumed that principles which may be valid for criticism of one art must necessarily hold good for another: that the function of criticism of poetry, for instance, is identical with the function of *Dramatic Criticism.* Special pleading is always open to suspicion, but it is a fact that there are vital differences between the art of the theatre as compared with most other arts, which have an important bearing upon the responsibility of the *Dramatic Critic.*

In the first place, in practically every other art form, the thing criticized and the criticism itself continue in more or less permanent co-existence. It is possible at any time, for instance, to read the literary work, or examine the picture, and to set against it the critic's comments, each man judging for himself whether they are, in his opinion, valid or not. That is not so in the case of the theatre, where the thing created is of the moment only, and ceases to exist (save as an impression on the minds or emotions of the audience) when the final curtain falls. It may be re-created the next day, but no two performances of the same play, by the same players, to a different audience, will be exactly the same.

Secondly, the theatre is about the only art form in which the artist is unable to see or hear for himself the finished creation. Therefore the artist in the theatre—the actor at least—needs criticism in a sense and to a degree quite different from say a writer or painter.

Thirdly, because of the evanescent quality of theatrical art, it is only to the extent that some facets of it can be caught in what is written about a performance that tomorrow can know anything of the theatre art of today. The *Dramatic Critic* is in a special sense writing in part for posterity—he is a recorder of theatre history while it is in the making.

In the fourth place, the *Dramatic Critic* has a power to destroy beyond anything that the critic of any other art can do. A play damned by the critics at its opening may be literally killed, never to appear again. A book or a picture will continue to exist whatever any critic may say about it—posterity may re-discover it, find virtue in it, and even give it a place among the masterpieces: it continues to exist. But not so in the case of a play, unless it happens also to be published—and the publishers are naturally less inclined to print an unsuccessful play than a successful one.

For these reasons the *Dramatic Critic* has a responsibility to something outside himself far beyond the responsibility of the critic of the other arts. I would not be disposed to argue at length against the art critic, or the literary critic, who maintained that his first responsibility in his writing was to himself as an artist, that it was his job to write of himself *à propos* of the subject discussed, that his function was to appraise results without going behind them, that the most important thing was his own literary form. At least he has a case. To whom, or to what else, can he be responsible? To talk about a responsibility to something as abstract as literature or 'a responsibility to art' is meaningless.

But—and this is the last vital difference between theatre art and the other arts—there is a 'body theatric' (in a sense in which there cannot be, say, a body of literature) to which the *Dramatic Critic* must, in my opinion, acknowledge responsibility. The nature of theatrical art, as something which cannot exist until a number of individual artists have co-operated in one joint creative achievement, is such, and the nature of its tradition, which can only be handed on by word of mouth, or through the medium of what is written *about* the theatre is such, that to speak of responsibility to the theatre is no meaningless phrase, but something real and important.

This, then, is a plea to the *Dramatic Critics,* to recognize in precept and in practice their prime responsibility to the theatre, to accept as their prime objective a desire to serve the theatre. When, and only when, that metamorphosis takes place, the theatre will have the critics it deserves and so sorely needs.

Harold Clurman
The Divine Pastime

HAROLD CLURMAN (1901–   ) has been one of the American Theatre's most eloquent spokesmen for a good part of this century. Director, critic, lecturer, and cofounder of the famous Group Theatre, he has always been as passionate as he is demanding. Although he has written numerous volumes of criticism, the essay that follows (The Introduction to *The Divine Pastime*) is as close to his "credo of a critic" as anything he has published.

◆ "Criticism is, has been and eternally will be as bad as it possibly can be." Thus spake George Bernard Shaw, the best theatre critic in the English language in at least the past hundred years. What he meant was that critics will never satisfy everyone concerned, that they will always make horrendous "mistakes," that they are bound occasionally to cause damage, and that the degree of their benefactions will always fall under the shadow of serious doubt.

What is a critic anyway? For the reader of the daily newspaper he is one who issues bulletins in the manner of a consumers' report. He is a sort of advance man, a freeloading publicity agent charged with the duty of instructing the prospective theatregoer as to what he should or should not buy. He is to tell his readers in no uncertain terms, "I like it" or "I don't like it."

If the reader were as careful in his perusal of printed matter as he is admonished to be about his diet, he would realize that in most cases the inference contained in the declaration "I like it" is of little value, in fact, is nearly meaningless. All three words are vague!

First: who is the "I" that speaks? Why should his assertion carry any particular weight? For him to exercise any decisive influence over me, should I not take the measure of the man, learn something of his intrinsic qualifications, his human disposition, his beliefs, his personal complexion? There are critics whose most emphatic encomia fill me with misgivings.

Second: what does the critic mean by the word "like"? In what way does he like it? I like pretty girls and I do not particularly "like" Samuel Beckett's work; yet I do not rush to a show which boasts a cast of pretty girls (I can meet them elsewhere) and I hope never to miss a Beckett play.

Above all: what is the "it" which the critic likes or dislikes? I like candy and I like meat, but before consuming either I should be able to distinguish between the two. The primary obligation of the critic is *to define* the character of the object he is called upon to judge. The definition itself may constitute a judgment, but insofar as they are distinct from each other the definition should precede the judgment. It is perfectly proper to rave about *Barefoot in the Park* as candy, and I can well understand the critic who damns Wedekind's *The Awakening of Spring,* but I can have little respect for him if he does not recognize that it is meat. It is certainly true that one man's meat is another man's poison, but the manner and reason for the choice may characterize the man.

To put what I have said another way: the reviewer whose reaction to a play is contained in some such ejaculations as "electrifying," "inspired," "a thunderbolt," "a mighty work," "a dismal bore," may in each instance be right, but his being right does not by itself make him a critic. For these epithets only indicate effects: pleasure or displeasure. The true critic is concerned with causes, with the composition of human, social, formal substances which have produced the effect. Strictly speaking, it is not even necessary that the critic name the effect; it is imperative that he take into account the sources from which it springs. In doing this the critic is faithful to the work he treats of, while at the same time he affords the reader some idea of what manner of man the critic himself is—which is a crucial consideration.

In estimating Shaw as a critic it does not upset me that he was captious about Wilde's *The Importance of Being Earnest*—he was wrong—and that he was much more receptive to the same author's *An Ideal Husband,* a play for which I have less regard. In both cases he said things of great interest and moment; I am more impressed by him in my disagreement than I am by the critic who pronounces *Any Wednesday* a "wow"—a statement which brooks no denial.

Theatre having become a luxury commodity with us, the person in quest of entertainment demands instantaneous guidance, and the daily critic is there to supply it with the necessary dispatch. His columns tend to make the pronouncement of opinion a substitute for criticism, so that very few of his readers have any idea of what criticism really is.

Newspaper editors are not especially interested in the theatre. Their views are generally similar to that of the ordinary playgoer. There is, thus, little inquiry into the qualifications of the person who is to occupy the post of theatre critic. If he is a competent journalist, is not so eccentric in his tastes that his recommendations are likely to disappoint or offend readers, the editor is satisfied. If, in addition, the critic can wisecrack and shape his opinions into formulas as efficient as an advertising slogan, the editor is delighted. What concerns him is circulation.

The daily critic is actually responsible to no one but his newspaper. In the context of our present theatre situation the critics of at least three or four of our dailies (the columns themselves even more than the people who write them) exercise far more power than anyone desires them to—power, that is, which affects sales. The critic may himself be embarrassed by the commercial influence he exerts. He will even go so far on occasion as to disclaim that he is a critic, protesting that he is simply a reviewer, that his word is hardly more important than the next fellow's. After all, as has often been remarked, he is usually constrained to write his review immediately after the performance in less than an hour. While such defenses are largely sincere, they contain some unconscious hypocrisy. The fact remains that most of the daily reviewers mistake their opinions for criticism. They are as much in the dark on the subject as their readers.

Criticism, to paraphrase Anatole France, is the adventure of a soul (or a mind) among presumed works of art. Just as the artist seeks to communicate his experience of life through the use of its raw materials and the specific means of his art, so the critic, confronting the resultant creation, sheds a new light on it, enhances our understanding of it, and finally ends by making his own sense of life significant to his readers. At best, the critic is an artist whose point of departure is another artist's work. If he is a truly fine critic, he will make his reader something of an artist as well. It is not essential that he also make him a customer!

Let us agree that the daily reviewer is rarely a critic of this kind because, for one thing, he has no time to be. One notices, however, that he infrequently has more to say about a play after a week's reflection than he said immediately after the performance. Some reviewers do not even desire more time. They trust that the rush from playhouse to typewriter will furnish them with the impetus to convey hot-off-the-griddle reaction.

For my part, I often do not know what I really think about a play as I leave the performance. Momentary satisfactions and immediate irritations frequently warp my judgment. My thoughts and feeling become clear to me only when I read what I have written! And then, I must confess, I sometimes alter my view, in the sense that I see plays—as I do people—in many different perspectives according to time and circumstance. The critic ought to proclaim the right to change his mind, just as an art work itself changes even for its own creator. Our relation to art ought not be static; it is a very human business.

To be candid, however, let us assert that most daily reviewers are not critics because they are not richly enough endowed with sensibility, thoughtfulness, personality, knowledge of art and life or literary skill to hold our attention for much longer than it takes to read their reviews.

It should not surprise us that great theatre critics—Lessing, Hazlitt, Lewes, Shaw—and even lesser ones of the same line are rarely employed as daily reviewers because men of this rank have prejudices about which they are as explicit as possible—prejudices, moreover, which are rarely those of the casual reader. And one of the authentic critic's main purposes is to enunciate or construct an attitude toward life—if you will, a "philosophy"—and to make it as cogently relevant as possible. This must necessarily scare a newspaper editor whose publication is designed to please "everybody," that is, from 400,000 to a million readers daily.

Criticism can never be wholly objective—though the critic should keep the "object" well in view—but our basic complaint is not that certain daily reviewers are too subjective but that too often they are themselves such puny subjects.

Critics of the mass-circulation weeklies are usually men who write in the vein of the daily reviewer except in that they employ a more specialized or more "pointed" vocabulary. The men who write for the smaller (usually liberal) weeklies aim to fulfill the requirements of true criticism, though too often—as sometimes in the case of George Jean Nathan—they believe they will attain this goal by defiantly reversing the daily reviewers' coin. To thumb one's nose at Broadway values is not in itself an artistic gesture. Still there is a value in upsetting settled and stupid habits of mind.

In the monthlies and the scholarly quarterlies, criticism generally becomes aesthetic debate or exposition, frequently valuable instruments in criticism. (Aristotle's *Poetics* is the classic model for this sort of criticism.) Often this proves to be drama, rather than theatre, criticism. It is necessary to make the distinction because criticism of drama is a branch of literary criticism (though to be sure drama, like poetry and the novel, has its own laws), while the theatre critic, who must be thoroughly aware of literary values, looks upon drama as it historically came into being—as a part of, but not the whole of, the theatre, which is an art in itself. There are men of sound literary judgment who are unattuned to the theatre, just as there are cultivated folk who have little real feeling for music or the visual media. One has only to compare Max Beerbohm's essay on Duse with Shaw's corresponding piece to become aware of the difference between a brilliant commentator on the drama and a complete theatre critic.

In the introduction to my earlier collected volume of theatre reviews and essays, *Lies Like Truth* (Macmillan, 1958), I said: "My notices in the weeklies tended to be milder than those I wrote for the monthly, and I suspect that I should be more careful to be kind if I wrote for a daily."

One may well ask how this statement can be reconciled with "honesty" and high standards. "My years of work as a producer and as a director," I went on to say, "taught me many lessons about snap judgments and the dangers of a too proud or rigid dogmatism . . . I would conduct myself in criticism . . . with due regard for immediate contingencies without ever losing sight of the larger issues and aims. Do not, I tell myself, squash the small deeds of the theatre's workers, trials and errors with an Absolute."

Can a person professionally engaged in the theatre also be a reliable critic? The simplest answer is to cite—I have already indirectly done so above—the names of some of the best critics of the past who have been craftsmen and critics in their respective artistic areas—a list I might extend further to include poets, musicians and painters. But I shall once again call upon Shaw to speak for me: "I do my best to be partial, to hit out at remediable abuses rather than at accidental shortcomings, and at strong and responsible rather than at weak and helpless ones . . . A man is either a critic or not a critic . . . He cannot help himself."

I shall go further. The fact that I am engaged in active stage work does not render me either timid and indulgent or resentful, malicious and vindictive. It makes me scrupulous and responsible. I am convinced that a critic of contemporary effort owes it to his job to be responsible to everyone in the theatre: the audience, to begin with, as well as to the dramatists, actors, directors, designers. In doing this he becomes responsible to the Theatre as a whole.

George Jean Nathan once cavalierly said that he did not care if every box office in the country closed. I do care. For the closing of the box office bespeaks closing of the theatre, and this would mean that we would end by being more culturally maimed than we are with the theatre in its present deplorable state. There can be no "masterpieces" where there is no production, no routine theatre activity. Even in Elizabethan times, without a box office, no theatre; without a theatre (and inevitably many bad plays), no Shakespeare to write for it.

I would encourage playgoing. (Do not lift your brows too high; it makes you look idiotic.) I would encourage it not by rave reviews of mediocre plays, not by discovering "genius" in every promising talent, but by being wholly committed to saying, with due regard to all the complexity of the elements involved, what I feel at each theatrical occasion I am called on to attend. Such treatment, which arises from a devotion to talent howsoever modest, will arouse interest in the theatre. Making extravagant claims for entertainment which one knows will prove remunerative, with or without critical ballyhoo, depresses such interest as much as does the neglect of promising, but not yet wholly ripe, efforts. I regard the writer to whom the practical economic, social and professional aspects of the theatre are totally alien as at best a curator of the drama, not as a true critic.

As to my own "philosophy" of life and the theatre: it must become apparent with the continuity of my progress as man and critic. It is for that rather than for my incidental recommendations—when I take the trouble to make them—that I write. Just as opinions, yours are as good as mine.

Recently I was introduced to a gentleman as a person about to stage a new play. "What do you think of it?" I was asked. "It's a good play," I answered. "Ah, I notice you are careful not to say it's *great,*" he remarked.

I then explained that in the history of the theatre from Aeschylus to Axelrod there were probably less than a hundred plays I would call indisputably great. Not all of Euripides, Shakespeare, Molière, Ibsen or Chekhov is great. Shaw, Pirandello, O'Neill, Brecht, Beckett, Genet are important but I hesitate to call them great.

The use of the designation, needless to say, depends on one's frame of reference. If one believes a play may retain its efficacy for, let us say, fifty years, one may reasonably call it great—though that is not the yardstick by which I measure. In contemporary American theatre criticism the word has come to signify gushing enthusiasm, similarly indicated by such a phrase as "the best play of several seasons." With us, the superlative is largely an implement of first aid to the box office.

Our theatre and its status among us are in such a sorry plight that when a reviewer labels a play "good" or "interesting," we take it to mean mediocre —hardly worth the expense of seeing it. Only a "money notice" is considered a favorable review—something having at least the force of a full-page newspaper ad. Criticism in such an atmosphere is perilously difficult. Theatre managers who complain about the reviewers do not want criticism; they want praise verging on hysterics. This generally holds true for playwrights and actors as well.

The reaction on the part of some critics to this journalistic inflation is to reverse the process: to preserve their critical chastity they assume an attitude of absolute severity. They will have nothing but the "best"; they insist on "the highest standards." One cannot be too extreme, they feel, in defense of Excellence.

Such a posture strikes me as no less false than the promiscuity of those addicted to raving about any presentation that can decently be commended at all. For while some absolute standard must be latent in the critic's mind if he is to give any play its proper place, it is not at all necessary or desirable to judge every new play on the basis of that ideal. There is even something inimical to art in such a practice.

"Masterpieces," says the poet W. H. Auden, "should be kept for High Holidays of the Spirit." That is certainly not to deny that we need organizations to keep masterpieces perennially in view. But what we must demand above all in plays is that they *speak* to us, stir us in ways which most intimately and powerfully stir our senses and our souls, penetrate to the core what is most truly alive in us. To do so plays do not have to have the stamp of universality or impeccable inspiration, or signs of top-flight genius. They have to be the consistent and persuasive expression of genuine perception, individual in origin, social in application. If Aeschylus, Shakespeare, Molière are prototypes of dramatic greatness, it must be evident that many second-, third-, fourth- and fifth-rate plays may also fulfill the function of usable art.

It is no special feat to determine greatness retrospectively. The critic who implies that nothing less than the absolutely first-rate will do is usually more pedant than artist. Immortality awards are best conferred by our descendants. "A 'high standard,' " said Henry James, "is an excellent thing, but we fancy it sometimes takes away more than it gives." We live more fully on what we create now than on what was created for us in the past. That is as true for audiences as for the makers and doers.

Since we are speaking of the total phenomenon of the theatre, rather than of drama alone, we must remind ourselves that masterpieces badly produced or produced at the wrong time and place cease to occupy their exalted position; in fact, they no longer serve the purposes of art. Under the proper circumstances, on the stage and in the auditorium, plays of more modest literary pretentions may excel them. I am often given to understand that Sophocles was a greater dramatist than O'Neill. I need no such instruction. It is nonetheless true that most productions of Sophocles (and of other Greek masters) have struck me as singularly empty, while certain O'Neill staged plays have impressed me deeply. To make this crushingly clear, on a recent radio program I informed the manager who sponsored both the 1964 Broadway *Hamlet* and *Beyond the Fringe* that I believed the latter contained the greater artistic value.

We have also learned that some dramatists of unquestioned stature—Goethe, Kleist, Racine, Strindberg—do not have the same impact in one country as in another, or make the impression they presumably should, even upon their own people at all times.

Talent of every kind, even small talent, must always be credited. That is particularly so of talent close to us in time and place. I do not suggest that we follow Herman Melville's injunction "Let America first praise mediocrity in her children before she praises . . . the best excellence in children of other lands." I submit, however, that a sense of the present and of presence are factors which it is unwise to overlook or underestimate. But the critical faculty does not consist only in recognizing talent; there must be also an ability to evaluate it. The American theatre is richly supplied (I almost said lousy) with talent, but too often talent not worthy enough to put to the best uses.

This raises an aspect of theatre criticism in which we are decidedly at fault. Our praise is usually the response to an effect, a register of stimulation. We applaud the person who produces the effect in an acclaim which ranges from a compliment to cleverness to the proclamation of genius. But what counts in talent is its specific gravity, its meaning, how and in what way it affects us, the human nourishment it offers us. Potassium cyanide is tremendously effective, but it is not food.

Everything—even the damnable—must be expressed in the theatre. I cannot hold anything to be true unless tested by its opposite. I need Beckett's negations if for no other reason than that they fortify me in my affirmations. I need Genet's "decadence" to sustain my health. I embrace the madness in certain modern dramatists to find my balance. To be sure, there is authentic "far-out" writing and there is fashionable simulacrum; it is the critic's task to distinguish between them. He must sift the stuff which composes each particular talent in relation to himself as a person representative of a certain public. "Entertainment," "good theatre," "beauty" are not enough. We must know what these virtues actually do, how they work. The critic's main job, I repeat, is not to speak of his likes or dislikes as pleasure or distaste alone, but to define as exactly as possible the nature of what he examines. And it is best to do this without the use of tags intended for quotes to be read on the run.

What I have said about the judgment of texts applies equally to acting and to those other ingredients which go into the making of a play in the theatre. ("To see sad sights," Shakespeare tells us, "moves more than to hear them told/For the eye interprets to the ear . . .") Most criticism nowadays is even more meager in regard to acting, direction and design than in evaluation of the texts themselves. Merit in acting is weighed chiefly by the degree of personal appeal it exercises. The actor is rarely judged for his relevance to the play as a whole since the play's meaning to begin with is frequently unspecified. To speak to the point about acting, the critic must judge the texture and composition of the role as the player shapes it through his natural endowment and through the authority of his craft.

Perhaps critics should not be held to too-strict account for neglect or oversight in the matter of acting, direction, etc., since most acting and direction on our stage today is rarely better than competent. In such cases a consideration "in depth" becomes supererogatory when it is not pretentious. Still, even with actors as eminent as Laurence Olivier, Alfred Lunt, Paul Scofield, Jean-Louis Barrault, or with directors as accomplished as Tyrone Guthrie, Peter Brook, Orson Welles, what our critics have to say usually comes down to little more than catchphrases, a bleat of unreserved enthusiasm or regretted disapproval. In this connection I must cite a fact first called to my attention by Jacques Copeau, the actor-director who strongly influenced Louis Jouvet, Charles Dullin and a whole generation of European theatre folk from 1913 to 1941: there have been fewer *great actors* in the history of the theatre than great dramatists.

No doubt I have often made hash in my reviews and essays of many of my own prescriptions. In extenuation I can only urge that while I am not sure I agree with an admirable literary critic I heard lecture many years ago in Paris who said, "The artist has every right; a critic only obligations," I always bear it in mind.

Richard Gilman
The Necessity for Destructive Criticism

RICHARD GILMAN (1925–   ) is professor of playwriting and criticism at the
Yale Drama School. He has been drama critic of *Commonweal* and *Newsweek* and
has written numerous books of dramatic criticism. In the essay reprinted here, he
argues that "destructive" criticism is not a negative force in theatre, but rather a source
of enlightenment.

◆ It was George Jean Nathan who in an uncharacteristic moment of
despair observed that drama criticism was probably the most useless activity
in the world. Play *reviewing* obviously does have an effect, although almost
never of an intellectual or aesthetic kind, but the criticism of drama seems to
drop into the most soundless of voids. The journalist-critic writes his pieces
—reasoning, cajoling, making analyses, presenting visions—and the machinery of the theatre grinds on in its heavy, automatic, self-perpetuating dream.
Broadway listens only to its own voice or to those voices from outside which
tell it what it wants to hear. And criticism is the one thing it has never wanted
to hear.

And yet if asked, Broadway, represented nowadays by at least one
negotiator who has gone to Harvard and who exhibits the weary patient smile
of someone who has been through all the sociologies of taste and heard all the
exhortations from Copeau and Artaud and Barrault, who knows the value or
at least the price of Brecht and the maximum titillating power of Ionesco or
Beckett, would more than likely reply that it certainly is willing to listen to
criticism, only *constructive* criticism, if you please and if you are capable of
providing it.

To which the critic, that horn-rimmed, golden-goose-killing neurotic,
that Kropotkin of the weekly or monthly or quarterly press, can only retort that
he doesn't please and isn't capable, for the simple reason that there is no such
thing as constructive criticism, in drama or any other art, the virulent illusion
that there is, or should be, being one of the chief reasons why the contemporary stage seems so entirely beyond redemption.

Some years ago Niccolo Tucci published a brilliant essay dealing with
the fallacies and deceitfulness inherent in the notion of constructive criticism.
His piece was about politics, specifically about the right and obligation of the
citizen to call his government on the carpet for its derelictions or wicked acts,
without necessarily having alternatives to put forward or anything positive to
say. But his central point—that the people who insist that criticism be con-

structive are invariably asking that it be kind, indulgent, boneless and corroborative, that it not be criticism at all—was and remains pertinent to areas far beyond politics.

I want now to examine the implications for drama of Tucci's idea, and along the way to look into the relations of the theatre with those persons whose profession, or trade, it is to comment upon what happens on our stages. We may discover that what is "constructive" in the lexicon of the theatre had indeed no real existence, while the so-called "destructive" element works, oddly enough, as a source of light.

Before proceeding, I want to repeat a distinction I shall employ from now on, that between reviewers and critics. Snobbish, if you will, indecorous, probably quixotic. But it seems to me that we are never going to get out of the miasma of deceit, self-pity and wishful thinking that rises from the theatre in this country as it does from no other medium, unless we begin to accept those distinctions that operate in actuality—in our case between actors and stars, dramas and hits, art and artisanship—and critics and reviewers.

Perhaps the greatest irony in a situation bursting with ironies is the reiterated idea that the critics are killing the theatre. Now we all know that when theatre people or the public refer to the "critics" they almost always mean the New York reviewers. It is certainly true that the critics, those persons whom the dictionary describes as "skilled in judging the qualities or merits of some class of things, esp. of literary or artistic work," have long harbored murderous thoughts about the condition of our drama, but their ineffectuality as public executioners is legendary. The reviewers, on the other hand, come close to being the most loyal and effective allies the commercial theatre could possibly desire. But not close enough, it would seem—the thing constitutes a case of an absolute desire encountering a relative compliance.

As a corollary of its demand for constructive criticism the theatre insists on absolute loyalty, and clearly receives a very high degree of it from the reviewers, who are all "theatre-lovers" to one or another flaming extent. And that brings us to our second irony. For "loyalty in a critic," Bernard Shaw wrote, "is corruption." This richly disturbing remark comes near the heart of so much that is wrong in the relationship between the stage and those who write about it from seats of power or seats of romantic yearning. From the true critic the theatre generally gets what can only be interpreted as gross infidelity, the reason being, as Shaw and every other major observer of drama makes abundantly clear, and as our own sense of what is civilized should tell us, that the critic cannot give his loyalty to men and institutions since he owes it to something a great deal more permanent.

He owes it, of course, to truth and to dramatic art. Once he sacrifices truth to men or art to institutions he is corrupt, unless, as is so frequently the case, he has never had any capacity for determining truth or any knowledge of dramatic art; for such men, corruption is clearly too grandiose a condition. But at least some of the reviewers are men of ordinarily developed taste and some intellectual maturity, and it is among them that corruption, in the sense not of venality or outright malfeasance but of the abandonment of a higher to a lower good, operates continually and in the name of that very loyalty which is worn like a badge of honor.

In "reviewerese," that peculiar language in which seven words—haunting, striking, gripping, charming, powerful, stunning and refreshing—do the heaviest duty, and in whose Golden Treasury the line "Momma, momma, momma, what a good solid show!" represents the ultimate in lyrical expression, the vapidity and perversion of values is spread out daily for all of us to see. But seldom has the dishonesty of popular stage reporting been so openly revealed and even trumpeted as it was by Walter Kerr, who is beyond question a critic fallen among reviewers, a man of wit, taste and useful ideas, whenever, that is to say, he is not busy sending telegrams to his mother.

With only the slightest indication that he was at all troubled by the matter, Mr. Kerr told a television audience that he felt he simply had to juice up his favorable notices, so that a mediocre work would come out entertaining, a passable one superior and a good one superlative. The reason was that if his language invariably matched his perceptions his readers, who were also of course potential theatregoers, would scarcely ever be encouraged to buy tickets.

Mr. Kerr left no doubt that he practiced what the naïve among us can only regard as a piece of high-level chicanery because of his passionate interest in the survival of the theatre. Such exclusive and truth-despoiling devotion is familiar to us in other areas, in advertising, for example ("my sometimes flagging faith that a dramatic critic is the servant of a high art, and not a mere advertiser of entertainments"—G.B.S.), or professional patriotism. We are forever coming up against this rationalization: if you want the theatre to survive, you have to lie on its behalf, you have to play the game, the name of which is "My-Theatre-Right-or-Wrong." How astonishing it is that the producers seem not to be aware that it is being played.

The truth is that their grievance against the reviewers stems from the fact that the game is not played as strictly as they would like. The reviewers do have standards, debased and flexible as they are, whereas the producers, with very few exceptions, have none, or at least none that are reliable. The result is that whereas each producer desires only that his particular offering be accepted and endorsed, the reviewers, some of whom may have to turn themselves into knots to do it, continue to judge plays and spectacles according to certain standards of professionalism, minimal criteria of humor, excitement, display, and quite shrewdly arrived-at norms of public acceptability and potential popularity (editors, Max Beerbohm wrote, "mostly engage for the criticism of plays men whose opinions coincide as nearly as possible with those of the public").

A double or elastic standard is better than nothing, which would seem to establish the public's debt to the newspapers for that much if nothing more. But the producers are also in the reviewers' debt, for without the latter's insistence that Broadway be Broadway, that it continue to serve, that is to say, a normative and exceedingly slowly changing idea of entertainment and popular enlightenment, the commercial stage would quickly enough degenerate into a condition of utter capriciousness, a flux in whose wash and roll the potential audience would find itself entirely without bearings and imposed on from every side.

What is much worse, from the managerial point of view, is that the sufferings and bewilderment of an audience from whom all guidelines have been snatched away, would eventually be translated into renunciation and flight. Just as its literary counterpart, the clientele of Womrath's, would largely give up reading if best-seller lists were to stop appearing, the Broadway audience, deprived of its caveats and assurances, its Hits, Smashes and Bombs, would give up going to the theatre rather than face the terrors of unpredictable experience and unheard-of sights. It would not be a question of merit: what is too good is surely as alarming as what is bad.

In fact, that is the point about the reviewers, that they exist, consciously or not, to keep Broadway functioning within staked-out grounds. They preserve it as the arena for theatrical enterprises which may neither rise above an upper limit determined by a line stretching between the imaginations of Lillian Hellman, William Inge and Richard Rodgers, nor beneath a lower one marked out by the inventiveness and sense of life of Norman Krasna, Harry Kurnitz and Garson Kanin. Whatever creeps into the spaces North or South of this Central Park of the imagination is adventitious, arbitrary, hermetic; if it is good, if it is art, if it is *Waiting for Godot*, its presence on the Street may confidently be ascribed to someone's idea of a joke that just might pay off.

Outside the theatre's hothouse, not part of its clubbiness, its opening-night ceremonies or its cabalisms, unconsulted about the honors it awards itself, and owing no more devotion to it than the literary critic owes to publishers or the art critic to galleries, the serious critic of drama is left free —to do what? To judge. "There is one and only one justification for the trade of drama criticism," Nathan wrote, "and that is to criticize drama and not merely apologize for it." And Shaw went further: "A critic is most certainly not in the position of a co-respondent in a divorce case: he is in no way bound to perjure himself to shield the reputation of the profession he criticizes. Far from being the instigator of its crimes and the partner of its guilty joys, he is the policeman of dramatic art; and it is his express business to denounce its delinquencies."

It is this idea of the critic as policeman that infuriates theatre people to the limit of their anarchistic temperaments. Their anger, as I have pointed out, is wrongly directed against the reviewers, who although they possess almost limitless powers of life and death are the Keystone Cops of the profession, whereas the critics, the FBI whose penal code is immeasurably severer and more uncompromising, possess almost no means of making their indictments stick.

Still, that may be a temporary matter. For there is a type of theatre person who senses that when the last shekel is in and the last platitude echoed, it will be the weekly and monthly critics, the best among them at any rate, who will have the last word, as Shaw wrote that posterity would remember the plays and performers of his time as *he,* and not the newspapers, evaluated them.

In whose pantheon now is Miss Hope Booth, "a young lady who cannot sing, act, dance or speak, but whose appearance suggests that she might profitably spend three or four years in learning these arts, which are useful on the stage"? And in which of our playhouses are the revivals of Sydney Grundy, Jerome K. Jerome and Arthur Wing Pinero, those manipulators of "dead machinery" who were the Inge, Schary and Chayefsky of their day? The nature of Shaw's "constructive" criticism was that it helped build tombs for all the lifeless drama of his time and thereby cleared the ground for something better.

Go through the three volumes of Shaw's criticism, covering as many London seasons, and you will find that not once in fifteen or twenty times was he anything but indignant at what he was called upon to see. Without pity he excoriated the theatre of the nineties, which sounds so much like our own, with its "dull routine of boom, bankruptcy and boredom," its performers' "eternal clamor for really artistic work and their ignominious collapse when they are taken at their word by Ibsen or anyone else," its lugubrious spectacle of "the drama losing its hold on life." It was only when once or twice a year something came along that did have a hold on life that Shaw's critiques turned enthusiastic and positive. But not "constructive"; you do not patronize or act generously toward artistic accomplishment—you identify it.

For if the critic is not the maker of dramatic art, he is the man most able to say what it is, and at the same time to establish the conditions in which it may flourish or at least gain a foothold. By being negative, *destructive,* if you please, toward everything else, he can help it outride the ephemera of "smash" and "riot" and "socko." And he will do his championing nearly always in the teeth of the coiners of those inimitable descriptive terms. To the handful of great journalist-critics the English-speaking stage has had—Shaw, Beerbohm, Nathan (for all his crotchets and his Francophobia), Stark Young and Eric Bentley—we owe most of our knowledge of the permanent drama of our time, and in most cases we owe even the opportunity to see or read it.

When the London reviewers were doing their best to drive Ibsen back to the depraved Continent (*Ghosts* was "unutterably offensive," "revoltingly suggestive and blasphemous," "a dirty act done publicly") it was Shaw, along with William Archer, who fought brilliantly and implacably to keep open the door to a resurrected drama. Later Nathan helped O'Neill past the roadblock of those newspapermen who characteristically admired his "power" while being terrified of his thematic and technical innovations. And more recently the truly heroic work of Eric Bentley, both in introducing us to the most vital contemporary and nineteenth-century European plays and in promulgating standards for a potentially mature American theatre, is a monument to the critical spirit at its untiring best.

Beerbohm once described what that critical spirit, which in relation to the stage seems never to be incarnate in more than three or four journalists at the same time, is perennially up against in its efforts to keep dramatic art alive. "My colleagues," he wrote, "have, for the most part, a primitive mistrust of strangers. They do not say, 'Here is new blood. Let us help it to circulate,' but, 'Here is new blood. Let us throw cold water on it.'"

Plus ça change . . . We know what it has been like trying to get our own new blood to circulate. The xenophobic response to the only interesting and significant works of the past fifteen years, the wretched, dismal inability even to begin to understand that a change is coming over some of the primary notions of drama as art, so that the stage may at least be enabled to catch up with painting and music and the movies—the whole depressing history is available to anyone who wants to spend a few hours in the newspaper branch of the New York Public Library.

Yet in reality it is not as depressing as it might have been, since it is relieved by one of those glorious streaks of irony which make the history and sociology of popular culture so much more entertaining than its products. The truth is that things do change; it is only the various kinds of spirit which remain the same. Thus the reviewers and the Broadway intelligentsia (the people who admire *J.B.* and keep one eye Off-Broadway for trends and applaud experiment whenever it is nonexperimental) have been considerably more open to the new drama than were Shaw's and Beerbohm's contemporaries to Ibsen and Hauptmann and Shaw himself. We may be forgiven for thinking it would have been a cleaner thing all round if they had remained closed.

After years of not getting Ionesco they discover him in *Rhinoceros,* his least characteristic and probably worst play. They recognize something in Beckett, but chiefly when Bert Lahr is around using his splendid talents to turn the piece into vaudeville; by now, having never understood him, they find Beckett old hat and yawn through all his newer plays. They haven't the faintest notion of what *The Blacks* is about, but extol its "theatricality" and ritualisms the way they would a Senegalese rain dance.

Having turned purple at *The Connection* and then been advised that it is the most interesting new work by an American in years, a number of them greet *The Apple,* an outstanding example of second-year jinx, with vastly increased respect. And they raise to demi-godhood the author of *Oh Dad,* and thereby demonstrate once again that to the eye of the freshman the sophomore is a dazzling sight.

But everything new, whether or not it is good and whether or not, if it is good, it is understood, is at the periphery. At the center the manufacturing and packaging of the familiar goes on, taking up most of everybody's time, including the critics, who have to come on the scene on second nights and prepare to undo, for their own readers and perhaps for posterity, what the reviewers have accomplished that morning. It may be the necessity of pointing out that *Gideon* serves a conformist idea of nonconformity and is full of spurious philosophy and neighborhood metaphysics. Or that *A Gift of Time* isn't merely "somewhat lacking in tension" but entirely ugly, with the ugliness that comes from substituting at every point the contrived and the debased for the living imagination.

Each season has its *No Strings,* the occasion on which the naked emperor is hailed as being most magnificently clothed, where the synthetic, the factitious, the false and the deracinated converge to form an exemplary reminder of the commercial theatre's flight from art and life *and* entertainment, if that was what you had modestly been looking for. (The fantastic dishonesty with which the racial theme is handled, and the consequent singling out of that very element for special praise, make for one of the best possible commentaries on our current situation; we are truly up to 1984 in the theatre, or a little beyond.)

Every season also has its tides of sycophancy on which float the reputations of certain star performers and against which the critic may want to throw himself as a minor countercurrent, so that Jason Robards, Jr., and Maurice Evans and Barbara Bel Geddes will not think that the seas are all that smooth. Or, turning around, he may want to say a word, if not of praise then of comfort, for the kind of inept but unpretentious Off-Broadway effort upon which the newspapers habitually unload all the scorn and vituperation which their pusillanimity or thralldom prevents them from delivering to those big houses on the Street which can seat five or six times as many of the bilked.

Well, who cares? Who is listening? Already the new season is upon us, the posters are up, the excitement and renewed hope and smell of possible success are in the air. The forecasts and previews are in the Sunday sections. We see that Willard Flange's new play, *The Tongue at the Roof of the Mouth,* described as a "study of backbiting in a Nebraska town," will be the first major work to open. Lillabet Paradise has written a drama based on the life of Jessica Dragonette, and it will star Frieda Zeitz-Kochmann, who has been enticed from retirement. Three musicals adapted from *The Origin of Species* will oepn within four days of one another.

The Leopoldville Art Theatre will be at the City Center with entirely revamped stagings of the classic Congolese repertoire. Harold Frond's Bjornson cycle resumes at the Sixth Street with the seventeenth offering in the series. A boxing match between a three-year-old spastic and his father's common-law wife will be the highlight of *You Got It, You Keep It,* the much-heralded new comedy by Alec and Bill and Frannie and Hobart and Pru Turnbull, which is being directed by Zoltan and Imre and Miklos and Istvan Chardash, with sets by Hammacher and Jim and Schlemmer Hotley. And Saratoga Wilson reports that there isn't a single mean or depraved character in his new work, scheduled for the same theatre as the long-awaited musical based on the life of . . .

We will recover. The committees will name the prize winners, the producers will issue a statement saying that the critics are certainly going to kill the theatre, which could survive even them if only the entertainment tax would be lifted. A noted director will write an article allowing as how all the theatre needs is a few old-fashioned hits, and another will write one denouncing people who forget that the business of the theatre is entertainment. Three reviewers will call it the best season in seven years, three will call it the worst in eight.

And the critic, to whom seasons are the least of considerations, will recover himself in silence, cultivating his sorrow, his anger and his narrow hope. And keeping his powder dry.

10

THE THEATRE AND SOCIETY

◆ . . . current social fantasy . . . . . . the spectator wants to understand . . . . . . interpretation of truth . . . . . . public dreaming . . . . . . instrument of social innovation . . . . . . volatile and unpredictable . . . . . . taken out of themselves . . . . . . integrally bound together . . . . . . self-control is the enemy of good theatre . . . . . . breach the taboo . . . . . . everyone wants to identify . . . . . . symbol-giving ceremonies . . . . . . a mirror . . .
. . . does not change the world . . .

Henri Ghéon
The Conditions of Dramatic Art

HENRI GHÉON (1875–1944) was a French poet and dramatist whose plays were modeled on the medieval mystery plays. In 1923 he was asked by Jacques Copeau to give some talks to the actors at Copeau's theatre, the Vieux-Colombier. These talks were published in the United States in 1961 under the title *The Art of the Theatre.*

◆ There is nothing equal to the stage as a school for humility. The author is essentially dependent on the possibilities of the actor. In accord with the style, with the laws of the dramatic action (plastic form, movement, development), he must further appeal to the costumer, the set designer, the electrician, the mechanic, the director—if he does not himself direct—above all, to the actors, I should insist here on the harm done to dramatic art when the perilous harmony of these instruments is shattered, when the inadequacy of the play, of the playwright's skill, tempts one or another—director, designer, actor—to work on his own. That is the reason for the too-frequent failures in our contemporary theatre. . . . Do we then conclude that when the spirit of the play has fused author and actors into a living whole and the curtain goes up, then at last the work has come to life? . . . No, not at all—as yet, nothing has been done: there has to be an audience.

For dramatic art is not achieved by an author writing his play in a corner, nor by a group of trained actors giving it life on the stage; it requires also an audience to receive it. It is author, actors, audience. We cannot eliminate any one of these three elements: they are integrally bound together.

You can imagine a picture that an artist paints for himself alone. You can imagine a poem that the poet recites to himself from morning to night but never repeats to other men. You can imagine a novel that has never been read, asleep in a desk drawer. But you cannot imagine a play, written, rehearsed, staged, finally produced, and then acted before empty chairs. At least when this does happen, it is far from pleasing to actors and author; for a play is not an end in itself. I mentioned above the strange liberty of novelist and poet in regard to their public. In our time this has turned into contempt for the public. It is true that to run after the public, to flatter its prejudices and weaknesses, is not the best way for an author to deepen and perfect his art. But it is quite another thing to despise the public, to discourage it, to slam the door in its face and refuse to speak to it. The writer who seeks publication wants to be read, otherwise he would write only to give form to his own ideas, his dreams; no need to go into print. All art is essentially social. But as I have also said, he who writes books is absolutely free to wait for his public. They may come or not, many of them or few, today, tomorrow, in ten years or in a century. It does not matter. The poem, novel, essay, remains printed on the pages of its book; it exists now and will not exist with any more reality on the day when it has ten thousand, twenty thousand, a hundred thousand readers. It is not influenced by the eventual reader; he cannot change it either before or after (I am not speaking of commercial literature); it is the reader alone who is influenced, more or less deeply, sooner or later. Great writers, like our classic writers, will show a certain elementary and courteous consideration for their public, being careful in grammar, syntax, logic, using language not too remote from common speech. But they know too that a book can be reread, picked up when one wishes, put aside again, returned to, opened and closed again; hence they will not dilute their thought because it is difficult, nor their style because it is elliptical. If the reader complains, so much the worse for him— he is not worthy to understand! No poem or novel or essay need be popular.

The case is quite different with dramatic work. It is like a book that is being read aloud, its pages turned remorselessly from the first to the last chapter. When a word has been spoken, it has been spoken; you cannot ask the actor to repeat it. That certainly would be a rich comedy, if you could imagine a difficult play punctuated by spectators rising in turn, demanding a replay of some fragment of the first act, a monologue in the third—they had missed the point at the time. The more intelligent—and those longing to seem intelligent—would protest with indignant "shushes!" Altercations, disorder, fist-fights! The drama would move off the stage into the house: action on the stage would stop. I am not fooling. Whether he pays for his seat or not, the spectator wants to understand, right on the spot, what the actor is saying. Hence the need of clarity, of intelligibility. The theatre is the very shrine of the manifest. This is the first servitude that the playwright must accept, willingly or not: no matter how exquisite, stylized, erudite, significant, image-flowered it may be, the language he uses must be understandable by all.

A second servitude is no less rigorous. We must go beyond the letter and the word to the object which they signify. It is no use for the words to be exact, the sentences well constructed, the ideas logically and clearly developed, if the thought or feeling touches no chord in the minds and hearts of the audience and calls forth not even a faint echo of that feeling and that thought! Still worse if they call out a contrary reaction. That can happen; in fact it happens frequently. Some weep, and others laugh at the same thing; two plays are being performed at the same time, one comic, one pathetic. Which is the true play, tell me? The one the author intended? In that case, let him keep it to himself. He is expressing feeling and thoughts to his contemporaries that they do not share. "Excuse me," you may object, "do any two men ever have even one emotion or one idea exactly alike?" Certainly not, in details. But in general, yes. For there are certain intellectual and moral values on which the majority agree in any real society: good and evil, true and false (I do not say beauty and ugliness; these are aesthetic values, and as such are subject to variation in the best of societies; let us not get involved in pure aesthetics, please). Agreement on what is good, agreement on what is true: the man who writes for the theatre must create at least that minimum of communion between his work and his audience. Only then will he touch feelings and win the assent he desires. A play really exists, lives and really lives, only when its lifespark leaps from the stage and from the playwright's soul across to the audience in a moment of vital contact. That is why Jacques Copeau said in a phrase I love to quote:

> There will never be a new theatre (meaning a reaction against today's falsified theatre in a return to tradition) until the day comes when the man in the audience murmurs in his heart and with his heart the same words spoken by the man on the stage.

Yes, the day when author and spectator—and I may add, actor also, for he is the hyphen between them—are one, and stand together on the same intellectual and moral ground. For communion we need such ground. But it can exist only in a truly organic society, by which I mean a society that has a center, a coherence and unanimity: it recognizes one good as *good* and one truth as *true*.

But if society is not organic, or if there is no society at all—what happens? Well, there will not be any theatre, or at the most a fragmentary, stammering, time-serving theatre. There will be no understanding, no communication, no communion. The play will have to crawl into the book, and wait for better days.

It cannot wait too long; for in the theatre, too long a delay in realization alters the concept itself. While the author is working on his play, unless he has at hand and under his control all the elements of language and technique as well as actors and audience, the validity of his "creative activity," as Maritain says, will be hopelessly falsified. He is not one, but two, or rather three; what matters is not only that many speak his name, but that all should answer him.

There is a school that conceives the stage as a room with one wall removed where something happens. I imagine it more as a platform set up in the midst of a crowd, a place of perpetual barter. A dramatic author must make a practical study of the conditions of that barter, discover its laws, make sure that it is possible, that he is not speaking a tongue alien to his public.

Thus dramatic art presupposes both in theory and in fact the existence of a homogeneous society, a "people" in the noblest meaning of the word. It is not a closed art, nor a long-range art, but an open, immediate art. Pity the author who feels within himself power to give substance to a dream that haunts him, yet who can find nothing outside to help him. It would be a miracle if he could create life in the present only by his hope for the future. True, there are certain great works that for special reasons did not succeed in their author's lifetime, even though they were essentially in accord with their age; their dramatic success was only a little deferred. But no plays of real vitality were misunderstood and rejected in their own day only to grip the emotions of an audience centuries later. Plays that survive or revive, as I have said, are plays that have once been alive.

Such are the essential conditions for drama. It depends on its own lifetime to exist or not. . . .

. . . The dramatist is imprisoned in the contingencies of theatre and of society; the character of his art is essentially social.

[*Translated by Adele M. Fiske*]

Ann Jellicoe
Some Unconscious Influences in the Theatre

ANN JELLICOE (1927–   ) is a playwright, director, and translator, and is currently the literary manager of The Royal Court Theatre in London. She is best known for her plays *The Knack* (1961) and *The Sport of My Mad Mother* (1956). The essay included here was a lecture she gave at Cambridge University in which she describes how each performance of a play is shaped by its audience.

◆   All art seeks to impose its own truth, and I want to consider some of the ways in which a dramatist tries to impose his truth upon us, how we are conditioned before ever we enter the theatre, the unconscious and unacknowledged forces operating upon us while we are there, finally I want to consider how the desire to impose truth may defeat itself.

It would be idle to try and define truth except to say that insofar as the artist is concerned truth is his personal view of fact and reality interpreted by him in terms of his art; but it may also be the demand of a work of art to be pursued to its absolute conclusion. The validity of an artist's view and interpretation of truth obviously depends upon his integrity, perception and skill as an artist. I am unwilling to discuss how far the artist's perception of truth may depend upon intellectual intelligence or upon that other artistic intelligence—the intelligence a sculptor may have in his hands for example.

But I would suggest that for most artists creating a work of art is also indissolubly searching for truth; and that art is less a process of creation than a process of discovery: the work demands and creates itself, the artist merely waits attentively for the work to reveal itself. But this also demands that the artist ask certain questions, answer certain problems in seeking to discover the nature of the work. And in his struggle the artist makes discoveries which release energy, excitement and enthusiasm which give his work power. The power of a work springs directly from its truth. The work having been created there is then an urgent desire to show it to other people. Artists must communicate. A work of art is not complete until it reaches its audience.

All art demands its audience but the audience is especially important in the theatre. In the theatre the audience cannot have an individual reaction, and their corporate reaction swamps individual judgement in a manner, and to a degree, I wouldn't have thought possible if I hadn't had the experience of travelling round the provinces on tour with my own play, seeing a familiar work with different audiences, and observing how those audiences affected my judgement of the work. The theatrical experience is not merely the experience of the play, but of experiencing it in company with the rest of the audience who colour the event to a degree of which one is largely unconscious.

But let us go back for the moment and consider one of the reasons why the audience goes to the theatre. The theatre audience is notoriously not a fair cross-section of the population. By and large they are newspaper readers. The theatre-going public is largely the readership of those papers giving most space to theatre criticism. Theatre people will tell you that the *Mirror,* the *News of the World* and *The People* mean little at the box office; but *The Times, Telegraph, Guardian, Financial Times, Express, Mail,* the two London evening papers and the three top Sundays all have great influence. One wants a good notice, or better still, a good selling notice, in any of them.

There is not much to choose between a good notice and a good selling notice, but for those concerned it may mean the difference between a degree of penury and considerable affluence. A good notice may finish by saying: 'There is nothing in this play which need deter the intelligent theatre goer.' A good selling notice may end: 'I urge you to see it.' A subtle degree of enthusiasm, but it means an immense difference in audience numbers. A really enthusiastic set of notices will bring huge audiences, all convinced they are going to see a good play. Whether it is in fact good is almost beside the point. The audience has been authoritatively told it's good, and by and large they will accept it as good; just as if they've been told it's funny they will tend to laugh. People look for what they have been told they will see. More subtly, if Harold Hobson says (as he has said) that Beckett is a greater writer than Sophocles then the audience who read Hobson are going to approach Beckett in a certain state of mind, for it has been strongly suggested that not merely is he a great writer, he is also a classic. It takes an awareness of the process and considerable confidence in one's own judgement to stand out against this conditioning.

More usefully critics will sort out an audience. Peter Lewis says in the *Mail* 'Rich uproarious belly laughs'. Of the same play Phillip Hope-Wallace writes in *The Guardian* 'Somewhat coarse humour'. One audience will be guided to the play, another will stay away. Obviously a certain kind of play will attract a certain kind of audience—intellectual perhaps at the Royal Court, less so at Drury Lane. An audience of common background and common age will react predictably to certain plays. Within the theatre certain factors are important. The business executives, doctors and lawyers in the stalls and dress circle have different values and may react differently from the teachers in the upper circle and the students in the gallery. Working as author or director I have often moved round a theatre during performance and noted that the stalls are indifferent while the balcony is enjoying itself. You will even find small pockets of reaction, their influence spreading for a few seats around and then falling off. The physical shape of a theatre is most important—too vast a subject to consider here; basically if you can't see or hear very well you may not be so deeply involved, unless there is a compensating strong audience reaction to lift you along—what one might call the gallery syndrome.

What does audience reaction mean? How does it work? What is actually happening when the audience reacts? It is a process that is taking place at this moment, for here I am, the performer, my status enhanced by an introduction, a raised position, the nature of the occasion when it is my privilege to speak. This all gives me power. And yet the very steps taken to protect my status imply my insecurity in this role. A process is taking place amongst you, of which you are probably unaware; you think you are forming an individual judgement, but I suggest you are forming a group judgement.

The first time I recognised this phenomenon and was able to isolate it was during the provincial tour of my play *The Knack.* The play opened here in Cambridge and the theatre was filled each night by young people who greatly enjoyed themselves. Without wishing to flatter I would say that under-graduates make good audiences, because the standard of intelligence is high, reactions are quick and lively; undergraduates tend to see a joke just before the point has been reached, thus they give themselves the extra, exquisite pleasure of having their suspicions confirmed. These audiences laughed a great deal and so did I. I watched the play three or four times sitting amongst them and laughed with them. I was aware that I wasn't totally in control of my reactions—self-control is the enemy of good theatre. The play did seem very funny, yet I'd lived with it for a long time and watched it many times in rehearsal, but with those first audiences it seemed quite fresh; I laughed at the play not as if I were seeing it for the first time but with a kind of fresh delight. Someone said to me, 'You laugh at your own play then?' and I had to confess I did; I excused myself by saying that the actors were extremely good—I genuinely did think this was the reason, and indeed the actors were good, but it was not the reason I laughed. The following week the play went to Bath —Bath in the late autumn when most of the summer visitors, such as they were, had departed. The audiences were thin and elderly, they were confused and outraged by the play, it was too quick and off-beat in style for them and they had no point of contact with the characters. Moreover, they found the play obscene; there were outraged letters in the local press about the obscene play which dealt with rape and kangaroo nipples and so forth; they couldn't make head or tail of it. Sitting in the auditorium amongst that audience, I did not want to laugh. More than that, the play appeared obscene to me. I had had a number of arguments with the Lord Chamberlain over certain lines which he had wanted to cut, but after discussion we were allowed to retain some of them. When these lines were said in Bath, and other lines which he had never even questioned, it seemed to me that the Lord Chamberlain was right—they were obscene. I began to think the Lord Chamberlain had a nice feeling for obscenity, but it was unpleasant: I had no wish to be the author of obscenity. There followed a good week in Cardiff. They told me the bar takings were the highest for years and I still wonder what that meant. But the play went well and my confidence was restored. Finally, *The Knack* came to London. The notices were good, but the audience were not given a strong lead. I was sitting in the audience watching the play and found myself thinking 'How could I ever have thought this play obscene? It's so innocent, it's so young.' Then, when the lights went up in the interval I noticed there was a large party of extremely sophisticated people in the row ahead of me; from their conversation they were clearly a group of people working in films.

I realised that, without having previously noticed them, and certainly not having been aware of them in the dark, their reaction was my reaction. It would almost be true to say that they had taken over my mind. There were a number of them, I was alone, their reaction was strong: 'How childlike, how innocent'; it became my reaction. Did this explain my laughing with the audience at Cambridge, and feeling of offence in Bath? I began to observe more carefully how each member of an audience is influenced by the reaction of those around them. And it now seems to me that no member of any audience of reasonable size can ever see a play in isolation. Their reaction is always coloured by the reaction of those around them. And not merely coloured: according to the nature of the audience, the play will appear quite different, will indeed be a different play, in Bath or London according to the audience with whom we see it. How many of us realise that, while play and acting may not change, what was a bad play when we saw it in Cheltenham last Wednesday may be splendid if we see it in Manchester next Friday?

The audience is the vital factor in the theatre, more volatile and unpredictable than play or actors, which are, after all, fixed entities. Even with improvised drama—and I don't mean improvised in rehearsal and then presented in a final form because the same rules still apply, but actually improvised in the presence of the audience—even with improvised drama the actor, though apparently in the dominating position, cannot take the audience other than where they are prepared to go. The way an audience will react will be determined by their particular make-up: a certain play will attract a certain audience. Once the audience is inside the theatre reaction will be affected by its physical shape. Finally the audience cannot react as individuals. The theatrical experience is essentially a buildup from within the audience in answer to the conditioning they have received about the play before they enter the theatre and the stimuli they receive from the stage.

There are objective standards in the theatre: a play may be original, forceful, truthful and well constructed but I think it is true to say that in the performance these standards are blurred and confused by the unconscious influences at work amongst the audience. You may judge a novel, for instance, as an individual, but there is no such thing as individual judgement in the theatre. You can indeed read a play and judge it as literature, but plays are not literature, they are performed by live actors to a live audience. A play read as literature is one thing, the theatrical experience is quite another. The theatrical experience is unconscious, subjective, powerful: an amalgam of the subconscious forces circulating amongst the audience, working from the stimuli they receive from the stage.

What is the nature of this stimulus? At its simplest a play is a device for capturing the audience's imagination and then taking it somewhere. What is imagination? How does it work? What does 'capturing the imagination' mean? May we concede that certain things do capture popular imagination—for instance, royalty, James Bond, John F. Kennedy, Danilo Dolci? The word 'capture' is significant, as if we were enthralled. These images, perhaps they are associated with status, money, fast cars, fine clothes, or with nobility of mind, high ideals, self-sacrifice; these are things we want to possess, actions we want to perform, status we wish to attain, ideals we want to follow. So the image possessing these qualities is attractive to us, and we readily allow it into our minds, we begin to play with it, to weave fantasies about it, picture ourselves in relation to the image, or imagine ourselves as the image. Basically one kind of imagination is based upon identification; certainly the words 'imagine' and 'imitate' share the same Latin root: to picture.

I was talking some time ago with an old sailor and he said, 'I went to the theatre once, it was in 1936. I thought I'd go because it was a play about the Navy.' He went because he had some idea that he would see an image of the life he knew and also, I suggest, because through identification he would be seeing himself. It wasn't simply that being a sailor he would easily imagine himself into the story, but through identification, seeing himself, he would be reassured that he existed and that his existence was significant. Possibly also, distancing himself from himself—seeing himself upon a stage going through certain experiences—would help to clarify his understanding of real life, reassure him as to the normality of certain stresses within himself, and possibly release certain of his tensions.

This explains all those drawing-room comedies with butlers and parlour-maids. They were designed for middle-class audiences with firmly entrenched and unquestioned values, who had perhaps one servant. The image of the class just above them was irresistibly attractive—in their scheme of values it was better to be a lord than a plain Mister, better to have a butler and a staff of servants than a mere housemaid. For two and a half hours the audience happily identified with Lady Kitty and Lord Chalfont, who were the image of what the audience wanted to be, and so they willingly and happily projected their dreams and desires upon this fantasy world. The point is that everyone wants to identify with those whom they feel are better than themselves. But what does 'better' mean? It may be more highly born, richer, more successful or perhaps more honest, more idealistic, more truthful, more courageous; or perhaps may be people whom the audience feel live more intensely and vividly than do the audience in their everyday lives.

These images, which society finds so attractive, may become powerful. They may indeed change the world. For we model ourselves on our chosen images, we begin to talk, dress, act and finally think like them. Jimmy Porter was such an image, James Dean another, Mick Jagger is another. I think it true to say that these helped to mould a generation. I don't think Jimmy Porter and James Dean were imposed upon the audiences of the fifties—and I doubt whether any image could be successfully imposed. It's rather that those who create a successful image recognise or sense some current social fantasy and give it a physical form. In a sense the audience creates the image; they create it to answer their need: the audience needs an image to imitate, upon which to project their imagination. By projection I mean that the audience begins to invest the images with their own fantasies and desires, emotional fears, anxieties and drives.

To give an example of what I mean by projection. Some months ago I was watching the Royal Court Theatre Studio, which was a group of professional actors who met regularly to experiment and extend their range. They were working with masks. There are two main types of mask, the comic and the tragic, and the technique of using them is a little different; here I am referring to the tragic mask. The tragic mask covers the actor's whole face, the face of the mask is expressionless, or rather, when held in the hand, has the expression the maker gave it; thus the actor cannot use the expression of his own face. Nor can he use his voice, for unlike the Greek masks, modern masks have no hole for the mouth; the open mouth of the Greek mask demands enormous proportions of the head and similar building up of the body—kothurni, high headdresses, padding, etc., which in turn is related to the size of Greek theatres. With the modern mask the actor appears utterly impoverished—no facial expression, no voice. He relies almost entirely upon the audience projecting its imagination. I was watching a simple scene between a mask and two speaking characters. The mask had lost the key of a tower in which her lover was imprisoned, the mask tried to get help to find the key, her anxiety was intense, at last someone understood, found the key and gave it back to her. At this point the mask smiled. The impression was so strong that I was jolted and looked more carefully, my identification was still strong enough to make me feel the mask really was smiling, I couldn't believe my eyes; they were indeed not to be believed, my intellect knew perfectly well that the mask was made of papiermâché and could not be smiling and yet my imagination projected a smile upon the mask. If imagination can make a rigid mask smile what can it not do? What is the limit of imagination in the theatre?

Another related observation: I was watching *Philoctetes* at the National Theatre and was struck by my reaction to Hercules' bow—at one moment I observed it with a detached professional interest as a well-made stage property, the next, my imagination having been caught, I began to invest it with power, it became a magical object to be handled with care and reverence, so that one was literally drawing in one's breath. This touches upon the central theatrical experience, theatrical dichotomy: you identify with the actor and yet you remain yourself. 'I am Hamlet, Prince of Denmark, yet I am also me sitting here in my seat.'

Theatrical dichotomy is the double experience that is at the heart of all theatre-going. The audience knows they are in a theatre watching a play that is make-believe, it's not really happening. They see before them actors on a stage who pretend to be certain people and pretend to be in a particular, developing situation; the actors invite the audience to join in this make-believe. And, given a good theatrical experience, the audience does indeed enter into the play, it allows itself to be carried away, but for most of the time the audience is well aware of reality. It doesn't lose itself entirely in the fantasy world. A double experience is taking place: the audience is caught up in the play and yet it's also aware that it's part of an audience sitting in a theatre. The audience plays at make-believe and knows that it is playing. If you increase the challenge to belief you also increase theatricality. In *A Midsummer Night's Dream* the dramatist has Oberon say, 'I am invisible and I will overhear their conference.' Oberon remains on stage and the actors behave as if he was not there. The audience then has the fun of seeing Oberon four-square in the scene and yet imagining him as invisible simply because he says he is and the other actors behave as if he is. Theatrical dichotomy is a comedian turning around in the middle of a revue sketch and talking directly to the audience, then going back into the sketch again—the reality conflicts with the play-acting and emphasises the two levels upon which the audience is experiencing. The challenge to belief may become finally so great that it is manifestly absurd —as is the case with the pantomime horse. This is so absurd that it demonstrates very clearly the true nature of theatre—theatre as play.

You can play with reality in this way in the theatre because you start with a self-evident basis of reality: live actors on a stage in front of a live audience. Films and television are essentially mechanical forms and they must first persuade you of reality; they are not real, so they must establish a standard of reality. Films and television are not magical because they can do anything. On film you can change a pine cone into a bag of gold, or make a man disappear—and this will actually happen before an audience's eyes, there is no challenge to the imagination. But in the theatre, as I've seen in pantomime, two thieves liable to be caught in a shop can say: 'Let's put this biscuit tin over our heads and then we'll be invisible, no one will see us.' And the other actors behave as if they cannot see them. It's ridiculous—as if putting a biscuit box on his head would make a man invisible. The audience knows the man is not invisible but enters into the joke that he is. The audience connive with the actors and with each other. They play together and in playing they enter into a particular relationship with the others in the theatre.

The audience goes to the theatre to be moved, to be 'taken out of themselves', to be 'carried away'. The good dramatist knows he must capture their imagination and hold it. To do this he uses any number of means, of which those of least use to him are intellectual. If the audience wants to be carried away the dramatist must induce surrender, so that he doesn't want to appeal to reason: rationalisation, objectivity—these are not states of mind which will help an audience to surrender. No. The appeal in the theatre must be to the senses, emotions and instincts. So we have colour, movement, rhythmical and musical sounds and use of words, and we have appeals to the half conscious and the unconscious: symbols, myths and rituals.

The hypnotic, or perhaps I should say psychedelic, qualities of sight and sound have been known and used in the theatre since earliest times, they have probably a more powerful direct effect upon the audience than any other stimuli, barring imagination. But speaking personally, I've long known of the power of sight and sound and the rules, such as they are, governing their use. On the other hand although my first play *The Sport of my Mad Mother* was built upon myth and ritual, it was written intuitively, I had no conscious idea of the means I was using. It's only in recent years that I've been able to analyse symbolism, myth and ritual, and in the time at my disposal I'd rather concentrate on them.

Symbolism has become a dirty word in the theatre since the war, probably because it was used in connection with the abstract, symbolic theatre of the thirties when symbols were made obvious and thrust down people's throats. This symbolic theatre developed as the poets' reply to the commercial theatre of the period which was almost wholly concerned with naturalism, materialism and the superficial display of manners. But symbolic theatre, being born of poets, was literary rather than dramatic. Let me digress and give an example of what I mean by literary. At one time I was running the Royal Court Theatre's Writers' Group, which met once a week in a free and easy fashion to improvise and allow writers to discover something about acting. One day a woman turned up when we were improvising upon the creation of the world. She didn't much like our attitude to the subject which was fairly tough and anarchic (which also means free and experimental), and said so. It seemed a good thing to let her try out her ideas. She set up a scene in which the Creator (herself) sat in the middle, whilst actors, representing the planets, revolved around her. Arnold Wesker and Edward Bond crouched down and revolved with generous seriousness. Her idea didn't work, not only because of the physical limitations of people but because it was a literary concept and not a theatrical concept. Later Arnold Wesker did a mime on the same subject with another girl. She sat inert and he began to mime life into her: he demonstrated each sense and then transferred it to her so that she was first roused and then gradually filled with life. This is a very theatrical concept and was later used in *I'm Talking About Jerusalem*.

The symbolic theatre then, was a literary theatre, and not very good at that. Symbolism came to be equated with a gutless abstract idealism, the kind of play where you don't have character but character types, and where every thought and every action has a wider symbolic application which is intellectualised: that is, made concrete in words so that the appeal is to the brain. But if symbolism is dead, symbols inescapably remain.

A symbol is a condensation of many kinds, and many layers, of experience. A symbol embodies an infinite number of ideas and associations more effectively and more economically than words, partly because a symbol is open-ended—each of us may read something different into a symbol and there is no limit to what we may read. But a symbol is also more effective than words simply because we don't as a rule consciously analyse what it means to us, it appeals subtly and insidiously, not to the brain, but to the less rational, less defined parts of our personality: to our emotions and memories.

A myth almost always embodies and illustrates in concrete form some human condition or confusion or perplexity: some tragedy, or mistake or mishap. Myths are the bodying forth, in stories, in images, of our longing, conflicts and fears, they give shape to the deepest human urges, often to unspoken, archetypal drives which cannot be formulated wholly in words. Myths deal often with urges so deeply rooted in human nature that they relate to our earliest infancy and to the earliest infancy of man, urges which have nothing to do with rational thought, and over which rational thought has little power. A myth speaks directly to the deepest parts of our nature.

One thinks of the myth of Hippolytus, the virginal young man torn to death by his own horses—horse of course being a sexual symbol. But it's quite possible to discover modern myths. I read recently of a fourteen-year-old girl who took her mother's birth control pills and ate them, putting aspirin in their place. As soon as the imagination begins to work on this story one senses the feeling of the ancient gods at play—a kind of meddling with power, so that any child born as a result should perhaps have remarkable and extreme qualities—be excessively ugly perhaps with some compensating special quality, or be marked out for some particular task.

Ritual is a device we use to give our lives scale and significance, to reassure ourselves as to the importance of our values, to celebrate such values. We create rituals when we wish to strengthen, celebrate or define our common life and common values, or when we want to give ourselves confidence to undertake a certain course of action. A ritual generally takes the form of repeating a pattern of words and gestures which tend to excite us above a normal state of mind. Once this state of mind is induced we are receptive and suggestible and ready for the climax of the rite. At the climax the essential nature of something is changed. As examples of rituals we may think of the mass, the marriage ceremony, the bestowal of diplomas, a coronation, etc. All these follow the same pattern, they reiterate a form of words and gestures inducing a mood of excitement and acceptance, when the audience is sufficiently receptive then the essential nature of something—some person, some relationship—is changed.

I would like to follow a specific example and try to illustrate the points that have already been made: the question of image-making in the theatre, of identification, of the appeal to the unconscious by means of symbolism, myth and ritual, and then I would like to show how all these well-laid schemes designed to seduce the audience may be turned inside-out if the dramatist doggedly pursues his idea of what he conceives to be the truth.

Let me take the story of Little Red Riding Hood, which so far as I know has had little dramatic treatment and is not one of the popular pantomimes. Perhaps we should go over the story briefly so that we may refresh our minds over certain details which may have been long since forgotten.

Once upon a time there was a little girl whose grandmother had given her a little red riding hood. The grandmother lived alone in the middle of a forest and one day Little Red Riding Hood's mother said to her, 'Grandma is ill, take this basket of food and bottle of wine to her, and, when you get into the forest, mind you keep to the path so that you don't lose your way or fall and break the bottle.' So Little Red Riding Hood set off. Once she was well into the wood, a wolf saw her and asked where she was going; when he heard she was on her way to her grandmother the wolf suggested that grandmother might like some of the wild flowers which were growing off the path. So Little Red Riding Hood wandered off the path deeper and deeper into the forest. The wolf hurried off to grandmother's house, gobbled up grandmother, put on her cap and spectacles and climbed into bed. Meanwhile Little Red Riding Hood had got lost and been put on her way by a friendly woodsman. When she arrived at grandmother's cottage she found the door open; inside was the wolf dressed as grandmother and sitting up in bed. 'Oh, Grandmother', said Little Red Riding Hood, 'what big ears you have.' 'All the better to hear you with', said the wolf. 'But grandmother, what big eyes you have.' 'All the better to see you with'. 'Oh, grandmother, what big teeth you have.' 'All the better to eat you with.' And at this the wolf jumped out of bed and ate up Little Red Riding Hood. But the woodsman, coming by to see that Little Red Riding Hood was all right, saw the wolf fast asleep after his meal. The woodsman was just about to kill the wolf when he realised that Little Red Riding Hood and her grandmother had disappeared and it occurred to him that the wolf might have eaten them. He slit open the wolf's belly and out popped Little Riding Hood and her grandmother. Little Red Riding Hood filled up the belly of the wolf with stones so that when he woke up he collapsed and died. And they all went home to mother and Little Red Riding Hood promised never to wander from the path again.

In *The Forgotten Language* Dr. Erich Fromm has analysed the symbolic and unconscious aspects of Little Red Riding Hood. He says: 'The little red riding hood is a symbol of menstruation, the warning "not to leave the path" and "not to fall and break the bottle" is a warning against the danger of sex and losing virginity.' The wolf's tempting Little Red Riding Hood into the deep forest is an attempt to seduce her. Fromm continues: 'The male is portrayed as a ruthless, cunning animal, and the sexual act is described as a cannibalistic act in which the male devours the female. This view is not held by women who like men and enjoy sex. But the hate and prejudice against men are more clearly exhibited at the end of the story . . . we must remember that woman's superiority consists in her ability to bear children. How, then is the wolf made ridiculous? By showing him attempting to play the part of a pregnant woman having living things in his belly. Little Red Riding Hood puts stones, a symbol of sterility, into his belly and the wolf collapses and dies. His death, according to the primitive law of retaliation, is punishment according to his crime, he is killed by stones, the symbol of sterility, which mock his usurpation of the woman's role.'

Perhaps this analysis explains why Little Red Riding Hood has never been as popular a subject for pantomime as say Cinderella or Aladdin. Putting it mildly, there is no one with whom men and boys might happily identify—the woodsman is a minor figure well off centre, but, more than this, men watching the performance are being asked to support an anti-male diatribe and would resent it. They might not know consciously why they didn't like the play, but they would react against it. In such a case they might well produce rationalisations; they might react by saying the play was boring, ill-constructed, pretentious, stupid—any rational reason would serve. Because, quite frankly, we are very often unaware of the real reasons why we reject something. And this includes drama critics. We may very often have valid, although unconscious, reasons for rejecting something—and I would agree with any man who refused to sit quietly through Red Riding Hood. The difficulty comes when we are unaware of our unconscious reasons for rejecting the play, and start rationalising them into false value judgements. It is really quite beside the point to call a play stupid, dull, boring or pretentious, if the real reason for our dislike lies elsewhere. It may indeed be a bad play objectively speaking. But I now distrust all negative criticism since there are so many subjective reasons why a play may be dismissed—reasons to do with our own nature rather than the nature of the play. The only kind of value judgement I do find myself able to trust is that of an artist who likes some piece of work—because an artist is knowledgeable and perceptive about his art and may be very clear as to why he likes the work. I'm afraid, if he dislikes it, an artist's reasons for dislike may be as subjective as anyone else's.

With Little Red Riding Hood as it stands I see little chance of a commercially successful play. I can imagine a socialist realist lesbian suffragette getting it up for a ladies evening, when it might indeed go with a swing. But if it were given a normal production it would be rejected out of hand because, of course, most drama critics are men.

I have said that art is a process of discovery rather than creation, to be more precise, apart from the vital intuitive leaps which an artist must make, the artist's most important job is to discover the right questions he must ask. Suppose one was becoming intrigued by the story of Little Red Riding Hood, to the point of beginning to write about it, what questions would one be asking oneself?

If you were a T.V. story editor—'The Writer's Best Friend' as, I think it was the Head of B.B.C. Drama said not so long ago—no doubt your question would be, 'How can this material be made more attractive to a general audience?' And surely the answer is not all that difficult. Our story editor will surely say that if the dramatist wants to engage the attention of the men in the audience he must strengthen and build up the character of the woodsman. It might be sufficient to have an opening scene demonstrating the power, skill, intelligence and general charm of the woodsman, and then, only when he is thoroughly established bring in Little Red Riding Hood. Thereafter the woodsman must appear regularly to maintain his hold on the audience's imagination. But I doubt if the story editor would consider that sufficient— the wolf is still too dominantly representing men in a most unflattering light. If you want men and boys to enjoy the play you must create an extra plot— quite as strong and possibly stronger than the present main plot. You might even have to introduce another character—the woodsman's little boy. Possibly the woodsman and the boy would be out to save the forest from spoliation by the wolf on the lines of Batman and Robin. Thus given a real hero, the woodsman, the wolf becomes unquestionably the villain and everyone in the audience can comfortably release their aggression towards him. They are free to hate the wolf and thus release the hate that is in all of them, and us, to some degree.

As regards myth and ritual, there is a text-book example of ritual in Little Red Riding Hood. The form of words in the ritual is established with the first two phrases 'Why grandmother what big ears you have', 'All the better to hear you with'. The form is confirmed in the second two phrases with a slight change of words which keeps the interest fresh and indicates further development. 'Why grandmother what big eyes you have', 'All the better to see you with.' With the third repetition the audience now knows the form of words and feels pleasure partly because it is in the know and so is flattered and put at ease, partly because of the sheer rhythmic seduction of the words, the two repetitions pointing to a third towards which the audience is, so to speak, leaning forward in expectation. The third repetition leads to the climax: Why grandmother what big teeth you have', 'All the better to eat you with.' Now the wolf's eating Red Riding Hood is not quite a surprise, because the wolf has already eaten the grandmother: the situation is clearly fraught with inter- est. The audience will be waiting for the climax, will suspect its nature. The reiteration of the verbal formula builds the tension yet holds back the climax, engendering more and more pleasurable excitement and anticipation. At the climax the excitement is released and the essential nature of something is changed.

As regards myth—myth being, at the moment, so fashionable—we can probably find something mythical in the forest: does it not represent the female principle—dark, secret, womblike, organic? Yet it is a threat to women. Men move in it freely and with confidence, they earn their livelihood from

it, it is a source of power: may this not reflect the male triumph over ma-
triarchy? Yet why does the grandmother live in the forest? Perhaps she per-
sonifies some older order of the organic female link with nature which still
survives and could threaten men?

Our story editor has now tilted the play to something more acceptable
to a general audience. The story seems solid with plenty of action. There are
figures with whom the audience may identify and an object on which they may
release their aggression. He has worked out ritual and some rather chic myth.
Finally the story is not going to offend anyone, it supports traditional morality,
so the audience is not going to have to come to terms with any new ideas, or
failing to come to terms with them is not going to have to find rational reasons
for their rejection. Well, there it is: efficient in a superficial kind of way.

Another man, not a story editor (that is, not a man brought in to botch
up a play and make it acceptable to an audience), might approach the material
quite differently. He may start writing something, messing around, enjoying
himself; but sooner or later he's going to feel dissatisfied and this feeling will
get stronger and stronger until he faces up to what's worrying him, whatever
it is. And he will have to stop what he's doing and start groping around trying
to discover what his problem is.

I think there is finally only one vital lesson for an artist, but all artists
must learn it and it's something they can only teach themselves. It is to know
when they are dissatisfied, to know that they must stop because they have lost
touch with some central vital thing. An artist must be ready to realise that
what he is doing has lost its point and ask himself why. To discover what he
is trying to express and then to sense if he has lost touch with it. An artist
is always trying for the absolute although I doubt whether he can ever be sure
that he has got there. Nevertheless, an artist in pursuing what he conceives
to be the truth feels a kind of peace and excitement the nearer he gets to the
centre of the problem.

I will now confess that while I earlier invented the character of the
story editor in order to demonstrate how not to approach a piece of work, it
was quite honestly my own initial approach. But, as always, there came a point
when one was dissatisfied with what one was doing, it seemed so superficial,
uninteresting and dishonest. And so I had to do what one always has to do:
face up to the questions which one hoped one would get by without facing.
In the course of this muddled questioning—and it is always muddled because
one has to follow false leads and so on—I began to make those creative
discoveries one always makes when one demands that one satisfy oneself as
regards truth. These discoveries always excite one so much that they give one
the energy to carry on, and they give one a line, an inexorable line which
dictates the form of the whole work. I must add that this process of questioning goes on until the work is finished, a kind of continuous checking that one
is being true to the inner nature of what one is doing.

So perhaps one might begin by asking, How is the wolf to be treated?
How is he to be shown upon the stage? As a real wolf—I mean an actual wolf?
Difficult. But consider the parallel of bull-fighting—I believe bull-fighting,

whatever its ethics, to be one of the most pure and exciting artistic forms—
the depth of the myth, the rigid courtly ritual containing violence and death.
But it is the very reality of death in the bullring which makes it non-theatrical.
Theatre doesn't deal with absolute reality, it deals with imaginative reality. So
no real wolf. Well, then, how are we to treat the wolf?—As he might be in
ballet perhaps? A man in costume suggesting the inner experience, the essence
of wolfdom? How seriously are we to take the wolf? Is he a comic villain? It
would be possible to have him funny and yet a real threat also. All depends
on the form of the play, or conversely this problem may decide the form.
Perhaps if we know how the wolf is to be treated we shall know the form and
style of the play.

   We try another point of entry. Why doesn't the wolf seduce Red
Riding Hood in the forest—why does he lure her off to gather flowers and then
leave her and go looking for the grandmother? There are only two possibilities
—either he does seduce her, or there is some really strong reason why he
doesn't. If he does seduce her then Red Riding Hood's later behaviour makes
her very interesting—if he doesn't, why doesn't he? Is he homosexual? Is she
unattractive? Then why did he lure her into the forest in the first place? Is
he kinky—preferring very old, possibly dead, ladies—and so lures Red Riding
Hood into the forest to get her out of the way?

   How can a wolf talk? Because the wolf is an extreme image of a certain
type of man.

   One can accept that Red Riding Hood couldn't tell the difference
between her grandmother and the wolf, although there would have to be a
particular reason for it in terms of character which would in turn affect the
whole play: Is Red Riding Hood short-sighted? Is she exceptionally stupid? Or
is she so shy, so well brought up by that mother of hers that although she
notices something wrong she doesn't like to say anything because it wouldn't
be polite. Or is it that she actually was seduced earlier in the forest?

   What I can't accept at present is Little Red Riding Hood's regurgitation. Either she is eaten—that is seduced, her virginity lost—or not. You can't
have it both ways. She can't be seduced and then regain her virginity. The
alternative: that she is actually eaten, and then rescued by the woodsman, is
only truthful if the woodsman is a figure of magical power—a god or demi-god
—someone with power of life and death.

   To return to the question of the wolf's leaving her in the forest. Is it
that the wolf realises that he can have both girl and grandmother? But why
doesn't he seduce Little Red Riding Hood in the forest and then go on to the
grandmother? Why does he wait until she gets to the cottage—how does he
know she'll come to the cottage?

   Right: now comes the leap, and at this point in thinking it out one gets
exhilarated. That's it. That's the falseness in the story. The original story lied
to make its point: the wolf does seduce Red Riding Hood in the forest. Once
I accept this, doesn't everything fall into place? She follows the wolf to the
cottage and the ritual dialogue takes on quite a different colour and becomes

sex play: 'Why grandmother, what big ears you have!'—then follows the second intercourse. It was she who followed him to the cottage, the first time he may have seduced her, the second time she seduces him. When the woodsman arrives Red Riding Hood buys her return into conventional society by betraying the wolf. By her betrayal we begin to recognise that the wolf is the outsider, the outlaw, the hunted man. Now we begin to glimpse the true mythical nature of the situation: the woman rooted in conventionality, who longs for excitement and adventure which her normal environment doesn't give her, she tastes the excitement and danger of consorting with the outlaw. But if she stayed with him she would have to abandon conventional society and she hasn't the courage for that, so she buys her way back into society by misrepresenting what happened—she says the wolf seduced her and this lie is accepted—this is her regurgitation.

This is the myth that Sidney Nolan found so fascinating in his series of paintings of Mrs. Frazer and the escaped convict: the conventional woman consorts with the wild man, who in his turn sees in her some promise of the comfort and secure happiness he has lost; when she has had enough and wants to return to her own kind, she turns on him and betrays him.

We have turned Little Red Riding Hood inside out. It started by glorifying women and denigrating men in an unhealthy and inverted way. But it did it by lying about the details of its story. As soon as the lie is exposed one sees that the woman, far from innocent, is the predator and the man is the victim.

Bearing in mind that the artist's view of truth must be coloured by his unconscious, the artist of integrity simply cannot ask himself whether this story would be popular or not, would appeal to women or not. Once he has allowed himself to be gripped by his material the artist must follow the subject where it will go giving it the shape it appears to demand. He cannot manipulate the story, except within very narrow limits, he can only discover its shape. If the story will disturb his audience he cannot help that (indeed disturbing the audience may be his unconscious aim, all artists want to be loved and accepted as much as anyone else, although this desire may take strange forms). The pursuit of truth is so fascinating and inexorable that the artist must follow.

Truth in this context may mean factually truthful, or truthful in terms of the artist's vision—in which case the product may be in fact a lie and insulting to the audience, but it remains a truthful picture of what the artist sees, and will have the valid, absolute quality of artistic truth.

Given a hypothetical great dramatist, this man is theoretically in a delicate position: if he abides by what he sees as truth, produces a truthful piece of work, it is almost certain to disturb his audience, because society—that is the audience—is always tending away from truth and the absolute, which are too uncomfortable to be borne for more than short periods. But if our great dramatist produces a piece of work designed to please his audience at the expense of truth then his work will lack power, and to an artist the power in his work is the whole point of working.

We have seen a situation in which the dramatist hopes that his audience is seduced into surrender by means of an appeal to imagination reinforced by sensual and emotional stimuli; their brains, their rational minds are lulled, their emotions, senses, instincts and memories are assaulted, stimulated, impregnated. It would seem in theory that the audience is defenceless. Receptive and open to any suggestion they must succumb to the artist, the skilful manipulator, who need only apply his technique to brainwash his audience and transform the world.

But art does not change the world much; it only changes the world when the world is ready to be changed. If art is reinforcing something that the audience wants to believe then it may be effective indeed. But by and large art has little direct influence and I think this is because although the artist may call upon the irrational and unconscious forces in his audience those same irrational forces will be their protection. As a general rule, until they get used to a new idea an audience will reject what a dramatist has to say if it challenges their preconceptions. If a play conflicts with certain of my preconceived ideas about art or morals then either I am going to have to reassess my ideas, which is uncomfortable and disturbing, or else I must in some way rob the play of its power.

In theory art has limitless power because so much of its appeal is to the unconscious, and it is the unconscious that rules the world despite the image we have of ourselves as rational beings. And of all the arts the theatre is probably the least resistible, not merely because it makes its appeal to so many facets of our personalities—senses, intellect, emotions—but also because the audience is in a way captive. It is much less easy to walk out of a theatre than it is to walk away from a picture; generally speaking in the theatre you are exposed to the experience from its start to its finish. But brainwashing is one thing, the theatre is another. It is going to take more than an evening's image-making, and more than a little myth and ritual to make us accept something which is at variance with our own fiercely defended unconscious values.

Martin Esslin
Drama and Society

MARTIN ESSLIN (1918–   ) was director of the BBC's Radio Drama department for thirty-seven years. In that capacity he brought to English audiences more new plays than any other single person. In recent years he has been Professor of Drama at Stanford University. Author of numerous books of criticism, this excerpt on the relationship of drama to its society was drawn from *An Anatomy of Drama,* published in 1976.

◆ . . . It is very revealing to see how over-propagandist drama defeats its own ends. For, unlike printed literature, which is consumed by individuals alone, the theatre is a collective experience. The reaction it evokes happens in public. Thus the message (political or otherwise) which a play contains always coexists with a demonstration of its reception by a social unit, the collectivity of the audience. In Nazi Germany certain plays which were acknowledged German classics and were regarded by the Nazis themselves as important elements in the cultural heritage of the nation, nevertheless had to be banned because audiences tended to applaud too loudly: for example, in Schiller's *Don Carlos* in which a powerful plea for freedom of speech is made. Similarly, totalitarian regimes can ill afford to have passages praising the leader and his works received by their audiences in sullen silence. They can tolerate even less having the theatres showing such plays standing empty. At the height of Stalinism the Soviet theatres were in that danger. Not, I think, because the population was hostile, but because the political message of most plays was so overdone, and so predictable, that everyone knew what it would be even before the curtain went up, and such plays therefore became terribly dull. The 'thaw' of 1965 in Poland and Hungary, and that of 1966 and 1967 in Czechoslovakia, was preceded by crises in the theatre. In order to fill the gapingly empty auditoria the authorities had to allow more popular plays, and these had to include classics dispensing a nationalistic or traditionalist message, as well as contemporary plays which dealt with topical themes by sly allusion or allegory and were instantly understood by audiences as containing a message of criticism of existing conditions. Although the electronic mass media and the cinema do not confront a collective audience and the actors in the same direct fashion, in the long term the social impact of drama in these media is similar: only here the reaction takes time to form. The rigid control of the cinema in totalitarian societies like Nazi Germany and the Soviet Union, and the even more restrictive use of drama in television and radio in such societies, amply demonstrates the concern of those regimes about the impact of drama.

Even in countries with greater overt freedom the theatre inevitably plays an important part in bringing into the open what are the burning issues of the time, such as capital punishment, social legislation and indeed the debate for and against socialism. In France, in the United States and in Britain the theatrical avant-garde has always been the spearhead of new trends of social and political thought. The theatre is the place where a nation thinks in public in front of itself. And in that context all sorts of matters assume political importance, for, ultimately, there is a close link between the general beliefs of a society, its concept of proper behavior and good manners, its view of sexual morals, and the political climate of a nation. Changes in manners and mores may ultimately change the very temper of politics.

An example, which is often quoted in this context is that of Shaw's *Pygmalion*. During its first performance in 1913, that fearful taboo word in English Victorian society, 'bloody', was for the first time pronounced upon the stage in front of a respectable audience. Basil Dean, the veteran producer, who was Beerbohm Tree's assistant at this occasion, has told me how everyone in the audience as well as behind the scenes dreaded the moment, which rumour had anticipated, when all the hitherto valid codes of polite behaviour would be broken. And when Eliza Doolittle had actually uttered the awful phrase 'not bloody likely', Dean tells me one could feel a sigh of relief rising from the auditorium of His Majesty's Theatre. The taboo had been broken, the heavens had not fallen, but something epoch-making had happened. Whether one welcomed the development or deplored it, from that moment the fabric of Victorian upper-class manners had begun to crumble. All that had happened was that a funny line had passed the lips of a favourite actress, Mrs. Patrick Campbell. On the surface, a less political event could hardly have been imagined. And yet, however long-term, however indirectly, it was certainly symptomatic of a big change in society.

It is clearly very difficult to measure the impact of such symptomatic events accurately. Is the fact that it has become possible to speak certain words in public merely an indication of a change which has already happened, or does it actually initiate the change? My guess is that there is a more complex link between these two alternatives. The change has happened in the minds of a few people, an elite, an avant-garde. But the fact that it is brought into the open and seen to be accepted without overt indignation or sanctions against those who have dared to breach the taboo then becomes a further powerful factor in dissolving the taboo in the minds of those who were still afraid to breach it. In the last half-century the theatre's part in destroying the taboos surrounding the frank discussion of sexual matters, homosexuality, the use of strong language regarded as blasphemous, etc., has been spectacular in the English-speaking world. The success—and the acceptance—of plays like *The Boys in the Band* was clearly both a symptom of change and an agent of further changes in attitudes. And social attitudes of this kind are also important political facts.

Northrop Frye has observed that in drama we invariably see at the beginning what amounts to a social order which is being disturbed and is, in one way or another, either overthrown or re-established, albeit in a different form. In *Macbeth* this is only too obvious. One king is murdered; another king takes his place and is in turn removed. Yet take a play of a quite different nature, *The Winter's Tale*. There a king's family—and thus a country—is disrupted and at the end order is restored under the auspices of the next generation. And even in the conventional French amorous triangle, a marriage is threatened by the appearance of the wife's lover and in the end either the marriage is vindicated and the lover expelled, or a new set-up is introduced, the old order overthrown. There are always social implications in any dramatic situation and in the resolution of any dramatic conflict simply because all human situations, all human behaviour patterns, have social—and therefore also political—implications.

Hamlet speaks of the theatre holding a mirror up to nature. I think in fact it is society to which the theatre holds up the mirror. The theatre and all drama can be seen as a mirror in which society looks at itself. This also is a fact which has social and political implications: for example, that at certain times the theatre tended to show only middle-class people to middle-class people demonstrates that in those times the lower classes were effectively excluded from society and therefore from the theatre.

The manners and life-style shown in the theatre inevitably become a potent influence on the manners and life-style of the times. Unconsciously we tend to reflect in our own life the attitudes, the accepted modes of behaviour, we have seen in the theatre, or for that matter in the cinema or on television. How do courting couples know what to say to each other when for the first time they are in a situation where they have to find the right words to break the ice or to declare their feelings? I am certain that unconsciously they will use dialogue or a style of approach they have seen on the stage or screen. And similarly with people who are faced with death, bereavement, victory or defeat in sport, etc. Of course, the playwrights who wrote the dialogues concerned have imitated dialogues they have observed in real life. Yet they have selected the manner of speech and the words which they felt most appropriate, so they have reinforced a certain way of behaviour as against another. When Shaw made Eliza Doolittle say 'not bloody likely' he was, of course, copying a phrase that was widely in use. But when it could be spoken in a theatre, society in a way was allowing itself to use it more openly. (Whether this was a good thing or not is quite a different matter.) As playwrights on the whole tend to be members of the more adventurous and advanced section of society, the theatre will inevitably be an instrument of social innovation and in that sense it is an institution subversive of the *status quo.* . . .

John Lahr and Jonathan Price
Re-Creations

JOHN LAHR (1941–   ), one of our finest critics, and JONATHAN PRICE (1941–   ), a concrete poet and teacher of drama, collaborated on one of the most interesting theatre books published in the last decade. In *Life-Show,* they took the metaphor of theatre and used it to probe deeply and provocatively into the dramatic details of contemporary culture. Both in its content and design, it opens up our thinking about the theatre in bold new ways.

◆   The play always brings us back to society. The same detailed analysis which clarifies the stage art can make sense of life scenes. Theater—along with sports, camping, travel—is mixed together under the umbrella term "recreation," which is synonymous with "exercise," "doing things." But play's function is much deeper than leisure; play is a kind of public dreaming. In a secular society, play becomes one of the few important symbol-giving ceremonies. Mircea Eliade has pointed out:

> The symbol not only makes the world "open" but also helps religious man to attain the universal. For it is through symbols that man finds his way out of his particular situation and "opens himself" to the general and the universal. Symbols awaken individual experience and transmute it into a spiritual act, into metaphysical comprehension of the world.
>
> *—The Sacred and the Profane*

Although on stage, some theater wants to reproduce the world as precisely as the child wants to reproduce home life by "playing house," play at its most delightful and profound is never "realistic."

Whether on stage or in a stadium, the area set aside for playing is special. We call it a *"play*ground." The space is symbolically sacred. The player and the spectator are both "taken out of themselves"; that is, the very act of playing re-creates a universe outside Time and historical place. Re-creation is a means of symbolically starting afresh.

In primitive societies, the sacredness we associate with child's play—that ability to see objects both as themselves and as signs of some higher order—is the central reality of the society.

> The religious festival is the reactualization of a primordial event, of a sacred history in which the actors are the gods or semi-divine beings.

> But sacred history is recounted in the myths. Hence the participants in the festival become contemporaries of the gods and semi-divine beings. They live in the primordial time that is sanctified by the gods.
> —*The Sacred and the Profane*

The idea of a people *living the universal* is nostalgic to technological man. He is often awed by the child's capacity for wonder, its ability to feel the spiritual in everyday; but even the adult attempts symbolic acts of renewal in his play.

> Modern man's private mythologies—his dreams, reveries, fantasies, and so on—never rise to the ontological status of myths, precisely because they are not experienced by the *whole man* and therefore do not transform a particular situation into a situation that is paradigmatic.
> —*The Sacred and the Profane*

Nevertheless, modern man's spiritual yearning is real; and its vestige is exhibited in many different kinds of performances. People follow their favorite performers on the screen or the field "religiously." We say they are "fanatics." Every form of play has its pantheon of "immortals." Baseball, Brecht, and the Bible have this single thing in common; they attempt imaginatively to reconstruct a world; they lubricate the imagination and force it to play.

Theater is one of the few ceremonies in modern life whose structure and artfulness sustain the child's-play impulse into adulthood, reviving the primal yearnings for psychic omnipotence. Theater is a testing, an exploration, a reiteration. Where the child wants to touch and to toy with objects to know them and learn, theater allows us to see objects as vessels containing hidden ideas. The playwright re-creates the world and makes the audience play according to his rules; but the viewer makes the connections and his presence wills the performance into being. In theater, as in all authentic play, he retains a sense of power. He is needed in the game; and it cannot be played without him. His response, to a large extent, controls the event.

Play is a rehearsal of the unknown as well as the familiar; a discovery as well as a confirmation. We say a playwright has a "point of view." The spectator must not only uncover that angle; but his whole experience of re-creation comes from that perspective. Like primitive rituals dramatizing the origins of the cosmos, theater creates a world whose vision can become exemplary. Images can transform consciousness and so renew life. Where the primitive performances are a crucial communal means of remembering the past and bringing the spirit world alive, modern man is always surprised when theater has any visceral effect on life. Our community is so large and cumbersome, so complicated by knowledge and technology, so often dedicated to escape—that rarely is theater seen to have a direct, visible effect on the society. But there are exceptions. Yeats's *Cathleen Ni Houlihan* was a heroic play that sparked participation in the Easter Rising of 1916 in Dublin. "The first night of Beaumarchais' *Marriage of Figaro,*" writes Conor Cruise O'Brien "was an episode—a real episode—in the French Revolution, and the dialogue of Bazarov in Turgenev's *Fathers and Sons* set the tone for more than one generation of Russian proto-revolutionists. The plebeians are always in some sense rehearsing the uprising."

Although what has become "sacred" in most modern theater is "commerce," the stage images can still speak directly to man's deepest yearnings and fears; the result can be cathartic. The riots in Dublin after the Abbey Theatre performed J.M. Synge's *The Playboy of the Western World* or the bedlam that broke out the first night of Alfred Jarry's *Ubu Roi* illustrates how the prophecy of a play can penetrate an audience's subconscious life and force a society into a recognition of its real condition. Most of our re-creations are merely recreations. They do not redefine us or extend our understanding of experience.

This is where stage play attains its dignity and importance. It distills and comments on the life-shows around it. Theater is not simply dealing with diversion, but with truth; not simply entertainment, but ethics. It expands consciousness. This process is a life force, and a tool for survival. Shakespeare absorbed the patterns of Elizabethan festival and found in them both the seeds of structure and content for many of his plays *(Twelfth Night, As You Like It, A Midsummer-Night's Dream).* Familiar spectacles are turned to an imaginative testing of boundaries and the function of festival in society. As Prince Hal says to Falstaff, the archetypal Lord of Misrule, "If all the year were playing holidays/To sport would be as tedious as work;/But when they seldom come, they wished for come. . . ." Playwrights from every century and society strive for this same compression. Wycherley outlines the hypocrisy in the Restoration show of manners; Brecht distills the patterns of history in his spectacles of war and politics; Beckett goes still deeper to show us the spiritual yearning behind our gaming instinct.

The playwright, the director, and the actor are engaged in ways of celebrating and revealing the living moment, re-creating the world to make an audience see and feel ideas in a new way. Plays are memory banks and culture probes. By observing the specifics of their mimetic craft, we—the spectators—can refine our relationship to the profound and dramatic interrelation of man with man, object, space, and society. The stage is the most ruthless, gorgeous exhibition of the dynamic of play that rules not only art, but every day.

Robert W. Corrigan
The Future of the Avant-Garde and the Paradigms of Post-Modernism

ROBERT W. CORRIGAN (1927–   ) concludes this volume with an essay that was originally delivered as the Avery Hopwood Lecture at the University of Michigan. The theatre always moves forward by returning to its old roots. In examining the characteristics of avant-gardism in theatre, the essay points to the emergence of a new post-modern theatre.

I like to think of artists as persons who cross the frontiers of our common life and through their work give definition to those boundary situations of the human mind and spirit. In this role they are makers of maps for the rest of the community, and these maps, in turn, celebrate the best and the worst, the most beautiful and most painful experiences that men have thought and felt. This metaphor of the artist as mapmaker is well known and widely accepted, but I am not so sure we can use it any more. You see, in recent years more and more artists have decided that cartography is a much too menial trade. They really want to be a combination of Christopher Columbus, Daniel Boone, and astronaut. What's more, they are rejecting their metaphoric role altogether. Many of them have decided that they actually are explorers. They think of their art not as something about life, but rather as an immediate social transaction which not only changes the world but also enhances their own humanity. Its aim is not to put reality at a remove through art, but to use art to remove barriers to reality. And this new image that artists have of themselves has created many problems—problems for confused audiences, for befuddled critics and scholars, and even for artists themselves.

Indeed, the thorniest problem in the art world today is the growing tendency in all of the arts to break down or dissolve those distinctions that have heretofore existed between art and life. This condition has occurred before in the history of Western culture, but only for brief periods of time and always as a local and aberrant phenomenon. Today it is already widespread and it continues to grow—some would say like a giant cancer, while others would describe it as a glorious liberation movement. The fact is, this tendency toward dissolution has been in process for a long time now and its coming was probably inevitable. But our awareness of this does not make it any less of a dilemma for most of us. In this essay I should like to discuss some of the more significant aspects of the problem not only so as to understand it better, but also because I wish to point to certain critical strategies which, hopefully, will resolve it.

Art and Paradigmatic Experience

All art is based on some form of what Karl Mannheim referred to as "paradigmatic experience." He defined such experiences as those "basic experiences which carry more weight than others, and which are unforgettable in comparison with others that are merely passing sensations." A paradigm is a model or pattern of order. It is a compelling vision of reality which creates —as it does in language—a hierarchy of being and value which permits us to shape and judge experience in its terms. Insofar as we believe in paradigmatic experiences, it is possible for us to say about an object, idea, or event, "this is true or false, good or bad, better or worse." Thomas Kuhn, in his influential book, *The Structure of Scientific Revolutions,* describes what happens in science in the same way. Scientific theories are, in fact, paradigms that are the most economic and complete models for synthesizing the known evidence about the physical world. In characterizing scientific advance, Kuhn describes those periods in which evidence begins to be assembled which the reigning paradigm cannot explain; that is, under the terms of the existing paradigm the new evidence appears anomalous and freakish. But it is the pressure of this anomalous evidence that characterizes scientific advance; calling not only for its acknowledgment, but demanding as well the invention of an entire new paradigm, or as Kuhn puts it, an explanation of what has by then become a "new world." When we deny the validity of paradigmatic experiences, or when the governing paradigms of a culture seem to have broken down, then nothing is revealed as having decisive importance. We are ruled by a kind of kaleidoscopic concept of life which, in giving equal significance to everything, attributes no radical significance to anything.

The same thing happens in the arts, and more particularly the theatre. Sophocles' theatre at Epidaurus, Shakespeare's Globe, the boxed living room with its fourth wall removed of Ibsen, Chekhov, and Shaw were emblematic. They both reflected and revealed the governing paradigms of their respective cultures. As these paradigms began to break down, not only was there a corresponding blurring of the definition of theatre space, but also the whole nature of theatrical performance underwent a metamorphosis. And it is no accident—as I hope to show presently—that the theatre of the past decade or so has been going through changes of the most revolutionary nature.

The most important shift in paradigms in the past several centuries, the shift which created what now we refer to as modernism, occurred in the second half of the 18th century and the first part of the 19th century when the Industrial Revolution combined with the political revolutions both in this country and on the continent to destroy the validity of those dominant paradigms that had governed Western art and thought since the Middle Ages, if not from the times of classical Greece. Today we can look back and see that this process had actually been going on at a gradual rate since the 15th century. But by the 19th century, our world was committed to the vision of a democratic egalitarianism and we could no longer accept—at least in principle—

a paradigm of social order based on a hierarchy of rank or class. Similarly, the industrial revolution had created the possibility of an economy of sufficiency which made it impossible for a paradigm based on an economy of scarcity to be maintained. This condition led to the emergence of new paradigms, the most important of those being the idea of unlimited economic growth through some form of industrial capitalism and the idea of progress as an alternative to Judgment Day. In the arts these major changes are reflected in the emergence of a marked pluralism of styles, a tendency to subordinate aesthetic style to more significant ethical and social concerns, the disappearance of genres, and the eventual devaluation of the art object. But most importantly, it created the idea of the avant-garde.

The Nature and Development of the Avant-Garde

We tend to forget what a recent idea this is. To the best of my knowledge, this Napoleonic military term was first used in reference to the arts by Saint-Simon in 1825. It is an ambiguous concept. On the one hand, all of the literature of the avant-garde reveals that it is at heart conservative and in a sense even reactionary. Avant-garde artists are "radical" only in the original sense of that word—they want to go back to the old roots. In using new techniques to return to these old truths, they hope to be more real and direct, to be more truly communal and involving. Thus, more often than not, what appears in their work to be a shattering of tradition is actually a reaffirmation of it.

But the avant-garde has also had a compelling need to repudiate the past, and particularly its own immediate past. Conceptually it is inextricably linked to the idea of progress, and its origins can be traced to the emergence of the Romantic Movement. It is interesting to note that before Romanticism, insofar as styles in art were categorized, they were invariably described as "schools." The notion of a school presupposes a master and a method, the criterion of tradition, and the principle of authority. Furthermore, the nature of a school is defined solely in aesthetic terms. Movements, on the other hand, are activist and future oriented. They are "moving" toward the realization of something. Whatever goal a school might have, it is transcendant; its central commitment is to the mastery of what has already been achieved, believing that such mastery combined with inspiration will create a future that need not, nor cannot, be precisely defined. The followers of a movement always work in terms of an end which resides in the movement itself. Moreover, this end exists beyond the limits of art and is essentially ethical and social rather than aesthetic in nature. For this reason movements conceive of culture not as increment but as creation.

Movements are inseparably linked to the idea of progress. Progress, which had heretofore been utopian and allegorical, had become by the beginning of the 19th century a realizable expectation. After the French Revolution, there was a decision to start a new calendar for human affairs. This was, in effect, saying that the metaphor of renewal was now seen as a reality so that, as George Steiner puts it, "the eternal tomorrow of utopian political vision became, as it were, Monday morning." And if it can be Monday morning, then the sooner we get started the better. The members of the avant-garde were the early starters, the cutting edge, the first wave—you name it. If culture is something created constantly anew, and if art is conceived as revolution and movement, then there has to be an avant-garde. We are just now coming to comprehend the full significance of this basic change in thinking about the arts and to assess its effects not only on what happened in the arts, but also on the way artists view themselves and their work.

The dominant characteristic of the avant-garde has been its antagonistic spirit. Avant-garde art always induces uneasiness. In fact, uneasiness may be the key word in the whole tradition of the new. A work of art is expected to throw us off balance; it should violate our sense of expectation. Now, in a way, all art has always done this, and it has been a source of its greatest power.

But the avant-garde artist is antagonistic in a profoundly different way. Because he or she is committed to originality rather than renewal, the new and the novel are the hallmarks of his or her creativity. Genuineness of vision is equated with avoiding what's been done before. Genuineness of craftsmanship implies a refusal to repeat old techniques. This creates one of the artist's biggest problems. He is always struggling with the burden of history. And this is more of a problem than ever today when increasingly all of humanity's diverse history is (or can be) experienced as something in the present tense. This is particularly true of the artist's relationship to the history of his or her art. For all of the avant-garde's desire to break down the distinctions between art and life, its efforts can only be understood in an art-historical context. In fact, in some ways, much avant-garde art is actually a form of art criticism.

However, there is probably an even more significant explanation for the antagonistic spirit of avant-garde art. One of the cornerstones of modernist thought is the belief that the present is valid only by virtue of its potentialities for the future. The avant-garde artist, like the commodities market, is always dealing in "futures." Because it believes (as all modernists do) that all potentiality can be actualized in the near future, the avant-garde rejects the past and, instead, embraces the vision of apocalypse. But it can never be totally successful in this. There is no escape from history. Hence the sense of equivocation that tends to characterize all avant-garde art. Earthworks or Happenings were attempts to get out of history, but the fact that they invariably had to be photographed or videotaped reveals the futility of the attempt.

Finally, however, it is important to understand that the avant-garde artist is not really opposing traditional forms of art; rather he is seeking a radically new experience. One in which the ideal can be made immediate and tangible; one that permits him to believe that the gap between the possible and the real—which heretofore had been bridged by works of art—can be closed. Thus, in rejecting art as a derivative experience in favor of the myth of art as an immediate experience, the avant-garde is constantly mixing aesthetic and ethical categories. And because of this confusion there is always pressure to break down the differences between art and life, to confuse them, to see them as the same.

The Breaking Down of the Distinctions Between Art and Life

This process has really been going on for a good part of this century. It was the central intuition of Dadaism. It was implied in Duchamp's found objects. It was the dominant dramatic idea in Pirandello's theatre, which in turn had a profound influence on the Theatre of the Absurd. It was hinted at by the atonal composers and became obvious in aleatory music. It was even one of the deaestheticizing premises of action painting. John Cage is probably its most articulate prophet, and over thirty years ago he said: "For too long art obscured the difference between life and art. Now let life obscure the difference between art and life."

But these were still minority views. The dominant tendency in the arts since World War I—and especially in the fifteen to twenty years after World War II—was to shrink the world to a rebellious gesture. The governing spirit during this time was one of protest and retreat and the work of most artists had become violent graphs of the cornered person. From such movements as the Theatre of the Absurd or abstract expressionism in painting, it is clear that humanity was defined by estrangement and solitude and not by participation in the life of society. Then in the 1960s, when all art forms seemed to erupt into the spasms of a mad St. Vitus dance, things began to change. It was then that the idea that art was not about life but was a form of life itself came to be the predominant view of the avant-garde. This happened, I think, because of a major shift in the artist's attitude toward technology. Technology came to be seen not as a dehumanizing enemy but as a great new resource that could be used in both material *and* spiritual ways so as to enhance the present and its possibilities. However, whenever we embrace anything—an attitude, an idea, even another person—we must remember that we are acted upon by the object of our embrace every bit as much as we affect it. There is no such thing as embrace with impunity. Thus, when the artist came to embrace technology not only was his work affected; his whole sense of himself was changed.

Probably the first noticeable effect of the artist's embrace of technology is that it gives him a radically new sense of choice. We know that each one of us has opportunities for choice that were unthinkable a generation ago, and more important, we know that we had better keep on making them. I think that the possibility for choice is at the very heart of the creative process; but when you also believe that one need not be bound permanently by his or her choices because new choices are made available to us every day, then your attitude toward what you create invariably changes. And this accounts—at least in part—for the growing dominance of the spirit of improvisation and impermanence in all of the arts. It is no accident that the era from 1960 until at least 1975 was so often referred to as "The Age of the Happening."

Today our artists are less and less concerned with creating lasting works of art. Because each day brings with it new choices, the artist comes to find joy in the creative process itself—indeed, involvement in the process of creating has tended to replace concern for the project or object that is made.

A catalogue of art and artists committed to process, improvisation, or impermanence would be almost endless, but the fact that there are so many does not mean that we don't have trouble with the phenomenon. Nothing underscores the ambiguity of this situation more dramatically than the fact that the Museum of Modern Art in New York has a permanent collection of disposable art. Nonetheless, I am convinced that one of the reasons all art seems to be moving toward performance (and that increasingly we are thinking about the arts in terms of performance) is due to the very ephemeralness of the theatrical event. This being the case, we should not be surprised that in the past couple of years some artists have carried this to even further extremes. Why bother making anything at all—especially since the marketing systems in all of the arts are so unashamedly corrupt? Rather than write plays, some playwrights give interviews before and after a performance no one has ever seen, to explain the meaning of what hasn't occurred. In the visual arts —at least in some quarters—there has been a noticeable shift away from the creation of tangible objects to calling attention to the attitudes by which art has been or can be made. In each of these instances execution has disappeared completely; philosophic attitude has taken precedence over unique form.

There is probably a more meaningful explanation for this bizarre situation of an art world without art. In the past, material objects were valuable because in an economy of scarcity what one made was more enduring than those who made them. Objects were sacred not only because they were unique and irreplaceable, but also because they represented an ideal of humanity which would endure beyond the life of any individual. Under such conditions people were as expendable as the materials were valuable. If the lives of a thousand had to be sacrificed in order to build a pyramid or a cathedral, so be it; such structures would last forever as eternal monuments to those ideals and aspirations by which people (or at least their monarchs) lived. But today we believe less and less in the permanence of matter, or, for that matter, in the stability of nature. After Hiroshima, how can we? Furthermore, in an economy of sufficiency, all materials are—theoretically, at least—expendable. Any object is replaceable, and our industrial technology has made it possible for us to replicate anything from a rare antique to the latest model automobile. In a society with such an economy, and with such a prodigal attitude toward human artifacts, the only unique and irreplaceable element is the person. As the life of the individual comes to replace the object or the performance as the only unique and irreplaceable creation in the universe, then increasingly the artist comes to think of his own physical and psychic being as the material from which and the medium through which he will shape his most meaningful, if not his only creations.

The effects of this conviction are clearest in the idea of life itself as a performance. Building upon the work of Erving Goffman, R. D. Laing,

Hugo Rahner, Jean Piaget, and Victor Turner, critics such as the three Richards (Poirier, Gilman, and Schechner) have been the leading spokesmen for this view, and Norman Mailer is the supreme embodiment of it. In the mid-fifties Mailer had reached a creative impasse and the novel form was no longer working for him. As he turned his attention to the turbulent events going on in the world, he came to believe that the most interesting source of art was the interaction between himself and those events. He no longer thought of writing as a mimetic act but rather as a "kind of combative enterprise analogous to war." Form was not a pattern imposed on experience, it was an account of one's engagement and struggle with it. For Mailer there was no longer any separation between living and creating. The artist himself is the work of art. He said as much when he maintained that "the first art work in an artist is the shaping of his own personality." It is important to understand that Mailer's running for mayor in New York City was an aesthetic, not a political act.

The Challenge to the Mimetic Idea of Art

Once the artist no longer believes that art and life are separate and distinct—albeit related—orders of experience, he must also question the mimetic nature of the artistic process. This is the most radical and profound challenge facing the arts today. Certainly the most widely held traditional belief of the artist's function is the one which asserts that the artist's main job is to take the chaos and complexity, the ambiguity, contradiction, and inconclusiveness of actual experience, and to impose on them a meaning and order by means of the unique powers of his temperament, the depth of his imagination, and his capacity to create form. That is, through words, tone, color, line, or image, he creates an object in which the inconsistencies of life experience are made whole and within the work are organically and coherently expressive. This view is based upon the essentially Platonic premise that reality can never be directly or totally known and that our awareness of it will always be limited; that there is a realm between conceptual certitude and the chaos of sense data which can only be bridged by approximate realities and provisional truths. Hence the need for fictive possibilities, for only fictions can mediate between what humanity desires or hopes reality to be and the way things actually are. I think one can safely maintain that this has been the dominant view in Western thought and art from the time of the Greeks until the middle of the 20th century.

When you challenge the Platonic view and replace it with the more existential belief that reality is whatever one experiences, then the relationship between art and life will begin to change. When Jackson Pollock said "Painting is a state of being," or when Mark Rothko insisted "a painting is not a picture of an experience; it is an experience," each of them was indicating that his concern was no longer with the finished work so much as with the *act* of painting. Thus, art becomes the occasion for a more heightened kind of participation in a reality which can be directly known. Today's artists have, with increasing frequency, substituted the myth of immediate experience for that of derivative experience. And the aim of advanced art in all its forms, as I said earlier, is not to put reality at a remove through art, but to use art to remove barriers to reality by presenting the complexity and ambiguity of life as directly as possible. These artists are not interested in producing works of art for people to mull over, but want to make the arts an immediately experienced transaction. The Aristotelian aesthetic of improving the audience's moral well being has been spurned in favor of professed involvement in social change.

The Collapse of Critical Judgment

I should like to touch upon one other aspect of the problem. Once you dissolve the distinctions between art and life, when the work becomes invisible as art by becoming at one with the environment, then how do you know what a work of art is and how to judge it? For the fact is, the aesthetics of direct experience is deaestheticizing. When the source of beauty shifts from the object of art to those who behold it, the whole idea of beauty becomes so relative, personal, and idiosyncratic that it soon ceases to have any real significance. Today, the question of "What is beauty?" doesn't seem very relevant and is seldom asked. For most of us, the more appropriate question is "What is art?" And the answer, of course, is that art is whatever someone who says he is an artist creates and calls art. Increasingly, our artists do not think of art as something reserved for the high holy days of the spirit; in fact, in their desire to make art and life more interrelated and mutually involved, the idea of "going" to a museum, a theatre, or a concert hall has become repugnant to them. I remember going to a performance of Robert Whitman's *Prune Flat* a number of years ago. It was given in a loft and the work was a film but the actors were acting live in front of the screen; it also had static visual images, strobe lights, and an electronic musical score. It all worked together in a synthetic way, and I thought it was a very interesting and moving experience. Afterwards, I went up to Mr. Whitman and in an old-fashioned way asked: "Wouldn't this have been better if it had been performed in a theatre?" He replied, "That's just the point. We don't want it in theatres. We want it in the loft where we made it, where we do it, where we are all together, where you are a part of us, where you're totally involved with us, where we live, where we eat, where we make love, where we are related together. We want to break down the gulf that exists between the artist and the audience. We want, in effect, to destroy audiences." If art is a life experience, then at best it is a game and all that is required to make an object into art is, as Jasper Johns put it, "its introduction into the art context." (Cage meant the same thing when he said: "So long as there is a concert situation there is a concert.")

If art is in fact a life experience and whatever an artist does is a work of art, then the qualities of art objects tend to become irrelevant in judging them. Indeed, even the objects become irrelevant; the only irreducible remainder of the idea of art is the figure of the artist. Such a condition invalidates the whole idea of aesthetics, and hence redefines the critic's role. When, as Harold Rosenberg observed, "art springs from ideas about art, rather than admired art objects, the evaluation of works cannot avoid being interpretative in a partisan way." It is no longer a question of aesthetics, but of ideology.

This explains one of the most remarkable characteristics of avant-garde art. When ideology is more important than objects, intention becomes more significant than results. This makes it possible to ignore, dislike, or hardly know the work of any given new movement in the arts and still comprehend it.

Without normative principles, the idea of criticism as a judicial act is impossible. And this is the situation we are in today. Our critics have ceased to be judges and have become guides and promoters. There will be plenty of work for them, since, as Hilton Kramer observed, "the more minimal the art, the more maximal the explanation." And if you think that is an exaggeration just look at any recent issue of *The Drama Review, Artforum,* or *New Sound.*

The Restoration of the Mimetic Nature of Art

If what I've said thus far is an accurate assessment of the present state of the arts, then it would appear that the future of the avant-garde as we have known it is at best problematic. But this is only partially true. I really think it is more a case of our mapmakers having gotten lost. They are reading the territory wrong and hence producing the wrong charts not only for themselves but for the rest of us as well. Back in 1925, Bertolt Brecht observed that "when one sees that our world of today no longer fits into the drama, then it is merely that the drama no longer fits into the world." What he meant by this was that the theatre had ceased to be meaningful to audiences because it was based upon outmoded premises. That is what is so clearly happening today. The reason the relation of art to life has become so askew is not something inherent in the arts, but because the ideas governing our experience—including our experience of works of art—have become both inadequate and false.

I believe what we have to face—and the evidence rises up to meet us everywhere, not least on our college campuses—is that the reigning paradigms of our modernist culture are not working or have already broken down. We certainly can no longer believe in an economy of limitless sufficiency when we know that the world's resources are being depleted at a faster rate than we can discover new ones. We didn't need Happenings, chance music, and self-destructing artifacts—all strategic denials of the future tense—to convince us that the idea of unlimited progress is no longer tenable. In short, as those paradigmatic experiences which gave rise to the idea of avant-gardism in the arts cease to be operative, it is reasonable to assume that the end of modernism is at hand, that Beckett's *Breath* is literally its last gasp! There is plenty of evidence to support this view, the most persuasive being the avant-garde's almost mechanical determination to carry on its own processes in a vacuum.

Today's vanguardism has become ritualized. It attacks nonexistent enemies and it heralds new advances when there is in fact nothing being advanced.

This condition doesn't worry me very much. For while it is true that our existing paradigms are collapsing, it is also clear that new paradigms are emerging to take their place. As and when they do, the hierarchies which are implicit in all paradigmatic structures will return and the mimetic nature of art can begin to function more easily. It is only during this time between reigning paradigms, when the principle of a syntactically organized vision of necessity gives way to more paratactical ("to exist side by side") conventions, that the distinctions between art and life tend to dissolve.

No one can say with certainty what the new paradigms of post-modern consciousness will be. I agree with Arthur Clarke that "the real future is not logically foreseeable." But I cannot help but notice that increasing numbers of historians, scientists, social scientists, literary and art critics, and anthropologists are beginning to discuss the future in terms of a transformation of human consciousness. And certainly much that is taking place in all of the arts confirms this transformation.

The Medieval Nature of the Contemporary Theatre

How is this process at work in the contemporary theatre? In the late 1960s, both the arts and the world were in a state of great turmoil. Looking back at that period from today's vantage point, we can see that it was a time of real revolution. And this was particularly true of the theatre. Conventions of performance and the performer/audience relationship were boldly challenged; the traditional structures of dramatic form were collapsed and reformed; the nature of actor training was reassessed; and the definitions of stage spaces were shattered as action moved off the conventional stage out into all kinds of heretofore alien environments. In short, it was a period of breaking out and breaking down. All of life seemed to have been theatricalized and the riots were a form of ritual madness. One thinks, for instance, of the trial of the Chicago Seven, which was certainly more an amalgam of Brecht, Artaud, Genet, and Ionesco than it was a court of law.

As it turns out, I think we were wrong about a lot of things a decade ago. I marvel especially at our blind *hubris.* We felt we knew all of the answers then. We had seen the rottenness at the core of the system and knew it for what it was. We were going to save the world by changing it, and the theatre and the other arts would be our weapon. We would stop the Viet Nam war; we would overthrow the authorities and power structures for whom we had nothing but contempt; and we would create new communities which would provide the energizing spirit for the new "greening of America." Well, it didn't work out that way. As I said earlier, the aesthetics of direct experience turned out to be deaestheticizing. The arts as a political weapon proved impotent. Like Mr. Nixon, we, too, experienced a "Watergate of the Spirit." It was—to use the title of a book describing the period—a *Time of Illusion.*

However, while the politicizing of the theatre in the sixties may have been short-lived and of dubious aesthetic distinction, it did, nonetheless, have a liberating spirit. It forced the theatre to redefine itself. It forced us to ask some basic questions, questions about the nature of theatre, questions about the always tricky relationship between art and life that exists in the theatre. We have had to grapple with these questions, with the result that our understanding of the theatrical event has been greatly enlarged. And my grappling with these questions has convinced me that the theatre of today is best described as having a medieval character.

Let me cite two examples to illustrate what I mean by this. One of the most influential books on the theatre published during the past decade was Peter Brook's *The Empty Space* (1969). Brook had many bold things to say about the theatre as we entered the 1970s, but the most audacious thing about the book was its title, *The Empty Space.* It is impossible for us to conceive of the Greek theatre at Epidaurus, Shakespeare's Globe, Molière's court, Ibsen's living rooms, or even Shaw's Edwardian drawing rooms as *empty spaces.* In the past, the place of performance was an emblem of either an actual ritual place or a model of the world, or some combination of the two. The space, shape, and nature of the classical Greek theatre was derived from "the sacred ground" of the god Dionysus. The Japanese Nōh theatre expresses symbolically the Buddhist cosmic myth. The Elizabethan theatre, based as it was upon the idea of "The Great Chain of Being," was conceived as a model of the world in which the drama of life took place. In the Golden Age of Spain, Calderon's "Great Theatre of the World" had a cosmological structure. Even the boxlike living room of the naturalistic theatre reflected a world view. The base root of the theatrical event is its transformational character, and when it has been most vital the empty space of the stage has been transformed into the "sacred place" of the play. To say "all the world's a stage" implies a governing cosmology and its attending metaphysic. But there have been transitional or medieval times when this has not been the case. I think of the Greek theatre after Euripides, the medieval European theatre when the mystery plays moved out of the church into the towns and countryside, the excessive Jacobean theatre closed down by Cromwell, and the ontologically barren and hallucinated world of Beckett's Gogo and Didi as they wait for a Godot who may or may not come. Living as we do in a time when there is no widely shared governing metaphysical view of the world, there is no way we can have an emblematic theatre—"a commonly shared sacred place," to use Eliade's phrase—similar to those of earlier times. This means that the stage is, in effect, an empty and neutral space and each production must begin at ground zero to create a new theatrical world governed by its own—and only its own—laws. What does this phenomenon tell us about the governing paradigms of modernism? Before answering that question let me mention my other example.

Theatre people all over the world often note the absence of first-rate playwrights in the contemporary theatre. Even the major writers (i.e., Williams, Miller, Pinter, Osborne, Beckett, Ionesco, Genet) of the two decades following World War II—who seem small when judged by theatre-historical standards—dwarf those writing today. At the same time that we bemoan the decline of the writer in theatre, everyone is passionately concerned with the actor and the actor's training. The most important theatrical ensembles of the past decade have been actor oriented. And our most significant theory and criticism is rooted in performance and not in dramatic literature. Again, the theatre's history can be illuminating. Whenever concern for the actor has taken precedence over the significance of the script, it has been a time of marked transition in cultural values. But history's most important lesson is that a renewed awareness of the centrality and nature of the act and radical transformations of theatrical space have invariably coincided, and this mysterious coincidence has always heralded cultural change.

Conclusion

I have argued that the collapse of the avant-garde in the arts is inextricably related to the breakdown of the paradigms of modernism which gave birth to the notion of the avant-garde in the first place. In the 1960s, many of us were trying to use the theatre to change the world. We failed for two reasons. One: we asked the wrong questions. We were too concerned with what the theatre was for and how it could be used rather than focusing our attention on what the theatre *is*. Second, and probably more important: we were so busy trying to change the world that we didn't notice that it was already in the process of doing so. The actor's regained centrality in the theatre and our reassessment of his nature and his role combined with the search for performance space that can be transformed into a sacred place, herald the fact that some fundamental changes in our culture have, in fact, already occurred.

If new paradigms based on the transformation of consciousness are in fact emerging, then those hierarchies so essential to the making and judging of art will do so also. Thus, even as the once creative and now debilitated notion of the avant-garde is transformed, we will begin to discover a great new vitality. Many cultural historians have pointed to the medieval nature of our times. If this is so, then perhaps there is a new Renaissance on the way—a renaissance which in the arts will be based on the restoration of the mimetic, a restoration that will invalidate those hallmarks of our present collapse, especially the widespread attitude of dilettantism and the belief that "being into things" is the equivalent of creation. I believe that the rebirth, if it comes —and I have faith that it will—will celebrate the qualities of energy and stamina, discipline and commitment. It will make us aware once again, although I am sure in new ways, that renewal is as dependent upon our capacity to maintain—even through the most excruciating boredom—as it is upon our ability to discover, that the idea of art as creation and as increment, while they may be in tension, need not be in dialectic opposition. In short, I think we may be coming to realize that our most profound discoveries are almost always things we already knew.